CYCLIST'S BRITAIN

CYCLIST'S BRITAIN

A complete guide to on- and off-highway routes

Pan/Ordnance Survey

First published 1985 by Pan Books Ltd, Cavaye Place, London SW10 9PG and Ordnance Survey, Romsey Road, Maybush, Southampton, SO9 4DH.
9 8 7 6 5 4 3 2 1

Conceived, edited and designed by Duncan Associates, 64 Fullerton Road, London, SW18 1BX with Mel Petersen & Associates, 5 Botts Mews, Chepstow Road, London, W2 5AG.

ISBN 0 330 28610 2

Typeset, printed and bound in Great Britain by Hazell Watson & Viney Limited, Member of the BPCC Group, Aylesbury, Bucks

● In England and Wales cyclists are permitted to ride on bridleways (**not** footpaths) which are designated as Public Rights of Way. In Scotland, however, no Public Rights of Way as such exist. While cyclists can in general ride on moorland and mountain paths taking due care to avoid damage to property and the natural environment, landowners may and do impose restrictions on access particularly during certain times of the year such as the grouse shooting season. The routes depicted in this book for off-highway riding in Scotland are no evidence therefore of a right of way and the **responsibility for gaining permission from landowners to cross their property rests with the cyclist.**

PAGE HEADINGS
Headings at the top of each page refer to the county or counties in which the *bulk* of the routing or mapping is located. For reasons of space, it has sometimes been necessary to abbreviate county names, eg Worcestershire for Hereford and Worcester.

Credits

INTRODUCTORY FEATURES
AND INVALUABLE ADVICE FROM

Richard Ballantine and The Bicycle Co-operative

Off-highway routes and cycle ways
Alan Mepham and Fred Goatcher of The Rough Stuff Fellowship; John Grimshaw and Nationwide Staff of the Railway Path Project

Principal contributors
Arnold Robinson, Bryan Colbourne, Anne Reid and Kenneth Innes, R. E. Harman, Chris Hutt, R. H. Kletz, Sheila Simpson.

This is a guide compiled by cyclists for cyclists. In a series of appeals published in *Bicycle Magazine* in 1983 and 1984, readers were asked to contribute their favourite rides, routes or tours, together with information that might benefit others using them; this book is the result; those who contributed are:

THE SOUTH-WEST
T. Cox, R. E. Harman, S. Thorpe, G. W. Lonsdale, Jane Corey, Bryan Colbourne, J. Babbidge, A. C. Longhurst, Chris Hutt, Simon Cook, Rory Savage, Arnold Robinson.

SOUTH-EAST ENGLAND
Michael Strivens, T. Wilson, R. K. Wild, Bryan Colbourne, R. E. Harman, David Weiss, P. K. Atkinson, Gordon Stokes, Arnold Robinson.

WALES
David Birchall, R. H. Kletz, Pauline and Ian Smith, R. E. Harman, G. W. Lonsdale, James Blair, Arnold Robinson.

MIDLANDS
Keith Hill, Julian Swindell, D. J. Rogers, Haydn G. Greenway, Sheila Simpson, N. Bassett, Jeffrey R. Eaves, John Holmes, P. K. Atkinson, M. A. Armitage, A. Ziemacki, S. Thorpe, F. Worrell, A. S. Turner, Arnold Robinson.

EAST ANGLIA
Sarah and James Mackay, Malcolm Osborne, Alfred S. Peacock, Adrian Taylor, Arnold Robinson.

NORTHERN ENGLAND
R. H. Kletz, Michael J. Taylor, Joy Greenwood, Peter Hall and Anne Calder, R. Beck, E. A. Jowett, John Holmes, Alan Richardson, Arnold Robinson.

SCOTLAND
R. Spooner, Kenneth L. Woodrow, Anne Reid and Kenneth Innes, Linda McColl, Colin A. Simpson, C. M. Smith, Lucy Ashdown and Robert Dale, R. H. Kletz, Gordon Black, T. Scoular, Arnold Robinson, Steve Deas.

Contents

England, Wales and Scotland are covered county by county in a sequence corresponding to the Ordnance Survey's grid reference system. This works from west to east, and from south to north. Cornwall, furthest west and furthest south, comes first. Grampian, furthest east and furthest north, comes last. For additional ease of reference, the book is divided into seven regional sections.

OS conventional symbols Routemaster

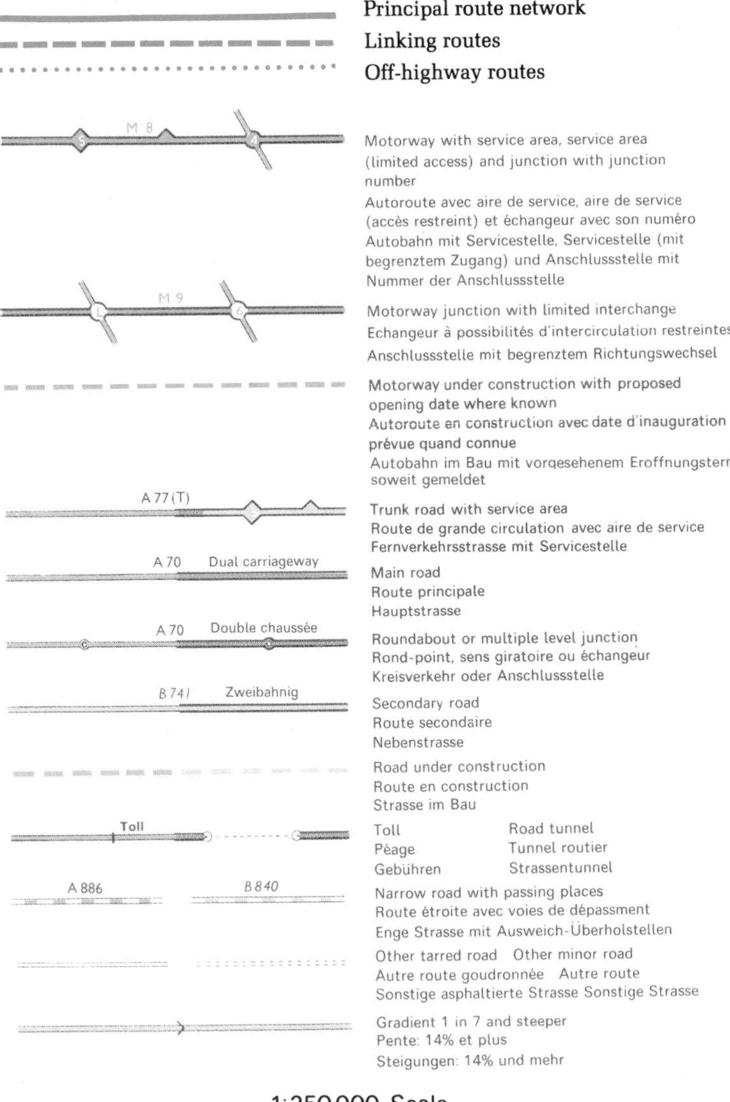

1:250 000 Scale

4 centimetres to 10 kilometres (one grid square)

Kilometres: 10 · 5 · 0 · 5 · 10 · 15

Miles: 5 · 0 · 5 · 10

1 kilometre = 0·6214 mile

1 mile = 1·61 kilometres

Landranger

ROADS AND PATHS

Main road

Minor road in towns, drive or track (unmetalled)

Path

RAILWAYS

Multiple } Standard gauge track
Single

Narrow gauge

Mineral line, siding or tramway

Bridge

Station

Level crossing

Tunnel

Cutting

Embankment

WATER FEATURES

Marsh

Lake or loch

Canal and tow path

Ferry foot

Ferry vehicle

Foot bridge

Cliff

Flat rock

Sand and mud

Sand and shingle

Low water mark

High water mark

GENERAL FEATURES

Electricity transmission line (with pylons spaced conventionally)

Quarry

Open pit

Wood

Orchard

Park or ornamental grounds

Bracken, heath and rough grassland

Dunes

Broadcasting station (mast or tower)

Bus or coach station

Church or Chapel with tower

Church or Chapel with spire

Church or Chapel without tower or spire

Glasshouse

Triangulation pillar

Windmill (in use)

Windmill (disused)

Wind pump

ABBREVIATIONS

PC	Public convenience (in rural areas)	P	Post office	NT	National Trust
.T	Telephone call box	*PH*	Public house	NTS	National Trust Scotland

RELIEF

Contours are at 10 metres VI or at 50 feet VI with values to the nearest metric equivalent

1:50 000

2 centimetres to 1 kilometre (one grid square)

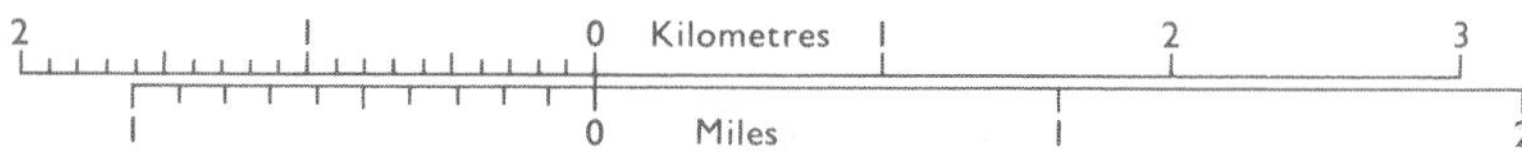

1 kilometre = 0·6214 mile

1 mile = 1·6093 kilometres

Using this book

Cyclist's Britain is for cyclists to use while actually on the road. Its Routemaster mapping, at a scale of 1:250 000, has allowed all the great cycle touring areas of England, Scotland and Wales to fit into one portable volume.

Routemaster mapping, produced by Ordnance Survey, the national map-making agency, shows all the classified roads (motorways, A- and B-roads) and practically the whole unclassified road system – in other words the byways and country lanes – of Britain. These last are, of course, the natural habitat of the cyclist: many lanes are no more than upgraded farm tracks; most are traffic-free, and many are remarkably beautiful.

The scale of Routemaster mapping does exclude some of the very smallest unclassified roads, and a few villages; similarly bridleways and many off-highway tracks used as public roads do not appear. For the inexperienced map-reader this can be an advantage: too much detail confuses; and for overall route-planning, the scale is invaluable because it emphasizes the essentials. However, bear in mind that Routemaster is essentially road mapping designed to take you anywhere you want to go on the public highways.

Like all Ordnance Survey cartography, it is highly accurate, based on detailed surveys: measurements of the ground combined with aerial photography. Ordnance Survey maps cover a wide variety of scales for different purposes, and in addition to the Routemaster mapping in *Cyclist's Britain*, there are excerpts from the outline edition of the Landranger series at a scale of 1:50 000 to show some off-highway routes in appropriate detail.

Hints on map-reading

There will be times when careful map-reading is required to get the best out of Routemaster mapping; in fact, many experienced cycle tourists, concentrating on a particular area, will appreciate using it in conjunction with the appropriate Landranger colour sheets. These show off-highway tracks and bridleways, and, with their greater detail, can help with route finding.

If you are a beginner at map-reading, practise in an area you know well. Familiarize yourself with the map's conventional symbols (given for use with this book on pages 8–9). Contour lines are the only features not entirely self-evident. They are surveyed lines showing the height of the ground above sea level, and with practice, the map-user can visualize from them the shape and steepness of hills.

Map-reading comes down to knowing where you are on the map when you set out, and then frequently checking your progress. Locating one's starting point is simple when setting out from a village or town, but when stopping to check position, beginners may find it helps to 'set' the map. This simply means turning the map so that its top edge points north.

Cycling along country lanes, it is usual to check progress by noting turnings as they pass – and of course towns and villages. With Routemaster mapping, one has to take into account the fact that some small turnings will not feature, and that signposting is sometimes inadequate, confusing or non-existent. To achieve a precise fix on your position, it is therefore necessary to understand scale, so that you can pinpoint position by measuring off miles actually covered on the map itself. On Routemaster, one inch (2.5 cm) represents approximately four miles (6.5 km) on the ground; on Landranger mapping, 1¼ inches (3 cm) represents one mile (1.5 km) on the ground. At an average cycling speed of say 12 mph (19 km/h) on flat ground you would therefore cover three inches of Routemaster or 9½ inches of Landranger mapping in one hour.

Despite being mainly road mapping, the Routemaster prepared for *Cyclist's Britain* also indicates major wooded areas, water areas, large rivers and railways – all useful for checking position.

The route network

Every stretch of road marked on *Cyclist's Britain* mapping by the solid green line is one that a contributor has ridden and found suitable, useful or enjoyable for cycling. The roads marked in this way are generally the most traffic-free, and often the least hilly. However, A- or B-road link-ups are common, and many of the routes are inevitably hilly. When these factors are particularly worth comment, the cyclist is alerted by a triangular symbol linked to a note in the text on the same page.

If improvising your own routes, it is worth bearing in mind that A-roads with two or more digits are generally the most peaceful, as opposed to trunk roads, indicated by a T in brackets.

The selected tours

Much of the fun of cycle touring is in the sense of freedom gained from planning your individual route; the network of routing in *Cyclist's Britain* has been made as extensive and generous as possible with just this in mind; possibilities for different types and lengths of rides are endless. At the same time, a number of selected tours have been picked out to introduce cyclists to the delights of each region. *They are merely a beginning*: adapt them to your own purposes to make new routes, and above all, devise your own original tours from the network.

The symbols

The mapping carries *two* systems of symbols. Those printed **dark green** are all keyed to a written comment or explanatory note in the text on the same page. They represent features singled out as of special relevance or interest.

Symbols printed **grey** are the Ordnance Survey's own, standard on Routemaster mapping. They highlight a wide range of features, and are not (except where converted to green), linked to a textual comment.

The dark green symbols, and accompanying text, are the result of extensive research by the book's contributors (about 60 different individuals) and by the editors. Expect some of the opinions expressed, therefore, to be subjective; and bear in mind that coverage is selective rather than exhaustive. The aim has been to produce a summary of relevant back-up information, plus selected highlights.

- **Bold place names** or geographical references in the text link to the same name or location on the map, and are an aid to locating the relevant symbol on the map.
- Remember that **early closing**, with its numerous local variations, affects many of the cycling shops and eating places listed.

Off-highway riding

There is no right of way for cyclists to *ride* on public footpaths. You may, however, ride on bridleways and on 'green roads' and tracks classed as public roads. *Cyclist's Britain* features a large selection of such routes, popularly described as 'rough-stuff', together with most of the specially built cycle ways in or near urban areas which were open at time of printing, or certain to open soon after. Many more such routes are planned for the future, and, with support from cyclists, organizations pressing for their construction may yet realize their vision of a nationwide network of safe off-highway escape routes from urban areas. (See p. 13.)

If planning to ride off-highway in Scotland, where the law of trespass is different to that in England and Wales, please note the warning on page 4.

Many of the off-highway routes in the book, particularly those in upland areas, are rough-stuff in the true sense: adventure routes to be undertaken only by the physically capable enthusiast. Many stretches will require dismounting or even wheeling, or shouldering the bike. Many will be impassable after wet weather, or much too steep to ride. Rough-stuffers should regard unexpected difficulties as integral to the charm of their pursuit.

However, *Cyclist's Britain* also shows plenty of easy, beginner's rough-stuff routing in lowland areas. Both types of riding attract growing numbers of people with a love of solitude and the urge to discover for themselves the remaining wild places of Britain. Don't let your enjoyment of rough-stuffing be spoilt by going out unprepared (see pages 12–15), and stay safety-conscious.

Cycle touring

Bicycles are quiet. You will not disturb the life of the countryside as you ride by. Moreover, cycling, like walking, puts you in intimate contact with your surroundings. You feel the wind blowing, you know its direction, and it may even bring you the scents of fields and gardens. You can listen to birdsong, notice the hedgerows in flower, and sometimes, all too vividly, feel the gradient of the hill you are climbing – or the exhilaration of a fast descent. In a sedentary and alienating age, cycling is one of the ideal recreations – a simple, refreshing way of seeing the world.

Starting points

If you have never ridden any distance before, don't worry: all you need to do is choose a route with terrain and mileage to suit you. A few short rides through gentle, preferably familiar, countryside and you will find yourself able to tackle longer rides if you feel inclined. The complete novice is well-advised to start with a guided, pre-planned ride.

It is also worth choosing routes that suit your bicycle. If you have a basic three-speed machine, then the easy terrain of East Anglia will suit you better than the steep hills of Dartmoor. If you are a regular commuting cyclist and own a ten-speed lightweight bike, you will have more scope. Roughly speaking, a novice cyclist can ride about 20 miles (32 km) in one day across mild terrain in complete comfort. The more experienced you become, the further you can comfortably travel. Bear in mind, though, that the length of a tour is of no importance at all alongside the enjoyment you obtain from the ride. Simply choose an area you want to explore, and ride at a pace that suits you. (Each regional section of *Cyclist's Britain* starts with a summary. Obviously, if the suggested route is 40 miles (64 km) long and you want the option of stopping after 20 miles, then check accommodation in the area so you can shorten the route to suit your ability.)

Access by train

If you live in the city or a long way from your chosen touring area, it makes good sense to travel there by train or car. Riding through miles of suburbs or dull countryside is a bad start to a tour. Rail links are highlighted on the maps in *Cyclist's Britain*, but British Rail have regulations on the carriage of bikes which change from time to time and need to be checked before an outing. In general you can take your bike on most trains at weekends free of charge, at the guard's discretion. Weekday rush hours are best avoided, and during the week you will have to pay a modest charge for your bike on high-speed trains, but not on most conventional trains. Ring your local station for details, and obtain the British Rail leaflet on the subject.

Safety

Inevitably, there are times when you will have to ride in traffic. Whole books have been written on the taxing business of city riding, but essentially you must ride with confidence in order to survive. Signal your intentions clearly and boldly, and make yourself conspicuous by wearing light-coloured clothing. At night, use a set of cycle lights together with a reflective body-covering such as a 'Sam Browne' belt.

Rough stuff

As well as routes on minor roads *Cyclist's Britain* includes a number of routes along tracks or bridleways. These can be tackled on a conventional machine, but off-highway riding – 'rough-stuffing' – is much easier if the bike is fitted with low, touring gears and sufficiently beefy tyres to give traction on loose or muddy surfaces. (Many sports machines are fitted with high gearing and smooth tyres which make them unsuitable for some off-highway routes.) If you are at all unsure of whether your bicycle is suitable for this kind of riding, ask at your local bike shop. Tyres and gear ratios can be altered. Recently, a new type of bicycle has appeared in the shops which is ideally suited to riding on rougher surfaces; this is the 'all terrain' or mountain bike which is designed to tackle conditions that would immobilize or destroy a conventional machine. Further information about these bikes appears on the next two pages.

Safety

Getting along out of doors is a matter of common sense and experience; but even if you have some experience, never forget that in upland areas conditions can change from good or fair to critical almost instantaneously, especially in regions close to the sea.

- Take wind- and waterproof clothing, gloves, an extra sweater, food, a torch, large-scale maps, a compass, whistle, basic tools and puncture repair outfit.
- For preference, don't go alone.
- Leave enough time for the crossing of passes. Check what time sunset will be; estimate the time you will need at the pace of the slowest group member.
- Ring the local short-term weather forecast or the local weather station for a weather report. Never attempt upland routes in poor visibility.
- Know the correct distress signal: six blasts of a whistle, or shouts, followed by a minute's silence, then repeated.
- Say where you are going before setting out, and report your return.

OFF-HIGHWAY ROUTES AND THE FUTURE OF CYCLING

Cycling is recognized as healthy, non-polluting, quiet and inexpensive – not only by cyclists but also by the public authorities. It is disturbing, then, that in many parts of Britain, but especially the built-up areas, cycling is – in fact has always been – under threat.

It is not surprising that many cycles are hardly used: parents forbid their children to ride, and the frail and elderly put their bikes away. So what can be done?

Cycling pressure groups generally offer four answers. First, give the cyclist some respite on certain main roads by introducing cycle lanes and preference at traffic signals. Second, identify and signpost safe cycling routes on roads with light traffic, and link them into networks by special features such as light-controlled crossings of major roads, paths through parks and contraflow cycle lanes. Third, reduce the speed and numbers of motor vehicles in residential areas by means of such traffic management devices as road narrowing, landscaping and 'sleeping policemen'. And finally, create routes separate from the road system, just for cyclists and pedestrians.

These off-highway routes are, and will be, increasingly welcomed and used by cycling novices, children, parents enticed back to cycling by their offspring, and the elderly.

The Railway Path Project has done much work in recent years towards building a nationwide network of such routes. The project is funded by the Department of Transport and the Manpower Services Commission to investigate, survey, publish, promote and in some cases to construct off-highway routes on disused railways, river banks, canal towpaths, forestry roads, footpaths and bridleways.

The original (1982) study, showing selected disused railways in England and Wales, is available from HMSO and Ordnance Survey. More recently, detailed proposals for South Wales, Greater Manchester, Liverpool and Cheshire, the Sheffield–Nottingham–Derby area and Scotland have been published. These are available from the Railway Path Project, 35 King Street, Bristol BS1 4DZ.

The Bicycle

1 **Rear brake** ...

1 *Rear brake* **2** *seat lug* **3** *saddle* **4** *front changer* **5** *gear levers* **6** *dropped handlebars* **7** *brake levers* **8** *front brake* **9** *rim* **10** *chain guard and chainring* **11** *bottom bracket* **12** *pedal with toe clips* **13** *chain* **14** *rear changer (derailleur)* **15** *rear sprockets (freewheel)* **16** *mudguards* **17** *rear luggage carrier.*

You can have a great deal of fun on an old conventional bike, but you do have to work harder than on a modern touring bike, which has been developed as the most efficient means of harnessing your energy.

If you do opt for a modern touring bike, the following features are the ideal.

Frame

The diamond (men's) frame is the strongest and gives the best ride. Ladies and 'mixte' frames are weaker and can flex alarmingly when heavily loaded. The lighter the frame, the better. See the illustration for hints on matching frame size to body size.

Gears

These are the key to easy riding. Touring bikes usually have ten gears, offering maximum scope for maintaining an even rate of pedalling over different gradients. The gears are operated by the front chainring in conjunction with five rear sprockets. Basically, the speed of the bike (or the ease with which it can be pedalled) is determined by the difference in numbers between chainring teeth and rear sprocket teeth. This difference, or ratio, is used in a formula to express gear number in inches:

$$\frac{\text{No. of teeth on chainring}}{\text{No. of teeth on sprocket}} \times 27 = x \text{ in gear}$$

For climbing hills with relative ease, a 30-in gear is desirable, and if carrying heavy loads, as low as 20 in. Most 'off the peg' bikes are in fact geared too high for touring.

Lowering the gearing on a three-speed hub gear bike is easily done by installing a larger rear sprocket. On cheaper ten-speed bikes, changes to the gear ratios are sometimes impossible, but more expensive bikes feature components designed for changes in gearing. A reputable bike shop should explain the options.

Handlebars

Dropped handlebars, while perhaps strange at first for the novice, are more versatile for road-riding than straight bars. They allow a variety of riding positions for increased comfort and efficiently distribute the body weight over the bike – improving bike stability, steering and spinal posture. Padded foam sleeves on the handlebars, or padded cycling mitts, reduce strain on the hands.

Seat

Sprung seats may initially appear the most comfortable, but their bounce wastes valuable energy which should go directly into pedalling. Leather, or plastic covered with leather, are the recommended saddle types because they can mould to your shape.

Pedals

Toe clips will greatly increase your pedalling efficiency by allowing you to pull up as well as pushing down. They also ensure that your feet remain on the pedals in the event of an unexpected bump or missed gear change. So long as you do not over-tighten the straps, you will be able to free your feet quickly when the need arises.

Mud-guards

It makes sense to keep mud and water on the road where they belong.

Mountain bikes

These machines, which are relatively new to Britain, evolved in California for racing down mountain sides. They have extremely light frames and extraordinarily strong brakes, tyres and wheels. They are ideal for riding on rough ground and unsurfaced tracks.

The frames have high bottom brackets, so that the correct frame size is two to three inches less than on conventional touring bikes. Handlebars are straight and wide for maximum steering control and a riding position that allows a wide view of events.

While developed specifically for riding rough terrain, mountain bikes are also excellent for high-street use. They are not as swift as a sports bike, but if fitted with road tyres can approach the same speeds. Narrowing the handlebars (to facilitate weaving through traffic) and fitting mud-guards are relatively easy undertakings for a competent bike shop.

Folding bikes

Don't dismiss folding bikes as purely a fad: they are a tidy way of complementing other forms of transport. 'Folders' are available for a range of purposes, from models with a single-hinged frame that weigh around 35 lb (16 kg) to ultra-compact lightweight models weighing 20 lb (9 kg) or less.

Setting up

Your bike should be set up with the top of the handlebars and seat at roughly the same level. Check your position by sitting on the bike and placing your heel on the pedal at its lowest point. If your leg is not straight, your seat should be higher. After some riding, you may find that the seat or handlebar positions need adjusting, especially for women who are often shorter from waist to wrists than men. Give the original arrangement a fair trial: it has been developed by experts.

Now you are almost ready to ride, but before setting off make sure everything is functioning properly. If the bike has been laid up for a while, go over it with a screwdriver and spanner, checking that all the parts are firmly attached. Lubricate the bearings and the chain.

- **Tyres** Check air pressure. The correct setting is usually marked on the tyre sidewall. Check the casing for cuts and embedded particles: a cause of punctures.
- **Brakes** Brake blocks should be firmly in place and aligned with wheel rims. Check that brake levers have sufficient clearance from the handlebars when the brakes are locked on, especially if you have dual levers.
- **Lights** Are they working? If battery-powered, are the batteries fresh?
- **Cables** Should operate smoothly. There should be no sharp kinks in the housings or frayed strands.
- **Wheels** Make sure they spin freely without excess side-to-side wobble or play in the bearings – indicated by a clicking noise when the wheel is pushed back and forth in a sideways direction.
- **Saddles and handlebars** Give them a twist to make sure they are firmly attached.

Clothes and Equipment

Even for a single day out, rainwear, a sweater, maps and food are all necessary gear. While it is possible to attach a few items to the carrier with a stretchy strap, the most effective way of loading a bike is with panniers. Rear panniers are quite sufficient for day-to-day use or short tours. If greater capacity is required for a long tour or cycle camping, front panniers should be added in order to distribute the weight equally over the bike. Front bar bags are a useful 'glove compartment' for maps, cameras and money; most detach easily from the bike and can be worn with a shoulder strap.

Lights

Lights are a must. Even if you intend to return before dark, still take them. You never know when you might be delayed, and it is both frightening and dangerous to ride on a pitch-dark country road without illumination. Both front and rear lights are mandatory. Battery-operated lights are handy for map reading; dynamo lights can give a stronger beam, but only operate when you are moving.

A red rear reflector and white front reflector are required by law, but you cannot have too many. Light-coloured clothing, a reflective Sam Browne Belt, ankle straps (which show up with pedalling movement) and reflectors attached to the bike are all sound investments.

Punctures and routine maintenance

It is useful to be able to manage a few minor repairs. If you are not naturally adept in this way, it is worth acquainting yourself with the essentials laid out in reputable manuals. Above all, know how to mend a puncture before you start out. It is no fun walking the bike home with a flat tyre. While puncture repair kits can be bought at any bike shop, always carry, in addition, a spare inner tube. It is much easier and quicker just to replace a tube than mend a puncture by the roadside. Beside the repair kit, you need two or three tyre levers for removing the tyre, and a pump. It is no use being able to repair a tube if you cannot pump it up afterwards. Finally, buy a few miscellaneous tools, such as a multi-headed spanner and a screwdriver, in case something else goes wrong. Even if you don't know a nut from a bolt, somebody else will. Recommended bicycle manuals: *Richard's Bicycle Book* by Richard Ballantine, a general introduction to cycling and a comprehensive maintenance guide (Pan, £2.95); *The Maintenance of Bicycles and Mopeds*, a light guide to maintenance (Reader's Digest, £1.50).

Food and drink

Energy being expended must be replenished, and experienced cyclists always carry some food, even if the route passes plenty of shops. When you push yourself hard, particularly in cold weather, your blood sugar content – the essential source of energy – can drop rapidly, leaving you exhausted and ill-tempered. If this happens, stop to eat some food and rest until your body has had a chance to recover. Contrary to advertising claims, chocolate and sweets do not provide quick energy; far better to eat something more substantial, finishing the meal or snack with fruit and/or biscuits. Always carry water (a bottle and rack to fit your handlebars are relatively cheap), and drink *before* becoming thirsty. Carry water, not fruit squashes – it quenches the thirst better; add some honey to boost your energy.

Clothes

How does one achieve sartorial elegance when cycling? For some, the answer is plus-fours, go-faster caps, and striped vests; but any casual clothing will do, provided it does not restrict movement. Cotton and wool, which allow perspiration to escape, are preferable to synthetics, and it is wise to wear clothes in layers that can be discarded.

- **Shoes** should be low-cut for ankle movement, with firm soles. Soft shoes allow the foot to flex, thereby wasting valuable pedalling power. Dual-purpose walking/cycling shoes with reinforced soles are available.

- **Socks** Synthetics make for sweaty feet. Wool keeps toes warm in winter.
- **Trousers/shorts** should allow easy movement. Flat seams, especially on the inside leg, are essential to avoid chafing. Custom-designed cycling shorts and trousers, while not exactly fashionable off the bike, are exceptionally comfortable for riding, and their high-cut back protects the kidney area from cooling.
- **Shirt/jacket** Wear them long to avoid inconvenient gaps at waist level. Collars and long sleeves prevent sunburn (British climate permitting).
- **Cycling gloves** are fingerless, with padded palms to help reduce numbness.
- **Helmets** Falls do not always involve a blow to the head, but when head injuries do occur, they are usually serious. Convention rather than sense probably determines the lack of helmet use in Britain. Of those available, the best combine a hard outer shell with ventilated and adjustable inner padding.
- **Rainwear** Most jacket and trouser suits unfortunately trap perspiration in as well as keeping rain out. Goretex fabric is completely waterproof while also allowing your body to 'breathe': the ideal but expensive solution. The traditional cycling cape keeps you fairly dry, but can disconcertingly act as a sail, especially when the wind is blowing in the wrong direction. Avoid rain hoods which restrict vision.

Theft and insurance

There are two types of cycle lock: serious and symbolic. Serious locks have a manufacturer's performance guarantee. If your bike is stolen as a result of the failure of the lock, you are paid the value of your bike up to a specified amount. Symbolic locks do not have a performance guarantee and most of them can be cut or broken in a matter of seconds. Serious locks are expensive, but the use of a symbolic lock invites the theft of your bike sooner or later.

Home insurance policies often cover bicycles, or can be extended to do so for a modest premium, and special bicycle policies are available from bike shops and cycling clubs.

1

THE SOUTH-WEST

Penzance is just five hours and 41 minutes from Paddington by the fastest trains, a journey time which disguises the remoteness and distinctiveness of Cornwall. Cyclists, in far more immediate contact with the countryside than motorists, are often the first to notice how different are many of the lanes and villages. The first are often narrow, and twist illogically – a motorist's nightmare, but a cyclist's dream. The second tend to be straggling and scattered, often more like settlements than villages. The neatly centred communities familiar elsewhere, and the more straightforward road patterns that go with them, are relatively rare here – an indication of how geographical position protected the ancient Celtic tribes of the south-west from the influence of Anglo-Saxon, and later, rulers of Britain.

The extreme western part of the Cornish peninsula, west from Penzance and St Ives, is perhaps the mecca of the cyclist's Cornwall. The coastal touring is famous, but there is also exceptional inland riding. The hills, though steep, are generally short.

East of Penzance, the Lizard peninsula is generally flat terrain well suited to family groups.

It is no coincidence that the route network in Devon and Cornwall east of the Land's End peninsula is essentially coastal. Inland, it is pretty enough, except where china clay mining disfigures the St Austell region; but riding within easy reach of the sea, where lush farmland borders rugged shores, is the great enchantment. The South-west Peninsula Coast Path is not practical for cyclists: only intermittent sections are bridleway, and, of course, the gradients are exhausting.

Dartmoor and Exmoor are the most obvious (if strenuous) cycling in Devon and Somerset, but no one serious about exploring the West Country should favour them at the expense of the country running from the Exe Estuary eastwards through South Dorset to Poole Harbour. Its atmosphere and dramatic coastal scenery can rival Devon and Cornwall; and Dorset really is a county off the beaten track.

Selected tours

A cross-section of the tours in this region, showing typical rides that can be put together from the route network in most localities; **further details, see pages 22–23.**

Day rides

1 Land's End peninsula
2 Quiet lanes and famous landmarks around St Ives and Marazion
3 Falmouth and Lizard
4 Pentire and the Camel Estuary
5 Western Dartmoor
6 South-east Devon
7 Exeter and Ottery St Mary
8 Dorset Hills and Blackmoor
9 Glastonbury and Wells

Two-day tours

10 Land's End Circuit
11 The South Hams
12 North-east Dartmoor
13 Axminster to Poole

Three-day tour

14 Exmoor Circuit

Seven or Fourteen-day tour

15 Four counties ride

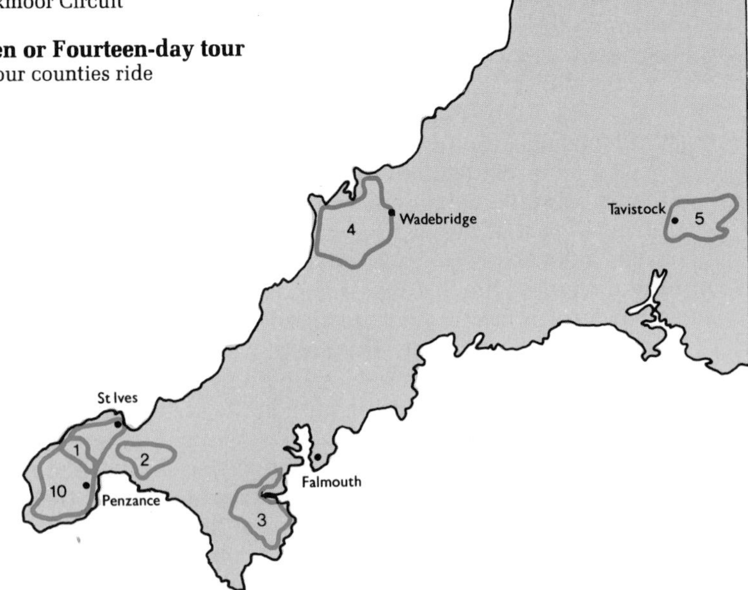

Selected tours

Selected Tours

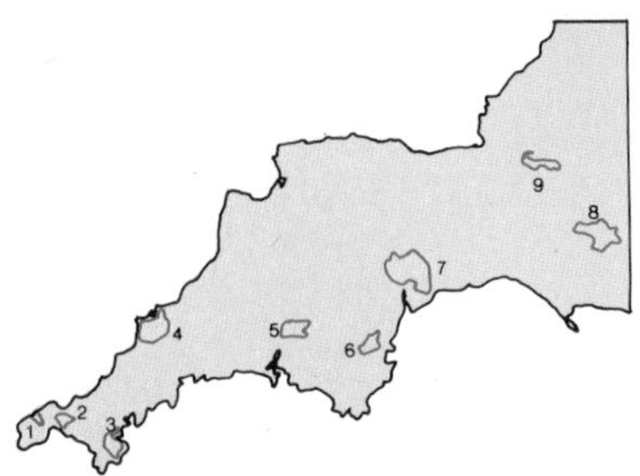

Day rides

1 Land's End Peninsula, north coast, south coast and inland, about 25 miles (40 km). An exceptionally wide range of scenery, from coastal cliffs to moorland and old mining scrapes; many prehistoric standing stones, hut circles and other remains. Medium-hilly, but most climbs moderate. *Penzance – Morvah – Treen – Newmill – Chyandour – Penzance;* **page 24.**

2 Quiet lanes and famous landmarks around St Ives and Marazion, about 15 miles (24 km). Opportunity to visit secluded Prussia Cove and St Michael's Mount. Mostly easy gradients; family cycling. *Lelant – St Erith – Leedstown – Townsend – St Hilary – Marazion–Crowlas–Lelant;* **page 24.**

3 Falmouth and the Lizard Peninsula, about 45 miles (72 km). Pretty coastal villages and pleasant views of the Helford River; many opportunities for diversions to visit beaches and clifftops. Short steep hills – some likely to be walked up – combined with relatively flat ground of the Lizard Peninsula; family cycling. *Falmouth – Helford Passage – Porthoustock – Coverack – Mawgan – Falmouth;* **page 26.**

4 Trevose, Pentire and the Camel Estuary, about 30 miles (48 km). Takes in some of the very best of North Cornwall: Trevose Head and Pentire Point are dramatically-jutting headlands, the Camel Estuary is fringed with a superb, sandy beach running nearly two miles (3 km) from Rock to Trebetherick and inland the St Breock Downs offer lovely, rolling countryside; family cycling. *Wadebridge – Trenance – Rock – Polzeath – Wadebridge;* **pages 27, 32.**

5 Western Dartmoor, about 30 miles (48 km). Few backroads cross the west side of Dartmoor, but this route gives some vivid impressions of the wilderness. A strenuous route: a long climb the first 4 miles (6.5 km) out of Tavistock, and another before the turn-off at Princetown. The ride round Burrator Reservoir compensates to some extent. *Tavistock – Princetown – Sheepstor – Buckland Monachorum–Tavistock;* **page 29.**

6 South-east Devon, about 26 miles (42 km). Samples some of the many excellent cycling lanes in this area; easy, few climbs. *Newton Abbot – Totnes – Staverton–Newton Abbot;* **page 30.**

7 Exeter and Otterton, about 50 miles (80 km). Gives the satisfaction of a relatively high mileage in a single day; for this part of Devon the gradients are generally easy. *Exeter–Cowley–Brampford Speke – Plymtree – Otterton – Clyst St George–Exeter;* **page 35.**

8 Dorset Downs and Blackmoor Vale, about 35 miles (56 km). Timeless and unspoilt Dorset countryside, the bleakness of the downs contrasting with the lushness of Blackmoor Vale; strenuous, steep climbs. *Blandford–Milton Abbas–Woolland – Kingston – Lydlinch – Manston – Stourpaine – Blandford;* **page 45.**

9 Glastonbury and Wells, about 45 miles (72 km). At Wells, one of the most beautiful English cathedrals, and at Glastonbury, the remains of the earliest Christian foundation in England. Plenty of easy cycling, but a long, moderately strenuous ride in parts. *Wells–Glastonbury–Maiden Bradley – Freshford – Monkton Combe – Paulton–Wells;* **pages 47, 49.**

Selected tours

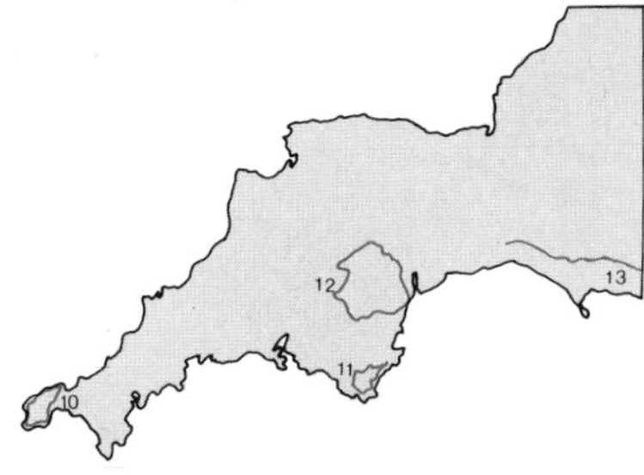

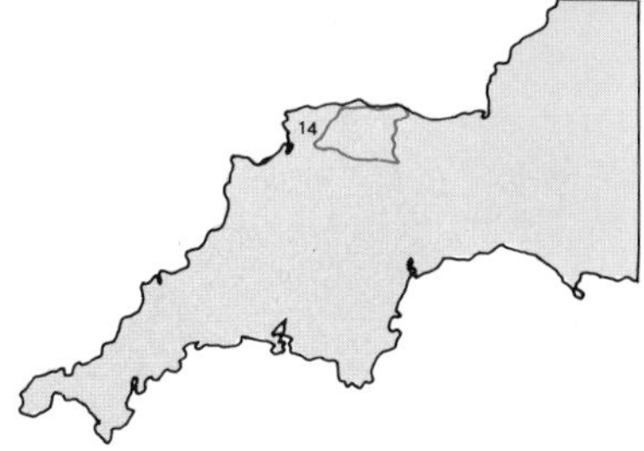

Two-day tours

10 Land's End Peninsula Circuit, about 45 miles (72 km). Windswept landscape and villages with a romantic, rough-hewn look; a survey of the most maritime region of Cornwall. Regular climbs on the coastal road, so progress is slow – and traffic is heavy in the summer holiday season. *St Ives–Penzance–Treen–Land's End–St Just–St Ives;* **page 24.**

11 The South Hams, about 40 miles (64 km). Some say the South Hams, the area south of the Dart, is the hardest area in England for cycling: hills are steep and frequent. The scenery, for those who appreciate it, more than compensates. The tour is a physical challenge – and the rewards are in proportion to the effort expended. Jawbone Hill out of Dartmouth is 1:3. *Dartmouth–Slapton–East Portlemouth – Churchstow – Bowden – Dartmouth;* **page 30.**

12 North-east Dartmoor, 50 miles (80 km). Contrasting scenery in this highly-attractive edge of Dartmoor; strenuous, with several long, steep climbs. *Newton Abbot – Ashburton – Postbridge–Widecombe–North Bovey–Bovey Tracy–Newton Abbot;* **pages 30, 34.**

13 Axminster to Poole, about 75 miles (120 km). Depending on your form, this is a challenging one-day ride or a full weekend. Both ends are served by main line railway stations; some steep hills. *Poole–Wareham–Dorchester–Eggardon Hill–Loders–Broadoak–Axminster;* **pages 36, 37, 38.**

Three-day tour

14 Circuit of Exmoor, 80 miles (128 km). Samples the cream of North Devon: a strenuous tour, low gears essential. *Minehead – Barnstaple – South Molton – Exebridge – Bridgetown – Winsford – Minehead;* **pages 40, 41, 42.**

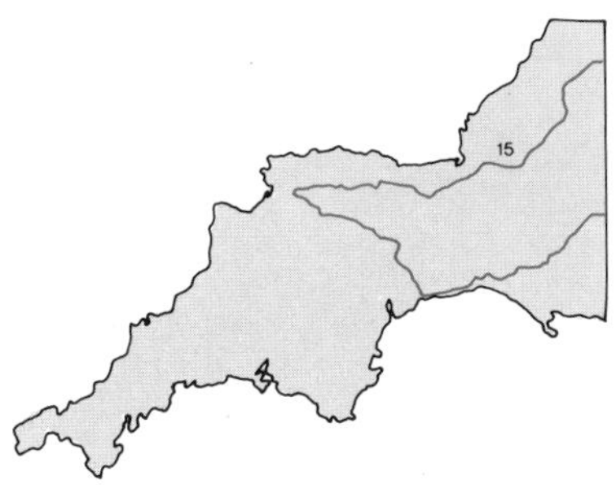

Seven-day tour

15 Four counties ride, about 280 miles (448 km). Seven days is a fast time for this tour; you could just as well take two weeks. *Salisbury – Burford – Pewsey – Marlborough – Lechlade – Cricklade – Malmesbury – Acton Turville – Bath – Wells – Street – Bridgewater – Elworthy – Lype Hill – Brayford – Barnstaple – George Nympton – Tiverton – Willand – Clyst Hydon – Ottery St Mary – Sidmouth – Seaton – Lyme Regis – Whitchurch Canonicorum – Broadoak – Bradpole – Cerne Abbas – Hazelbury Bryant – Sturminster Newton – Shaftesbury–Stratford Tony–Salisbury;* **pages 35, 36, 37, 40, 41, 42, 43, 45, 46, 47, 48, 49;** remainder of tour in next section.

West Cornwall

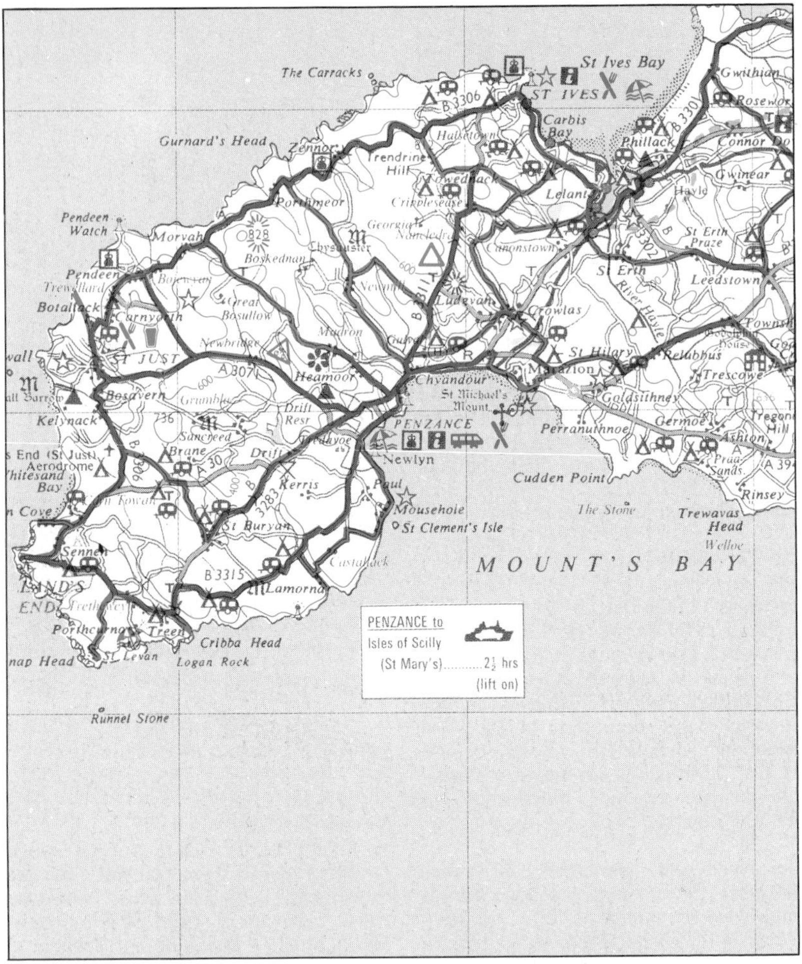

PENZANCE to
Isles of Scilly
(St Mary's)..........2½ hrs
(lift on)

- [△] Some A-road stretches difficult to avoid in this confined area, but only regular traffic build-up is on the **B3311**. Many unavoidable climbs.
- [train] **Penzance**, western terminus of the Paddington–Cornwall InterCity service, London 4¾ hrs.
- [X] Choices, with some Sunday opening, at **St Ives**, **Penzance** and **St Just**.
- [pint] The Star, **St Just**.
- [hill] Superb downhill run **to Penzance**.
- [beach] **Porthcurnow** pretty cove; **St Ives** extensive sands; **Penzance** fine promenade.
- [viewpoint] The conspicuous rocky outcrop of **Carn Galver** is worth the climb.
- ☆ **St Michael's Mount**; **Mousehole** ('Mouzel'), typical Cornish fishing village; **Land's End**; **St Ives**, seaside town and artists' colony.
- ▲ **Land's End (St Just)** Penzance (0736) 788437; **Penzance** 0736 2666.

Land's End

South Cornwall/The Lizard

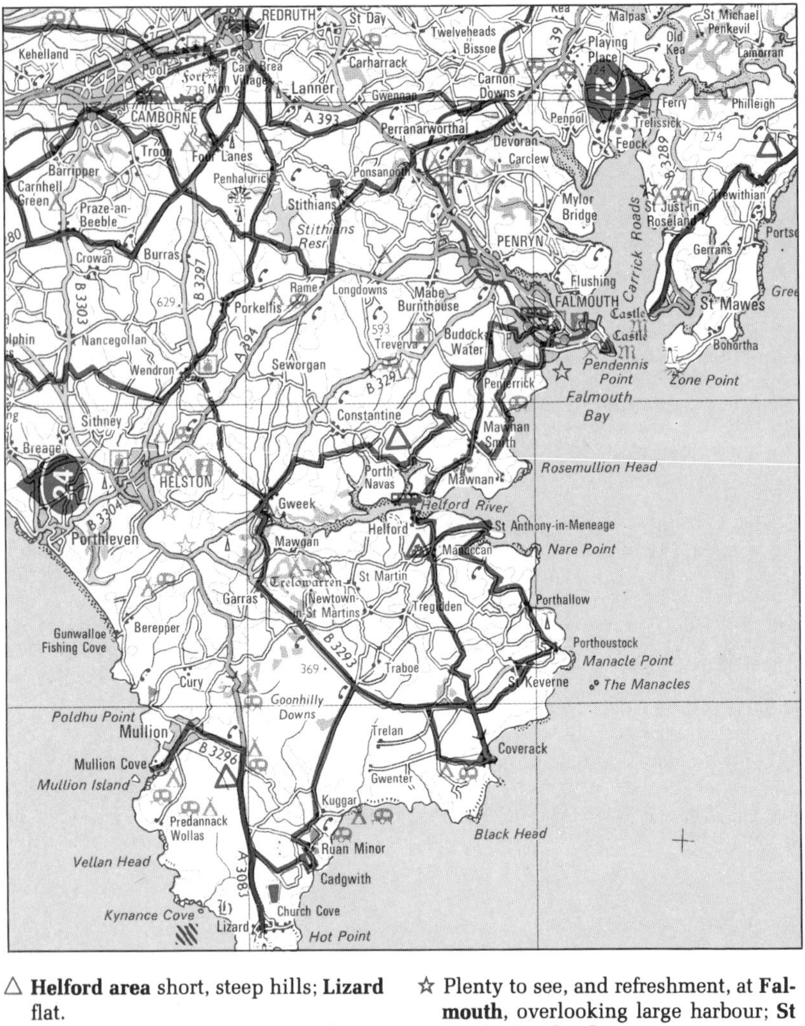

△ **Helford area** short, steep hills; **Lizard** flat.

Most InterCity trains stop at **Camborne** and **Redruth**; **Helford River** and **St Mawes** ferries carry bikes.

Golden Lion Inn, **Stithians**; Housel Bay Hotel, **Lizard**.

Pretty coastal villages and lovely views of creeks around the **Helford River**; study Landranger Sheet 204 for diversions to beaches and coves.

☆ Plenty to see, and refreshment, at **Falmouth**, overlooking large harbour; **St Just in Roseland**.

Walk to **high point of Carnmenellis**.

Lizard Point, the English mainland's southernmost tip.

Camborne Sports, 71 Trelowarren Street.

▲ **Coverack** St Keverne (0326) 280687; **Pendennis Castle** Falmouth (0326) 311435.

Mid Cornwall

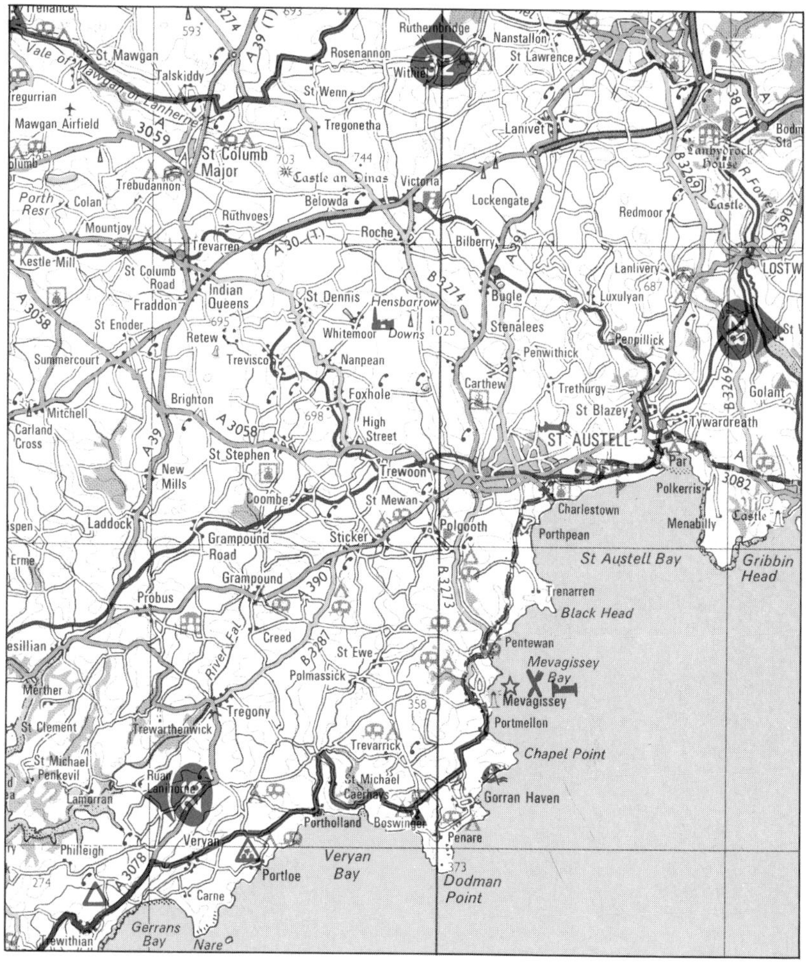

△ This 4-mile (6.5-km) section of the **A3078** is generally acceptable, barring peak times. The highest points of this exciting coastal route with fine views are only about 300 ft (91 m) but they do mean many short, steep ascents.

Recommended diversion down to **Portloe**, delightful fishing village but steep descent/ascent.

Choices at **Mevagissey**.

Gorran Haven has a sandy beach.

☆ **Mevagissey**, narrow streets, often closed to motor traffic, but cycles are no problem. A gem on the coast.

China clay country, **St Austell** region.

St Austell Barlows, Market House.

Mandalay Hotel, School Hill, **Mevagissey**, (0726) 842435.

▲ **Boswinger**, Mevagissey (0726) 843234. Well situated 16 miles (26 km) from St Mawes, popular with cyclists.

South Cornwall

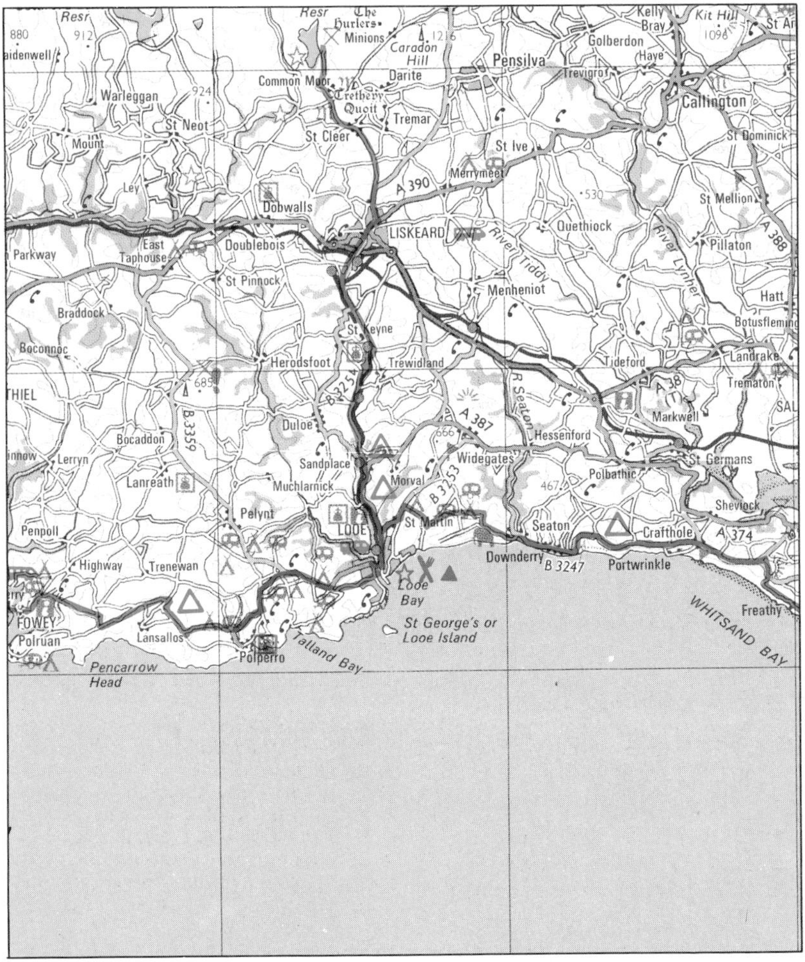

△ **Looe–Liskeard**, gradual climb up valley; **Looe–Fowey**, three strenuous climbs, otherwise mostly gentle; **E from Looe**, easy.

Most InterCity trains stop at **Liskeard**, from where the branch line connects with **Looe**. The Looe–Liskeard ride is therefore easy to assist by train, making the extension via St Cleer up to Bodmin Moor a comfortable day's outing. The **Boddinick Ferry** is the recommended crossing to Fowey – fork left at top of hill approaching Boddinick to avoid the usual queue.

☆ **East** and **West Looe**, twin villages, face each other across the Looe River. Most of the shops and refreshment places are in East Looe.

Narrow backroad beside river **N of Looe**, excellent cycling.

Polperro Smugglers' Museum.

Pixies Holt, East Looe, (05036) 2726.

South Devon/South-west Dartmoor

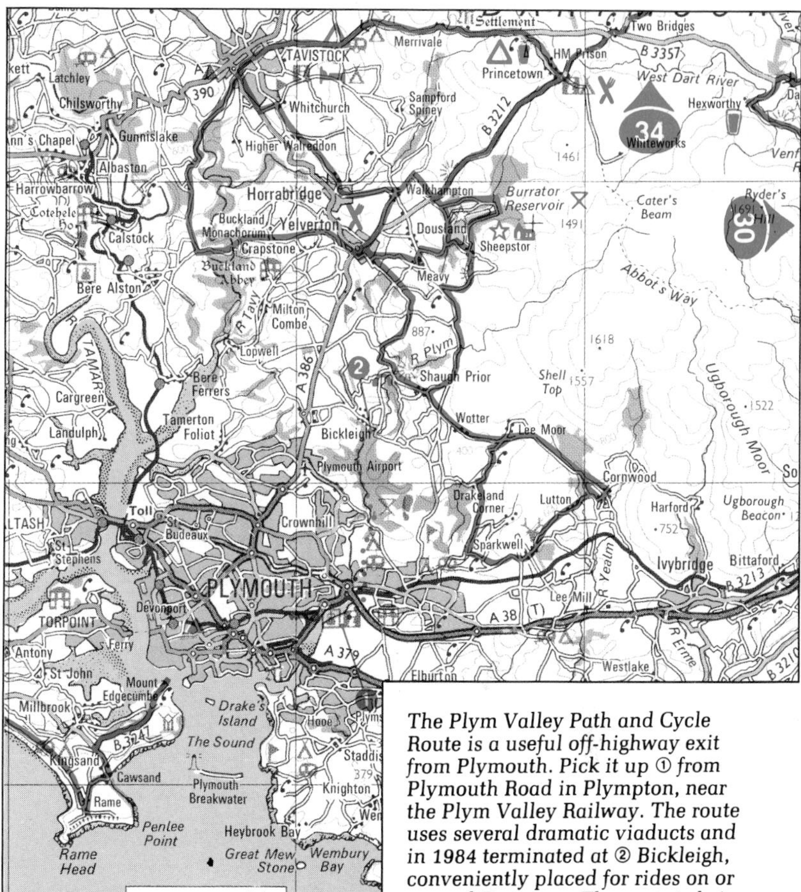

The Plym Valley Path and Cycle Route is a useful off-highway exit from Plymouth. Pick it up ① from Plymouth Road in Plympton, near the Plym Valley Railway. The route uses several dramatic viaducts and in 1984 terminated at ② Bickleigh, conveniently placed for rides on or around Dartmoor. The route is being extended – so explore progress N of Bickleigh.

△ A long climb – 4 miles (6.5 km) – out of **Tavistock**, and another before the turn-off to **Princetown**.

Merrivale has a pleasant pub; popular, family pub/hotel at **Hexworthy**.

Princetown is not an inspiring place (it owes its existence to the prison), but refreshments available; also at **Yelverton**.

Burrator Reservoir is beautifully situated, with excellent picnic places.

☆ **Sheepstor**, an attractive village hidden in a fold of the hills, has an interesting 15th-C priest's house.

Shaugh Bridge, beauty spot, walks.

Plymouth Battery Cycles, 125 Embankment Road.

Tavistock is an ideal centre for touring W Dartmoor, but its youth hostel is closed. **B & B** Mrs H. Newton, 12 Old Launceston Road, 0822 5294.

▲ **Stoke, Plymouth**, (0752) 52189.

South Devon/South-east Dartmoor

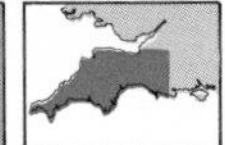

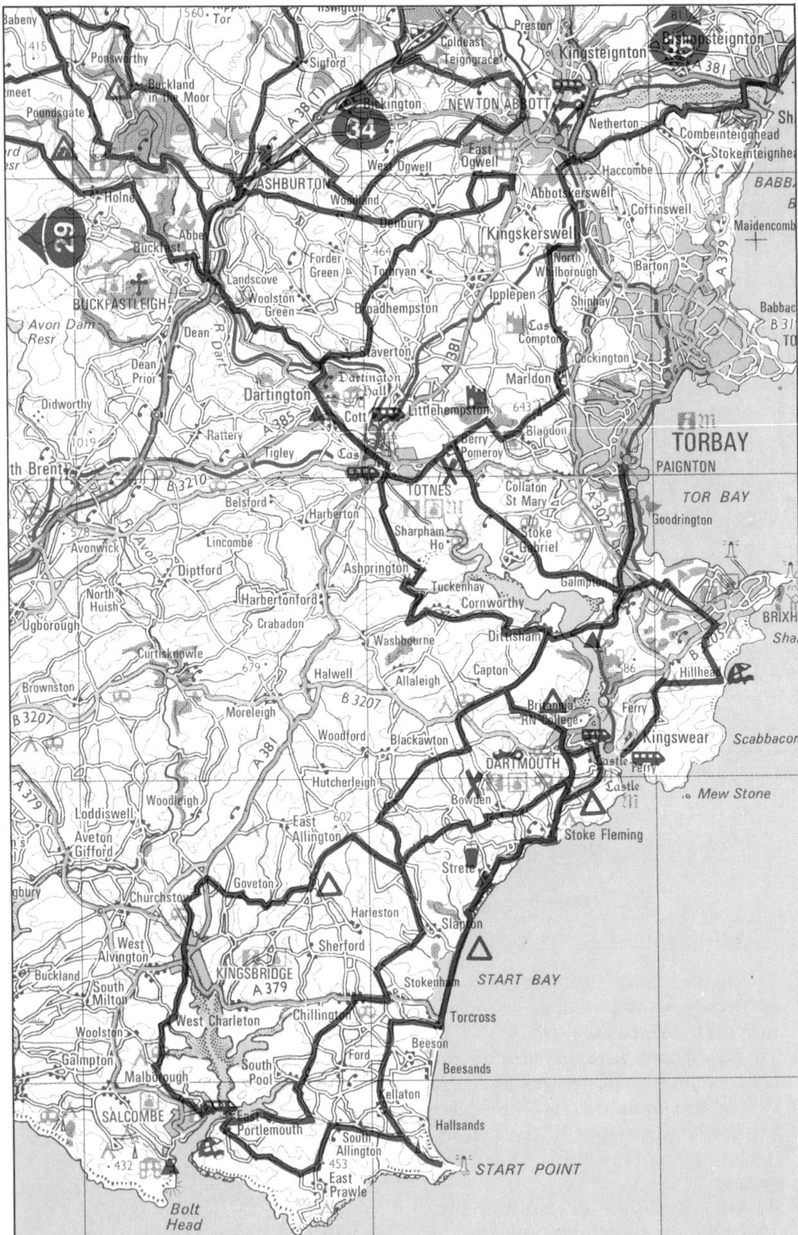

Babeny
Ponsworthy
Buckland in the Moor
Poundsgate
Sigford
Coldeast
Teigngrace
Preston
Kingsteignton
Bishopsteignton
A 381
Bickington
A 38 (T)
34
NEWTON ABBOTT
Netherton
Combeinteignhead
Stokeinteignhead
Haccombe
East Ogwell
West Ogwell
ASHBURTON
Woodland
Abbotskerswell
Coffinswell
Holne
29
Buckfast
Denbury
Kingskerswell
Maidencombe
A 379
464
Forder Green
Torbryan
North Whilborough
Barton
Landscove
BUCKFASTLEIGH
Woolston Green
Broadhempston
Ipplepen
Shiphay
Avon Dam Resr
Dean
R Dart
Cas Compton
Staverton
Cockington
Dean Prior
Dartington Hall
Dartington
Marldon
Didworthy
Cott
Littlehempston
643
A 385
Rattery
1019
Blagdon
Berry Pomeroy
TORBAY
PAIGNTON
Tigley
Cas
B 3210
TOTNES
Collaton St Mary
TOR BAY
Belsford
Harberton
A 3022
Goodrington
578
Avonwick
Sharpham Ho
Stoke Gabriel
Lincombe
Avon
Diptford
Ashprington
Galmpton
North Huish
Harbertonford
Tuckenhay
Cornworthy
Ugborough
Crabadon
Dittisham
B 3205
Washbourne
Curtisknowle
679
Halwell
Capton
586
Hillhead
Brownston
Allaleigh
B 3207
Moreleigh
Britannia RN College
Ferry
Woodford
Blackawton
Kingswear
Scabbacombe
A 381
DARTMOUTH
Castle
Ferry
Castle
A 379
Hutcherleigh
Mew Stone
Loddiswell
Woodleigh
Bowden
East Allington
602
Stoke Fleming
Aveton Gifford
Strete
Goveton
Churchstow
Harleston
Slapton
West Alvington
Sherford
Buckland
KINGSBRIDGE
A 379
START BAY
South Milton
Stokenham
Chillington
Torcross
West Charleton
Woolston
Beeson
Galmpton
Ford
South Pool
Beesands
Malborough
Kellaton
SALCOMBE
East Portlemouth
Hallsands
South Allington
453
432
START POINT
East Prawle
Bolt Head
Prawle

South Devon/South-east Dartmoor

△ **Dartmouth, Old Mill Creek**, steep with nasty hairpin near bottom; **Dartmouth, Jawbone Hill** (A379) 1:3; **A379 Stoke Fleming to Torcross**, avoid in summer (marked because it is flat, and, with a following wind, gives a fine ride past Slapton Sands – otherwise keep to the quiet inland lanes); **SE Dartmoor area** is especially strenuous, also the area S of the Dart – the **South Hams** – some of the hardest cycling in England, but worth it for the scenery.

Most InterCity trains on the Paddington–Plymouth service stop at **Newton Abbot** and **Totnes**. Totnes Riverside Station is a terminus of the private Dart Valley Railway, bikes not accepted; Dartmouth and other towns are well-served by the branch line. **Dartmouth–Kingswear vehicle ferry** accepts bikes, the passenger ferry does not; **Salcombe to East Portlemouth ferry**, bikes accepted, but must be carried down steps to jetty – regular service, increased at peak season

Dittisham ferry accepts bikes – summon by ringing bell.

Dartmouth and the Dart

Strete Start Bay Inn; **Ashburton** London Inn, good bar food, own ale.

Dartmouth Useful choices of cafés, restaurants and pubs; **Totnes** excellent choices, and vegetarian restaurant near top of High Street.

Dozens over whole area, but this **descent from the moor** is truly exhilarating.

East Portlemouth has a sandy beach; Man Sands, **S of Brixham**, secluded.

The present **Buckfast Abbey** was erected by the monks of this Benedictine foundation in 1907–38.

Berry Pomeroy, property of the Dukes of Somerset, is a fine ruin.

Newton Abbot Tower Cycles, Wolborough Street; **Dartmouth** Foot, Townstal Post Office.

▲ **Salcombe** 054884 2856; **Start Bay, Strete**, summer hostel, postal bookings only to YHA SW Regional Office, Belmont Place, Devonport Road, Stoke, Plymouth PL3 4DW: **Maypool, Galmpton** Churston (0803) 842444; **Dartington** Totnes (0803) 862203.

North Cornwall

The disused Padstow–Wadebridge railway line provides a rideable way on cinder track. Although not officially dedicated to use by cyclists, bikes are permitted. Access outside Padstow at Tregonce ① and at Wadebridge ② as indicated. The county council has real hopes of acquiring the stretch from Wadebridge to Bodmin.

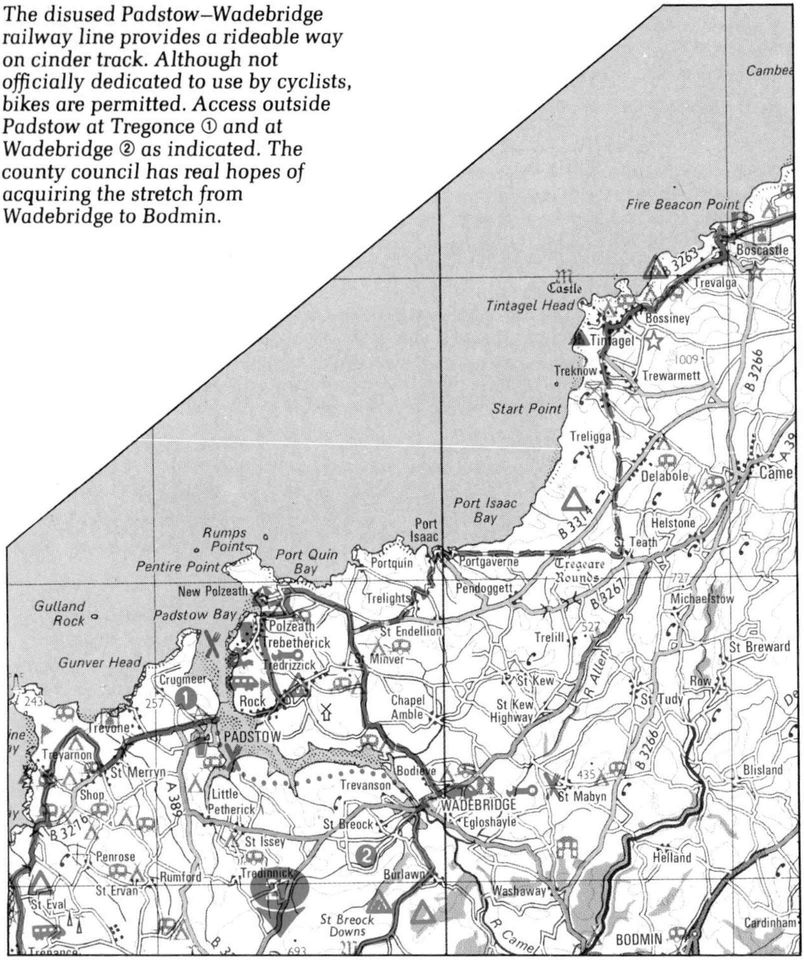

△ **St Breock Downs**, sharp gradients, elsewhere variable but with plenty of level cycling. The **B3314** is a fair linking route, but avoid at peak times, or use the marked alternative. To continue SW **to St Ives**, use B and unclassified coast roads.

Rail access limited to the branch line terminating at **Newquay** about 5 miles (8 km) SSW along the B3276. **Padstow–Rock** ferry accepts bikes.

Padstow and **Wadebridge**, choices, Sunday opening; **Polzeath** cafés.

St Breock Downs; **Camel Estuary**; **Tintagel/Boscastle**, rugged scenery.

Daymer Bay signposted from Trebetherick; **Polzeath** surfing beach.

☆ **Tintagel**, **Boscastle**.

Wadebridge The Cycle Shop, 2 Cros Street.

▲ **Boscastle** 08405 287; **Tintagel** 0840 770334.

North Cornwall/Devon

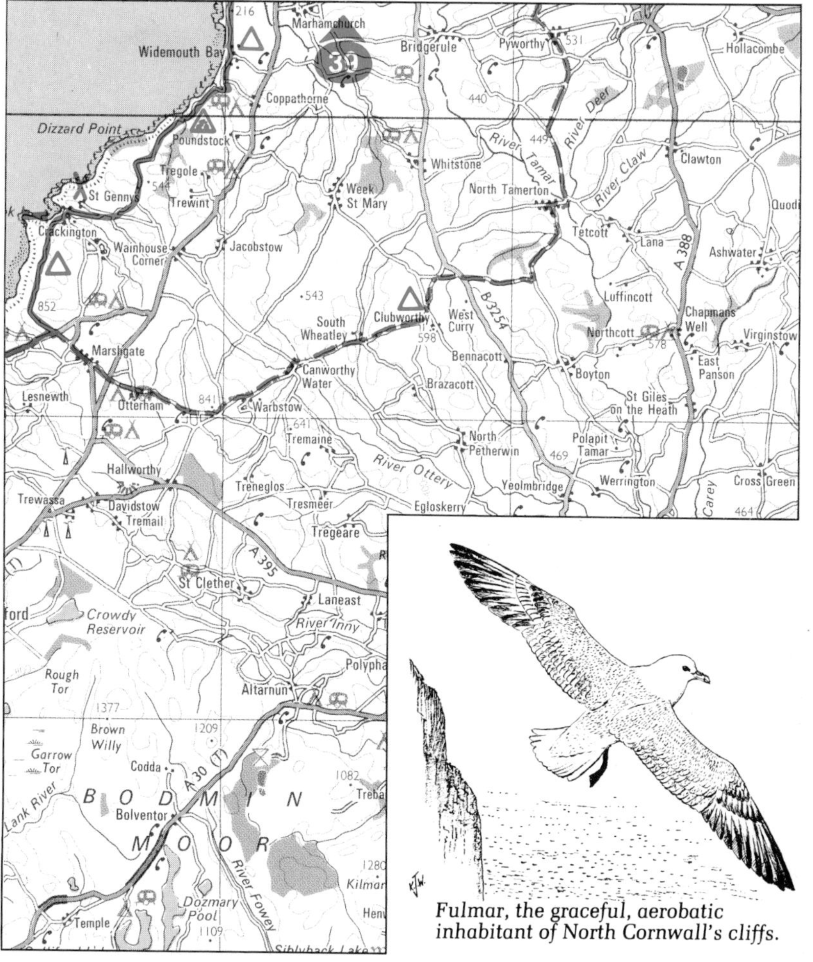

Fulmar, the graceful, aerobatic inhabitant of North Cornwall's cliffs.

△ Extremely hilly between the turn-off from the **B3314 near Marshgate and Widemouth Bay** – 1:3 and 1:4 gradients: short level stretch N of **Widemouth Bay**. The **inland route**, crossing the valleys of the Ottery and the Tamar, is hilly in parts, but has less traffic than even the quiet unclassified lanes along the coast.

Limited along this **coastal section**.

Totterham area Views back to high points on Bodmin Moor – Rough Tor and Brown Willy.

Outstanding scenery and views compensate for the climbs on **coastal route**. Allow time for uphill work, and stopping to admire.

Crackinton Haven Mrs Roberts, 26 Lundy Drive, St Gennys (08403) 410 and Coombe Barton Hotel, St Gennys 345 (latter reasonably priced, but above B & B level). Many camp sites.

Mid Devon/North-east Dartmoor

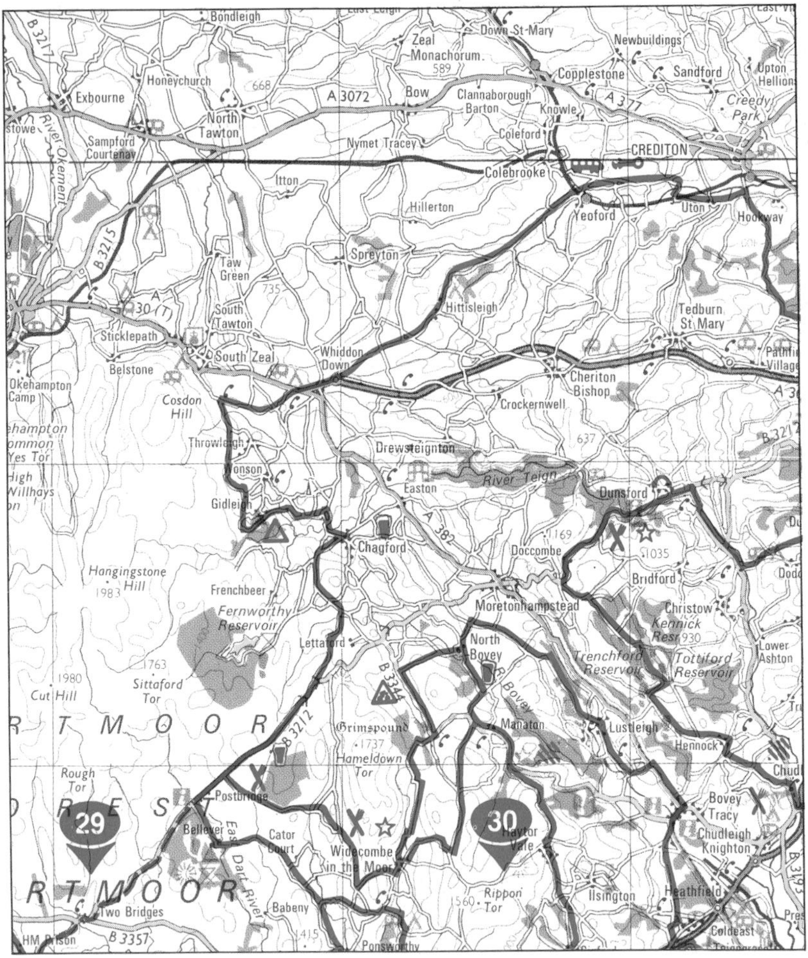

△ Strenuous on this flank of Dartmoor; approaching **Chagford** from Gidleigh expect hair-raising descents.

🚌 **Crediton** on the Barnstaple branch line.

✗ **Widecombe**, **Postbridge**, choices plus hot drinks machine outside Post Office; **Bovey Tracy**, café at foot of main street; **Steps Bridge**, café.

🍺 **B3212 NE of Postbridge** Warren House Inn, famous hostelry; **Chagford**, choices; **North Bovey** Ring of Bells.

⚠ Fine contrasts in this part of **Dartmoor** – rugged moorland, wooded valleys.

☆ **Widecombe**, walks to Lustleigh Cleave, pretty wooded ravine, and Becky Falls; **Chudleigh Rock**, and cave, worth exploring: take bike lamp.

∩ **Steps Bridge**, footpath along Teign.

🔧 **Crediton** The Cycle Shop, 100 High Street.

▲ **Steps Bridge**, Christow (0647) 52435.

East Devon/Exe Estuary

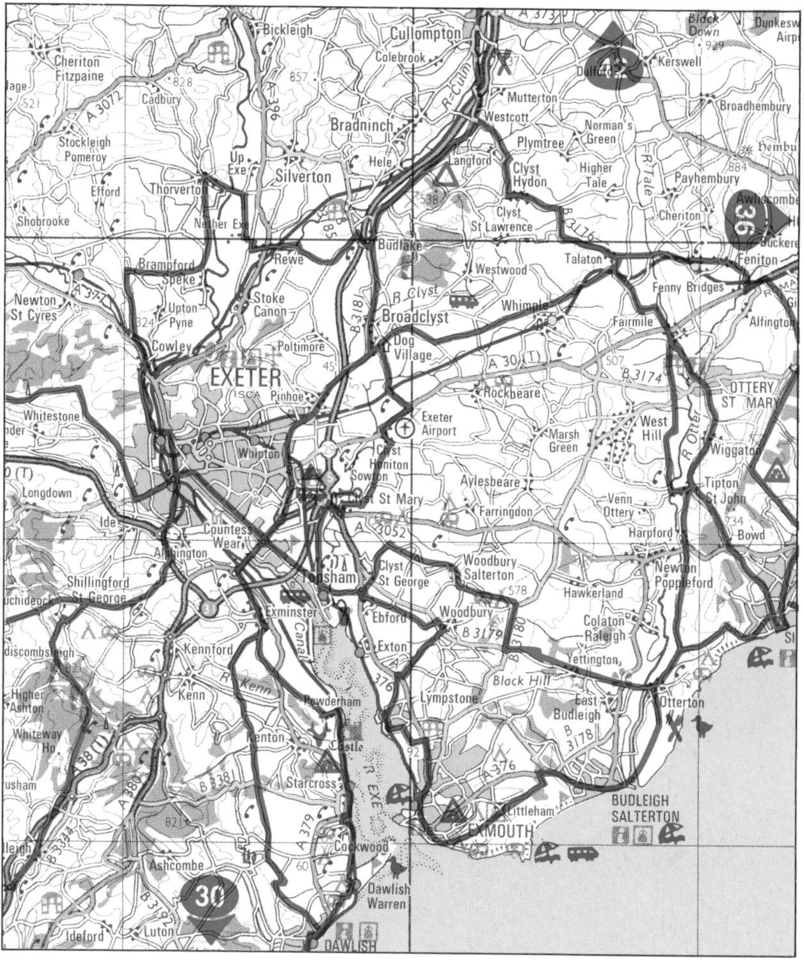

△ **B3181** little used now and generally flat by West Country standards; routes E of Exeter are generally level.

Exeter, junction of three InterCity lines; **Topsham** and **Exmouth** on branch line, for return to Exeter.

Otterton Mill Café (and craft centre); **Cullompton** Bull Ring café in Market Square.

Bridge Inn, **Topsham**, famous for wide choice of real ales.

Unclassified road SE of **Ottery** superbly situated on escarpment crest; **The Front, Exmouth** is pleasant.

Powderham, fallow deer.

Exe Estuary, birdlife; **Dawlish Warren** is a bird reserve; **River Otter Nature Reserve**.

Budleigh and **Sidmouth** have pebble beaches; **Exmouth** has a sandy beach.

Exeter Norton Cycles, 141 Fore Street.

▲ **Exeter** Topsham (039287) 3329.

East Devon / West Dorset

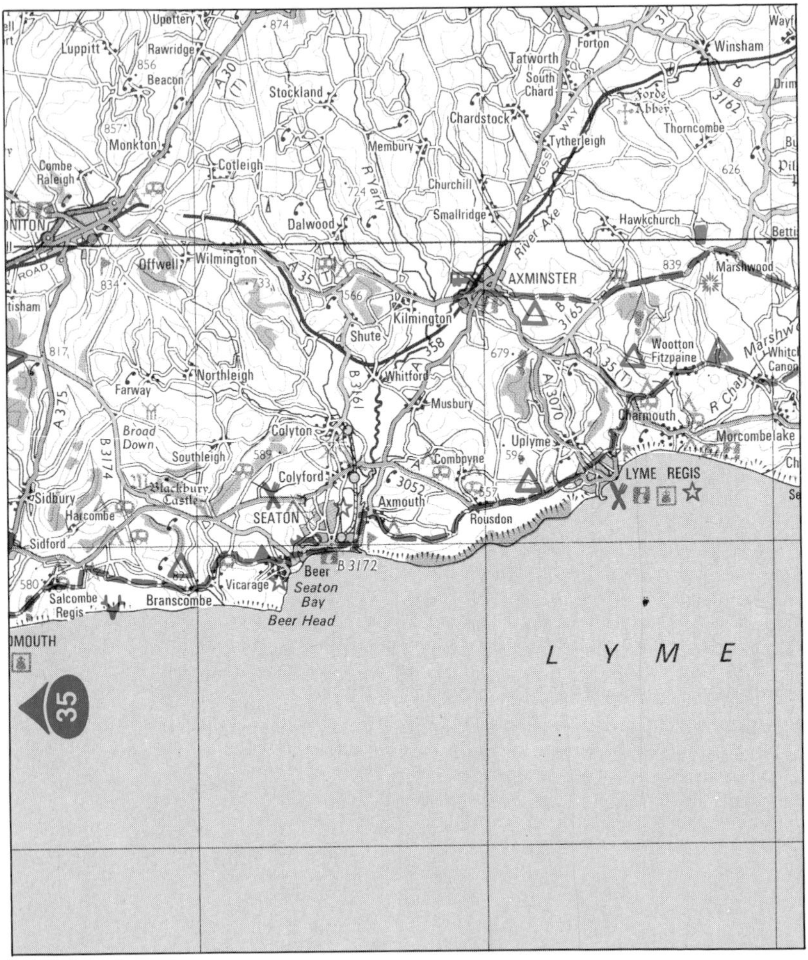

35

Sidmouth to Lyme, narrow, hilly lanes, some traffic at peak season; Stammery Hill, long ascent; **approaching Lyme from Rousdon**, near **Axminster**, long ascent, but **Lyme eastwards** mostly level.

Axminster InterCity connections.

Lyme and **Seaton**, choices.

B3165 near Marshwood, Bottle Inn.

E from Seaton, remote, narrow, pretty lanes.

Near Salcombe Regis, donkey sanctuary – guaranteed, more donkeys together than can be seen in a lifetime.

Seaton, resort with usual amenities, fine coastal walks, restored tramway; **Lyme Regis**, charming old fishing town and resort; **Beer**, superb model railway at Peco factory.

Lamberts Castle hill fort, walks.

Seaton Ayres, 86 Queen Street.

Beer Seaton (0297) 20296.

South-west Dorset

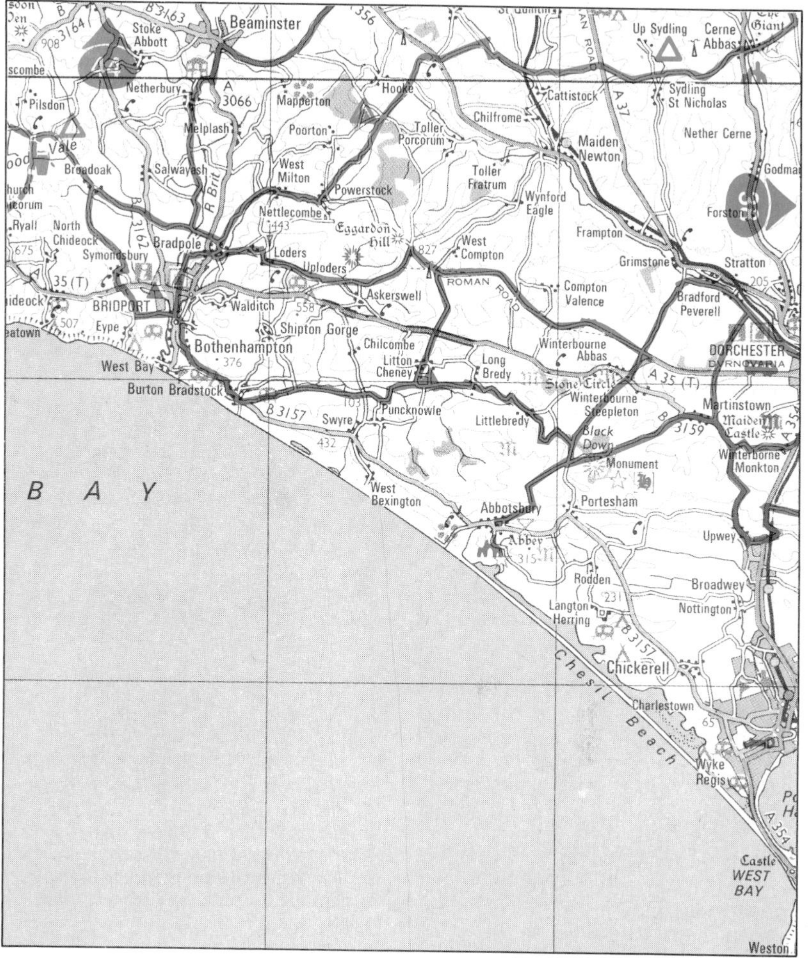

△ **Near Broadoak**, steep ascent; **Sydling St Nicholas–Cerne Abbas** long ascent.

Dorchester InterCity connections to London, branch line to N Dorset and Somerset.

Near Broadoak, pub serving meals.

Inland lanes, sense of remoteness.

Eggardon Hill, walks, views.

Maiden Castle, vast earthworks, superb walking circuit.

Hardy's Monument, to the officer in Nelson's fleet; **Cerne Abbas**, the virile giant, carved in chalk hillside, is probably an ancient fertility symbol.

Abbotsbury abbey ruins and swannery with about 800 birds; **Cerne Abbas** abbey ruins, associations with St Augustine, wishing well.

Weymouth Samways, 44 Crescent Street.

▲ **Bridport** 0308 22655; **Litton Cheney** Long Bredy (03083) 340.

South-east Dorset

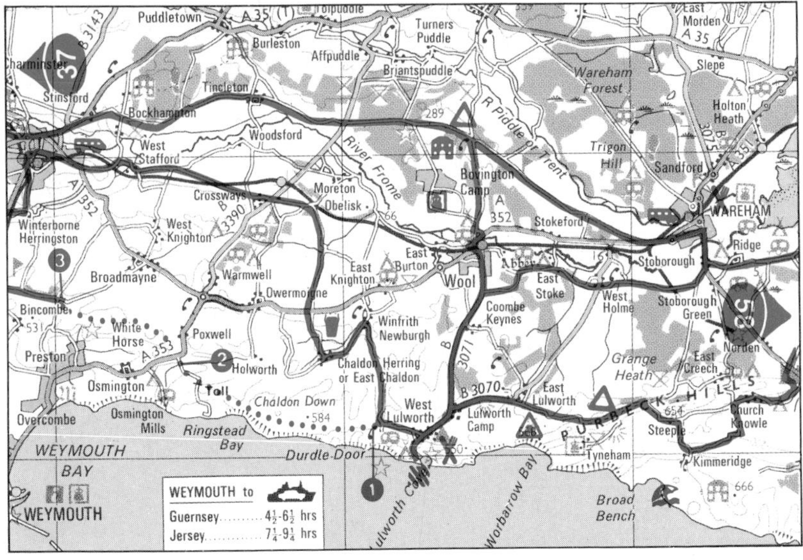

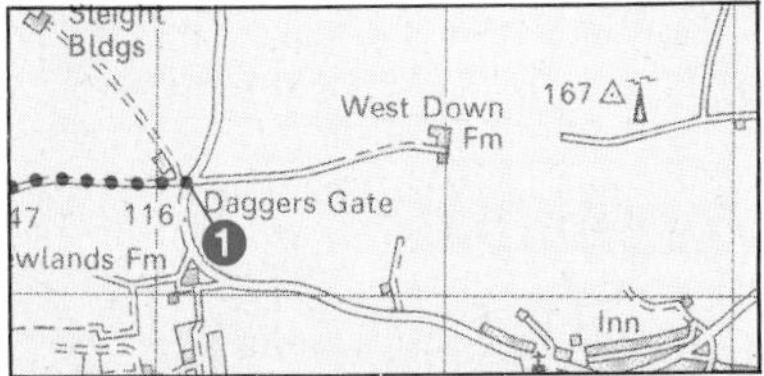

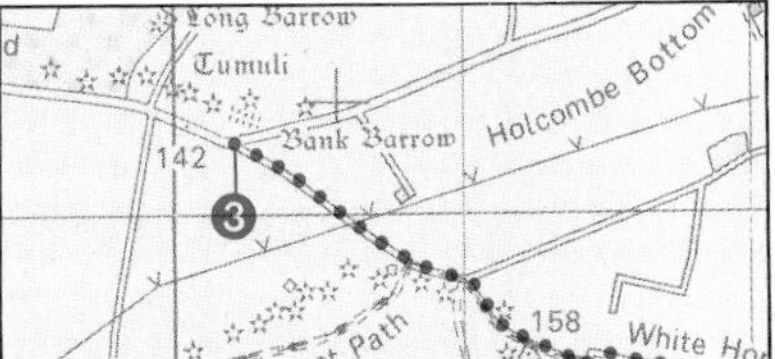

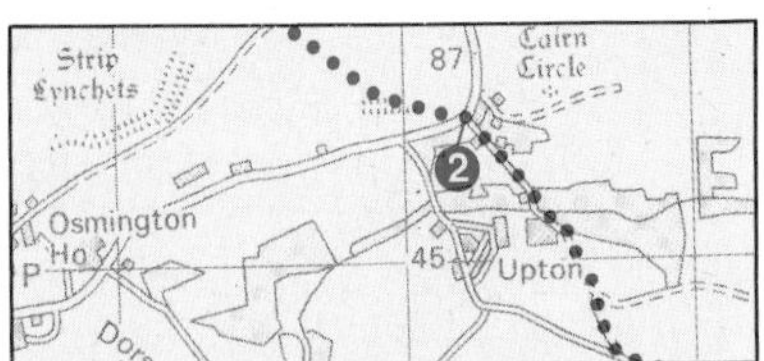

A grassy track, mostly rideable, leads W from Daggers Gate ①. In 5 miles (8 km) cross the A353 as shown ②. After a further 3 miles (5 km) rejoin tarmac ③ near Came Wood. Continue straight ahead another 2 miles (3 km) to meet the A354.

△ **Coastal route** extremely hilly, regular sharp ascents; **inland route** not nearly so demanding, or rewarding.

Dorchester and **Wareham**, on the London–Weymouth main line.

West Lulworth and **Wareham** have cafés, cheap eating places.

Sailor's Return, serving Pompey Royal bitter, is a warren of tiny rooms – building little changed since 16th C.

The switch-back coastal section from **Chaldon Herring to Steeple** is truly dramatic; views.

Signposted detour to **Clouds Hill**, cottage used by T E Lawrence.

Tank museum, **Bovington Camp**.

Lulworth Cove, crowded in summer, as is cliff path W to Durdle Door.

Access to beach from **Kimmeridg**e coastguards' cottages.

▲ **West Lulworth** 092941 564.

North Devon

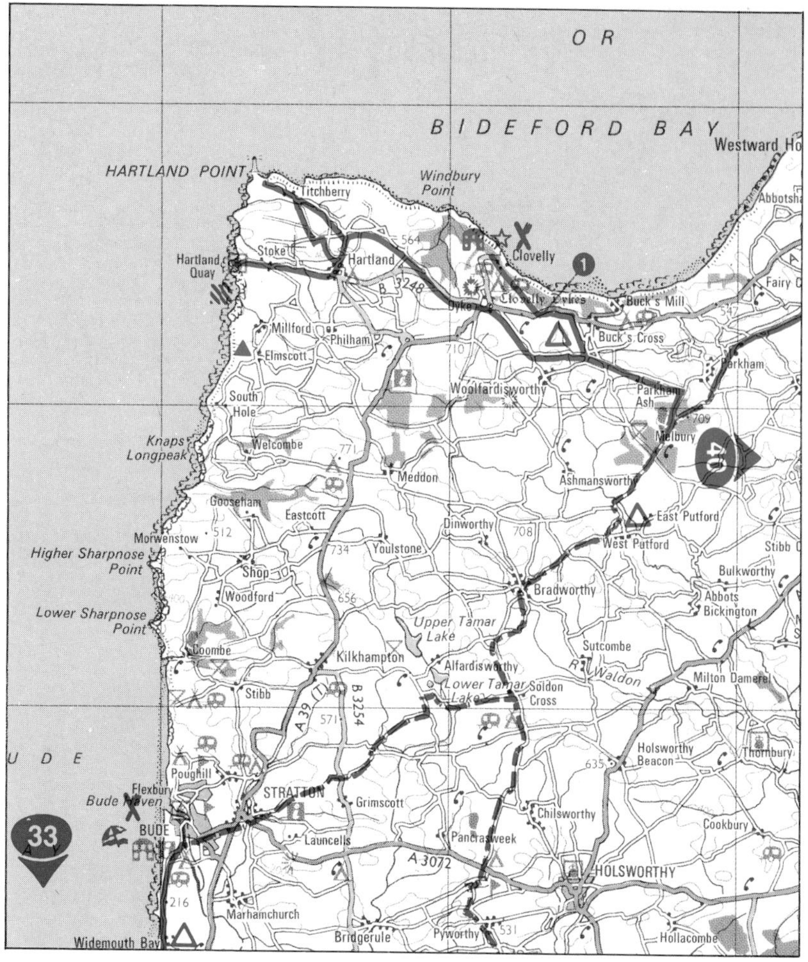

① A final approach to **Clovelly** can be made by turning off along the lovely Hobby Drive, running through woods and along cliff edges.

△ The short section on the congested **A39** is unfortunately unavoidable; short but steep climbs N of **West Putford**, elsewhere moderate gradients on inland route. The routing is mainly on lovely Devon lanes, banked and hedged; wildflowers in spring.

Choices at **Bude, Clovelly**.

A fine sandy beach at **Bude**, and superb scenery N and S; ideal place to walk the Devon North Coast Path.

Rugged scenery at **Hartland Point**.

☆ **Clovelly** is one of the most engagingly situated fishing villages in the SW, hardly two cottages on the same level. Much of interest – walks, boat trips, historic house, Iron Age camp.

▲ **Hartland** 02374 367.

North Devon/Exmoor

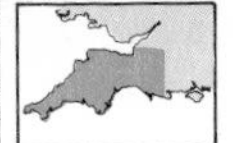

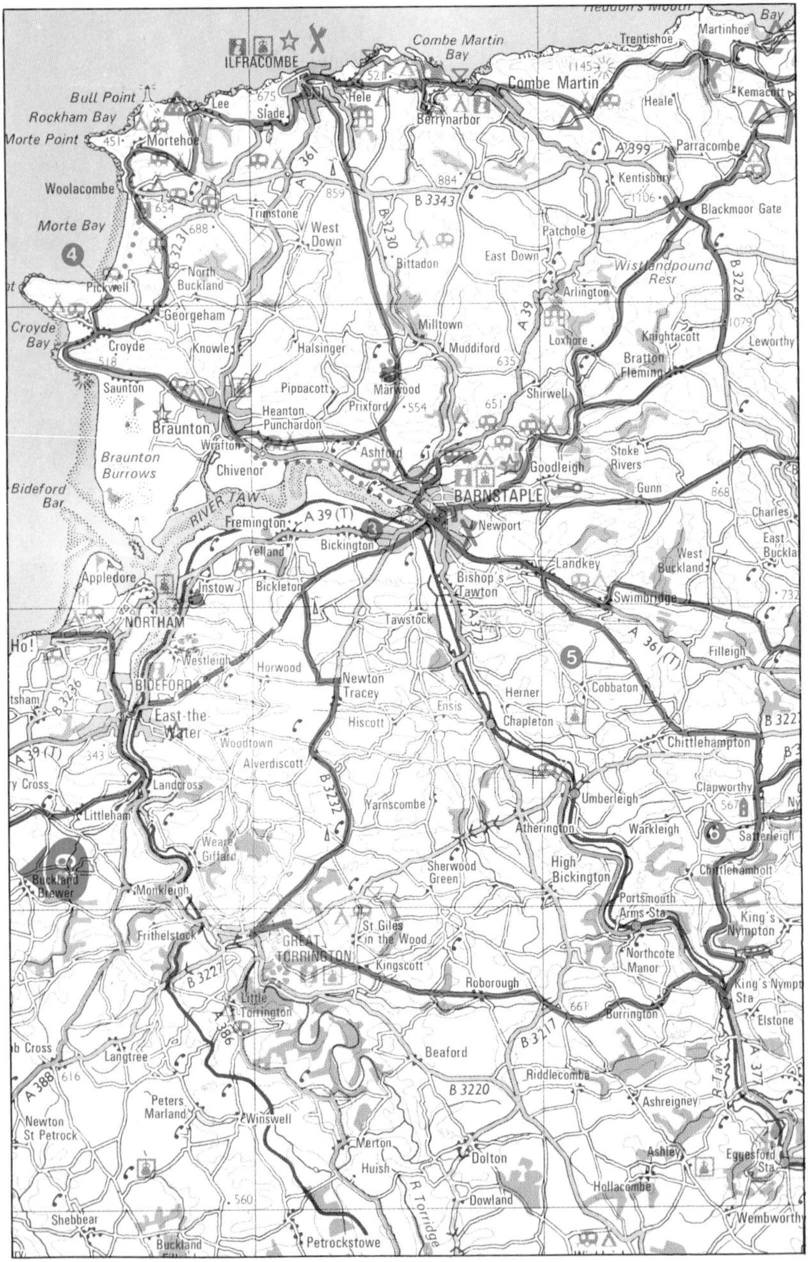
Bay
Combe Martin
Bay
Trentishoe
Martinhoe
ILFRACOMBE
1145
Combe Martin
521
Kemacott
Bull Point
Lee
675
Hele
Heale
Rockham Bay
Slade
Berrynarbor
Morte Point
451
Mortehoe
A 399
Paracombe
A 361
Woolacombe
884
Kentisbury
859
B 3343
654
1106
Blackmoor Gate
Trimstone
Morte Bay
688
West
Down
Patchole
B 3231
B 3230
East Down
North
Buckland
Bittadon
Wistlandpound
Resr
B 3226
Pickwell
Arlington
Georgeham
A 39
Croyde
Bay
Milltown
Knightacott
1079
Croyde
Knowle
Halsinger
Muddiford
Loxhore
Leworthy
518
635
Bratton
Fleming
Saunton
Pippacott
Marwood
Shirwell
Prixford
554
651
Heanton
Punchardon
Braunton
Wrafton
Ashford
Braunton
Burrows
Chivenor
Goodleigh
Stoke
Rivers
Bideford
Bar
Gunn
868
RIVER TAW
BARNSTAPLE
Charles
Fremington
A 39 (T)
Newport
East
Yelland
Bickington
West
Buckland
Landkey
Appledore
Instow
Bickleton
Bishop's
Tawton
Swimbridge
Tawstock
NORTHAM
A 377
A 361 (T)
Filleigh
Ho!
Westleigh
Horwood
BIDEFORD
Newton
Tracey
Herner
Cobbaton
B 3236
Ensis
East-the-
Water
Hiscott
Chapleton
B 3227
Woodtown
Chittlehampton
A 39 (T)
343
Alverdiscott
Landcross
B 3232
Clapworthy
Umberleigh
567
Littleham
Yarnscombe
Atherington
Warkleigh
Satterleigh
Weare
Giffard
High
Bickington
Sherwood
Green
Chittlehamholt
Buckland
Brewer
Monkleigh
Portsmouth
Arms Sta
King's
Nympton
St Giles
in the Wood
Frithelstock
GREAT
TORRINGTON
Northcote
Manor
Kingscott
B 3227
Roborough
King's Nympt
Sta
Little
Torrington
661
Burrington
Elstone
A 386
B 3217
Langtree
Beaford
A 377
616
A 388
Riddlecombe
R Taw
B 3220
Peters
Marland
Ashreigney
Newton
St Petrock
Winswell
Merton
Ashley
Eggesford
Sta
Huish
Dolton
Hollacombe
560
R Torridge
Dowland
Shebbear
Wembworthy
Buckland
Petrockstowe

North Devon/Exmoor

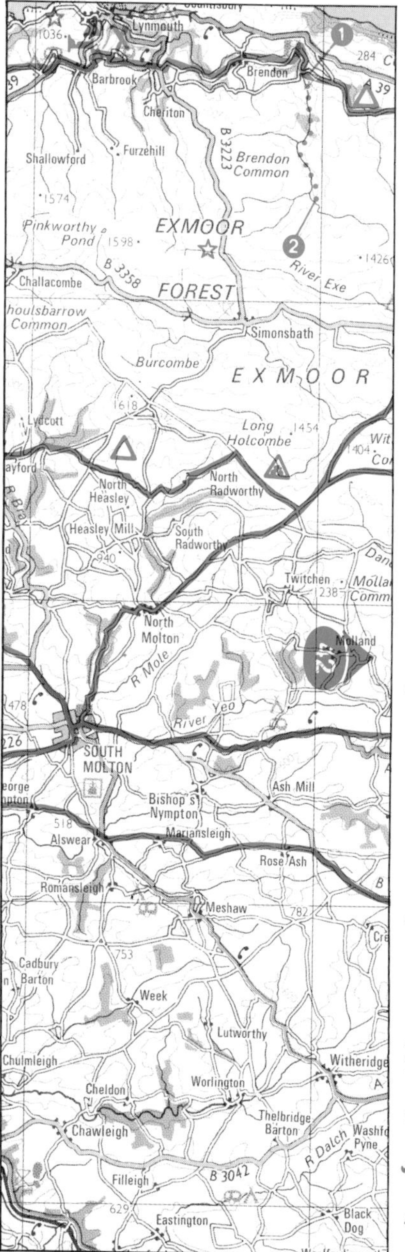

① A bridleway starting at Malmsmead follows the W bank of Badgworthy Water to ② its junction with Hoccombe Water. Do not ride further – the bridleway is a footpath from here. Landranger Sheet 180 shows other bridleways W and E over Exmoor.

③ In Barnstaple a cycleway leads from the S end of Fairview Road near the Rugby Club along the River Taw to Braunton.

④ Bridleway to Woolacombe: do not attempt after wet weather, but excellent if dry.

⑤ Several side roads not marked on map.

⑥ Look carefully for road to George Nympton. Much of the route network is typical Devon lanes – high banks, hedges on top, restricted visibility. Ride appropriately. The A39 is heavily congested at peak times. Hills unavoidable in Exmoor region, but gradients generally moderate except **Barnstaple–Lynmouth** via coast, 1:4 gradients, and **Brayford eastwards**, exceptionally strenuous. Lane near **Woody Bay** extremely narrow.

Barnstaple and King's Nympton on branch line from Exeter.

Barnstaple, **Lynmouth** (plus Lynton, off map) and **Ilfracombe** offer choices, even out of season and Sundays; Hunter's Inn, on unclassified road approaching **Martinhoe**, an attractive hotel, bar, meals, coffee; **Blackmoor Gate** usefully sited café and hotel.

Brayford eastwards is beautiful, Exmoor at its benign best, worth every pedal push; **Barnstaple–Lynmouth**, outstanding coastal scenery, opportunities to explore beaches.

Fine coastal views.

Opportunities along whole **coastal stretch**: **Robber's Bridge**, beauty spot.

☆ **Exmoor**, superb walking; **seaside towns** as marked.

Barnstaple The Cycle Centre, 8 The Arcade.

▲ **Instow** 0271 860394; **Ilfracombe** 0271 65337; **Lynton** 05985 3237.

North Somerset and Devon/Exmoor

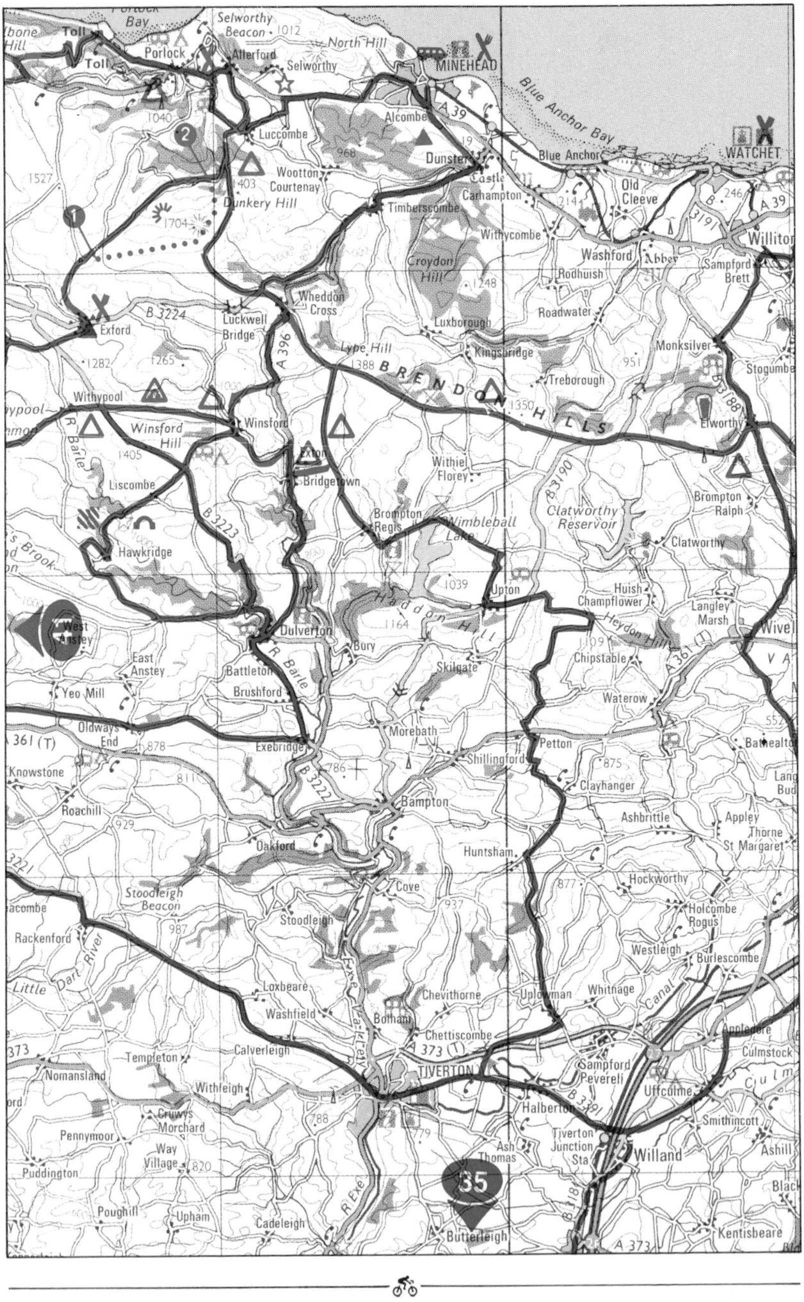

West Somerset/Quantock Hills

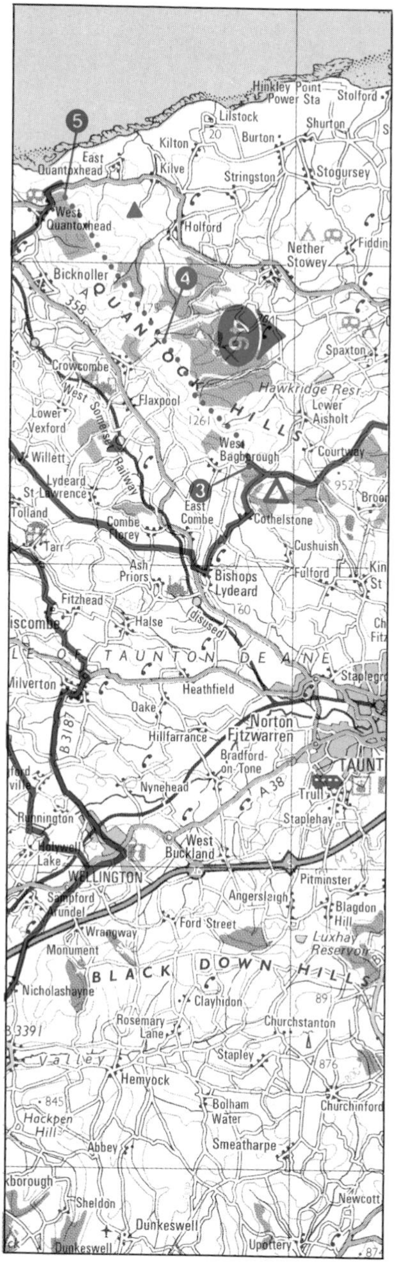

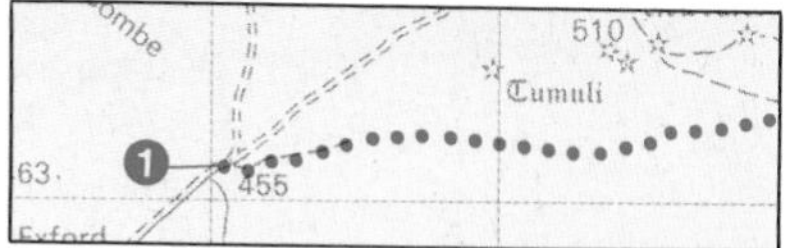

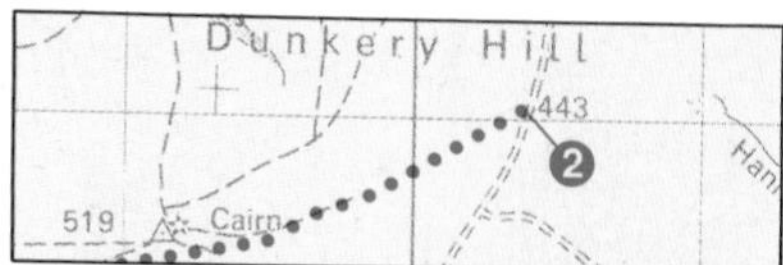

① A bridleway leads from the junction of unclassified roads on Exford Common up the W spur of Dunkery Beacon, joining the Dunkery Gate–Webber's Post road at ②.

③ Fine bridleway route along ridge of Quantock Hills: go through West Bagborough, up steep hill to T-junction. Turn left and follow the ridge via Wills Neck (highest point), cross the Crowcombe road ④ by Beacon Hill and descend by side of wood to A39 near W Quantoxhead ⑤. Mostly rideable.

△ **S of off-highway route, Dunkery Hill–Luccombe**, long, steep descent; **Porlock Hill** is 1:4, by-pass using toll road is still steep; two strenuous ascents as marked on **Brendon Hills**; **Withypool**, **Exton** and **Elsworthy** steep ascents; **ascent of Quantocks** short and steep from W, less steep from E.

Taunton InterCity connections with Bristol and London.

Choices in and out of season at **Watchet**, **Minehead**, **Porlock**, **Exford**.

Elworthy Raleigh Cross, good food.

Winsford area Open moorland, outstanding when heather in bloom.

Superb views across Bristol Channel to Wales.

☆ **Selworthy**, a 'model village'. Walks signposted to Selworthy Beacon.

Tarr Steps, ford and ancient Clapper Bridge – beauty spot, fine walks.

▲ **Exford** 064383 288; **Minehead** 0643 2595; **Crowcombe Heathfield** Lydeard St Lawrence (09847) 249; **Holford** 027874 224.

Somerset/Dorset

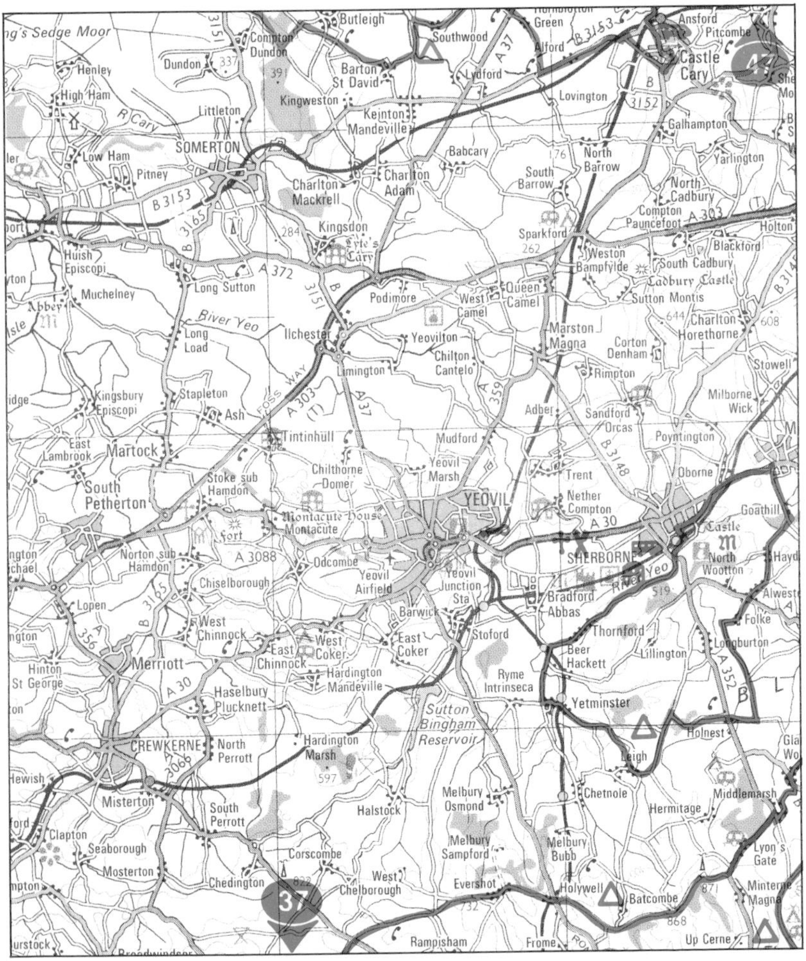

△ The **Sherborne–Leigh–Sherborne** loop is generally level, an easy family outing; unclassified roads; **Evershot–Lyon's Gate** are strenuous; unclassified roads **Butleigh–Castle Cary**, level cycling.

🚆 **Sherborne** and Yeovil Junction are on the Salisbury–Exeter main line; **Castle Cary**, is on the branch line connecting with Weymouth via Yetminster.

✗ Limited choices in **Sherborne**.

✝ **Sherborne Abbey Church's** fan-vaulted interior is not to be missed. A town of fine mellow stone buildings.

𝔪 **Sherborne** Ruins of bishops' castle (c. 1100); the present **Sherborne Castle**, built in part by Sir Walter Raleigh.

☆ The church clock at **Yetminster** chimes 'God Save the Queen'.

🔧 **Yeovil** PDE Cycles, Wessex Road; Yeovil Cycle Centre, South Western Terrace.

Dorset/Wiltshire

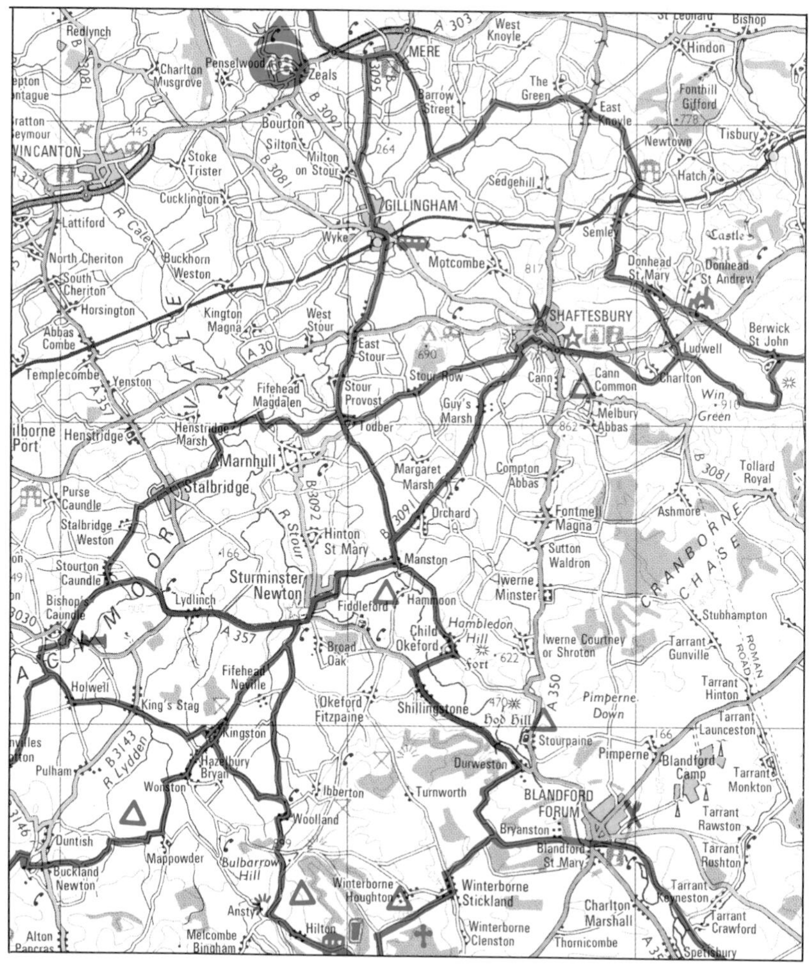

△ **Buckland Newton–Sturminster Newton**, fairly level; **Blandford Forum–Woolland**, strenuous; long climb up **Bulbarrow Hill**; **A350 at Blandford** congested at peak times – divert on unclassified roads as shown; similarly for the **A30** W of Shaftesbury; **Child Okeford–Todber** mainly level.

🚌 **Gillingham**, on the Salisbury–Exeter main line.

✗ Limited at **Blandford**, **Shaftesbury**.

The pub at **Milton Abbas** (see next-but-one entry) is excellent.

From **Bulbarrow Hill**.

Milton Abbas (name just off map to S), is a model village built when the 1st Earl of Dorchester removed the original to improve his view.

☆ **Shaftesbury**, superbly situated on a 700-foot (25-m) spur. Abbey ruins.

Bishop's Caundle Mrs S. Friar, 096 323 273.

Avon/Somerset

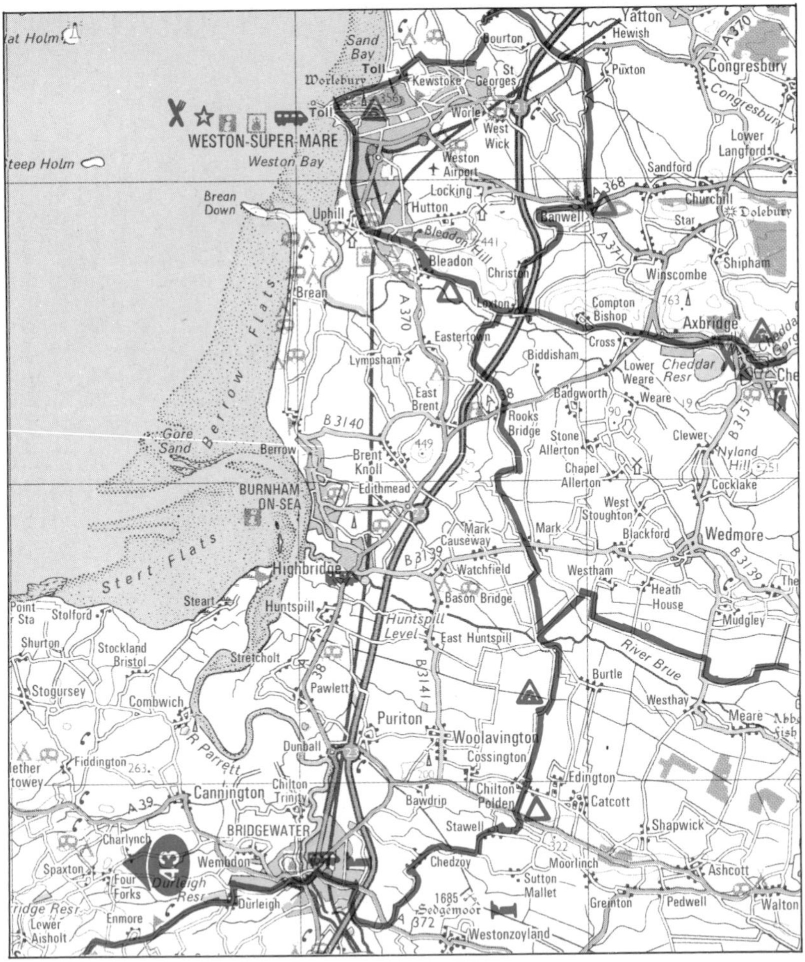

△ Except for the B3135 through **Cheddar Gorge**, traffic is scarce on the routes marked. However, crossing the **A368 at Banwell** needs care, also the **A39 at Chilton Polden**; climbs around **Bleadon**, and on to W end of the Mendips.

Weston-super-Mare, **Highbridge** and **Bridgwater**, on the Bristol–Taunton main line.

Weston-super-Mare to Kewstoke toll road, overlooking the Bristol Channel; superb level cycling on the flat land between the **River Brue and Chilton Polden**.

Choices at **Weston-super-Mare** and **Cheddar Gorge**, Sunday openings.

☆ **Weston-super-Mare**, seaside resort, piers, Winter Garden, esplanade.

Cheddar Gorge, caves open to public.

Bridgwater Hunts, 58 Monmouth Street, 0278 56424.

▲ **Cheddar** 0934 74294.

South Avon/North-east Somerset

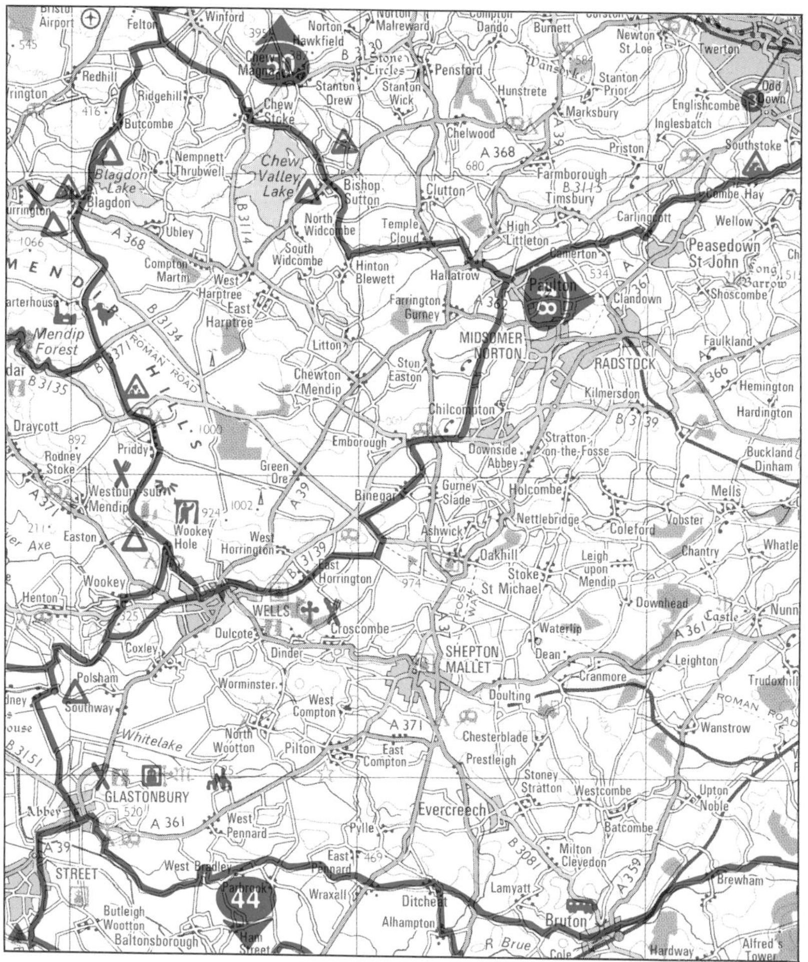

△ Steep ascents/descents at **Bishop Sutton**, **Blagdon**, **Burrington Combe**, **Wookey Hole**; **Wells–Glastonbury** exceptionally flat.

🚌 **Bruton**, on the Taunton–Reading main line.

✕ Choices at **Glastonbury**, **Wells**, **Burrington** (pub/café open Sundays); **Priddy campsite**.

⛰ Fine undulating section on **Mendips**; superb descent in **Burrington Combe**.

☀ From **Mendips**, the Somerset Levels.

⛪ **Glastonbury Tor** 550 ft (170 m) with remains of 15th-C church tower; abbey remains and rural life museum nearby.

Wookey Hole, cave, Madame Tussaud's storeroom and paper mill.

✝ **Wells Cathedral**, one of the smallest and most beautiful in England.

Charterhouse Roman lead workings, nature reserve.

▲ **Street** 0458 42961.

Wiltshire/Avon

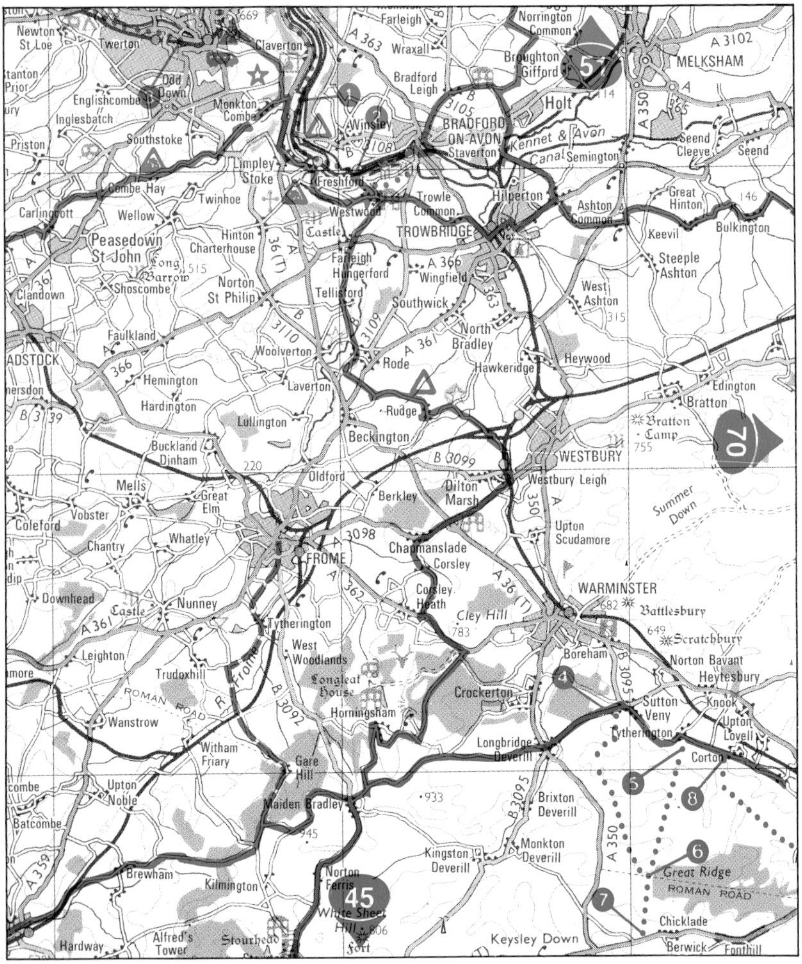

① Access to the Kennet and Avon Canal towpath at Dundas Aqueduct and ② Avoncliff Aqueduct. Bath – Dundas is an all-weather surface but Dundas–Avoncliff deteriorates when wet. Towpath avoids steep climbs into Bath; licence required, apply British Waterways Board. ② links with signposted Wiltshire Cycleway.

③ Access to Bath–Bristol Cycleway is signposted in Brassmill Lane.

④ Useful bridleways lead over the Downs from Sutton Veny and ⑤ Tytherington, joining ⑥ at wood and ending ⑦ on the A303 near Chicklade.

⑧ Terminus of the Wilton–Warminster off-highway route, see page 61.

△ Level **towpath**.

Bath, on London–Bristol main line.

☆ **Bath**, one of *the* West Country tourist destinations, a Georgian city.

▲ **Bath** 0225 65674.

Bath

Avon/Gloucestershire

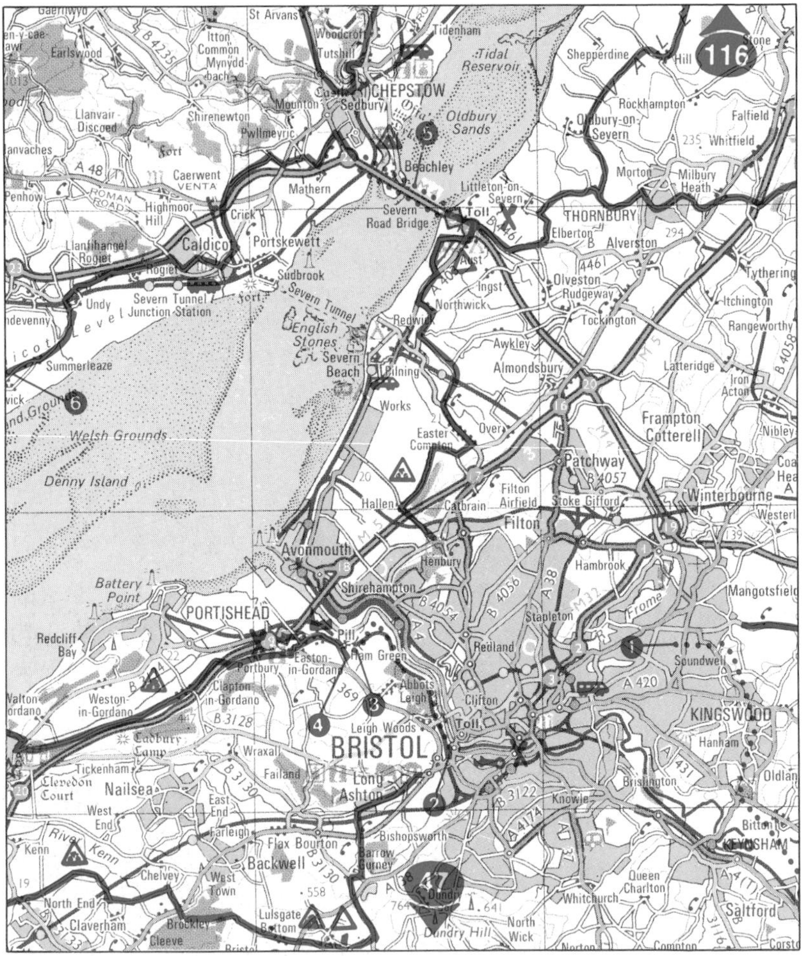

① Access to Bristol–Bath Cycleway in Thicket Road, Staple Hill.

② Access to Bristol–Avonmouth Cycleway at bottom of Rownham Hill. Near end ③ dismount and walk across field – restricted right of way. ④ Access at Ham Green Hospital.

⑤ Cycleways beside Severn Bridge.

⑥ Route continues on unclassified roads to Transporter Bridge, Newport.

△ Climb through **Brockley Combe**; use footpath to avoid **M4 Junction 21**.

Bristol (InterCity); **Severn Beach** (not Sundays); **Chepstow**; **Severn Tunnel.**

Choices in **Bristol**; motorway services open 24 hrs at **Aust** and **Gordano**.

Hallen–Severn Bridge exceptionally flat, also **Brockley–Clevedon**.

☆ **Clevedon**, Victorian seaside town.

P. C. Simpson, 76 High Street, **Portishead**; Rawlings, 7/9 Bath Hill, **Keynsham**.

N Avon/W Wiltshire/S Gloucestershire

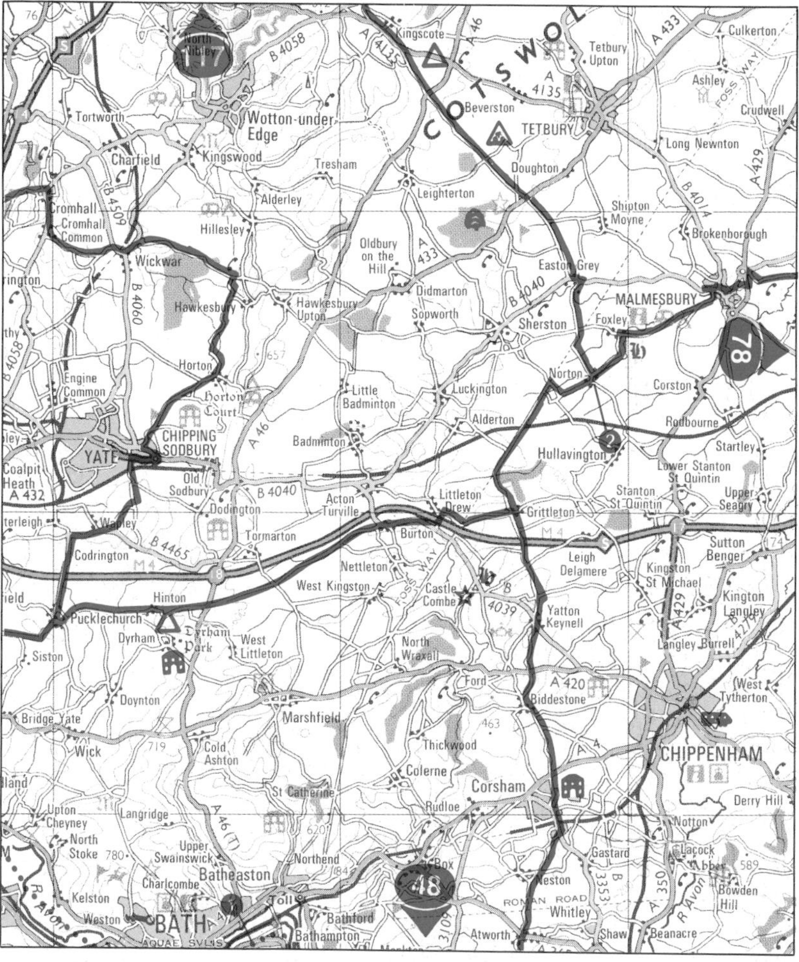

① Kennet and Avon Canal towpath, level route out of and into Bath, but licence required (see page 47): access from Beckford Road (A36) in Bath.

② Link with Wiltshire Cycleway.

△ Steep climb up on to Cotswolds at **Hinton**; **A4135** has little traffic.

🚂 **Chippenham**, on the Swindon–Bath main line.

⛰ Lovely gradual descent from **Kingscote to Westonbirt**.

🏛 Dyrham Park, a late 17th-C mansion with some fine paintings; **Corsham Court**, notable collection of paintings.

☆ Much photographed and filmed, **Castle Combe** was a major weaving centre in the Middle Ages; 14th-C cross.

🌲 **Westonbirt Arboretum** is a fine example of its kind, originally planted 1829.

🅷 **Malmesbury**, a pleasant town.

🔧 **Bath** Johns Bikes, 1 Cleveland Place East, London Road.

XVIII
Miles from
Poole Gate
II Mile
from

2

THE SOUTH-EAST

Perhaps it is too easy to be pessimistic about recreation in this heavily populated region. It may be lumbered with London's encroachments on the home counties, and the ribbon of south coast housing developments that stretches almost without interruption from Hastings to Poole; but cyclists, in particular, should look beyond the warts, for in few parts of Britain is it easier to escape quickly and convincingly from the urban sprawl. Communications, radiating from the capital, are plentiful; and the chief playgrounds – typically the South Downs and the Chiltern Hills – can seem, in atmosphere, wonderfully remote from the metropolis.

For novice riders and family groups, the New Forest is probably the mildest cycling, but its unclassified and B roads are only tolerably traffic-free at holiday time; real peace is to be found by exploring the countless Forestry Commission tracks. Landranger mapping (scale 1:50 000) is not really detailed enough; use the O.S. New Forest Outdoor Leisure Map (number 22) which covers the whole area at 1:25 000. There is more family cycling the other side of Southampton in the Meon Valley area. Continuing east, there are the South Downs, but with relatively few lanes at the Chichester end. In East Sussex and Kent the range broadens out, with opportunities for exploring the valleys between. The South Downs Way, a bridleway its whole length, is one of England's finest off-highway cycling opportunities, but remember it lies on chalk – excellent going when dry, sticky if wet.

The Hampshire and Surrey Hills are modestly demanding, sometimes underrated touring country, with a lovely mixture of landscape. Again moving east, the Weald of Kent divides into two parts: the High Weald, dominated at 600 feet (183 m) by Ashdown Forest; and the Low Weald, almost flat.

The Wiltshire and Berkshire Downs are altogether more open and bracing, and they carry another fine off-highway route, the Ridgeway Path. Finally the Chilterns – classic chalk country – provide demanding cycling barely out of earshot of London.

Selected tours

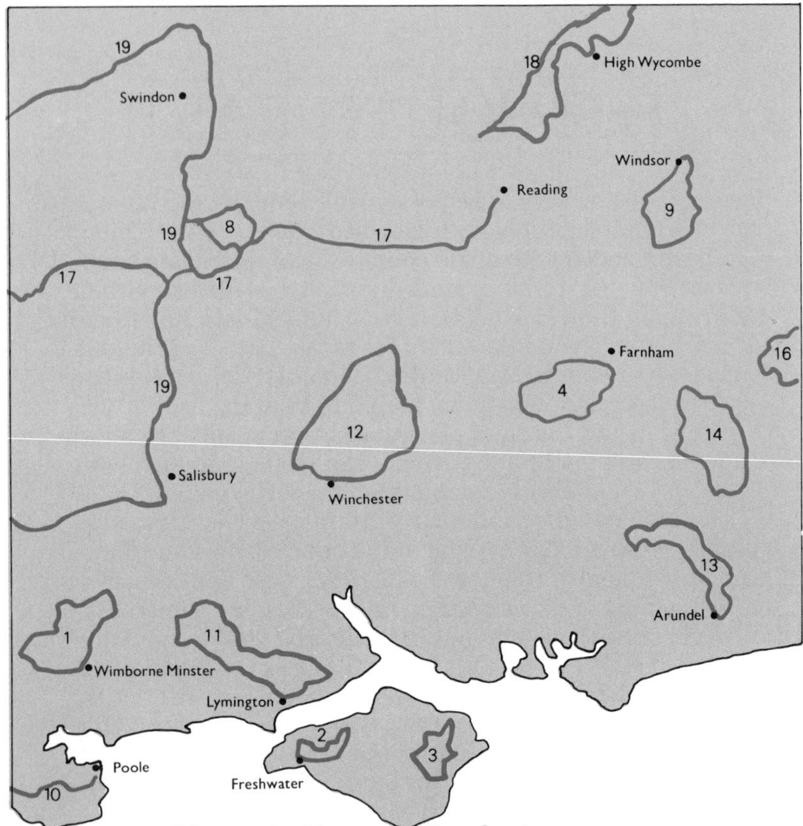

A cross-section of the tours in this region, showing typical rides that can be put together from the route network in a range of localities; **further details, pages 56–7**.

Day rides

1 North-east Dorset and Cranborne Chase
2 Isle of Wight, Yarmouth and Freshwater area
3 Isle of Wight, east end
4 Frensham Pond and Alton
5 Lingfield and Forest Row
6 Stately homes in the Kentish Weald
7 Sevenoaks and the North Downs
8 Kennet Valley and Savernake Forest
9 Windsor Great Park

Two-day tours

10 Poole to Axminster
11 The New Forest
12 The Test Valley
13 Arundel, Petworth and Midhurst
14 Godalming and Billingshurst
15 Croydon to Brighton
16 The Surrey Hills
17 Reading to Bath
18 The Chiltern Hills

Seven days or longer

19 Four counties ride

Selected tours

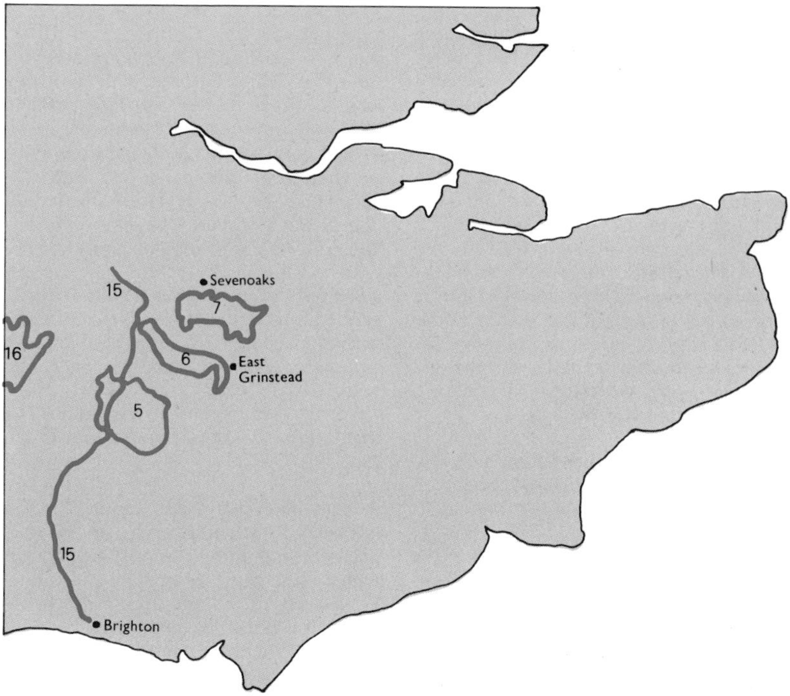

Sevenoaks
15
7
16
6
East Grinstead
5
15
Brighton

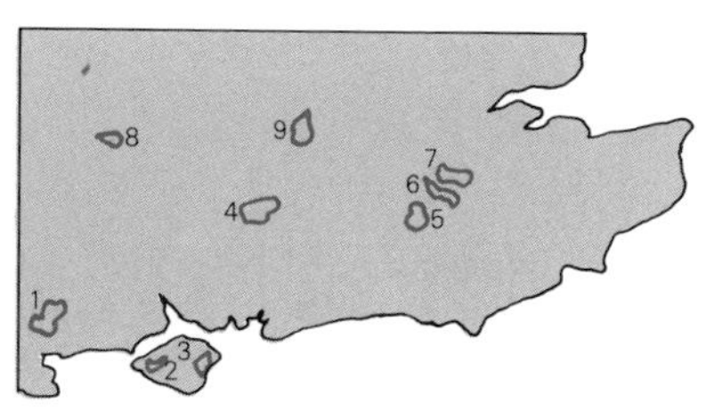

Day rides

1 North-east Dorset and Cranborne Chase, peaceful villages, woodland and quiet unclassified roads in rural Dorset, about 32 miles (51 km) – for some this will be quite a demanding day: mostly gently undulating, but some hills on the west side of the loop. *Wimborne Minster – Tarrant Crawford – Tarrant Rushton – Cranborne – Horton–Wimborne*; **pages 58, 61**.

2 Isle of Wight, Yarmouth and Freshwater area, 20 miles (32 km), a true day ride, but expect climbs, unavoidable on the Isle of Wight, and worthwhile for the views. A pleasant off-highway ride on an adequate surface (disused railway track) leads south the whole way across the island from Yarmouth, then superb views as you climb the island's central spine. Excellent rough-stuffing alternative in

Selected tours

immediate vicinity: the Tennyson Trail – see mapping – is quite smooth going once on top. Superb views of the English Channel and Solent. *Yarmouth – Freshwater – Calbourne – Newtown – Yarmouth*; **page 59**.

3 Isle of Wight, east end, 20 miles (32 km). The South-east corner of the Isle of Wight has lovely, rural scenery which often strikes people as a miniature version of the 'real' England across the Solent. A steam railway, restored and in running order, an ancient manor house and, as a starting and finishing point, the seaside resort of Ryde. *Ryde–Havenstreet bridleway to Arreton – Alverstone – Brading–Ryde*; **page 60**.

4 Frensham Pond and Alton, peaceful riding either side of the A31, about 28 miles (45 km). Some delightful unclassified roads in this western edge of Surrey, a busy but attractive country town and a village with a magnificent green. Frensham Great Pond lies in typical Surrey heathland. *Farnham – Tilford – Alton–Well–Farnham*; **page 73**.

5 Lingfield and Forest Row, through parts of Ashdown and Worth Forests, about 30 miles (48 km). Relatively easygoing, with only one or two difficult hills and some convenient stopping places; plenty of historical and architectural interest. *Lingfield–Ashurstwood–Forest Row–Sharpthorpe–West Hoathly–Turners Hill–Pound Hill – Copthorne – Burstow – Otwood – Horne – Newchapel–Lingfield*; **pages 67, 75**.

6 Stately homes in the Weald of Kent and Surrey, about 30 miles (48 km). A loop based on Oxted, taking in some of the best parts of rural Surrey and Kent, with Hever Castle, Chiddingstone Castle and Penshurst Place all on the route, which is also well served with pubs. Hills are few, and gentle. *Oxted–Limpsfield–Marlpit Hill – Chiddingstone Causeway – Penshurst – Chiddingstone – Hever – Edenbridge–Oxted*; **page 75**.

7 Sevenoaks and the North Downs, about 39 miles (63 km). Completed in a day, this is a sporting challenge, and novice riders or family groups will probably want to divide the ride into two, east and west of Sevenoaks. Strenuous, with almost continuous climbs and descents. *Sevenoaks – Knole – Ivy Hatch – Sevenoaks Weald – Ide Hill – Westerham Chevening – Dunton Green – Otford – Kemsing–Seal–Sevenoaks*; **pages 75, 76**.

8 Kennet Valley and Savernake Forest – gentle downland and woods east of Marlborough, about 25 miles (40 km). A straightforward day ride, easy or gently undulating country throughout. *Marlborough – Ramsbury – Hungerford – Great Bedwyn–Marlborough*; **pages 71, 79**.

9 Windsor Great Park, about 25 miles (40 km). A leisurely ride, remarkably peaceful and pretty for this part of the home counties. *Windsor – Ascot – Windlesham – Virginia Water – Datchet–Windsor*; **pages 73, 81**.

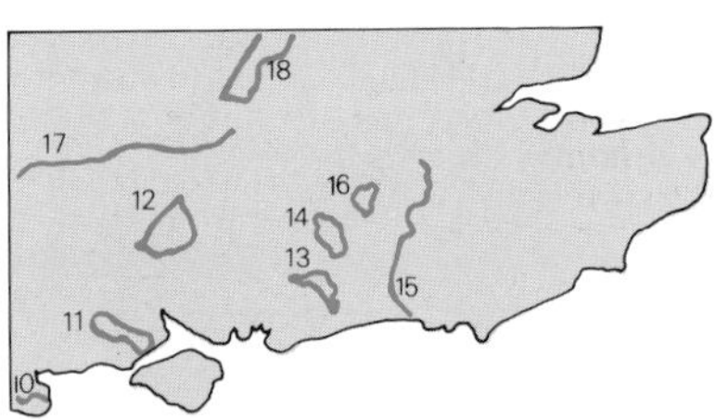

Two-day tours

10 Poole to Axminster through South Dorset, about 75 miles (120 km), with alternative routes also marked through the same area, and extensions possible as far as Exmouth (see The South-west). Excellent access by rail at both ends makes this a useful straight-line route, and it can be cycled in reverse. *Poole–Church Knowle–West Lulworth–Chaldon Herring – West Stafford – Dorchester – Martinstown – Long Bredy – Bridport – Symondsbury – Marshwood –*

Selected tours

Axminster; **page 58** and in The South-west **pages 36, 37, 38**.

11 The New Forest, about 46 miles (74 km) or, with an extension, 58 miles (93 km). Takes in much of the best of this beautiful landscape of heath, close-cropped lawn' and magnificent woodland. Easy cycling almost throughout, ideal for novices and family groups. *Lymington–East End–Bucklers Hard–East Boldre–Brockenhurst–Linwood–Ringwood – Burley Street – Sway – Lymington*; **pages 59, 62**.

12 The Test Valley, based on Winchester, with lush rural countryside and pretty villages, about 45 miles (72 km). *Winchester–Itchen Abbas–Cheriton–Whitchurch – Wherwell – Leckford – Crawley–Winchester*; **pages 63, 71, 72, 62**.

13 Arundel, Petworth, Midhurst – the west end of the South Downs, about 45 miles (72 km). Superb cycle touring through varied country and some interesting towns; based on Arundel; some pleasant off-highway sections. *Arundel–Burpham – Amberley – Rackham – Fittleworth – Petworth – Midhurst – Graffham – East Lavington – Bignor – Bury–Arundel*; **pages 64, 65**.

14 Goldalming and Billingshurst, rural Surrey south of Guildford, about 39 miles (62 km). Could be a fairly energetic day ride, but this is such ideal cycling country that taking it leisurely will give the most enjoyment; based on Godalming, headquarters of the Cyclists' Touring Club. *Godalming – Hambledon – Chiddingfold – Wisborough Green – Alford – Dunsfold – Hascombe – Godalming, with an alternative through Cranleigh*; **pages 65, 73, 74**.

15 Croydon to Brighton, a classic route to the south coast, about 50 miles (80 km). *Sanderstead – Warlingham – Crawley Down – Worth Abbey – Handcross – Twineham–Poynings–Brighton*; **pages 66, 67, 75**.

16 The Surrey Hills, a tortuous, hilly route of about 38 miles (61 km) which no cyclist in the south-east should miss: lovely villages and exceptional viewpoints. *Reigate – Leigh – Newdigate – Holmzbury St Mary – Gomshall – Westhumble – Betchworth–Reigate*; **page 74**.

17 Reading to Bath, roughly tracing the course of the Kennet and Avon Canal, about 68 miles (109 km). Fairly level cycling through fine country, with helpful railway access either end. *Reading–Greenham – Hungerford – Burbage – Alton Priors – Roundway – Keevil – Trowbridge – Freshford, then (with permit, see page 48) canal towpath into Bath or hilly alternative*; **pages 80, 71, 70, and page 48 in The South-west**.

18 The Chiltern Hills, about 84 miles (134 km). An energetic weekend up and down these chalk hills with their fine hanging beech woods. *Streatley–Stoke Row – Henley – Fingest – Saunderton – Loosley Row – Cholesbury – Aldbury – Ivinghoe – Aston Clinton – Pitch Green–Cookley Green–Ipsden–Goring–Streatley*; **pages 80, 81** and the Midlands section.

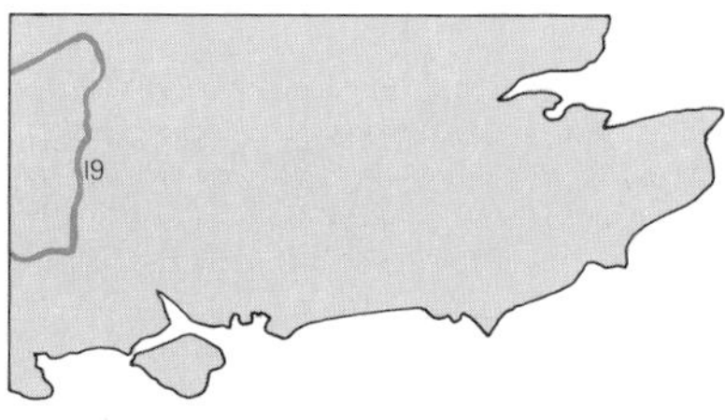

Seven days or longer

19 Four Counties Ride (continued from The South-west), about 280 miles (448 km). Seven days is a fast time for this tour: you could just as well take two weeks. Much of the best of Wiltshire, Somerset, Dorset and Devon. **Full route summary on page 23**.

South Dorset

① and ② access to bridleway along chalk ridge of Nine Barrow Down – alternative to B3351 in summer.

③ Access to Poole–Wimborne Minster disused railway at Stanley Green Industrial Estate and ④ drive to Canford School.

△ **Purbeck Hills westwards**, steep climbs/descents; elsewhere easy, especially the **Avon Valley**.

Bournemouth and **Poole**, InterCity services; **Sandbanks** ferry accepts bikes.

Choices at **Swanage** and **Wareham**, limited choice **Wimborne**; **Corfe Castle**, cream teas; **Studland**.

Square and Compass Inn, **Worth Matravers**.

Studland Bay, extensive sandy beach.

Poole Shepherds Cycles, 319 Ashley Road; **Bournemouth** George Dixon Cycles, 244 Charminster Road.

▲ **Swanage** 0929 42213.

South Hampshire/Isle of Wight

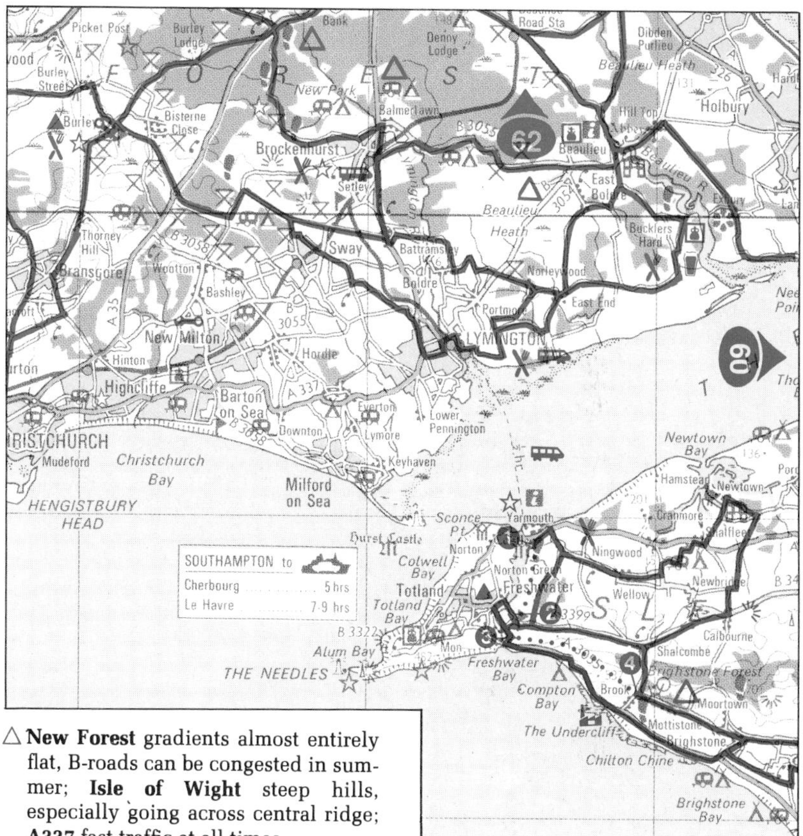

△ **New Forest** gradients almost entirely flat, B-roads can be congested in summer; **Isle of Wight** steep hills, especially going across central ridge; **A337** fast traffic at all times.

Brockenhurst, frequent InterCity connections, branch line to **Lymington**; **Lymington–Yarmouth** ferry accepts bikes.

Lymington and **Yarmouth**, choices; **Bucklers Hard**, Mulberry Tea rooms; **Burley**, **Brockenhurst**, some choice.

Bucklers Hard the Master Builder's Arms.

Beaulieu National Motor Museum, Palace House and abbey ruins; **Bucklers Hard** Maritime Museum.

☆ **Yarmouth**, yachting port; **Brockenhurst** and **Burley**; **New Forest**, heath and woodland.

New Milton Wareham Brothers, 36 Station Road.

▲ **Burley** 04253 3233; **Totland Bay** Freshwater (0983) 752165.

① Right out of The Square, left on to A3055, then second right, Victoria Road, which runs into Station Road. Through old station, down platform, and right on to bridleway/disused track. ② Right on to road at stone bridge. Access to Tennyson Trail bridleway ③ is in Southdown Road near golf club signposted 'F32 Shalcombe'; at next sign continue on Tennyson Trail. ④ Right through gate, then right on to main road.

Isle of Wight

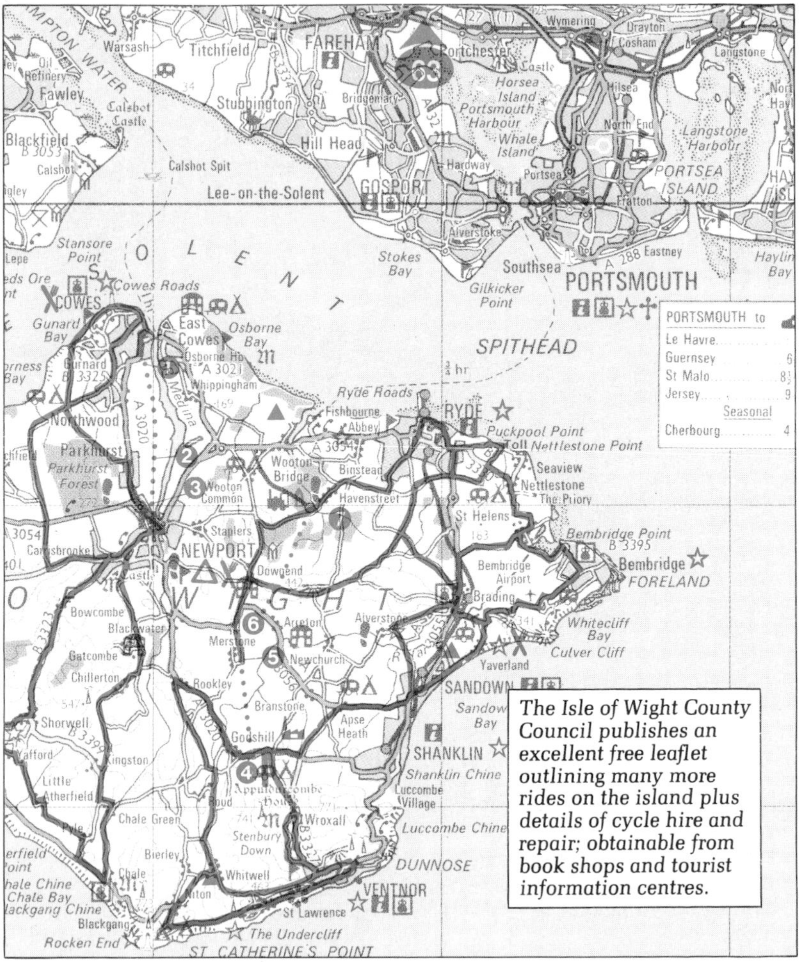

The Isle of Wight County Council publishes an excellent free leaflet outlining many more rides on the island plus details of cycle hire and repair; obtainable from book shops and tourist information centres.

① Access to Cowes–Newport Cycleway marked in Medina Industrial Estate by rectangular cycling sign, ② at Stag Lane and ③ from Dodnor Lane, 1 mile (1.5 km) N of Newport town centre.

④ Bridleway to Budbridge Manor leads off left just after Godshill. Pass Manor and turn right where two paths meet; after 50 yards (60 m) continue on tarmac lane; continue on bridleway to Horringford, ⑤.

⑥ Bridleway (N18) leads off near steam railway; straight on at next sign, exit on road, ⑦.

△ Away from A-roads, light traffic; many climbs but usually short.

Ⅹ Choices **as marked**, and others.

☆ **Cowes**, yachting; **Shanklin, Ventnor, Ryde** and other seaside resorts.

▲ **Wootton Bridge** 0983 882348; **Sandown** 0983 402651; **Whitwell** Niton (0983) 730473.

Wiltshire / Hampshire / Dorset

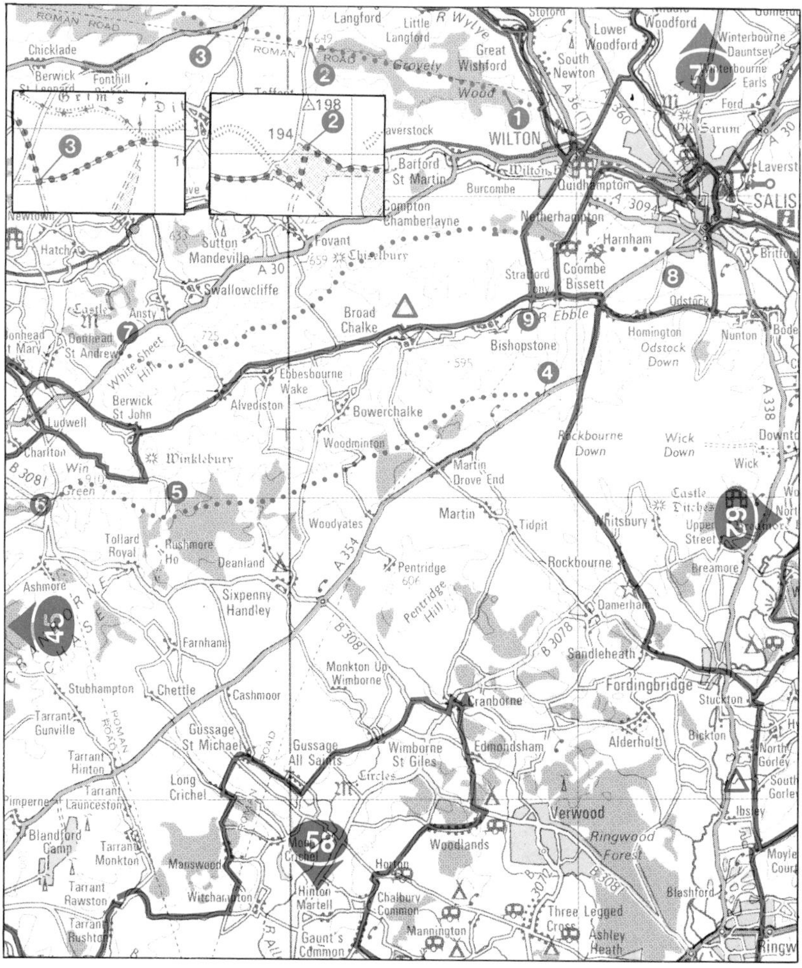

① Near railway bridge turn left up stony track for Grovely Ridge route; ② and ③ as indicated on Landranger excerpts.

④ Ox Drove branches off right near Hill-crest Kennels and filling station. Easily followed to ⑤ junction sign-posted Win Green Hill, ⑥. Some tarmac, but generally *mud after rain*.

⑦ Old coach road follows the Herepath, access from A30 opposite Donhead St Andrew turning. Track is easily followed to ⑧ the A354. Ride from W to E – gradual descent from White Sheet Hill (surface badly eroded).

△ **Fordingbridge – Ringwood** and **Coombe Bissett–Ebbesbourne Wake** are generally easy cycling; elsewhere long climbs. **Salisbury** difficult for cyclists, lanes indicated hard to locate on leaving.

⊶ **Salisbury** Hayball, 35 Rollestone Street.

▲ **Cranborne** 07254 285.

South Hampshire/New Forest

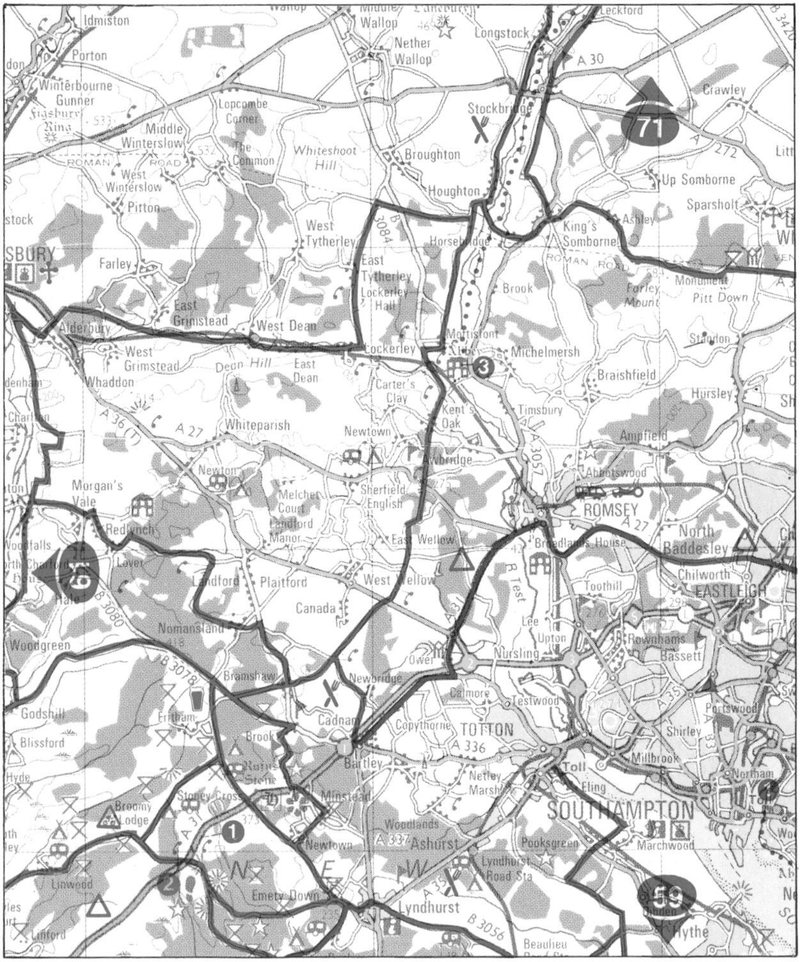

① A31 can only be crossed from S to N here; tunnel under A31 at ②.

③ Access to Test Valley disused railway at Mottisfont Car Park, off A3057 and A3057 at Fullerton (Old Station site).

④ Access to Southampton E shore route, Victoria Road.

△ Avoid **A31** at all times; **N Southampton** is a linking route only; near **Godshill**, ford with slippery surface, footbridge alternative.

Romsey, Southampton – Salisbury branch line.

Choices **Lyndhurst, Cadnam, Stockbridge.**

Fritham, unspoilt pub, Pompey Royal.

N of A31 fine New Forest scenery.

Rufus Stone, memorial to King William II ('Rufus') killed while hunting.

Romsey, Abbey Cycles, 12 Bell Street.

▲ **Salisbury** 0722 27572; **S'oton** 0703 769607.

South Hampshire

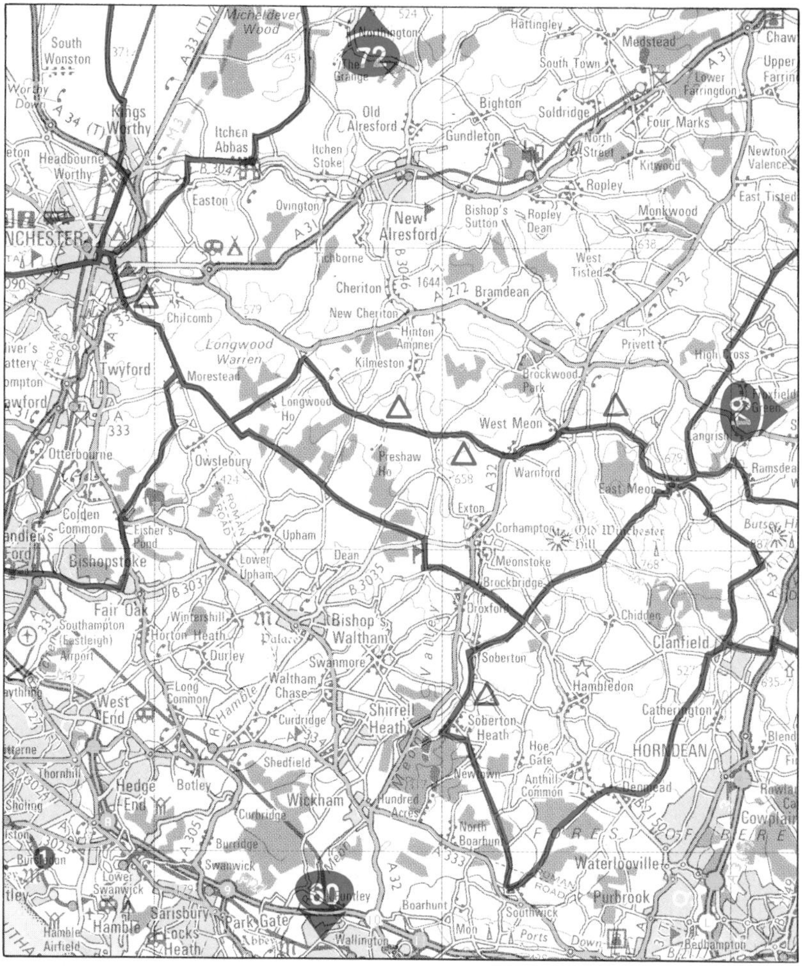

① Access to Southampton E shore cycle route from Weston Parade.

△ Climbs leaving **Winchester** E or W; **Winchester–West Meon**, rolling country but not hard cycling, except the climb from **Warnford** if travelling W; **West Meon** eastwards, twisting lanes, mostly hedged, with some short hills; **Meon Valley** area much level cycling.

Winchester on the London–Bournemouth InterCity main line.

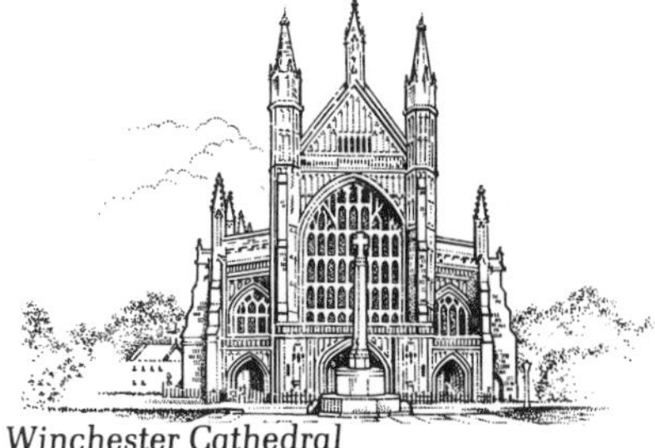

Winchester Cathedral

Hampshire/West Sussex

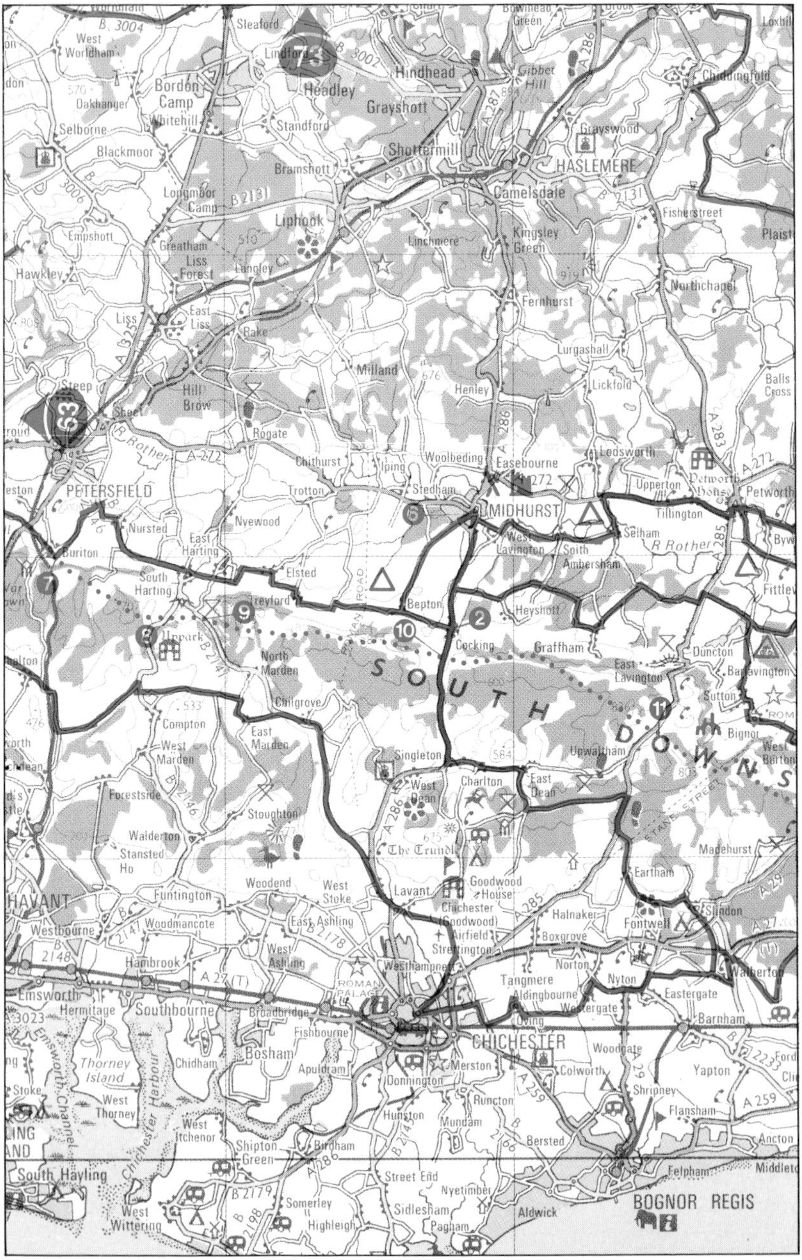

West Sussex/Surrey

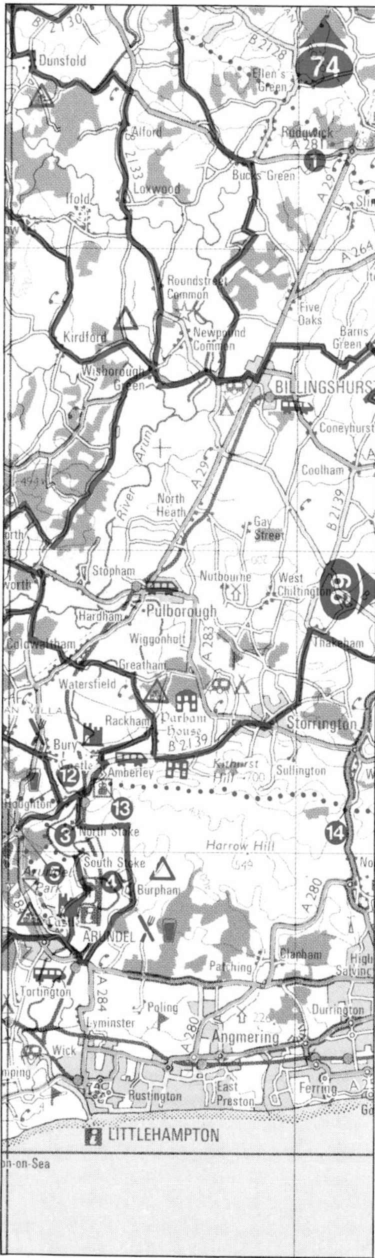

① Guildford–Steyning railway path – for access see pages 66 and 74.

② Unclassified road not marked on map leads direct to Heyshott. If travelling E, difficult to locate because it is obscured by buildings on the A286.

③ Bridleway, located at gate at end of South Lane, runs along River Arun, mostly rideable; joins ④ surfaced road at South Stoke.

⑤ Cycling permitted through Arundel Park – access at Whiteways Lodge roundabout.

⑥–⑭ Access to South Downs Way. See page 69.

⑮ Links with the West Sussex County Council/Cyclists' Touring Club excellent *Countryside Cycling* routes. Pack of six (£1.00) from local bookshops and tourist information centres.

△ **Billingshurst** area gently undulating; **Petersfield–B2139** short, sharp climbs, narrow twisting lane; climbs whichever way out of **Arundel**; **Petworth** and **Midhurst** area, gently undulating.

Chichester on the Portsmouth–Brighton main line; **Arundel, Amberley, Pulborough** and **Billingshurst** on the Victoria–Littlehampton line.

Café tea garden by river at **Amberley Station**; café at N end of **Midhurst** main street; café and riverside tea garden at **Arundel**.

Houghton, ancient inn; **Arundel**, choices.

Arundel–North Stoke beautiful downland run, also **Amberley–Greatham**; **Arundel Park**; idyllic lanes **below N scarp of downs**; **Dunsfold** area lovely woodland stretches.

Arundel and **Amberley**, latter not open to public; **Midhurst** Cowdray Castle ruins.

Petworth (Nat. Trust), notable façade, park; Turner associations; **Parham** fine Tudor house, exceptional setting; **Amberley** picturesque village.

Bignor Roman villa.

▲ **Arundel** 0903 882204.

West Sussex

① Access to Guildford–Steyning railway path (Guildford–Itchingfield section) at railway bridge under A264 near junction to Itchingfield and Christ's Hospital. ② Access to Itchingfield–Steyning section of same route at Christ's Hospital and ③ Steyning. Well used by horses – avoid after rain.

④ Access to Worth Way off road to Turners Hill at site of old level crossing and ⑤ from B2028: turn into Grange Road, at end turn left and then right into Burleigh Way; second right into Woodland Drive, first left into Hazel Way and second right into Cob Close.

⑥ This section of Forest Way (East Grinstead–Groombridge) ends at a dismantled bridge. Clamber down bank to A22. To continue turn right into Forest Row, first left (Lower Road) and left at end into Station Road. The next section begins ⑦ at E end of the disused station yard.

⑧ to ⑰, access to South Downs Way. See also page 69.

⑱ Route passes through Handcross village and crosses the A23.

△ **Forest Row–Sharpthorne** long climb, but picnic area at top for resting; steep climb into **Turners Hill**; **Steyning** up to down is 1:6; **Poynings–Brighton** skirts foot of Devil's Dyke, but hilly.

Brighton, InterCity services, London; **Worthing** on Brighton – Portsmouth main line; **Horsham** and **Crawley** on Littlehampton–Gatwick branch line.

Ditchling Beacon, second highest point on the South Downs.

Cissbury Ring and **Devil's Dyke**, ancient hill forts and ramparts.

Burgess Hill A. Hole, 39 Cyprus Road; **Worthing** John Spooner Cycles, 21 South Farm Road.

▲ **Truleigh Hill** Steyning (0903) 813419; **Patcham** Brighton (0273) 556196; **Telscombe** Brighton (0273) 37077; **Newhaven** Fort Newhaven Brighton (0273) 513600/514217; **Alfriston** 0323 870423.

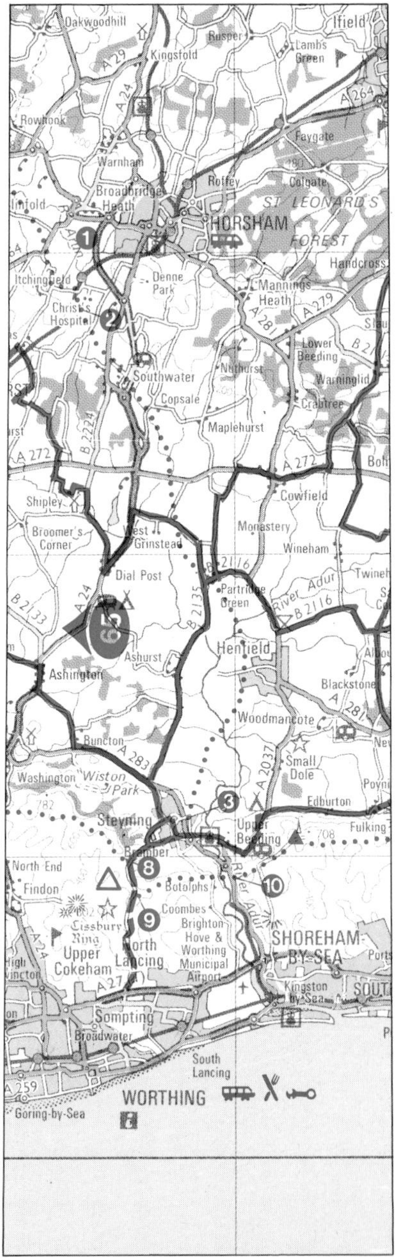

West Sussex/East Sussex

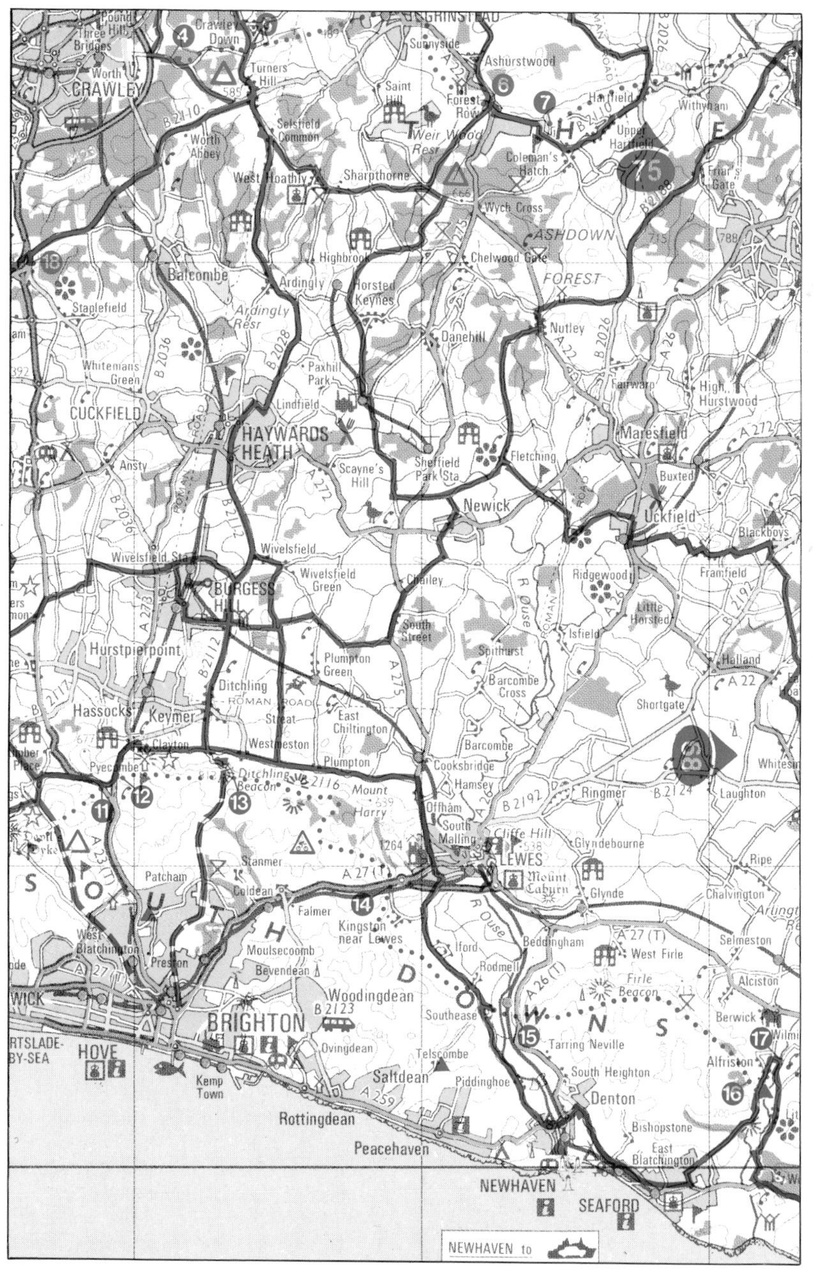

East Sussex

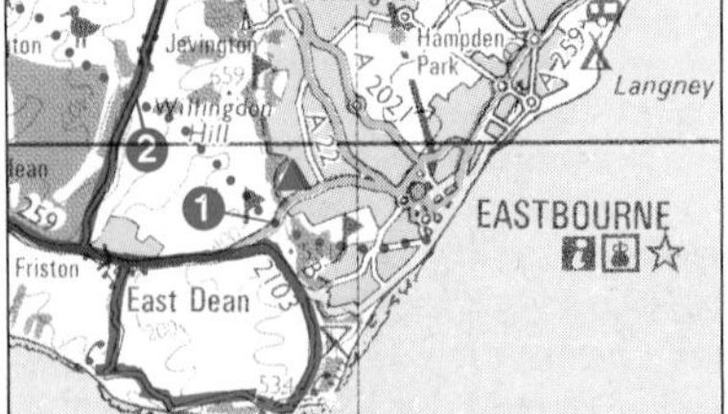

① and ② access as indicated to the South Downs Way. Eastbourne is its E terminus. The Way is adequately signposted the whole of its 80 miles (129 km) to Buriton near Petersfield, with entry points at road junctions usually well signposted. Large-scale maps are, however, strongly recommended: Landranger Sheets 197, 198 and 199 cover the whole route; OS Outdoor Leisure Map, Brighton and

East Sussex/Kent

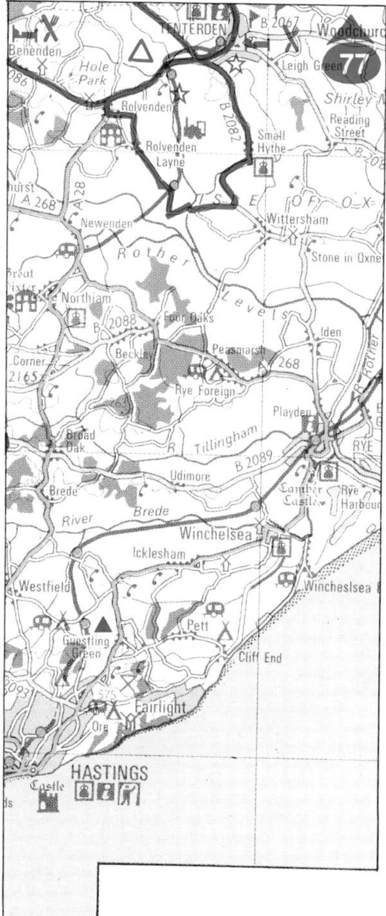

Sussex Vale, shows the route between Rodmell and Steyning. The track is not all rideable, it is extremely steep in parts and great care should be taken after rain: the chalk surface becomes slippery.

③ and ④ obvious access to unsurfaced road through Bedgebury Forest, mostly rideable.

△ The route centred on **Tenterden/Goudhurst** (latter, page 76) is gently undulating, with few really steep hills; the circuits based on **Battle** are fairly strenuous, especially the unclassified roads which dip in and out of small valleys; unclassified road leaving **Bateman's**, heaviest climb on route.

Battle and other stations on the Charing Cross–Hastings line.

Knolly's Café and Castle Cafeteria, **Bodiam; choices of café at **Battle**, **Robertsbridge**, **Tenterden**; most pubs serve bar meals.

Superb forest ride through the National Pinetum, **Bedgebury Forest**; lovely rural scenery **Sedlescombe–Ewhurst Green** and lane from **Bateman's to Ashburnham/Ponts Green.**

☆ **Tenterden Steam Railway**, regular trips in summer months; **Ewhurst Green**, one of several picturesque villages in the area.

Bedgebury National Pinetum is an impressive collection of conifers and rhododendrons.

14th-C moated **Bodium Castle**, admission charge (but not to grounds).

Bateman's 17th-C house, formerly home of Rudyard Kipling.

Battle Abbey founded by William the Conqueror; due S, site of Battle of Hastings.

Heathfield Cycle Revival, Mutton Hall Hill, A265.

No youth hostels near routes, but B & B plentiful: agency at tourist information office, **Tenterden**; camp sites – see grey symbols.

▲ **Beachy Head** Eastbourne (0323) 20284; **Guestling** (near Hastings) Pett (042486) 2373.

Bodiam Castle

Wiltshire

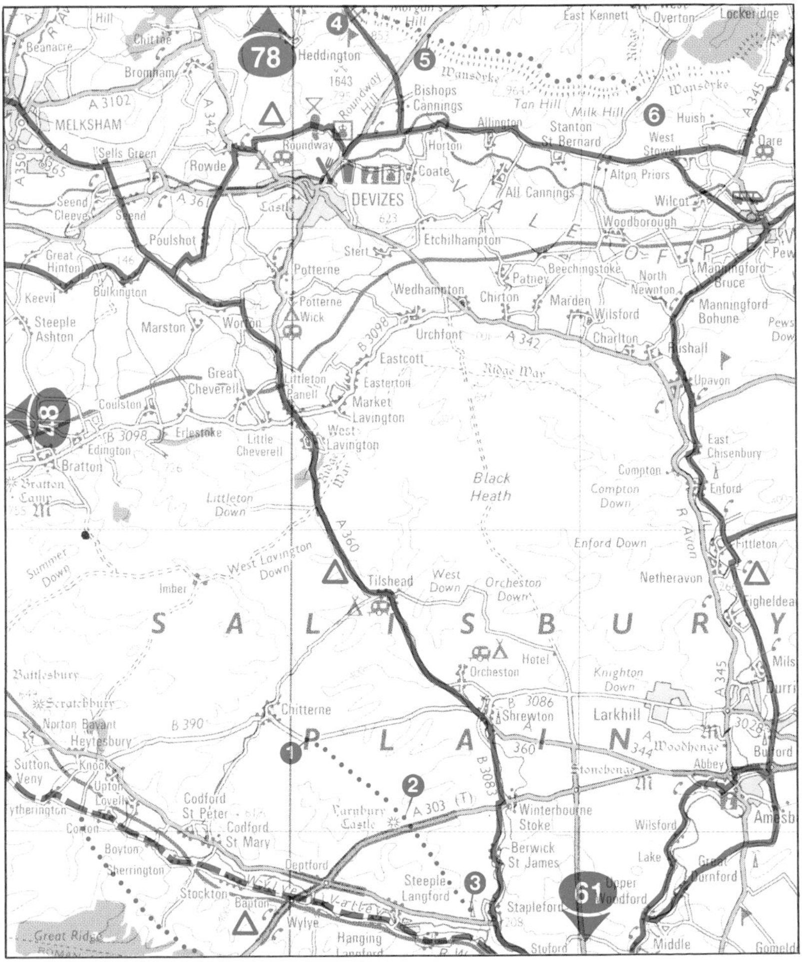

① Access to broad track about 1 mile (1.5 km) SE of Chitterne at top of hill. ② Cross the A303 and exit ③ at Stapleford. Rideable throughout, but very muddy patches after rain.

④ Access to Wansdyke bridleway at picnic site about 1½ miles (3 km) NW of A361 and ⑤ from the A361. Exit ⑥ on unclassified road about 2 miles (3 km) N of Alton Priors. For further possibilities see Landranger 184.

⑦ Access to Test Valley route at old station site.

△ **A360** fast but scattered traffic; **Upavon – Middle Woodford** some climbs; **West Stowell–Great Hinton** relatively level; **Wylye Valley** suitable for families and novices.

Pewsey, InterCity services London/Exeter.

Devizes, choices; Wadsworth's 6X is brewed in this pleasant market town.

Wiltshire/Hampshire

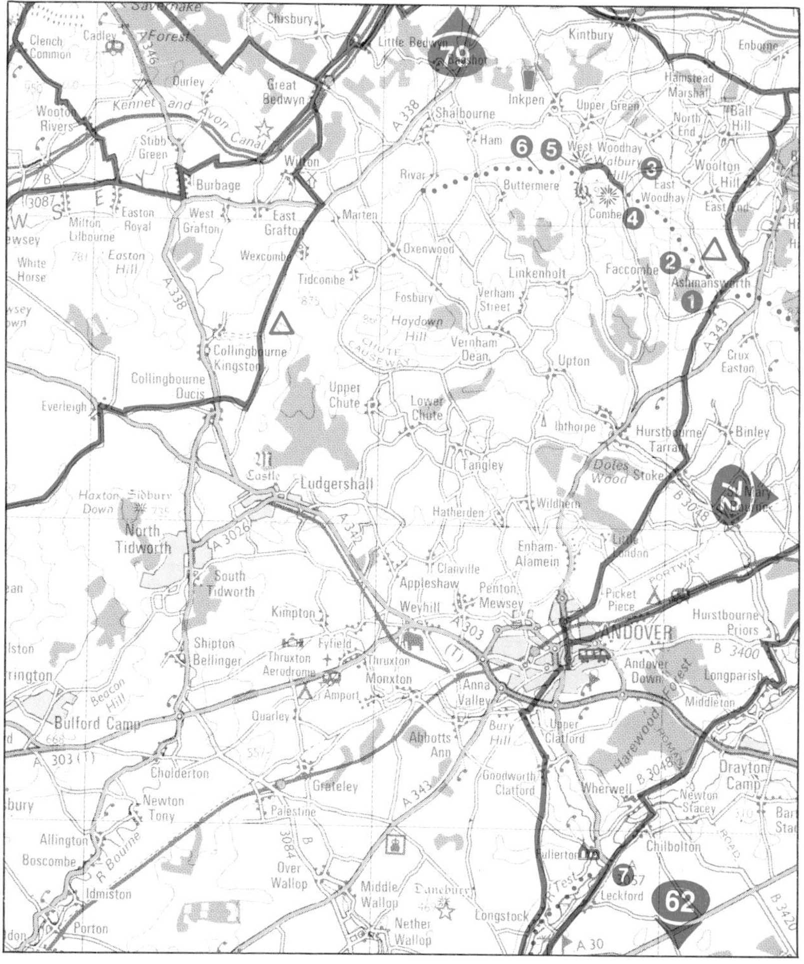

① Access to Inkpen Ridgeway (see page 72) at minor road above Ashmansworth. To continue W, go N on road for 300 yards (274 m) and fork left ② up track. ③ Track meets road near T-junction; turn right at junction and where road swings right carry straight on ④ over Walbury Hill. ⑤ Cross road and make for Inkpen Beacon, obvious by the gibbet ⑥. Waymarked Wayfarers Walk or WW.

△ Unclassified roads **Wexcome–Fittleton**, climbs/ascents, also **Andover–Newbury**.

Andover, on the London–Salisbury main line.

The Swan at Inkpen – real ale.

Walbury Iron Age hill fort covers no less than 80 acres (32 ha).

The original gibbet was erected in 1676 to hang George Broomham and his mistress.

Hampshire/Berkshire

① Access to the Inkpen Ridgeway waymarked Inkpen Beacon. ② Cross B3051, and go over Watership Down. ③ Cross lane and ④ A34. Route generally well waymarked as Wayfarers Walk or WW. An interesting track, probably now superior to the Ridgeway itself in surface and scenery.

△ Long climbs/descents S of **Kingsclere** and S of **Ecchinswell** (Watership Down). **Aldermaston–Greenham** generally level – part of Reading–Bath route following roughly the course of the Kennet and Avon canal.

Basingstoke and **Newbury**, InterCity services to Reading, London.

N of Whitchurch, remote, peaceful.

Superb views **as marked**.

Silchester Roman town, museum.

Stratfield Saye, Duke of Wellington's house.

▲ **Overton**, Red Lion Lane (no tel.).

E Berkshire/NE Hampshire/W Surrey

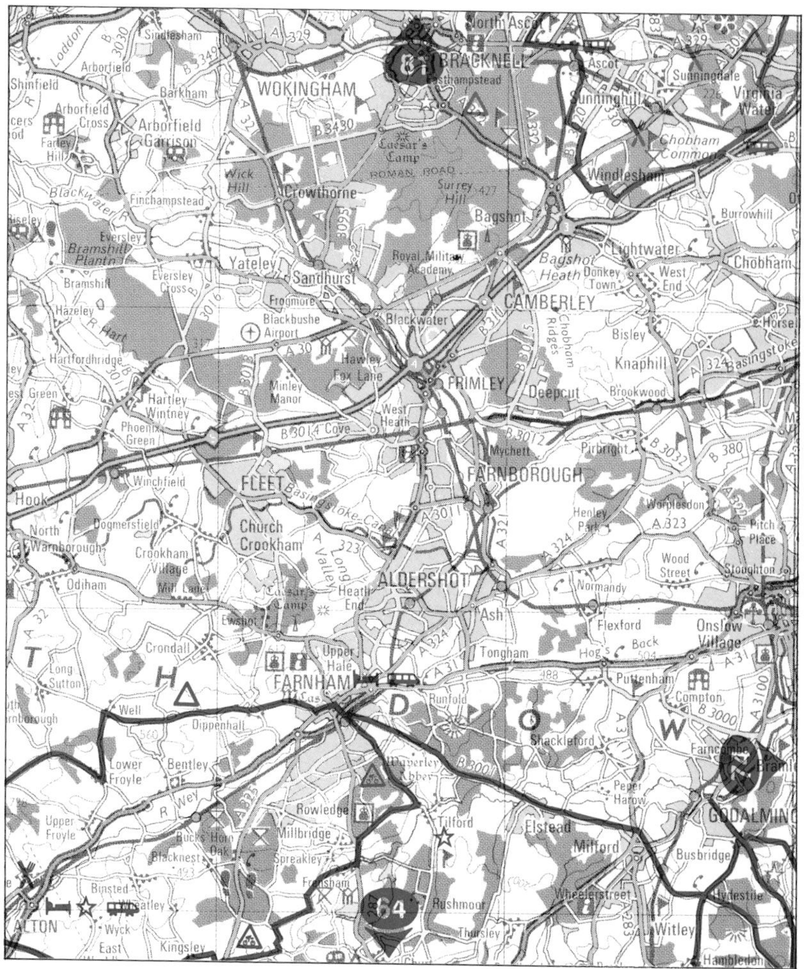

△ **Bracknell** is friendly to cyclists: extensive urban cycleway facilities; the **Alton–Farnham** loop is undulating with occasional steeper climbs and descents; the **Virginia Water–Ascot** loop is easy, gently undulating.

🚌 Frequent suburban services (London terminus, Waterloo) to **Virginia Water**, **Ascot**, **Farnham** and **Alton**.

✗ Café and pub meals at **Alton**; limited choices **Sunninghill**, **Sunningdale**.

▲ **Farnham–Tilford** delightful, also **Frensham–Kingsley**.

☆ **Tilford** village is just off the route but worth a detour – large green, attractive houses, notable oak tree; **Alton** is busy but congenial – Curtis Museum (agricultural exhibits), church with Civil War bullet marks on door.

🔧 **Godalming** Weale, 25 Church Street. Nearest youth hostel is at Hindhead (page 64) but B & B **Farnham**, **Alton**.

Surrey/Greater London

① Access to the Guildford – Henfield disused railway line off A281 between Shalford and Bramley by former level crossing.

△ A very hilly circuit with three major climbs: **Leith Hill**, going **N from the A25** and **Box Hill**.

🚌 **Reigate**, on the Guildford–Tonbridge line, or nearby Redhill Station.

✕ Popular café at **Box Hill**; most pubs in the area serve bar meals.

⛰ Outstanding viewpoints, typically at **Box Hill** and **Leith Hill**. Latter, at 965 feet (294 m) is highest point in SE England – on clear days, views to St Paul's in London and of ships in the Channel.

☆ **Reigate**, castle, 18th-C town hall; **Leigh**, medieval houses.

▲ **Holmbury St Mary** Dorking (0306) 730777; **Tanners Hatch** Bookham (0372) 52528.

Surrey/Kent/Greater London

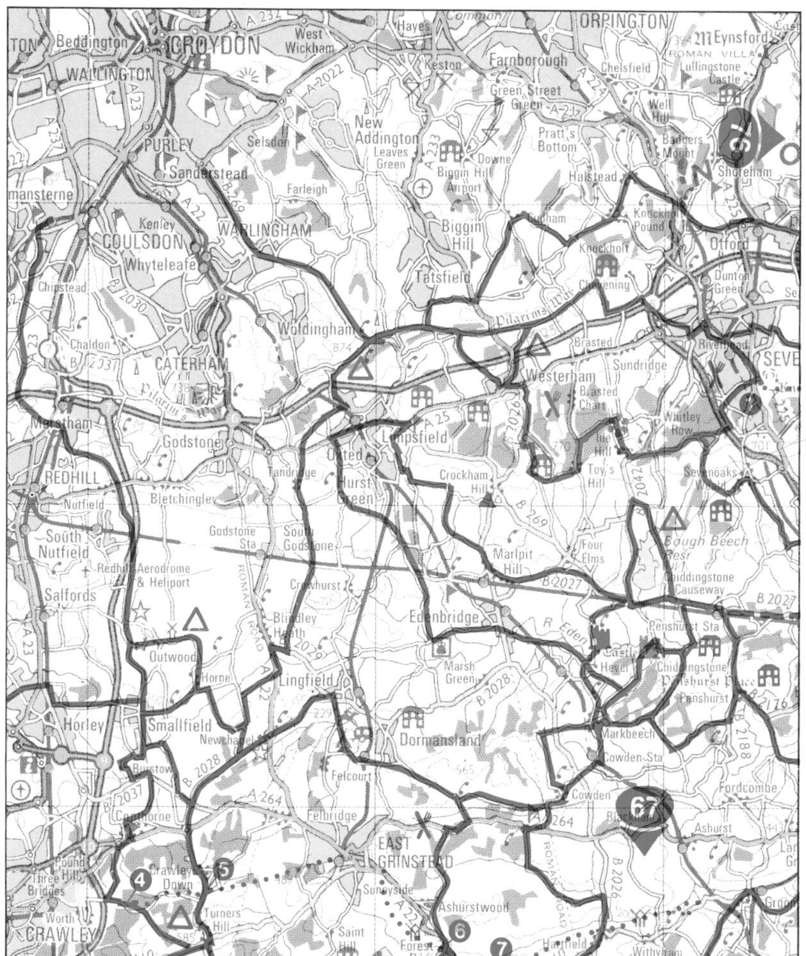

① Access to Worth Way (see page 66) and ② at car park on NW side of East Grinstead Station.

③ Join Forest Way at roundabout off A22 or ④ at site of missing bridge, Groombridge Road.

△ **Oxted–Penshurst** circuit, a few gentle hills; steep climb just before the mill at **Outwood**; steep hill into **Turners Hill**; 1:5 hill with blind hairpin just **N of M25 at Oxted**; **North Downs/Sevenoaks** area strenuous.

✗ Cafés on green at **Westerham**; **Sevenoaks** and **East Grinstead**, limited choices.

🍺 **S of Penshurst** at Smart's Hill the Spotted Dog has good food, views.

🏰 **Hever**, the Astor stately home.

🏛 **Chiddingstone Castle**, **Penshurst**, **Chartwell**, historic houses all worth long visits.

▲ **Crockham Hill** 0732 866322.

West Kent

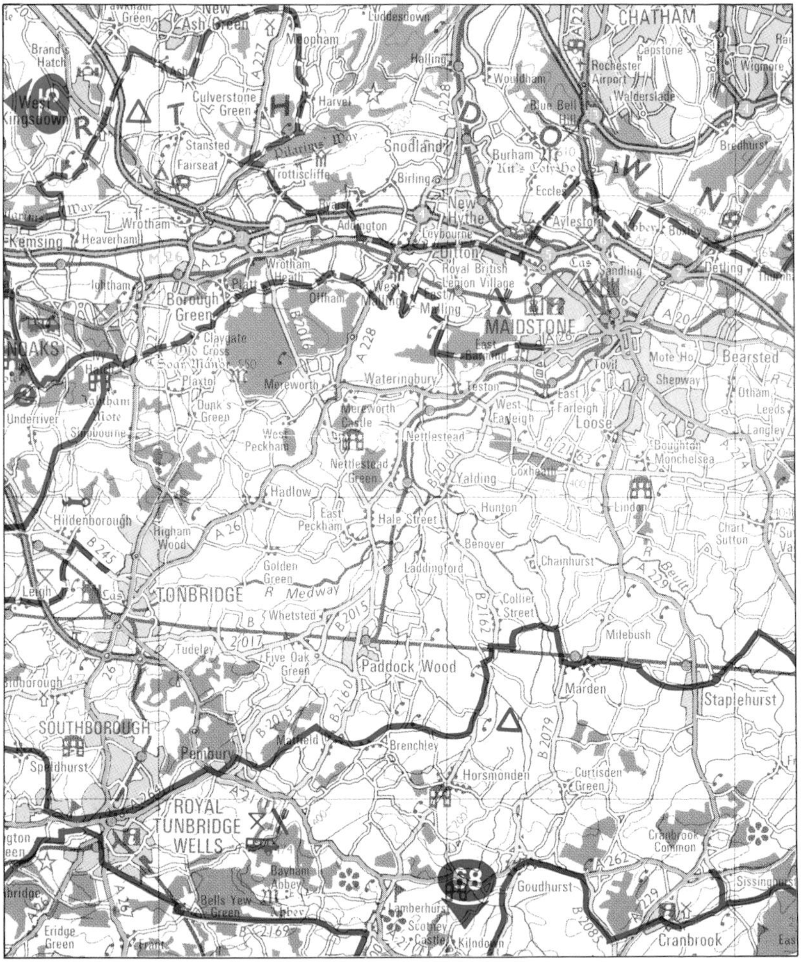

① and ② obvious access to the park surrounding Knole (you may be requested to walk along part of the drive).

△ Unclassified roads between **Royal Tunbridge Wells and Staplehurst** easy and level; **Kemsing–Meopham** climbs.

Sevenoaks on the London–Hastings main line, InterCity services, likewise **Royal Tunbridge Wells Central**; **Maidstone West** on the Victoria–Ashford suburban line.

Choices **Maidstone**, **Tunbridge Wells.**

Through park at **Knole** and **unclassified roads to Ightham Mote**, dignified rural settings; **Ivy Hatch**, small and picturesque, a happy stopping place.

Knole, the enormous 15th–17th-C house, fine state rooms, deer park; **Ightham Mote**, moated house.

Hildenborough Cycle Centre, 13b Brookmead.

▲ **Kemsing** Sevenoaks (0732) 61341.

Kent

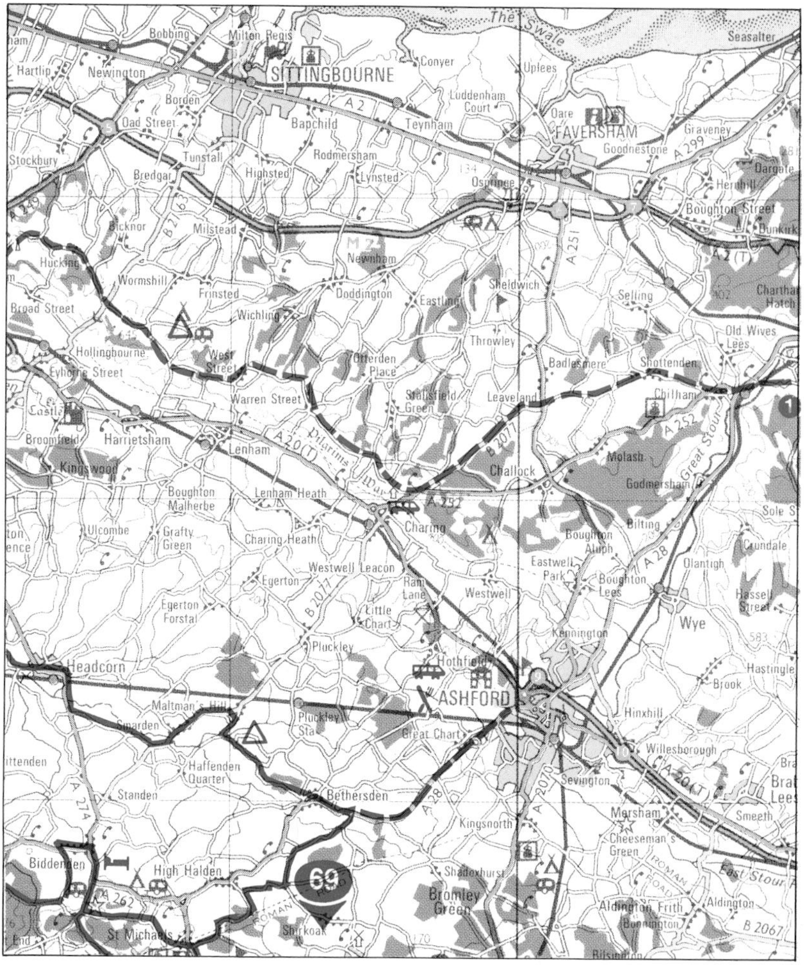

① For Canterbury, continue on unclassified roads roughly parallel to Stour.

△ **North Downs routing** undulating, some ridge riding; **Headcorn–Ashford** generally level.

Ashford on the London–Dover main line, InterCity services; **Charing**, suburban services from Victoria.

Choices in **Ashford**, limited in Biddenden.

Useful B & B agency at **Biddenden.**

Harebell, left, and wild thyme, right, familiar on the downland in summer.

North Wiltshire

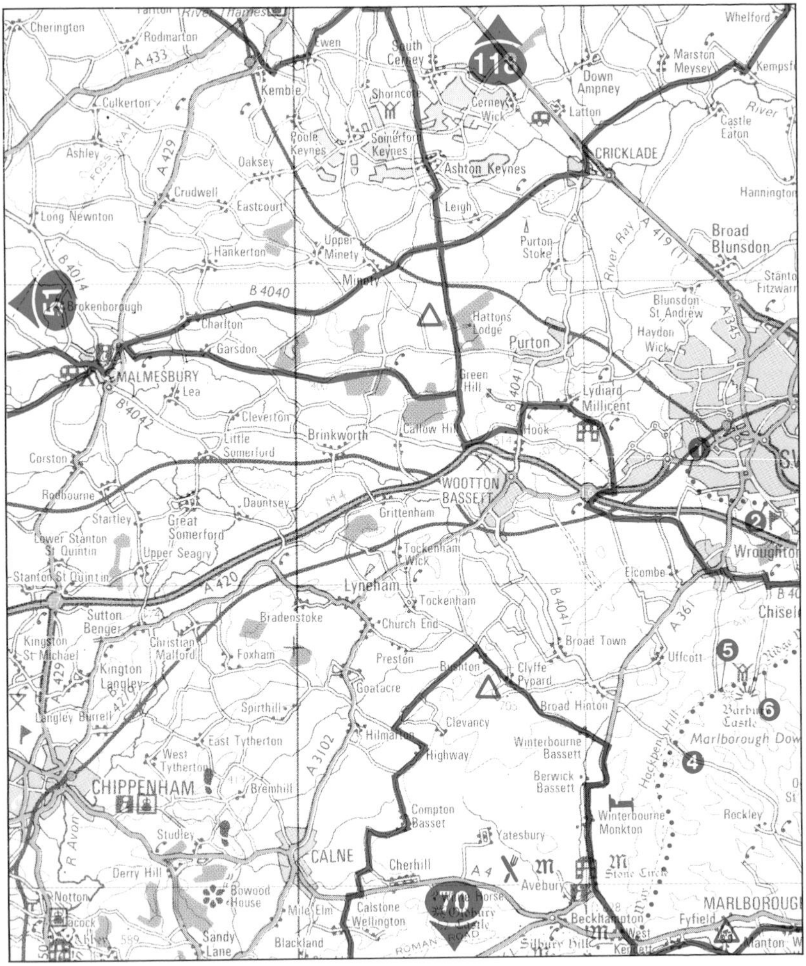

① Access to Toothill–Swindon Old Town disused railway path at underpass and ② at industrial site on Swindon Old Town Station site.

③ Link to signposted Wiltshire Cycleway.

④ to ⑥ Access to the Ridgeway Path obvious and usually well waymarked where it crosses roads. See page 79.

△ **Clyffe Pypard** heavy climb, and climbs generally on downs, though height is maintained several miles at a time; **N of M4** gradients generally level.

Choices at **Marlborough**, limited choice at **Avebury**, otherwise little.

Manton westwards, fine downland.

Avebury's stone circle rivals Stonehenge for visitor numbers; other attractions include church, museum.

Avebury The Rectory, Avebury SN8 1RF, B & B; also at **Marlborough, Winterbourne Monkton.**

N Wiltshire/S Oxfordshire/W Berkshire

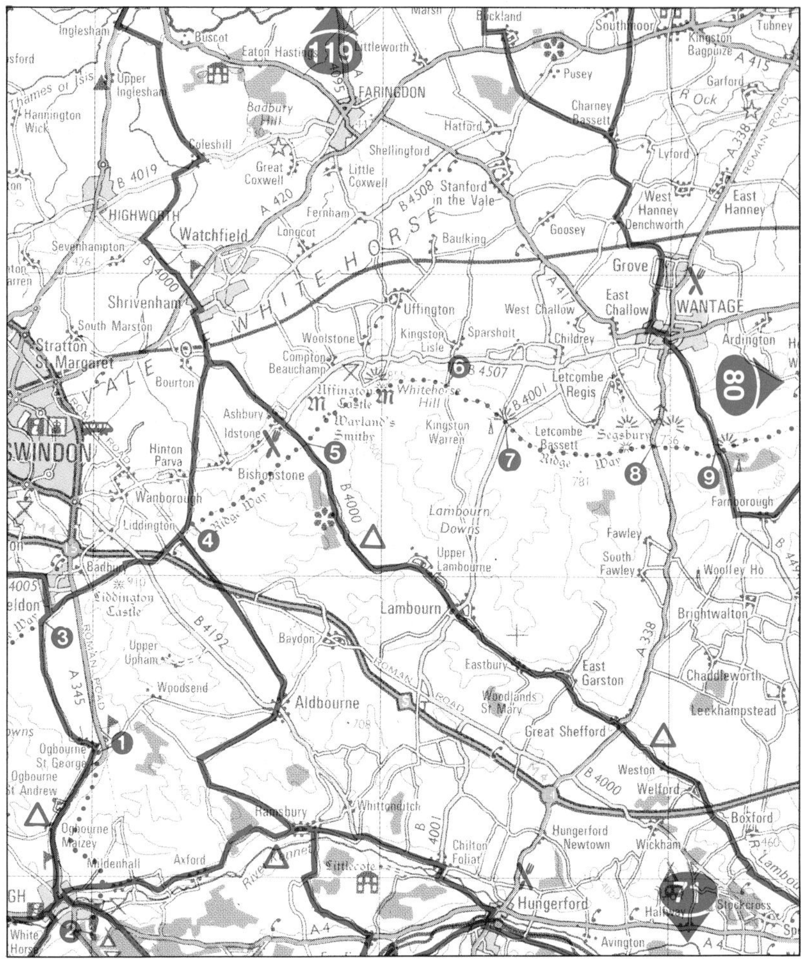

① Access to Ogbourne St George–Marlborough disused railway route off road just before it passes under A345 and ② at footbridge over cutting by Corporation Depot (opening 1985).

③ to ⑨ access to the Ridgeway Path obvious and usually well waymarked where it crosses roads. It is a bridleway as far as Streatley near Goring; the stretch N of the Thames is footpath only. Popularity has resulted in bad erosion of the surface in parts.

△ **Marlborough–Hungerford** easy; **Marlborough – Chiseldon** moderate for a downland crossing; **Welford – Lambourn** fairly level; **Lambourn – Ashbury** climbs.

🚆 **Swindon**, frequent InterCity services.

✗ Choices at **Hungerford, Wantage**.

𝔪 **Uffington** White Horse, hill fort; **Wayland's Smithy**, chambered burial barrow.

South Oxfordshire/East Berkshire

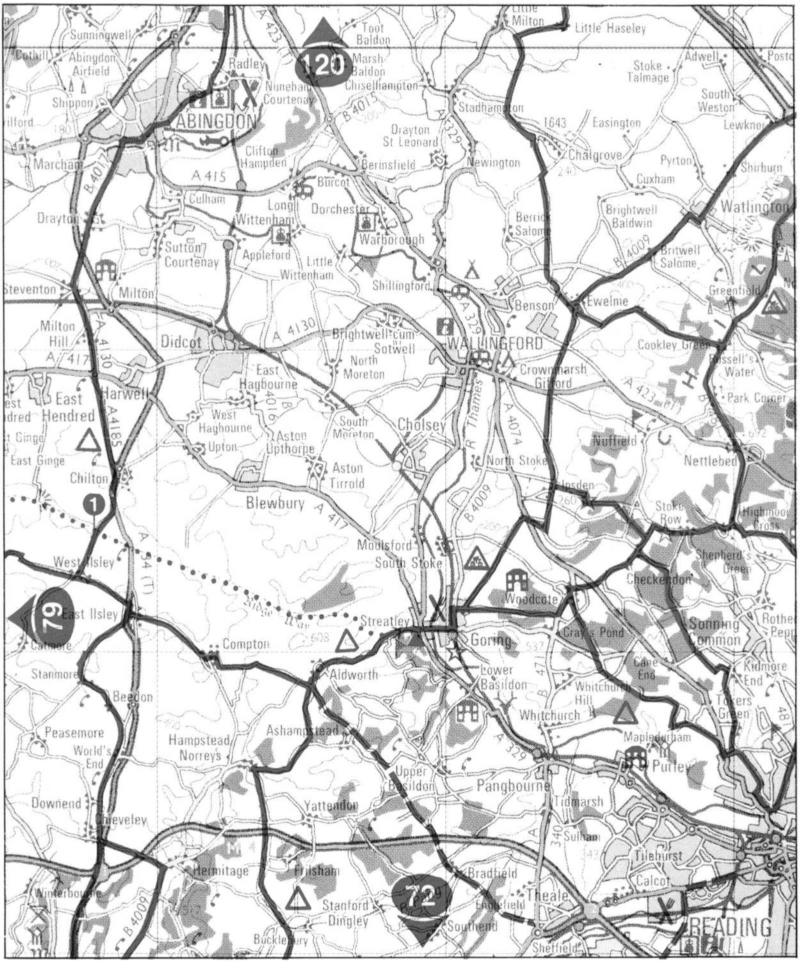

① Access to the Ridgeway Path obvious and usually well waymarked where it crosses roads. See page 79.

△ **Streatley–Aldworth** steep hill; **Abingdon – southwards** moderate; **NE of Reading** some short, steep ascents; **S of Frilsham**, ford or footbridge.

(train) **Reading** frequent InterCity services; **Didcot, Goring**, Reading–Oxford main line.

(X) Choices in **Reading**; limited choices, **Abingdon**; tea shops at **Goring**.

(▲) Thames Valley at **Goring**; along the N escarpment of the **Chilterns**.

(house) S of **Ipsden** Brazier's Court, mock-Gothic house once inhabited by Ian Fleming, creator of James Bond.

☆ **Goring** boat trips on the Thames, superbly steep-sided here.

(key) **Abingdon** H & N Bragg, 2 High Street.

▲ **Streatley** Goring-on-Thames (0491) 872278.

East Berkshire/South-east Buckinghamshire

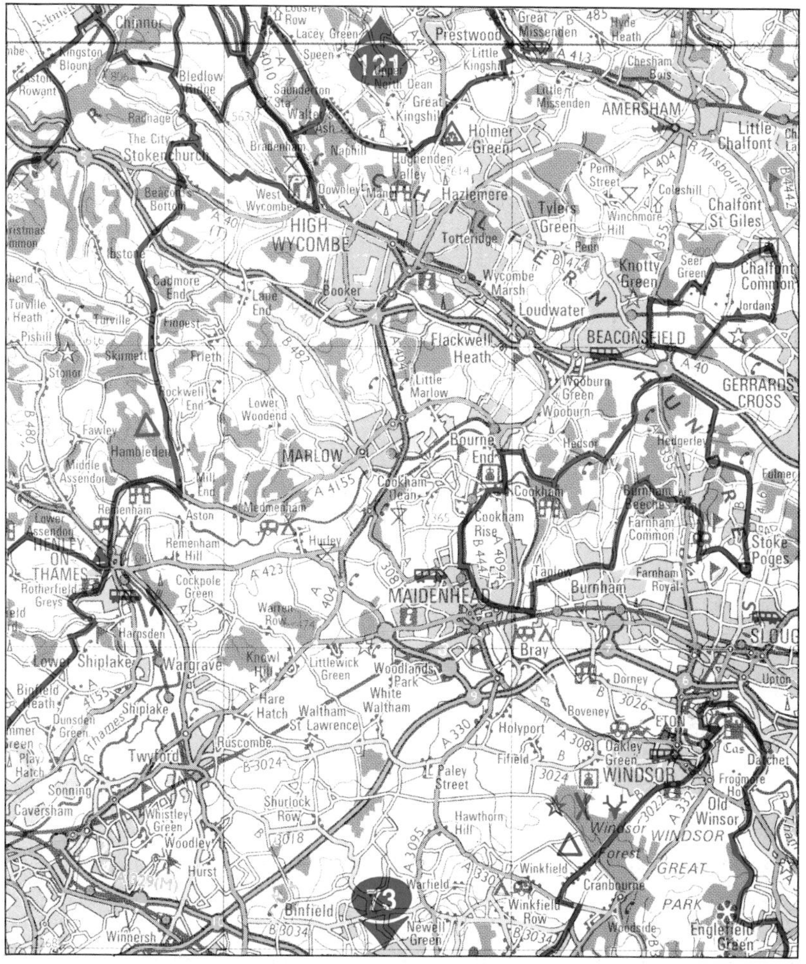

△ **SW–NE across the Chilterns** unavoidable ascents; **Windsor Great Park** area gently undulating.

Maidenhead and **Slough** on the London – Reading main line; suburban services from Marylebone to **Beaconsfield** and **Great Missenden**; **Windsor & Eton** service either from Paddington changing at Slough or from Waterloo via Staines. **Henley-on-Thames** on branch line from Twyford.

Choices at **Windsor** and **Henley**.

Hambleden–Fingest, lovely Chiltern hills and valleys; similar fine countryside in the **Hughenden/Great Missenden** area.

☆ **Windsor** Castle, St George's Chapel.

Windsor Safari Park.

Amersham Dees, 39 Hill Avenue.

▲ **Bradenham** Naphill (024024) 2929; **Henley** 04912 572060; **Jordans** Chalfont St Giles (02407) 3135.

3
WALES

There is hardly a better excuse for buying yourself a proper touring bike than a first visit to Wales. You will be going there mainly because you love mountains, and while it is a fair generalization that the main roads running along the valley floors are relatively level, it is also generally true that they are busy – sometimes appallingly so.

The minor and unclassified roads are of course the key to the true joys of cycling in Wales. In some parts of the country, notably Mid Wales, they form considerable networks and they are the key to the uplands. Often wildly remote, they are more likely to be cluttered with sheep than cars; they make few concessions to easy gradients, and low gearing will never be so much appreciated.

This does not only apply to the major mountain ranges. The Arans and the Berwyns, the Black Mountains and the Brecon Beacons are classed, by some, as no more than major hill groups; but they will bring the unfit and ill-equipped to their hands and knees as surely as any other super-strenuous riding in the British Isles.

Not included in this section are two quite large portions of Wales. Most of the industrial south is unsuitable for cycling because of the heavy traffic concentrated along the main roads along the valley floors. And the old county of Pembroke (now just the south-west corner of Dyfed) may have a wonderful coastline, but it is best appreciated on foot; inland is mostly unexceptional.

Selected tours

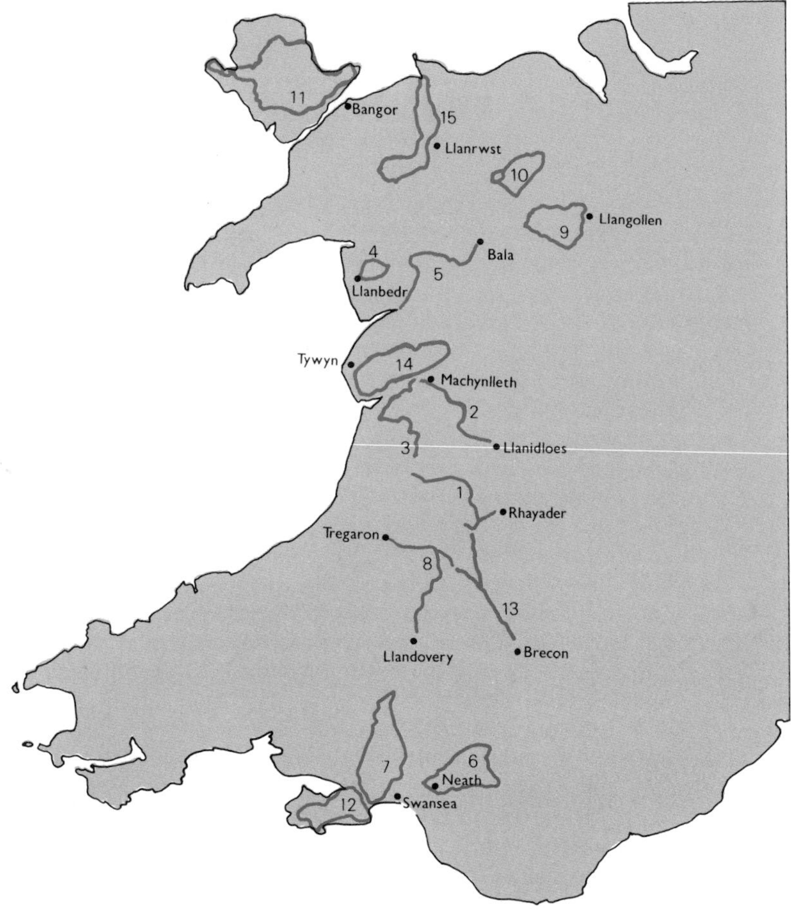

A cross-section of the tours in this region, showing typical rides that can be put together from the route network in localities; **further details, pages 86–7.**

Day rides

1 The Elan Valley
2 Upper Severn Valley
3 Ponterwyd to Machynlleth
4 The Roman Steps
5 Bala to Dolgellau via the Mountain Road

Two-day tours

6 The Vale of Neath
7 Swansea–Carreg Cennen loop
8 The Towy Valley
9 Wayfarer circuit from Llangollen
10 Clocaenog Forest
11 Anglesey

Three days or longer

12 Gower Peninsula
13 Deserted Mid Wales
14 Dovey Forest and Tal-y-llyn
15 Heart of Snowdonia

Selected tours

Day rides

1 The Elan Valley, a relatively easy ride in Mid Wales, about 26 miles (42 km). Although there is a direct route by mountain road from Rhayader to Devil's Bridge, it omits the beautiful Elan Valley with its impressive dams and fine reservoirs surrounded by forests. The route as given lays fair claim to being one of the finest in Mid Wales. *Rhayader–Craig Goch Reservoir – Yr Allt – Cwmystwyth – Devil's Bridge with an optional diversion to Claerwen Reservoir;* **pages 94, 96.**

2 Upper Severn Valley, Llanidloes to Machynlleth, about 24 miles (38 km). Like several other routes in this section, this is a linear ride: the views are so good that cycling it in both directions is a pleasure, and the north terminus, Machynlleth, has reasonably regular train connections with Shrewsbury and the Midlands. *Llanidloes – Staylittle – Dylife–Machynlleth;* **pages 96, 98, 99.**

3 Ponterwyd to Machynlleth, lovely, desolate Mid Wales scenery, and a link between Mid Wales and the south part of the Snowdonia National Park, about 24 miles (38 km). There is, however, 6 miles (10 km) of the often busy A487 – though two diversions on quiet unclassified roads can be made to break it up. The alternative is to take the off-highway route further inland from Nant-y-Môch Reservoir under the west flanks of Plynlimon: much more challenging (some walking is involved), but truly peaceful. *Ponterwyd–south shore of Nat-y-Môch Reservoir – Cwm Ceulan – Talybont – Glaspwll–Machynlleth, or off-highway route indicated north from Nant-y-Môch Reservoir;* **pages 94, 98.**

4 The Roman Steps, a challenging expedition, highly unsuitable for family groups, through a wild pass deep in the rough Rhinogs, about 30 miles (48 km). It is best to tackle this classic rough-stuff route from west to east, so the heavy climbing comes before the gentler descent. Harlech, as the starting point, is well served with public transport, but the other end is not, so incorporate the route in a longer tour, or plan an overnight stop. *Harlech–Llanbedr–Roman Steps–Moel y Feidiog–Llanuwchllyn–Bala;* **pages 100, 101, 102, 103, 104**, which also feature the alternative and even rougher route across the Rhinogs, the Bwlch Drws Ardudwy.

5 Bala to Dolgellau via the Mountain Road, about 32 miles (51 km). Relatively easy gradients, and an unforgettable 15 miles (24 km) mainly downhill through the Coed y Brenin Forest. Public transport rather far from each end, so incorporate the route in a longer tour and plan overnight stops. *Bala–Llanuwchillyn–Moel y Feidiog–Cefndeuddw–Dolgellau;* **pages 104, 101, 100.**

Continued on page 86.

Selected tours

Two-day tours

6 The Vale of Neath, based on Neath near Swansea, about 45 miles (72 km). A strenuous route involving 3,000 feet (915 m) of climbing. Could be a day's training loop for the fit sporting cyclist. Uses some mileage on A-roads, but except for a short stretch of the A465, traffic levels are low. For steep climbs and long descents, ride the loop clockwise. *Neath – Melincourt – Hirwaun – Treherbert – Croeserw – Neath;* **page 89.**

7 Swansea and Carreg Cennen Castle circuit, north from Swansea to the edge of the Black Mountain area, about 53 miles (85 km). Could be a single day for the fit – generally easy cycling, though the north tip of the loop is hilly. Carreg Cennen Castle makes a pretty and atmospheric stopping place, and there is a pleasant off-highway stretch. *Swansea – Pontardulais – Betws – Trapp – Gwaun-Cae-Gurwen – Pontardawe – Glais–Swansea;* **pages 88, 89.**

8 The Towy Valley, Llandovery to Tregaron, about 30 miles (48 km). Family groups would certainly want to take two days on this hilly route with some interesting diversions for exploration. The valley, which has undergone major changes in recent years with the construction of the Llyn Brianne Reservoir, is a complete ride in itself (well served by some dramatically situated youth hostels) or a linking route between other touring areas of Wales. *Llandovery–Cilycwm–Ystradffin–Tregaron, with diversions to Abergwesyn and through the Camddwr Valley;* **pages 92, 94.**

9 Wayfarer Circuit from Llangollen, about 34 miles (54 km). One of the most adventurous cycle rides in Wales (unsuitable for family groups) and for many almost a pilgrimage. It involves crossing the Berwyn range on an off-highway track, at whose summit is a memorial to a much-respected cycling enthusiast and writer. As rough stuff goes, the Wayfarer Pass is relatively easy, and sometimes over-popular. *Llangollen – Llanarmon Dyffryn – Ceiriog – Wayfarer Pass – Cynwyd – Corwen – Llangollen;* **pages 104, 146.**

10 Clocaenog Forest, with the Brenig and Alwen Reservoirs, about 35 miles (56 km). At the height of the holiday season, when coastal North Wales and Snowdonia are crowded to capacity, this route is a chance to enjoy quiet backroads – but it is strenuous. *Ruthin – Bontuchel – Nilig – Llanfihangel – Glyn Myfyr – Derwen–Ruthin, with an extension to the Brenig and Alwen Reservoirs;* **page 109.**

11 Anglesey, starting and finishing at Llanfairpwll or Holyhead, about 76 miles (122 km). Easy cycling makes this rather high mileage for North Wales a possibility for family groups. The route has been devised to pass many of Anglesey's most fascinating ancient monuments and access by rail is simple from the Midlands. *Llanfairpwyllgwyngyll – Holyhead – Beaumaris – Menai Bridge – Llanfairpwll;* **pages 106, 107.**

Selected tours

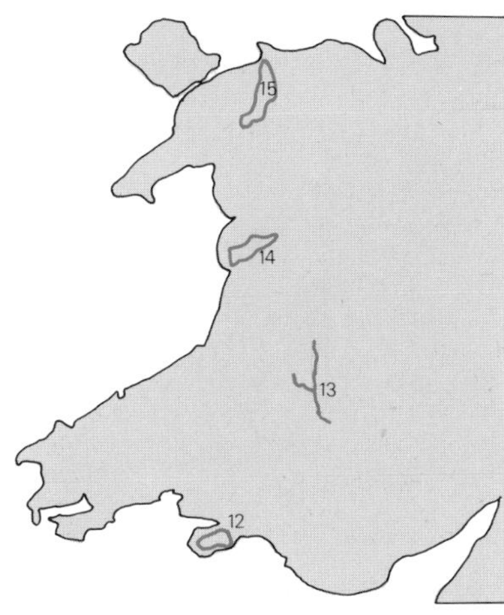

Three days or longer

12 Gower Peninsula from Swansea, about 40 miles (64 km) with opportunities to extend the tour. An ideal way of exploring the beautiful Gower; suitable for family groups if taken at the right pace. Dramatic coastal scenery on the south side of the loop, but pleasant cycling on the north, too. *Swansea – The Mumbles – Port-Eynon – Cheriton – Upper Killay–Swansea, with extensions via Rhossili and Three Crosses;* **pages 88, 89.**

13 Deserted Mid Wales, linking Brecon, Tregaron, Rhayader and Builth Wells, about 96 miles (154 km). This route – together with numbers 1, 2, 3 and 8 – is proof that Mid Wales is classic cycle touring country. It is sad that in few other parts of Wales can you experience virtually traffic-free back roads through desolate but beautiful scenery. This is a challenging ride, possible in one day for the fittest sporting cyclist, but also an excellent family ride if planned properly and taken slowly. The contributor, a member of CTC's Bristol group, has covered portions of the route on a tandem tricycle with his five-year-old son as 'stoker' – but found a 22-inch bottom gear useful. *Brecon–Upper Chapel–Abergwesyn–Tregaron–Ysbyty Ystwyth–Cwmystwyth–Rhayader–Builth Wells–Upper Chapel–Brecon;* **pages 93, 94, 95, 96, 97.**

14 Dovey Forest and Tal-y-llyn, the Dovey Estuary and Cader Idris region, about 45 miles (72 km), comprising two circuits of 22 miles (35 km) and 34 miles (54 km). The two circuits give the option to tackle the route over one, two or even three days according to the riders' abilities. A wide variety of fine scenery, and excellent access by rail. *Machynlleth–Aberangell – Corris Uchaf – Tal-y-llyn – Tywyn – Aberdyfi – Machynlleth, with the option to make the shorter circuit via Plas Llwyngwern;* **98, 99, 100, 101.**

15 Heart of Snowdonia, Conwy Valley, Betws-y-coed and Capel Curig, about 50 miles (80 km). Cycling on A-roads is unavoidable in this part of North Wales, but here is a route designed to give, at least on some sections, the appropriate sense of remoteness. But it does require a demanding 3-mile (5-km) rough-stuff section of which only about ten per cent is rideable. *Llandudno Junction – Graig – Betwys-y-coed – Dolwyddellan – Capel Curig – Trefriw – Llandudno Junction.*

West Glamorgan/Dyfed

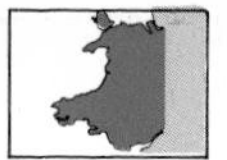

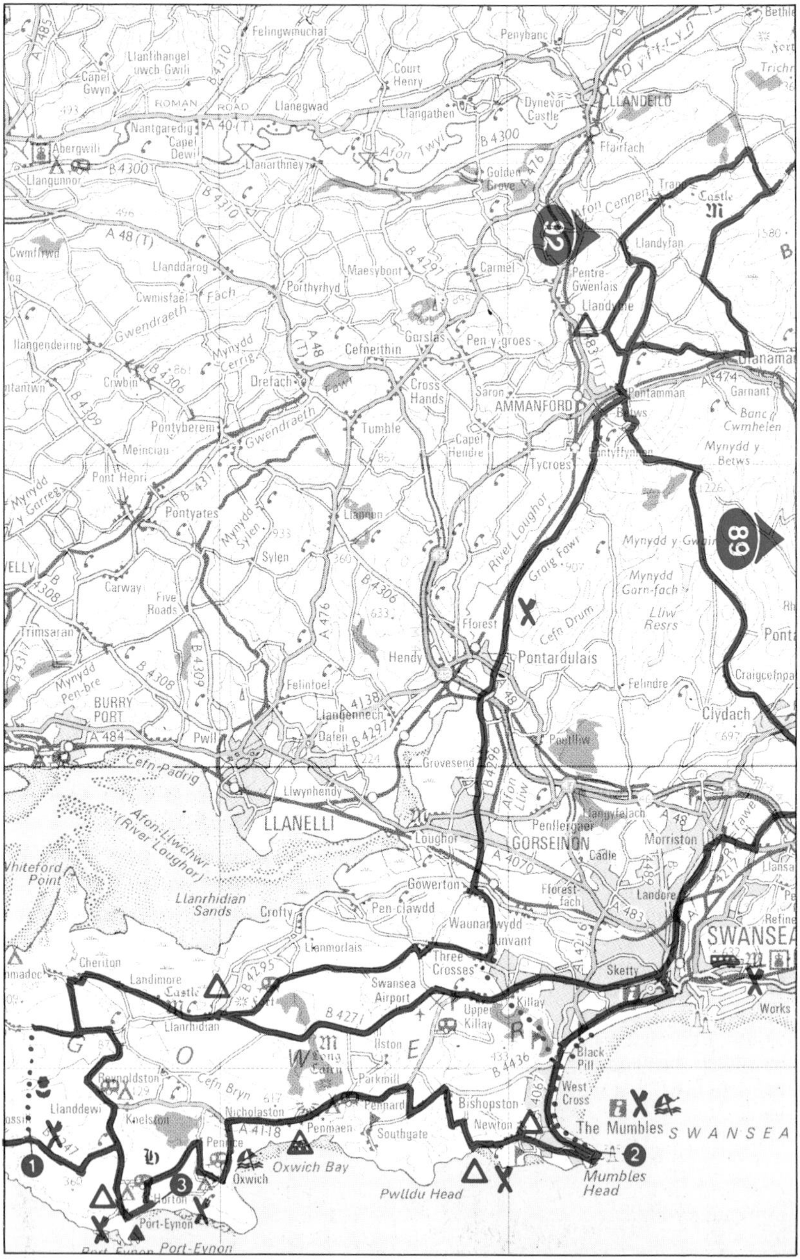

West Glamorgan/Mid Glamorgan

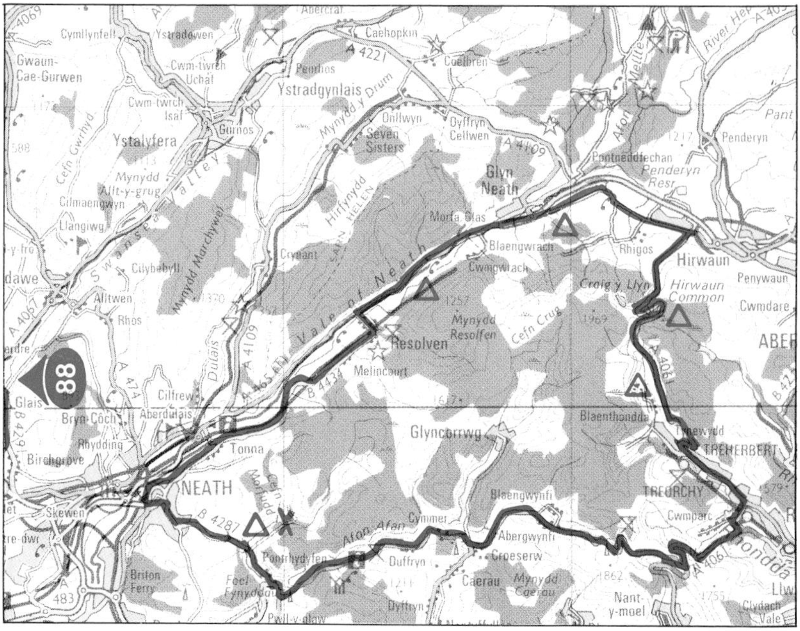

① Bridleway route along summit of Rhossilli Down. The bridleway along its foot, leading off right in under ½ mile (0.8 km), is less strenuous.

② Black Pill to Dunvant disused railway line: tarmac surface as far as Killay in 1984, extensions to Dunvant planned.

③ Unsurfaced track along beach to Port-Eynon saves steep climb.

△ **The Mumbles** area hilly; **N side of Gower Peninsula** easier than S side; climbs at **Caswell Bay**, W of The Mumbles, and **Port-Eynon**; the circuit based on **Neath** is a challenging ride, about 3,000 feet (915 m) of climbing: ride it clockwise for steep climbing and long descents, the other way round for easier climbs and steep descents; some A-road cycling on Neath circuit, but traffic generally light. Hard climbs near **Glyn Neath** and **S of Hirwaun**; **N of Ammanford**, alternative route with fords.

🚂 **Swansea**, some InterCity services from S Wales, London and the Midlands.

✗ Cafés as marked on **Gower Peninsula** – choices generally limited on N side; **Swansea–Ammanford** and **Neath** circuits, choices limited.

⛺ **The Mumbles – Port-Eynon**, scenery and views; **S of Hirwaun** wonderful straight descent.

𝔪 **Carneg Cennen Castle**, picnic site.

The Mumbles and **Oxerith**, sandy beaches.

▲ **Port-Eynon** Gower (0792) 390706 – by beach in an old lifeboat station.

Razorbills, seen from Gower cliffs.

Gwent/Wye Valley

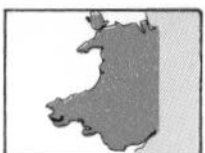

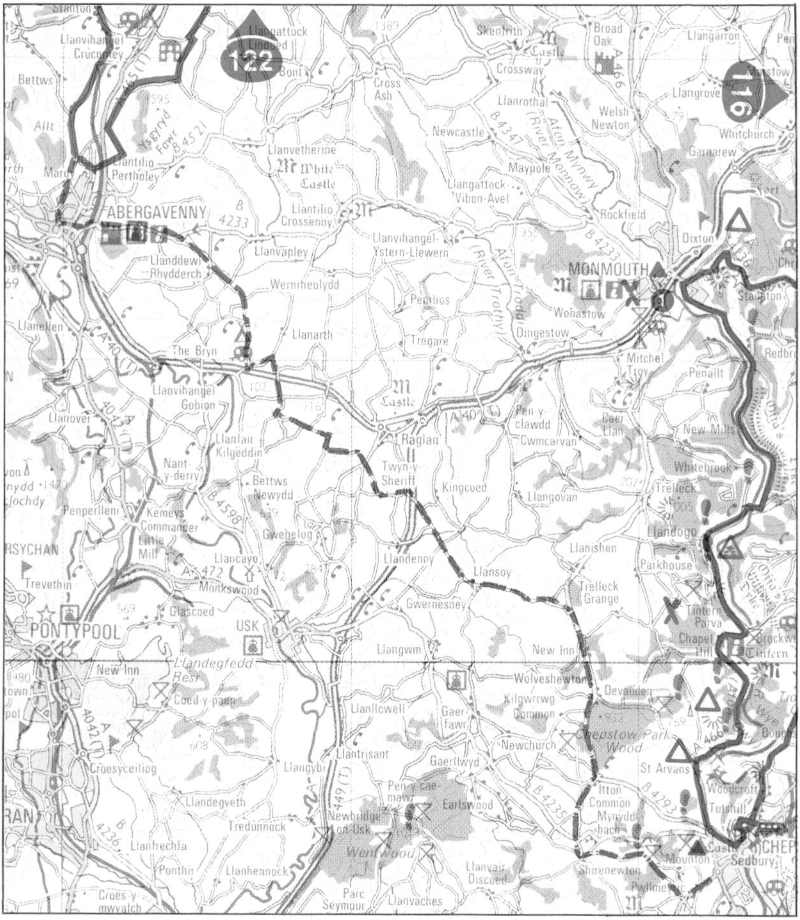

① To avoid one way system on leaving, walk along Wyebridge St and use underpass to cross A40.

△ **A466 Wye Valley** is busy, but great cycling: ride it out of season if possible. Strenuous climbs N from **St Arvans** and **Monmouth–Staunton**.

Chepstow on the S Wales main line.

Choices **Tintern, Parra, Monmouth**; also in many Wye Valley villages.

Wye Valley, exceptional viewpoints.

From **A466** a lane leads to Wynd Cliff, a sensational vantage point.

Abergavenny Brecon Beacons National Park exhibition at Tourist Information Centre, Monk Street; **Monmouth** Nelson relics.

Tintern famous romantic abbey ruins; **Monmouth Castle** 12th-C Great Tower survives, plus Great Castle House.

▲ **Chepstow** 02912 2685; **Monmouth** 0600 5116.

The Wye Valley

Dyfed/Powys/Black Mountain

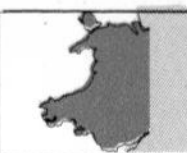

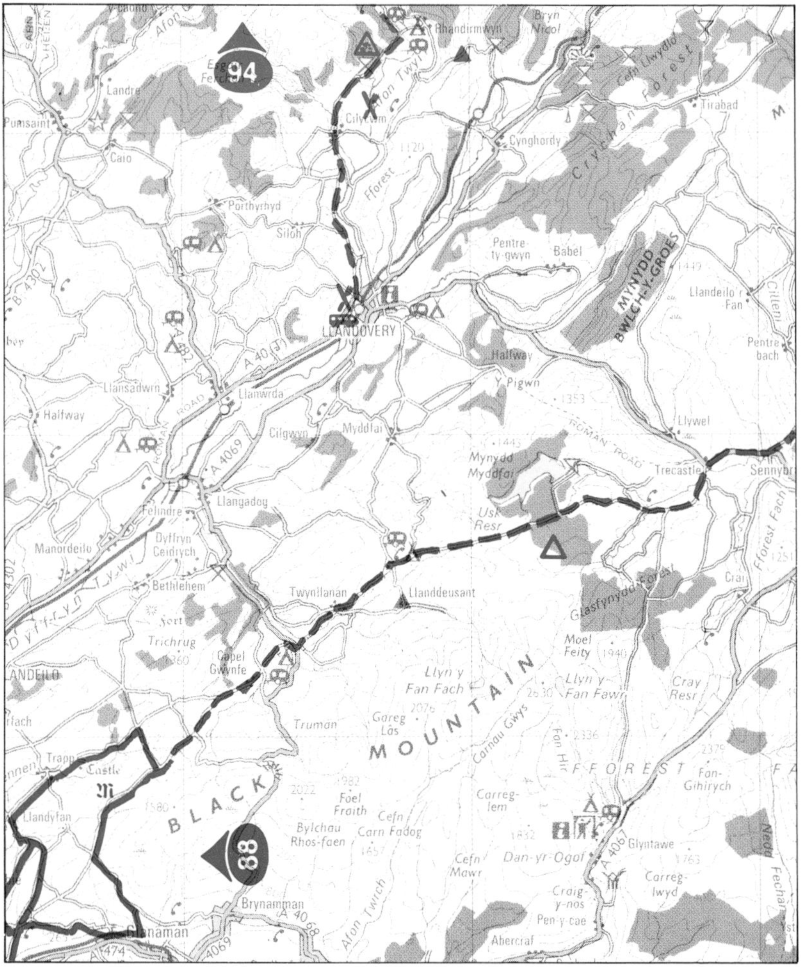

△ **Brecon – Llandovery** undulating but climbs **Trecastle–Usk Reservoir**.

Llandovery on the Mid Wales line.

Limited choices (pubs, cafés) **Llandovery**; pub meals, **Cilycwm**.

Mountain scenery **N of Llandovery** gains in grandeur with every mile.

▲ Bryn Poeth Uchaf (**Rhandirmwyn**) Cynghordy (05505) 235. Isolated farmhouse lit by gas. Access difficult by cycle, obtain YHA instructions.

Bryn Poeth Uchaf Youth Hostel

Powys/Brecon Beacons

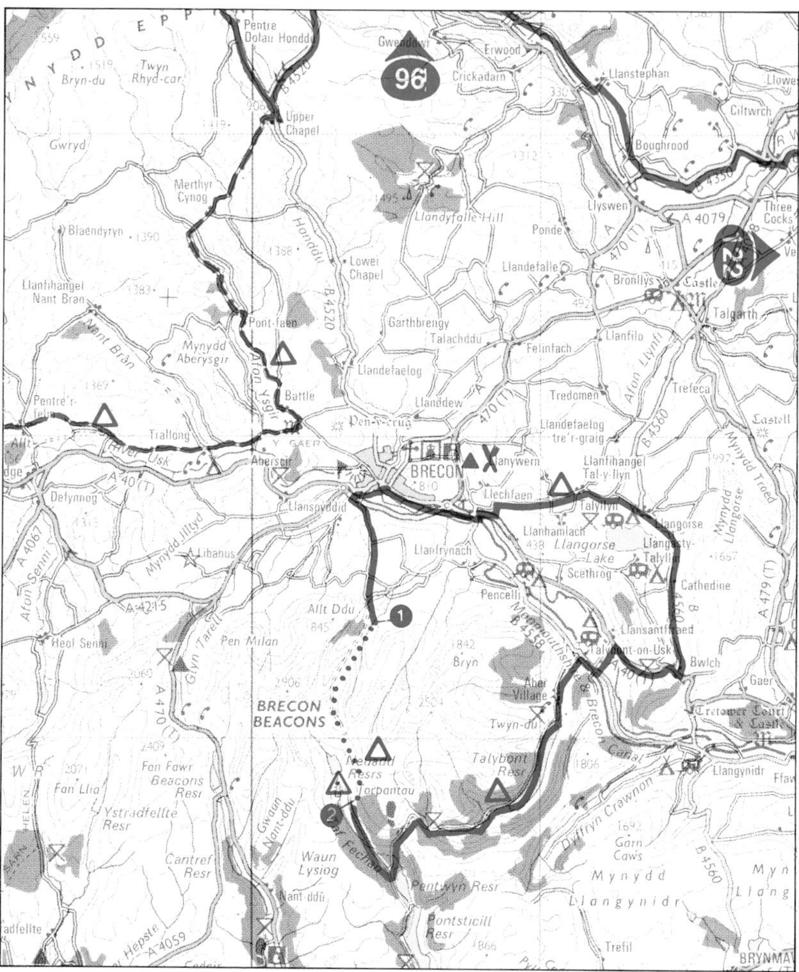

① Take the second right after Bailea Farm for access to the unsurfaced road crossing the Brecon Beacons. Road soon peters out into a stony track leading up through trees and a gate on to the hillside. A fine expedition, through the heart of the Beacons, but strenuous: one section at S end is through a stream gulley – no choice but to dismount and push. Best views travelling N to S. Access ② from unclassified road NW of the reservoirs.

△ The **unsurfaced track** leads through a gap in the Beacons, but heavy climbing nonetheless; routes N, E and W **out of Brecon** variable; level stretch along **Talybont Reservoir**.

✗ Limited choice, **Brecon**.

⚠ The **rough stuff** is a superb way of seeing the Brecon Beacons, but poor visibility means wasted effort.

▲ **Llwyn-y-Celyn** Brecon (0874) 4261.

Dyfed/Powys

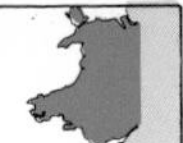

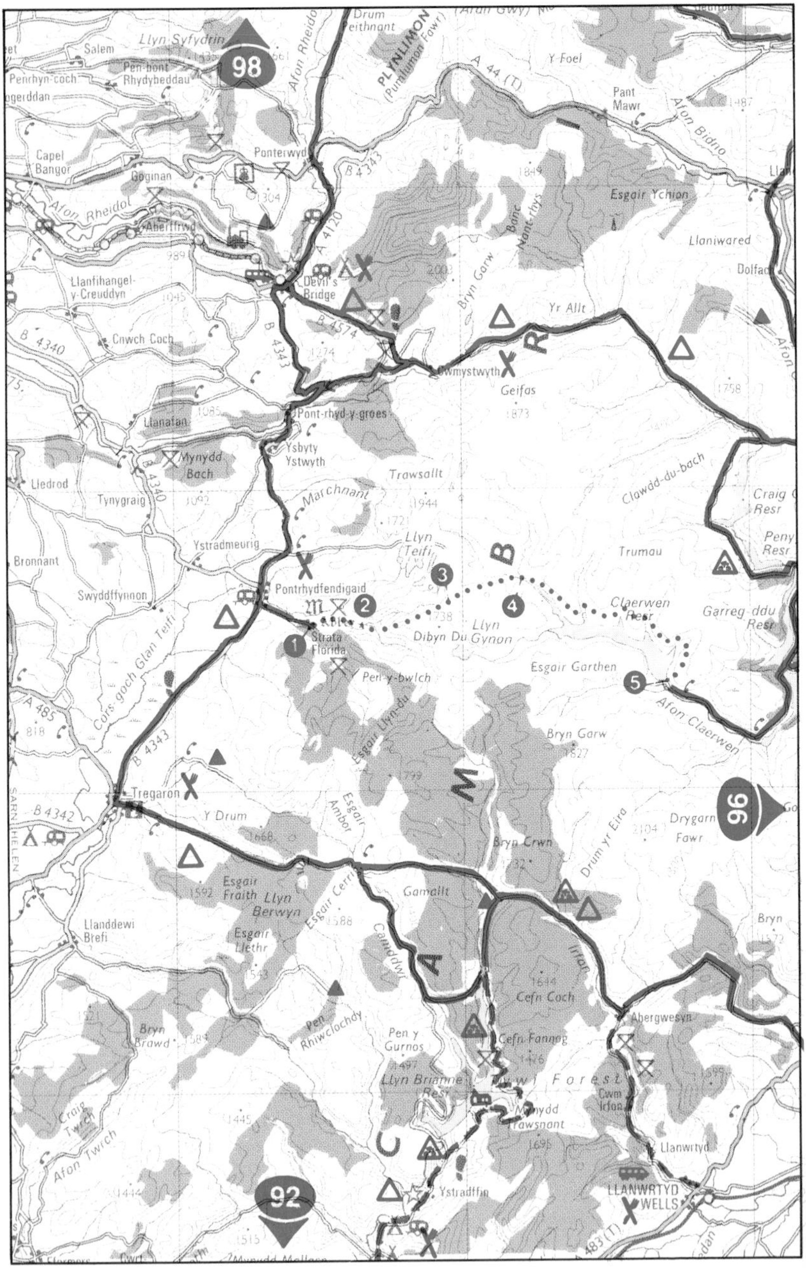

Llyn Syfydrin
Salem
Pen-bont Rhydybeddau
Penrhyn-coch
98
Drum Peithnant
Afon Rheidol
PLYNLIMON (Pumlumon Fawr)
A 44 (T)
Y Foel
Pant Mawr
Afon Bidno
Capel Bangor
Ponterwyd
B 4343
Goginan
Afon Rheidol
Aberffrwd
A 4120
Esgair Ychion
Banc Nant-rhys
Llaniwared
Dolfach
Llanfihangel-y-Creuddyn
Devil's Bridge
Bryn Garw
Yr Allt
B 4574
B 4340
Cnwch Coch
B 4343
Cwmystwyth
Geifas
Pont-rhyd-y-groes
Llanafan
Ysbyty Ystwyth
Mynydd Bach
Lledrod
B 4340
Trawsallt
Clawdd-du-bach
Tynygraig
Marchnant
Craig Goch Resr
Llyn Teifi
Ystradmeurig
Peny Resr
Trumau
Bronnant
Pontrhydfendigaid
Swyddffynnon
Strata Florida
Llyn Dibyn Du
Llyn Gynon
Claerwen Resr
Garreg-ddu Resr
Esgair Garthen
Pen-y-bwlch
Afon Claerwen
Cors-goch Glan Teifi
A 485
Esgair Llyn-du
Bryn Garw
B 4343
Tregaron
B 4342
SARN HELEN
Y Drum
Esgair Ambor
96
Drygarn Fawr
Drum yr Eira
Bryn Crwn
Gamallt
Esgair Fraith
Llyn Berwyn
Esgair Cerrig
Llanddewi Brefi
Esgair Llethr
Camddwr
Irfon
Cefn Coch
Bryn
Abergwesyn
Pen Rhiwclochdy
Bryn Brawd
Pen y Gurnos
Cefn Fannog
Llyn Brianne Resr
Tywi Forest
Craig Twrch
Mynydd Trawsnant
Cwm Irfon
Afon Twrch
Llanwrtyd
92
Ystradffin
LLANWRTYD WELLS
483 (T)
Mynydd Mallaen

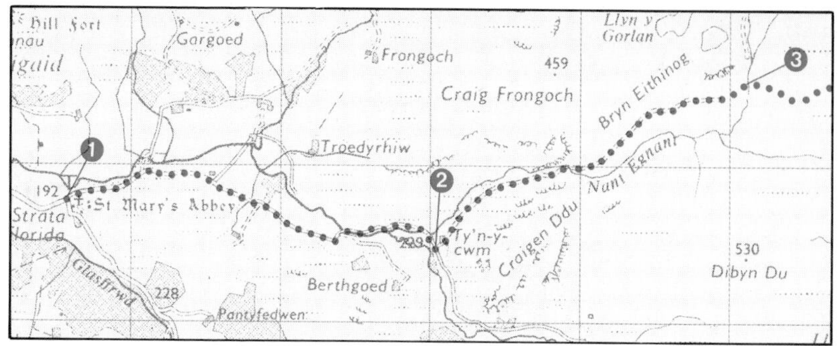

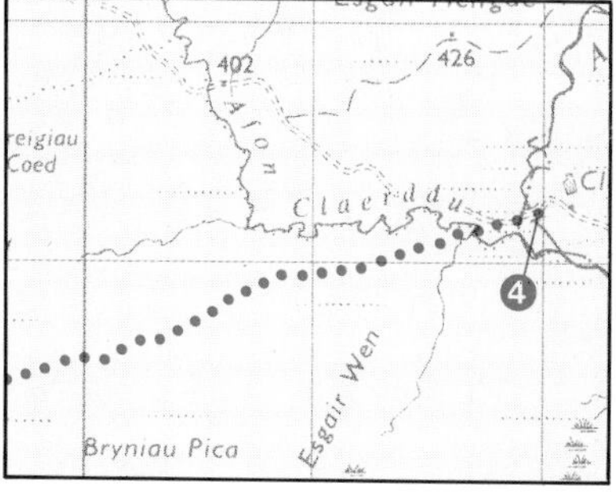

① From St Mary's Abbey, Strata Florida, gain access to the rough track leading over the hillsides of the Elan Valley by taking the farm road to the left of the abbey. In about 2 miles (3 km) turn left ② through Ty'n-y-cwm farmyard and continue out into the valley, climbing to ③ the S tip of Llyn Egnant. Contour round the left hand side of the hill in front and then make for the derelict farm of Claerwen, landmarked by a clump of trees, ④. Before the farm, ford the Afon Claerddu and cross the bridge over the Afon Claerwen. At farm, follow the track along the N shore of Claerwen Reservoir to unclassified road ⑤ by AA box. See warnings on page 13.

△ Continual climbing from **Towy Bridge via Ystradffin** past the reservoir; mountain road **W of Tregaron** very steep climbs/descents; **NW from Abergwesyn** 1:6 and steeper climbs, including 'Devil's Staircase', approaching 1:4 – road until recently unsurfaced track, narrow, with passing places and no shelter; **from Yr Allt** severe gradients to SE, while travelling W a long descent **to Cwmystwyth**; **Cwmystwyth–Devil's Bridge** 2 mile (3 km) climb then descent; major climbs and descents **Tregaron–Devil's Bridge**.

Llanwrtyd Wells on the Mid Wales line; **Devil's Bridge** terminus of Aberystwyth narrow-gauge railway.

No refreshment at all between Towy Bridge and Tregaron; limited choice **Llanwrtyd Wells**; pub meals **Towy Bridge**, **Tregaron**, **Pontrhydfendigaid**; cafés **Cwymstwyth** and **Devil's Bridge**.

N from Ystradffin some of the best mountain scenery in Wales; superb **reservoir sections** as marked; **NW from Abergwesyn**, bleak, wild.

▲ Blaencaron (**near Tregaron**) Tregaron (09744) 441 – all water fetched from stream; Tyncornel (**E of Llandewi Brefi**) no telephone, apply Youth Hostel, Tyncornel, Llandewi Brefi, Tregaron, Dyfed; Dolgoch (**S of Abergwesyn–Tregaron road**) Tregaron (09744) 680; Ystumtuen (**Devil's Bridge**) Ponterwyd (097085) 693; Nant-y-Dernol (**N of reservoirs**) Llangurig (05515) 246. (Warden is farmer who answers phone from 12.30–1.00 only.) Obtain access instructions.

Powys

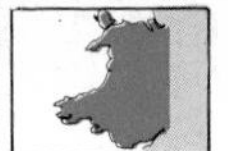

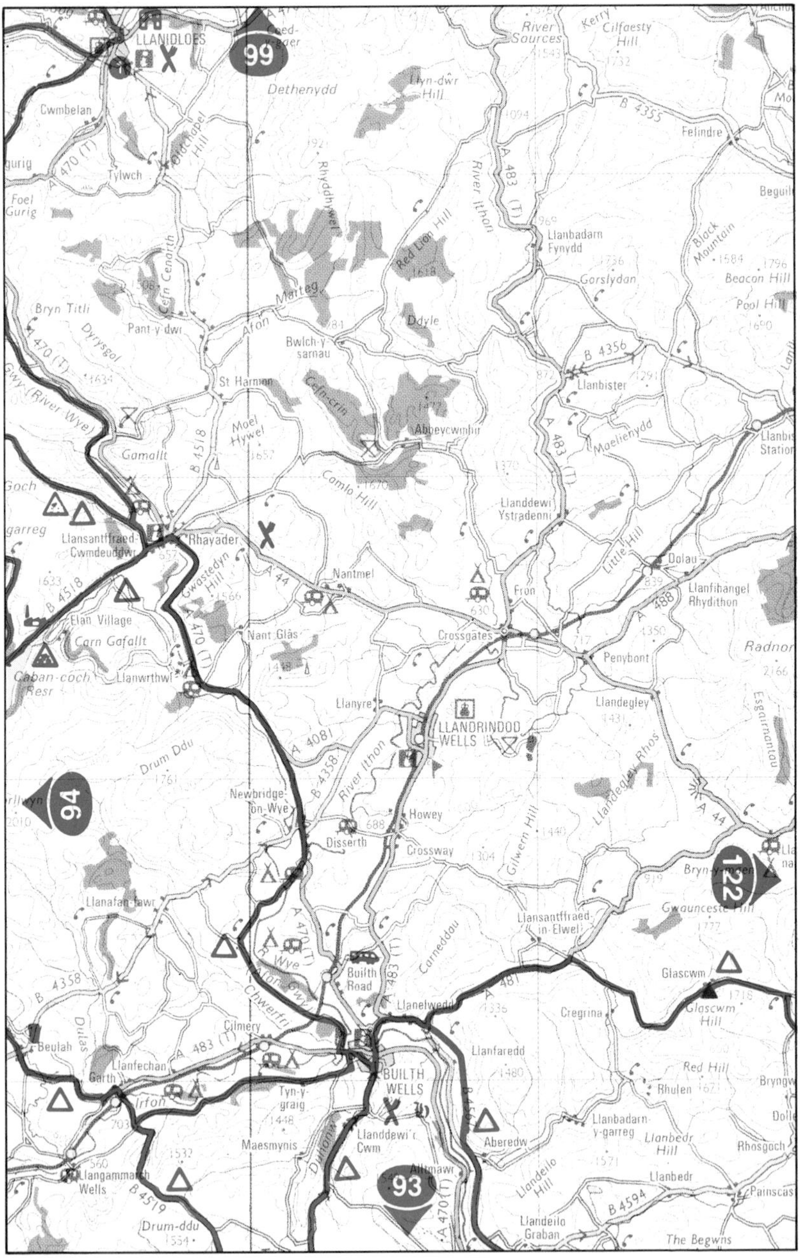

LLANIDLOES
Coed-y-gaer
99
Dethenydd
Llyn-dŵr Hill
River Sources
Kerry
Cilfaesty Hill
B 4355
Felindre
Cwmbelan
Oldchapel Hill
A 470 (T)
Tylwch
Foel Gurig
Rhyddhywel
A 483 (T)
River Ithon
Red Lion Hill
Llanbadarn Fynydd
Black Mountain
Beacon Hill
Pool Hill
Cefn Cenarth
Gorslydan
Bryn Titli
Afon Marteg
Pant-y-dwr
Dyrysgol
Bwlch-y-sarnau
Ddyle
B 4356
Llanbister
St Harmon
Cefn-crin
Gwy (River Wye)
B 4518
Moel Hywel
Abbeycwmhir
Maelienydd
Gamallt
Camlo Hill
Llanbister Station
Llanddewi Ystradenni
Llansantffraed-Cwmdeuddwr
Rhayader
Little Hill
Dolau
Gwastedyn Hill
A 44
Nantmel
Fron
Llanfihangel Rhydithon
Elan Village
Carn Gafallt
A 470 (T)
Nant Glâs
Crossgates
A 488
Penybont
Radnor
Caban-coch Resr
Llanwrthwl
Llanyre
Llandegley
LLANDRINDOD WELLS
A 4081
Drum Ddu
Llandegley Rhos
Esgairnantau
94
B 4358
River Ithon
Newbridge-on-Wye
Howey
Disserth
Crossway
Gilwern Hill
A 44
122
Bryn-y-maen
Llanafan-fawr
Gwaunceste Hill
Llansantffraed-in-Elwel
Carneddau
A 483 (T)
B 4358
R. Wye
Afon Gwy
Builth Road
Chwerfri
Glascwm
Llanelwedd
A 481
Cregrina
Glascwm Hill
Dulas
Cilmery
Beulah
A 483 (T)
Llanfaredd
Llanfechan
Garth
BUILTH WELLS
Red Hill
Irfon
Tyn-y-graig
Rhulen
Llanbadarn-y-garreg
Llanbedr Hill
Maesmynis
Llanddewi'r Cwm
Aberedw
Rhosgoch
Llangammarch Wells
Alltmawr
93
Llandeilo Hill
Llanbedr
B 4519
A 470 (T)
B 4594
Painscastle
Drum-ddu
Llandeilo Graban
The Begwns

Elan Valley

① To leave Llanidloes, cross the Severn from the Market Hall and immediately turn left, continuing on this unclassified road through Glan-y-nant, then turn right through Hen Neuadd.

△ **B4567 N** and **S of Aberedw** is generally level, tracing course of River Wye. The **A470 N from Builth Wells** is not usually busy, and fairly interesting cycling; the marked alternative tracing the Wye is generally easy, but longer. **SW of Rhayader**, gradual climb to the reservoir; **NW from Rhayader** becoming strenuous – see page 94. **SE of Beulah** short linking stretch of A483, then **B4519** climbs to nearly 1,500 feet (457 m) over firing range; unclassified road **Glascwm** moderate, largely following river valley, **B4520 S of Builth Wells** crosses MOD firing range, subject to closure for short periods.

Builth Road on the Mid Wales line.

Builth Wells choices (cafés), and hot running water in the public lavatories; cafés in **Rhayader** and **Llanidloes**. Llanidloes is last chance for refreshments or provisions until Machynlleth is reached.

Pub at **Beulah**.

NW from Rhayader increasingly bleak and impressive; approaching **Elan Valley**, reservoirs from Elan Village especially beautiful at any season.

Caban Coch Reservoir and Dam at the junction of the Elan and Claerwen Valleys forming a vast man-made lake system.

Builth Wells, market town, once important for its location on the cattle route to England.

Llanidloes The half-timbered Market Hall dates from around 1600, probably the only free-standing market hall in Wales.

▲ **Glascwm** Hundred House (09824) 367.

Dyfed/Powys

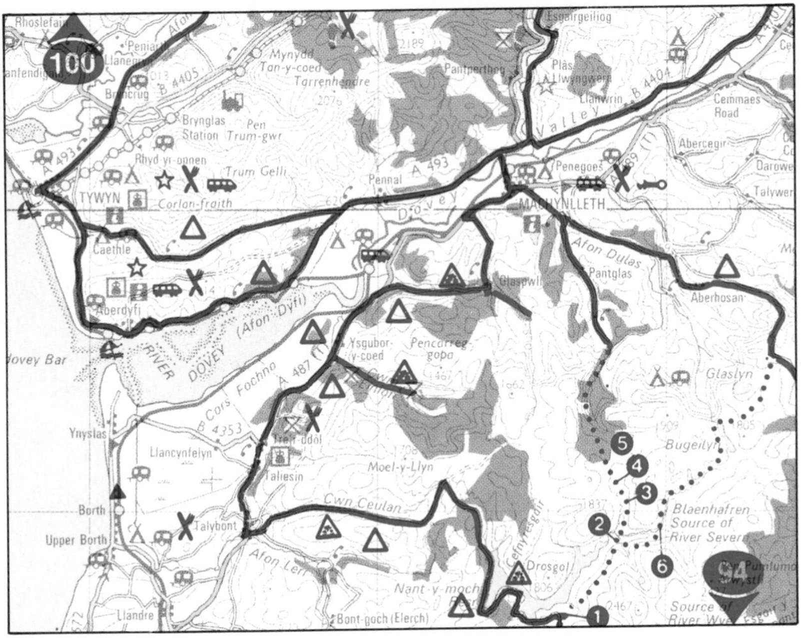

△ The **A487** is busy, avoid at peak times or use the off-highway alternative shown opposite. The main road does, however, give access to two worthwhile diversions: one, a tarmac lane, leads roughly E from the hamlet of Furnace just S of **Ysgubor-y-coed** – strenuous climb and tricky descent; the other leads roughly E up Llynfant Valley from the A487 about **2 miles (3 km) N of Furnace** – look carefully for a narrow, almost concealed unclassified road: steep climbing. Easy riding **along the Nant-y-môch Reservoir** but then road climbs. Take care on descent through **Cwm Ceulan** – stray sheep and other hazards. The **Dovey Estuary road** is easy. The unclassified road running **SE of Tywyn** (through Happy Valley) towards Pennal avoids the A493, but a steep climb towards end of valley. A long climb through **Dylife**; drawn-out, sometimes steep descent **Dylife to Machynlleth**.

Machynlleth and **Dovey Junction** on the Shrewsbury – Aberystwyth line; **Aberdyfi, Tywyn** and other stations on the Cambrian coast line. The Aberdyfi–Machynlleth service is infrequent.

Pub meals and cafés at **Talybont, Machynlleth, Aberdyfi, Tywyn**; café at **Tre'r-ddôl**; pub meals at **Abergynolwyn**; otherwise scarce.

The **detours off the A487** explore delightful valleys; **Nant-y-môch Reservoir** section is enchanting and the descent down the **Cwm Ceulan** outstanding – in an area of superb cycle touring.

Sandy beach at **Aberdyfi**, shingle and sand at **Tywyn**.

☆ **Aberdyfi** is a beautifully situated seaside town; sailing; at **Tywyn** is the Tal-y-lyn Railway Centre, narrow-gauge railway trips inland.

Cycle repair and hire in **Machynlleth**.

▲ **Borth** (097081) 498.

Dyfed/Powys

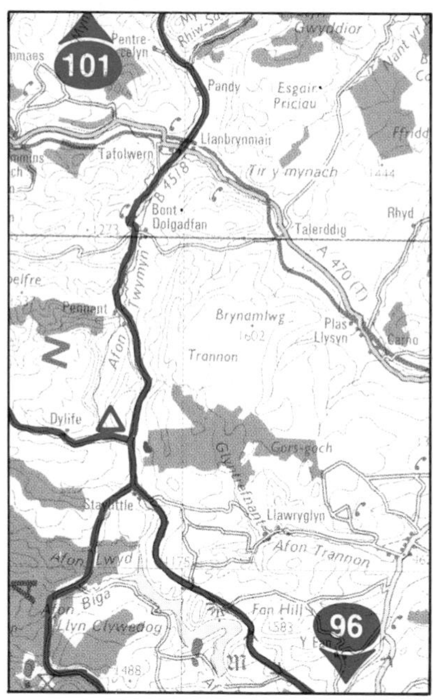

① At the corner about ⅓ mile (0.5 km) E of Nant-y-môch Dam, strike N down the track, crossing the Afon Hengwym ②. At ③ bear right and dismount (track classed as footpath). ④ Ford or footbridge over river. ⑤ Enter forest and continue N, ignoring side turnings, eventually joining tarmac lane to Pantglas. From ② a bridleway leads E along the Hengwym's S bank. Cross river at ⑥ and continue NW on (at first) ill-defined way past Bugeilyn and Glaslyn – see Landranger 135 – to connect with unclassified road NW of Dylife. *Strenuous; see warning, page 13.*

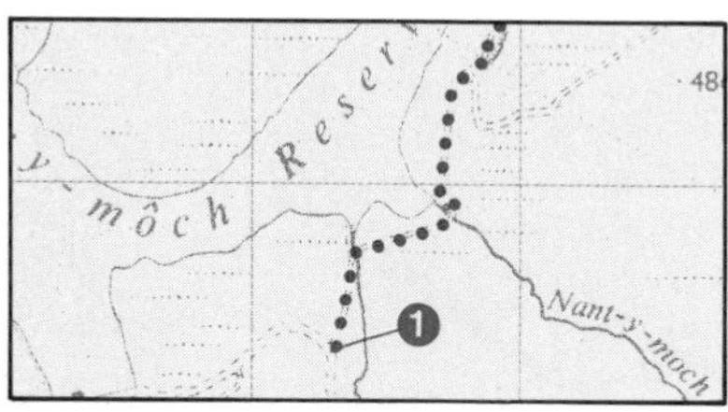

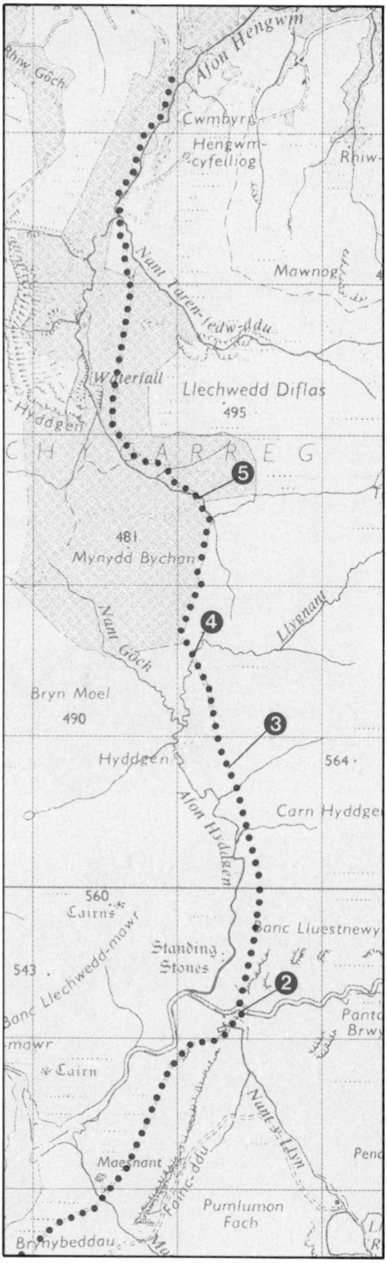

Gwynedd

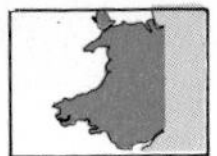

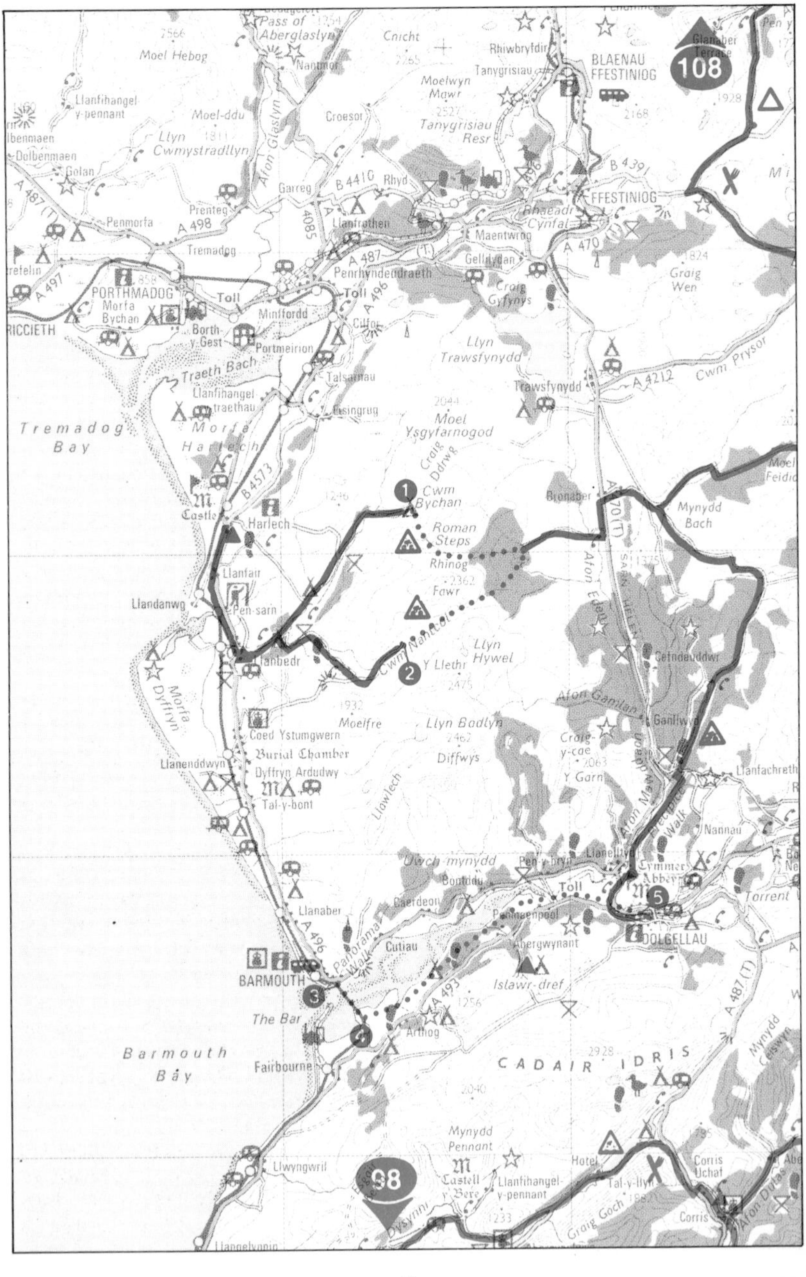

Pass of Aberglaslyn
Moel Hebog
Cnicht
Nantmor
Rhiwbryfdir
Tanygrisiau
BLAENAU FFESTINIOG
Glanaber Terrace
108
Moelwyn Mawr
Llanfihangel-y-pennant
Moel-ddu
Croesor
Tanygrisiau Resr
Llyn Cwmystradllyn
Afon Glaslyn
Dolbenmaen
Golan
Garreg
B 4410
Rhyd
B 4391
FFESTINIOG
Prenteg
Penmorfa
A 498
Llanfrothen
Rhaeadr Cynfal
Maentwrog
Tremadog
A 487
A 470
Gellilydan
Graig Wen
PORTHMADOG
Penrhyndeudraeth
Toll
Morfa Bychan
Minffordd
Craig Gyfynys
CRICCIETH
Borth-y-Gest
Portmeirion
Llyn Trawsfynydd
Traeth Bach
Talsarnau
Trawsfynydd
A 4212
Cwm Prysor
Llanfihangel-traethau
Eisingrug
Moel Ysgyfarnogod
Tremadog Bay
Morfa Harlech
Craig Ddrwg
B 4573
Cwm Bychan
Bronaber
Mynydd Bach
Castle
Harlech
Roman Steps
Rhinog Fawr
Llanfair
Afon Eden
Sarn Helen
Llandanwg
Pen-sarn
Cwm Nantcol
Llyn Hywel
Llanbedr
Y Llethr
Cefndeuddwr
Morfa Dyffryn
Afon Gamlan
Ganllwyd
Moelfre
Llyn Bodlyn
Coed Ystumgwern
Burial Chamber
Diffwys
Craig-y-cae
Llanenddwyn
Dyffryn Ardudwy
Y Garn
Llanfachreth
Tal-y-bont
Llawlech
Afon Mawddach
Precipice Walk
Nannau
Uwch-mynydd
Pen-y-bryn
Llanelltyd
Bontddu
Cymmer Abbey
Caerdeon
Toll
Torrent Walk
Llanaber
Penmaenpool
Panorama Walk
Cutiau
Abergwynant
DOLGELLAU
A 496
BARMOUTH
A 493
Islawr-dref
The Bar
Arthog
A 487 (T)
Barmouth Bay
Fairbourne
CADAIR IDRIS
Mynydd Pennant
Hotel
Corris Uchaf
Llwyngwril
98
Castell y Bere
Llanfihangel-y-pennant
Tal-y-llyn
Dysynni
Graig Goch
Corris
Afon Dulas
Llangelynin

Gwynedd

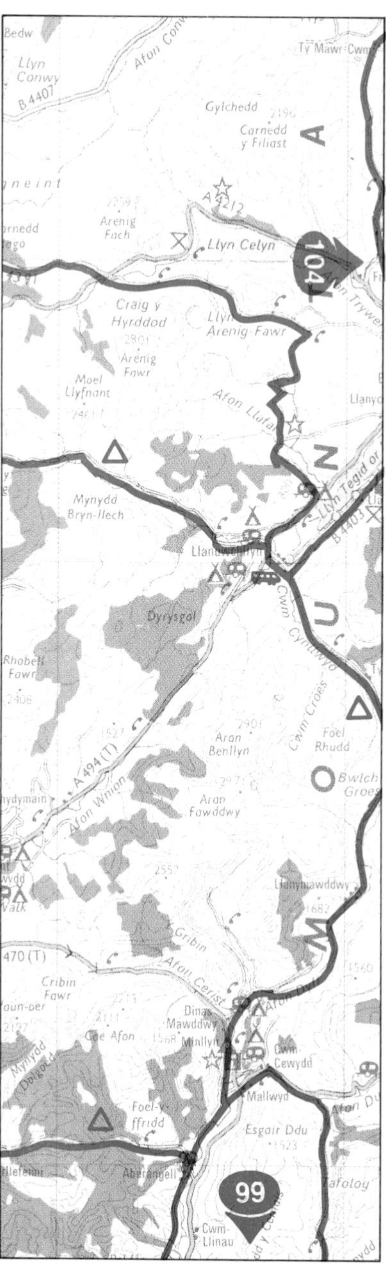

① and ② The Roman Steps and the Bwlch Drws Ardudwy, classic rough-stuff routes linking Harlech and the coast with the A470 via the Rhinogs. Full details on Landranger 1:50 000 mapping, see pages 102–3.

③ Access to the Barmouth–Dolgellau disused railway line route at the toll bridge, ④ at Morfa Mawddach Station and ⑤ from the Riverside Park, Dolgellau, via flood embankment and footbridge.

△ **Wfrom Llanuwchllyn** is a 7-mile (11-km) climb followed by a 2-mile (3-km) descent, some further climbing, then mainly descent for the last 15 miles (24 km) to Dolgellau; **W from Aberangell** (towards top of climb through village turn left on to Forest Drive) surfaced road ends after 1 mile (1.5 km): unsurfaced but hard track, mostly rideable, with a strenuous ½-mile (0.8-km) climb followed by a 2-mile (3-km) descent; **S of Pen y Bedw** exceptionally steep descent; **Bwlch Groes**, one of the highest public roads in Wales, fearsome in winter.

Blaenau Ffestiniog, terminus of the branch line from Llandudno Junction; **Barmouth** and numerous stations on the Cambrian Coast line; **Llanuwchllyn**, terminus of the Bala Lake narrow gauge railway.

Choices – pub meals and cafés – at **Dolgellau**; useful café after miles of empty country at **junction of B4407 and B4391** E of Ffestiniog; Tal-y-llyn Hotel **on the B4405** pub meals in superb surroundings.

The whole area is a cycle tourist's dream, but outstanding stretches are the long descent on **unclassified roads** to the **NE of Dolgellau**; **Aberangell westwards** past Tal-y-llyn; the **rough stuff** – see pages 102–3.

▲ **Kings** (near Dolgellau), Dolgellau (0341) 422392; **Dinas Mawddwy** 06504 279; **Corris** 065473 686; **Harlech** 0766 780285; **Llanbedr** 034123 287.

Gwynedd

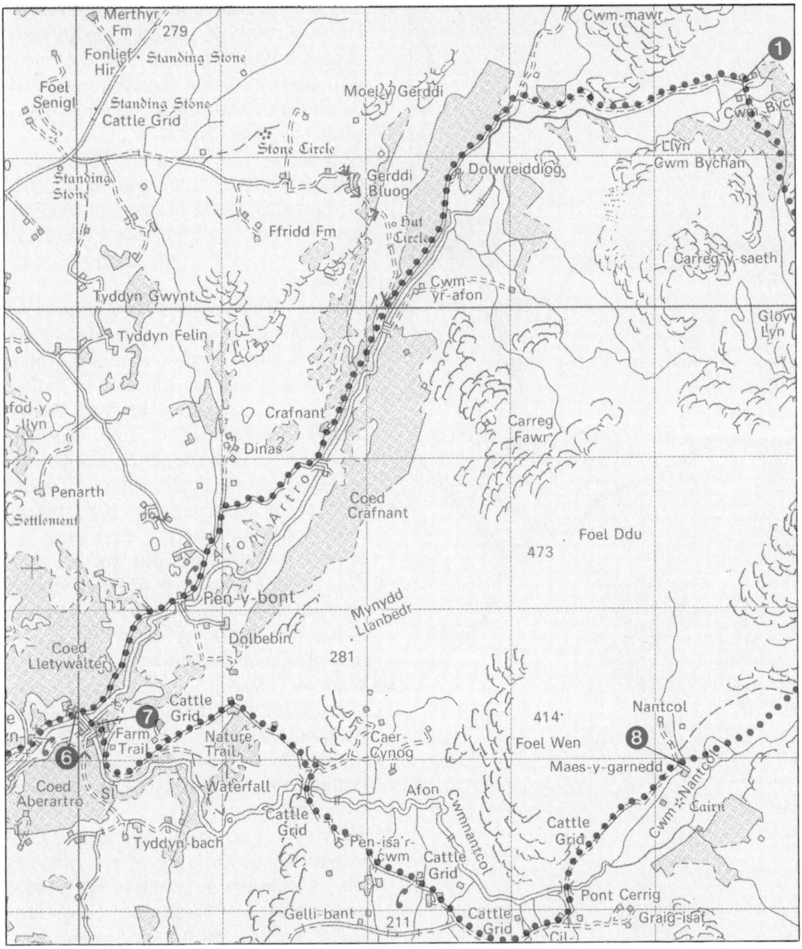

The Roman Steps are supreme rough stuff, only for the fit and well-equipped: see warnings on page 11. Expect to dismount, and to carry your bike for at least 2½ miles (4 km).

① After riding through beautiful oak woods along the Afon Artro, and passing Llyn Cwm Bychan turn right through the gate in the dry stone wall before reaching the farm. Dismount and follow the path through woodland and across rocky terrain, and in ¾ mile (1 km), beyond a stone wall, reach ② the Steps. Shoulder your bike and climb the rocky staircase. The descent from ③ the top of the pass down the E slopes is relatively gentle, and the landscape less wild. Follow the narrow path through heather to Coed y Brenin Forest (boggy under trees). Cross the first Forestry Commission track ④ and ⑤ turn left at the next

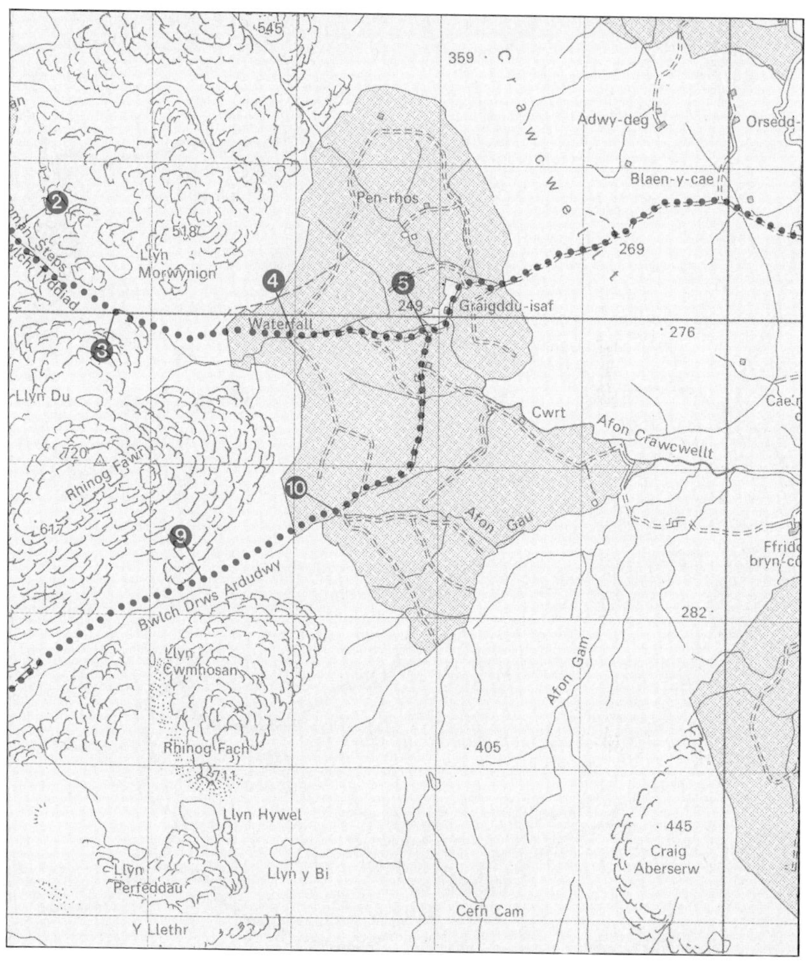

track when the farmstead of Craigddu-uchaf comes in sight. Pick up the tarmac road beyond the farm for an exhilarating descent to the A470.

Bwlch Drws Ardudwy is a lonelier alternative to the Roman Steps, some say more ruggedly beautiful; it involves wheeling and at times carrying the bike for at least 3 miles (5 km).

⑥ Turn right off the Llyn Cwm Bychan road 1 mile (1.5 km) from Llandbedr across the ancient stone bridge and in 100 yards (90 m) ⑦ turn left for the narrow gated road to Cwm Nantcol. From where the road ends ⑧ dismount and follow the path as it twists for 1½ miles (2.5 km) across the heather to the great natural amphitheatre below Rhinog Fawr. A staircase of rough stones leads to the top of the pass ⑨. Follow path to Coed y Brenin, and forest track ⑩ to Craigddu-uchaf.

East Gwynedd/South Clwyd/North Powys

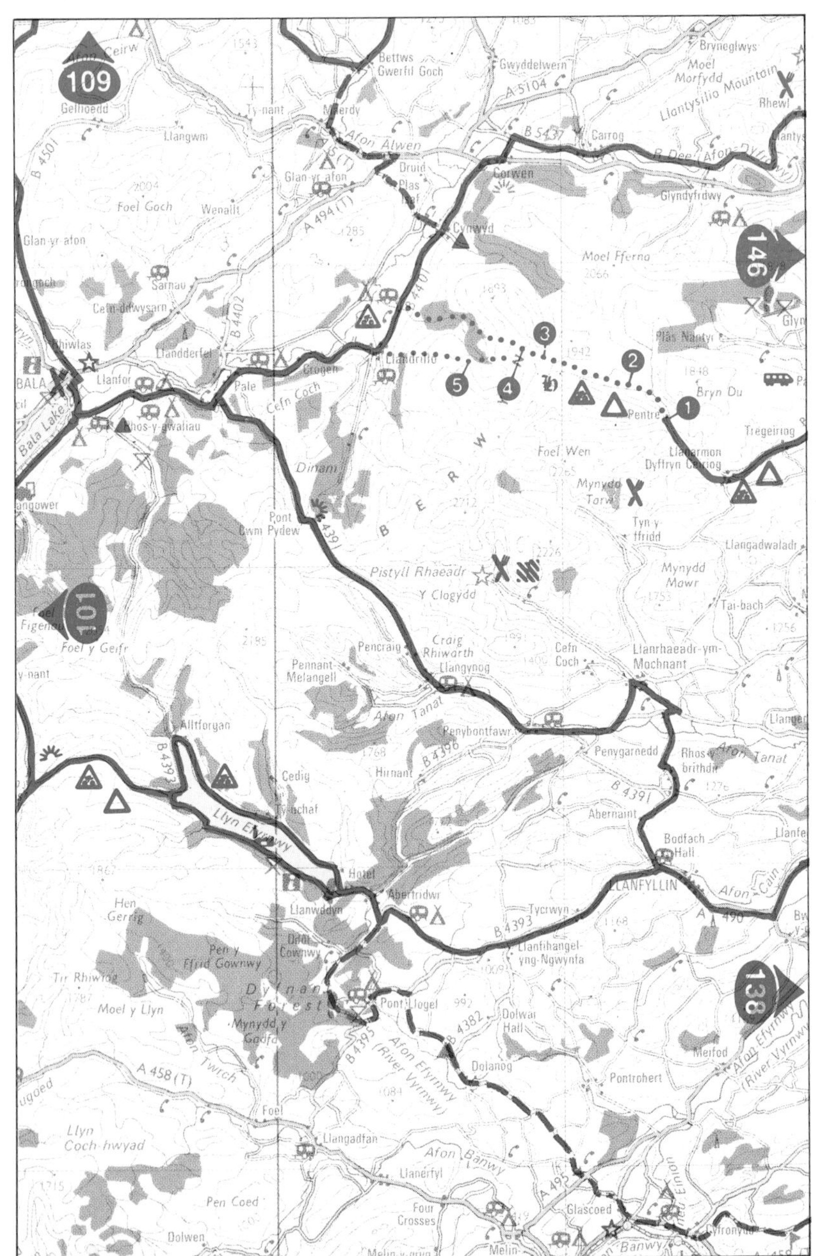

East Gwynedd/South Clwyd/North Powys

① 'The Wayfarer' is a relatively easy rough-stuff crossing of the Berwyn Mountains, but as with other mountain routes it is only for the fit and properly equipped (see page 11). It involves pushing the bike uphill for about 1 mile (1.5 km). In Pentre ① follow the lane towards the isolated farm of Sych-cae-rhiw, but at the fork before the farm keep left along the track which begins to climb Nant Rhydwilyn. Beyond a gate, you are on the moorland slopes of the Berwyn. The track climbs, then drops to a stream ② which is crossed on a modern bridge. Over this, railway sleepers form a platform across marshy ground, but with low gearing it is possible to ride for much of the ¾ mile (1 km) to the summit of the pass, except near the top where the going becomes really rough and steep. At the summit ③ sign the visitor's book in the metal box weighted down with stones. Close by is Wayfarer's Memorial (see note below). If Cynwyd is your goal, keep to the right ④ where the track forks about ¼ mile (0.5 km) from the memorial. The track, now mostly rideable (but gated), descends steadily to the riverside meadows of the Dee Valley to connect with the B4401.

If Llandrillo is your goal, fork left at ④. The track, an old drove road, is rougher than the route to Cynwyd, but more interesting. All but ¾ mile (1 km) is easily rideable. Cross a stone bridge ⑤ and splash through the number of tiny streams which cross the path before finally descending into Llandrillo.

△ **Unclassified road W from Lake Vyrnwy**, a steep climb up the first part of the Eunant Fawr Valley – but a cooling stream with many small waterfalls runs close by. **B4500 to Llanarmon Dyffryn Ceiriog** is easy riding; strenuous **rough stuff** – see directions above.

Nearest stations are Ruabon and Chirk, on the Shrewsbury–Chester branch line, see page 146.

Pub meals at **Llanarmon**; small tea room at **Rhewl**; pub meals and cafés at **Bala**; useful café at **Tan-y-pistyll**. Elsewhere facilities are sparse, carry provisions.

Llanarmon has two hospitable inns.

The Wayfarer **rough-stuff** route across the Berwyns is a memorable if popular route. Enthusiasts have been known to add some adventure by doing it on a moonlit summer night, breakfasting in Corwen or Bala; the **B4500 from Glyn Ceiriog** (just off map) to Llanarmon is especially beautiful; the **Dee Valley** is charming and the country **W from Lake Vyrnwy** impressively desolate; if time allows, a circuit of **Vyrnwy** is worthwhile.

B4391 extensive views across Berwyn Mountains; junction of unclassified roads **W of Lake Vyrnwy** fine view down the steep valley to Dinas Mawddwy.

Wayfarer's Memorial, a plaque set in the rock at the **top of the pass**, makes the Wayfarer route a pilgrimage for cyclists. 'Wayfarer' was the pen name of W. M. Robinson (1877–1956), the cyclist who loved touring the Welsh countryside and inspired many with his accounts of it in cycling magazines. The memorial and visitor's book are maintained by the Rough Stuff Fellowship against the odds: even here, there are vandals.

Fine waterfall at **Tan-y-pistyll**, well worth the detour.

Astonishing Victorian gothic dam architecture on **Lake Vyrnwy**, and attractive lake supplying drinking water to the Birmingham area.

☆ Narrow gauge railways at **Bala** and **Heniarth**. Bala is an excellent touring centre for North Wales.

▲ **Plas Rhiwaedog** (near Bala) Bala (0678) 520215 – 17th-C manor house; **Cynwyd** Corwen (0490) 2797 – former water mill.

Gwynedd

① Access to Bangor–Bethesda disused railway line route from the old A5 as it crosses the river and ② Glasinfryn.

③ Access to the Caernarfon–Bryncir disused railway line route at Caernarfon Castle and ④ Llanwnda (Hen Castell). ③–④ is asphalt. The route terminates at Bryncir about 5 miles (8 km) N of Criccieth.

△ Avoid the **A4086** at peak times; steady climb up the **Llanberis** pass, but recommended direction of travel is Llanberis to Capel Curig (see page 108) because going the other way at speed spoils the views.

Llanfairpwllgwyngyll or **Holyhead** on the Crewe–Holyhead main line.

Choices of pub meals and cafés at **Bangor**, **Caernarfon**, **Llanberis**, **Menai Bridge**, **Beaumaris** (name not on map) and **Holyhead**.

Sandy beach and good swimming at **Lligwy Bay** near Din Lligwy; excellent sandy beach and fine sand dunes at **Aberffraw**.

Caernarfon Castle, chief of the chain of famous Welsh castles built by Edward I was started in 1283. **Beaumaris Castle** is another of Edward I's castles, never completed, but the concentric planning and moat are nonetheless impressive.

Anglesey is famous for its ancient monuments and the route takes in **Bryn-celli-du** burial chamber, 2000 BC; Bodowy burial chamber, N **of Bryn-siencyn**, cover stone on three uprights; Ty-Newydd burial chamber, **N of Bodorgan Station**, with its massive cover stone on three uprights; **unclassified road S of South Stack**, a well-preserved collection of circular huts from the Roman period; Trefignath burial chamber **S of Holyhead**; and **Din Lligwy**, a fortified Iron Age village.

Dramatic cliffs with sea bird colonies can be viewed from the RSPB observation tower at South Stack on **Holyhead**.

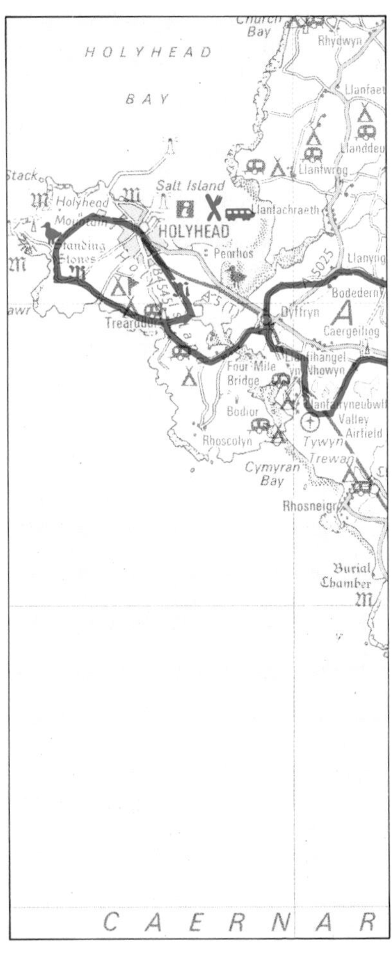

Menai Bridge, Telford's elegant suspension bridge of 1826, with a span of 579 feet (176 m) between towers.

Llanfairpwyll was extended by publicity-seeking Victorians into the longest place name in Britain.

Plas Newydd (Nat. Trust) **off the A4080**, 18th-C mansion and gardens, fine setting.

▲ **Bangor** 0248 353516; **Llanberis** 0286 870280; **Snowdon Ranger** Waunfawr (028685) 391.

Gwynedd

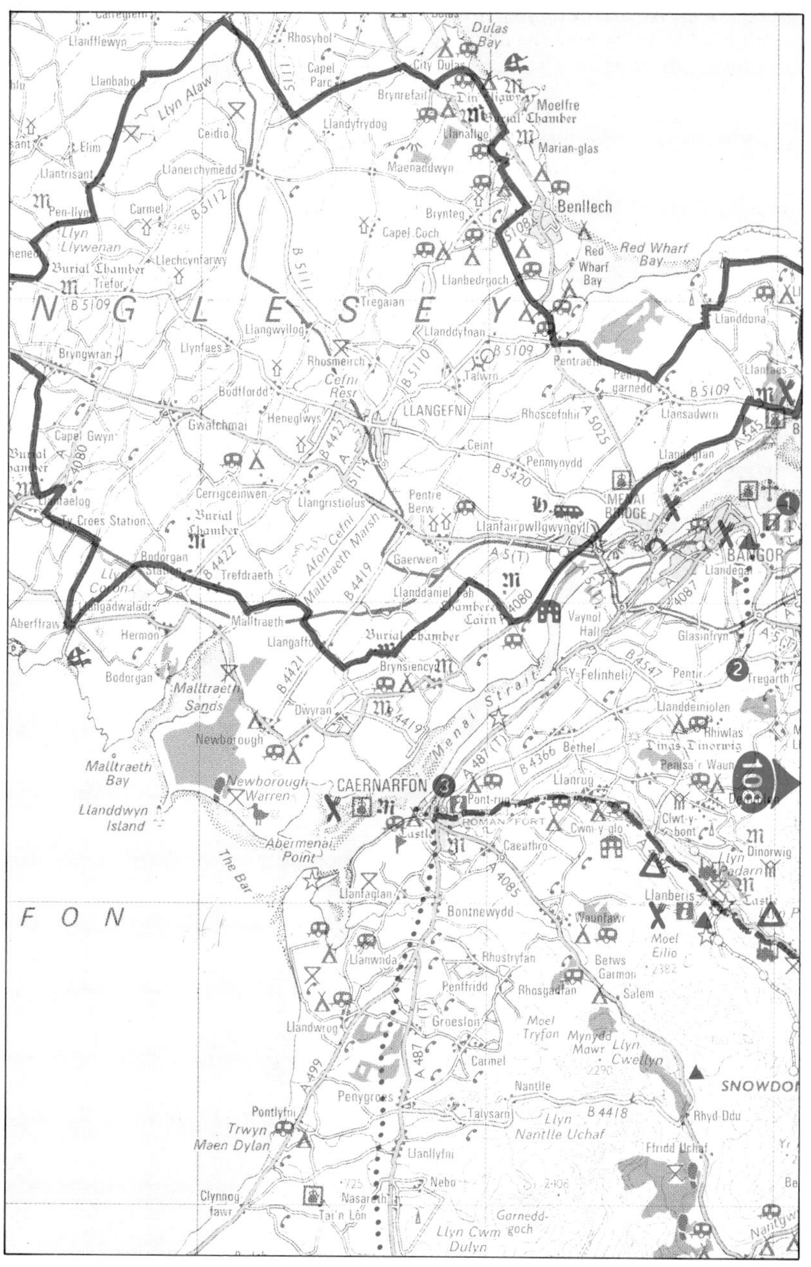
Rhosybol
Dulas Bay
Llanfflewyn
Capel Parc
City Dulas
Llanbabo
Llyn Alaw
Brynrefail
Din Lligwy
Moelfre
Burial Chamber
Llandyfrydog
Llanallgo
Ceidio
Marian-glas
Elim
Llanerchymedd
Maenaddwyn
Llantrisant
Benllech
Pen-llyn
Carmel
B5112
Brynteg
Capel Coch
B5108
Llyn Llywenan
Red Wharf Bay
Red Wharf Bay
Burial Chamber
Llechcynfarwy
B 5111
Trefor
Llanbedrgoch
B 5109
Tregaian
N G L E S E Y
Llanddona
Llangwyllog
Llanddyfnan
Llynfaes
B 5109
Bryngwran
Rhosmeirch
Pentraeth
Llanfaes
Talwrn
B 5110
Cefni Resr
Pen-y-garnedd
Bodffordd
B 5109
LLANGEFNI
Rhoscefnhir
Llansadwrn
Gwalchmai
Heneglwys
A 5025
Capel Gwyn
B 4422
A 545
A 4080
Ceint
Llandegfan
Penmynydd
B 5420
Cerrigceinwen
Llangristiolus
Pentre Berw
MENAI BRIDGE
Llanfaelog
Burial Chamber
Ty Croes Station
Llanfairpwllgwyngyll
Afon Cefni
Malltraeth Marsh
BANGOR
Bodorgan Station
B 4422
Gaerwen
A 5(T)
Llandegai
Llyn Coron
Trefdraeth
B 4419
A 4087
Llanddaniel Fab
Chambered Cairn
A 4080
Llangadwaladr
Vaynol Hall
Aberffraw
Hermon
Malltraeth
Burial Chamber
Glasinfryn
Llangaffo
A 5(T)
Bodorgan
Brynsiencyn
B 4547
Pentir
Tregarth
Y Felinheli
Malltraeth Sands
B 4421
Menai Strait
Dwyran
B 4419
Llanddeiniolen
Newborough
Rhiwlas
Dinas Dinorwig
A 487 (T)
B 4366
Bethel
Malltraeth Bay
Penisa'r Waun
Newborough Warren
CAERNARFON
Llanrug
108
Llanddwyn Island
Pont-rug
Clwt-y-bont
ROMAN FORT
Cwm-y-glo
Castle
Abermenai Point
Caeathro
Dinorwig
The Bar
Llyn Padarn
A 4085
Llanfaglan
Llanberis
Castle
F O N
Bontnewydd
Waunfawr
Moel Eilio
2382
Rhostryfan
Llanwnda
Betws Garmon
Penffridd
Rhosgadfan
Salem
Moel Tryfan
Groeslon
Mynydd Mawr
Llyn Cwellyn
Llandwrog
A 487
2290
Carmel
A 499
SNOWDON
Nantlle
Penygroes
Pontllyfni
Talysarn
B 4418
Rhyd-Ddu
Trwyn Maen Dylan
Llyn Nantlle Uchaf
Ffridd Uchaf
Llanllyfni
725
Nebo
2408
Clynnog fawr
Nasareth
Tai'n Lôn
Garnedd-goch
Llyn Cwm Dulyn

North-east Gwynedd

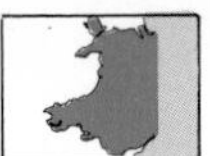

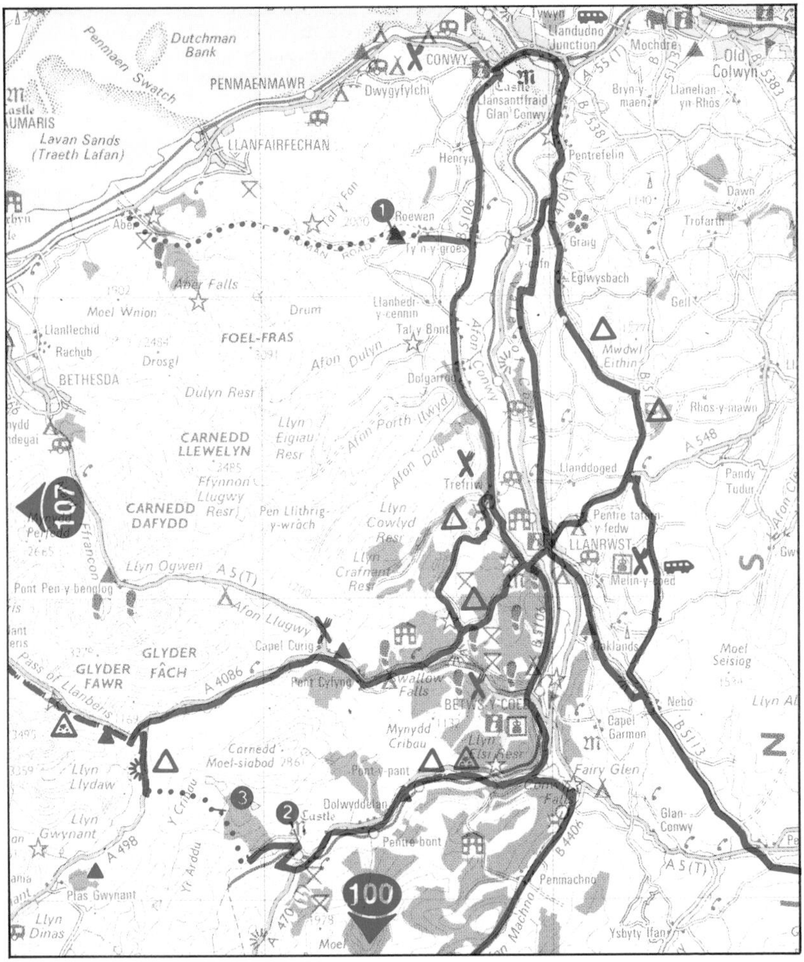

△ **SE from Graig**, hilly but quiet alternative to the A470; **A470 S of Betws-y-Coed**, steady climb; climb going N to **junction of A498 and A4086** E of Pass of Llanberis; climbs on the **B5113**; heavy climb **N from Swallow Falls**; steep descent **to Trefriw**.

🚌 **Llandudno Junction** on the Chester–Holyhead main line; **Llanwryst** and other stations on the Blaenau Ffestiniog branch line.

✗ Choices at **tourist centres** marked.

⚠ **Llanberis Pass** and Lledr Valley (**A470 S of Betws-y-Coed**) are outstanding.

𝔪 Picturesque 13th-C **Conwy Castle**.

▲ **Lledr Valley** Dolwyddelan (06906) 202; **Bryn Gwynant** (off A498) Beddgelert (076686) 251; **Pen-y-pass** (Pass of Llanberis) Llanberis (0286) 870428; **Capel Curig** 06904 225; **Roewen**, contact the regional YHA office, Colwyn Bay (0492) 31406.

North Clwyd

Access to Roman Road (see page 108) linking the Conwy Valley with the A55 ① just past the Roewen youth hostel. Track easy to follow, but expect a steep descent before Aber. The rough-stuff route linking the A470 and the A4086 is only about 10 per cent rideable, but usefully placed, and with remarkable views of Snowdon. Turn sharp left ② at entrance to hamlet of Blaenau Dolwyddelan (not on map). Continue to the third gate on this lane, then another 100 yards (90 m) and turn right to the farm of Coed Mawr. Go through the gated stock yard and join the rough track, later becoming a path, which is waymarked. In 1 mile (1.5 km) cross the rough bridge, climb past conifers to ruins of stone building and at junction of tracks head left towards the pass of Bwlch-y-Ehediad ③. Begin the descent and expect a very steep drop from the first trees of the oak wood. Continue through woodland to the gateway in the wall bordering a meadow, and continue to the A498.

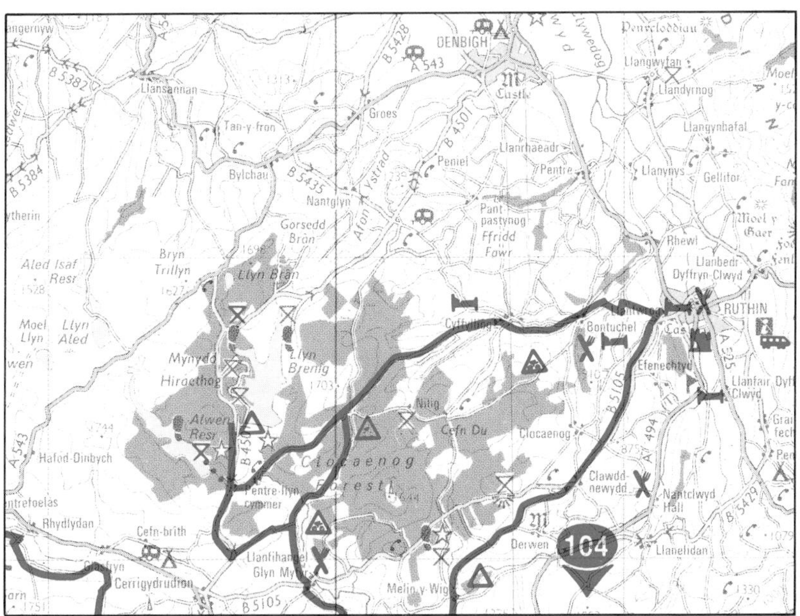

△ Strenuous, with almost continual climbs and descents, some very steep; particularly hard work on the **B4501 S of Brenig Reservoir** and **NE from Melin-y-Wig**.

Rail access is poor: nearest station is Penyffordd on the Wrexham–Wirrall branch line, about 15 miles (24 km) E of Ruthin. A peaceful alternative to crowded NW Wales in high season.

Ruthin has a café and choices for pub meals; pub meals at **Bontuchel**, **Llanfihangel Glyn Myfyr** and **Clawdd-newydd**. No refreshments around Clocaenog Forest or the reservoirs.

From Bontuchel alongside the Afon Clywedog, the **Clocaenog Forest** and the **Alwen Valley** are outstanding.

13th-C **Ruthin Castle**.

At both **reservoirs**.

B & B at **Ruthin**, **Bontuchel**, **Cyffylliog** and **Llanfair Dyffryn Clwyd**.

4

MIDLANDS

There are many definitions of the Midlands; none are perfect, but here is one for the English 'heartland' defined by the boundaries drawn in this book.

In the extreme south-west is Gloucestershire. Its sheep-farming uplands and mellow stone towns, together with the Forest of Dean and the lower Wye Valley, are the main attractions for the cyclist. To the east of Gloucestershire comes most of Oxfordshire, followed by the northern half of Buckinghamshire, both more or less undulating landscapes, given over to agriculture, and containing much that is made for cycling. Some of Hertfordshire and southern Bedfordshire complete this southernmost belt of the Midlands.

The next layer of counties to the north, again working from west to east, consists of Hereford and Worcester, Warwickshire, Northamptonshire and the western half of Cambridgeshire: also mainly agricultural landscape, but with some fine, wild country easily accessible west of Hereford.

Above that second belt come Shropshire, most of Staffordshire, the metropolitan county of West Midlands, South Derbyshire and Leicestershire. Shropshire is an outstanding cycling county, with a formidable network of unspoilt lanes. West Midlands is not entirely urbanized, and the industrial centre known as The Potteries, in and around Stoke-on-Trent, is confined to Staffordshire's north-west corner. Between and around these scars is generally level, easy cycling, through country that for most people is the clearest expression anywhere of 'Englishness' in landscape.

The most northerly belt is Cheshire, north Derbyshire, Nottinghamshire, Lincolnshire, plus some of Greater Manchester and South Yorkshire. Here, at the southern end of the Pennines, is the Peak District, superb but demanding cycling: go against the grain of the hills and you can face a punishingly rapid succession of steep climbs. Not so obviously dramatic, but great cycling country in its own right, is the East Midlands, mostly level, and much of it unspoilt.

Selected tours

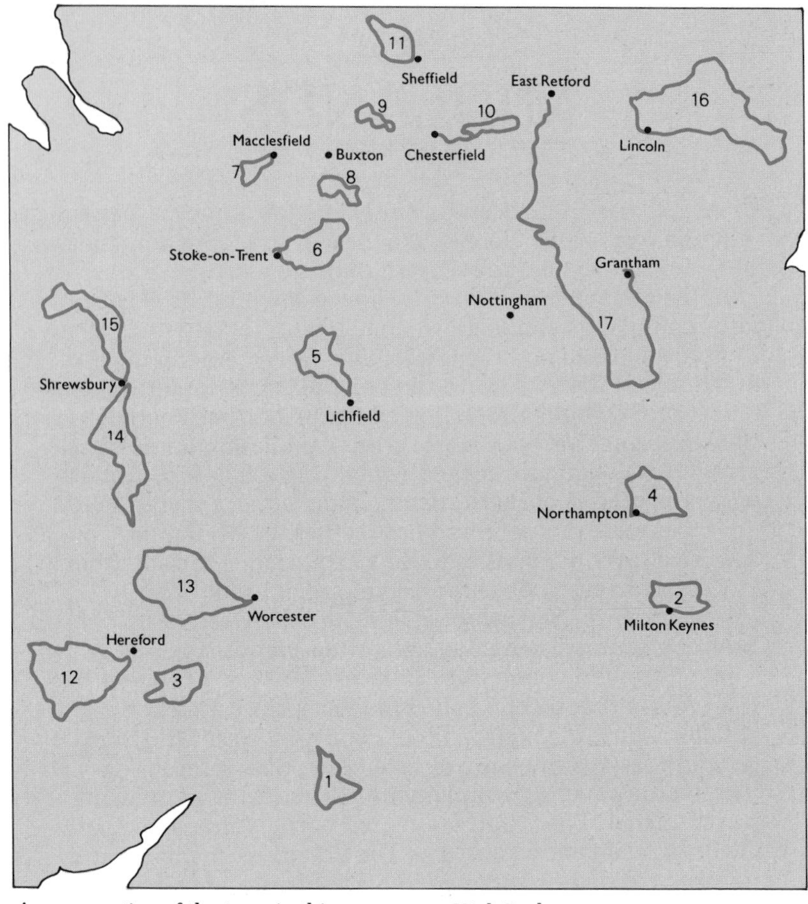

A cross-section of the tours in this region, showing typical rides which can be put together from the route network in a range of localities; details, **pages 114–15**.

Day rides

1 Cotswolds/Coln Valley
2 Bedford and Woburn
3 East Herefordshire, the upper Wye
4 Northampton circuit
5 Cannock Chase
6 Staffordshire Moorlands
7 Cheshire lanes
8 Peak District, Hartington and Flash
9 High Peak
10 Chesterfield, Clumber and Welbeck
11 North-west of Sheffield

Two-day tours

12 The Gospel Pass
13 The Teme Valley
14 Shropshire Highlands
15 North-west Shropshire
16 Lincolnshire circuit

Three days or longer

17 East Retford, Oakham, Stamford and Grantham.

Selected tours

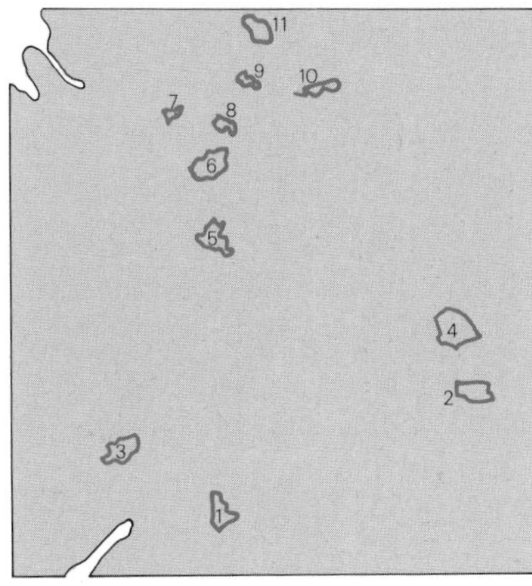

Day rides

1 The Cotswolds and Coln Valley, based on Cirencester, about 34 miles (54 km). Generally easy, but some steep hills in the upper reaches of the Coln Valley – a happy introduction to this lovely area for a family group. The Coln Valley is timeless and peaceful, with a succession of beautiful villages; and you can visit Chedworth Roman villa. *Cirencester–Hatherop – The Colns – Withington–Baunton–Cirencester*; **page 118**.

2 Bedford and Woburn, country lanes in the Bedford and Woburn Abbey area, about 47 miles (75 km). An easy, family ride, despite the relatively high day's mileage, with just a few isolated steep hills. Chance to visit famous Woburn Abbey, also the collection of vintage aircraft and cars at Old Warden. *Bedford – Salford – Woburn – Flitwick – Clophill–Old Warden–Bedford*; **pages 131, 176.**

3 East Herefordshire (Hereford and Worcester) and the upper Wye Valley, about 38 miles (61 km). Two modest stretches of walking are required to cross the Wye on intriguing little suspension bridges – but the effort is rewarded by this rich, unspoilt country with the Wye meandering through. Excellent at any time of year, but especially in spring when the wild flowers are out. *Ledbury – Woolhope – Hoarwithy – Sellack – Foy – Ross-on-Wye – Kempley – Dymock –Ledbury*; **page 124.**

4 Northampton circuit, based on Wellingborough, about 44 miles (70 km). Easy cycling on peaceful roads, passing Pitsford Reservoir, excellent birdwatching, and Salcey Forest, a peaceful wooded area by the M1. *Wellingborough–Mears Ashby – Brixworth – Holdenby – Great Brington – Bugbrooke – Hartwell – Horton – Wollaston – Wellingborough*; **pages 130, 131, 135.**

5 Cannock Chase, south-east of Stafford, about 35 miles (56 km). Cannock Chase, a former hunting ground, is on a plateau rising to 800 feet (244 m). There are some steep climbs, but this is still a straightforward day's ride. Bracken, heather and forestry contrast with the surrounding Midland plain. *Lichfield–some off-highway routing in the Chase – Milford – Blithfield Reservoir – Lichfield*; **pages 146, 147.**

6 Staffordshire Moorlands, between Stoke-on-Trent and the Peak District, about 42 miles (67 km). Local people feel that this area, rubbing shoulders with the Peak District, is underestimated. Not strenuous, but quite taxing: start early. *Stoke-on-Trent – Cheadle – Waterhouses – Manifold Valley Path – Grindon – Butterton – Bradnop – Basford Green – Stanley – Bagnall – Stoke*; **pages 148, 149.**

7 Cheshire lanes between Macclesfield and Sandbach, about 40 miles (64 km). Real solitude on some deserted lanes not far south of Manchester. *Sandbach – Brereton Green – Marton – Macclesfield – Withington Green – Swettenham – Sandbach*; **page 156.**

8 Peak District, Hartington and Flash, about 25 miles (40 km). A very strenuous ride through the upper reaches of the Dove and Manifold Valleys, climbing to Flash, the highest village in England. Rugged Peak District terrain, panoramic

Selected tours

views, with the last few miles through pastoral countryside. *Hartington–Pilsbury – Longnor – Flash – Fawfieldhead–Brund–Hartington*; **page 157**.

9 High Peak, the Hope Valley and Edale, about 28 miles (45 km). Hope Valley and Edale are the heart of the Peak District, with splendid scenery and marvellous views. A popular tourist area, but the route avoids most of the traffic; some bridleway riding. *Hathersage – Castleton – Edale – Aston – Thornhill–Hathersage*; **page 157**.

10 Chesterfield, Clumber Park and Welbeck Abbey, about 38 miles (61 km). East of Sheffield is some pleasant cycling country overlooked by many cyclists, who think it is spoilt by the proximity of the mining industry. With careful planning, as on this route, the black spots can be avoided. *Chesterfield (Calow)–Palterton – Bolsover – Elmton – Creswell – Welbeck Abbey – Clumber Park – Carburton – Norton – Whaley – Bolsover – Palterton – Calow*; **pages 158, 159**.

11 North-west of Sheffield into the northern Peak District, about 30 miles (48 km). A hilly route, but taken gently, still suitable for families or groups. *Sheffield–Low Bradfield – Langsett – Wortley – Grenoside–Sheffield*; **page 162**.

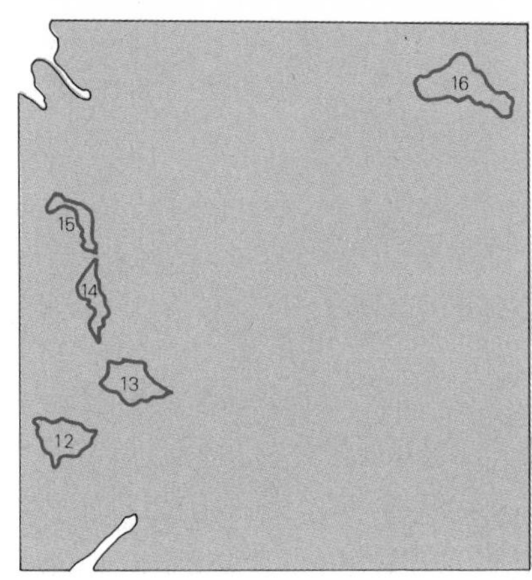

Two-day tours

12 The Gospel Pass, Hereford into the Black Mountains and back, about 65 miles (104 km). The starting and finishing sections at Hereford are easy, but the rest is strenuous. A sporting day's ride, or a weekend out for the average cyclist, taking in the popular Llanthony Valley (best visited out of the holiday season). *Hereford – Lulham – Dorstone – Hay-on-Wye – Capel-y-ffin – Llanthony – Pandy – Pontrilas – Kilpeck – Grafton*; **pages 122, 124**.

13 The Teme Valley, west and north-west from Worcester, about 65 miles (104 km). A relatively unknown area offering truly peaceful country riding. Opportunity to visit cider mills in action if doing the route in late summer or autumn. *Worcester – Bransford – Pencombe – Tenbury Wells – Martley – Worcester*; **pages 124, 126, 133**.

14 Shropshire Highlands, Shrewsbury south to Ludlow, about 60 miles (96 km). An arduous ride taking in some serious hill country. Ludlow is an unspoilt town dating largely from the middle ages. *Shrewsbury – Bridges – Church Stretton – Acton Scott – Dinchope – Norton – Ludlow – Sutton – Peaton – Tugford – Gretton – Longnor – Shrewsbury*; **pages 138, 139, 132, 133**.

Selected tours

15 North-west Shropshire, Shrewsbury and Oswestry, about 55 miles (88 km). Apart for some climbing around the border area, this is an easy ride and could be completed in a day. Passes through Shropshire's lake district, and some atmospheric border country. *Shrewsbury – Leaton – Ellesmere – Chirk – Oswestry – Lower Frankton – Yeaton – Forton – Shrewsbury*; **pages 139, 147, 146, 138**.

16 Lincolnshire Circuit, about 70 miles (112 km). A tour designed to capture the flavour of one of England's most underestimated areas. Takes in the gentle Lincolnshire Wolds, chalk hills rising slightly above the surrounding flatland, but with surprisingly dramatic views. Unspoilt rural scenery more or less throughout, and some fascinating old villages. *Lincoln – Gautby – Horncastle – Old Bolingbroke – Harrington – Donington on Bain – Tealby – Market Rasen – Hackthorn – Scampton – Lincoln*; **pages 160, 161, 165**.

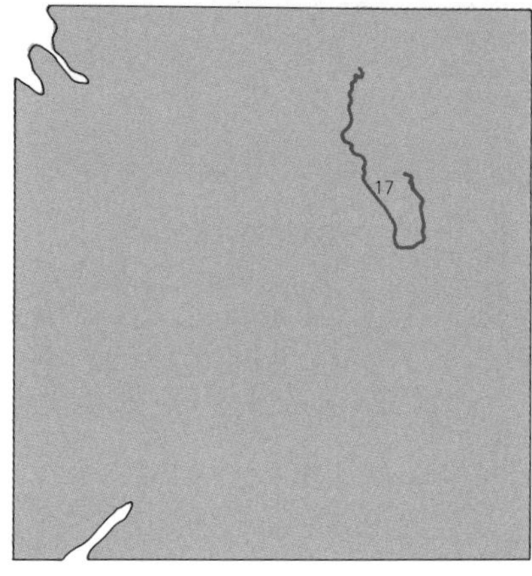

Three days or longer

17 East Retford, Oakham, Stamford and Grantham: Lincolnshire, Leicestershire and Nottinghamshire, about 95 miles (152 km). An absorbing tour of the east Midlands, including some idyllic cycling country; the starting and finishing points are easily connected by train whichever way the route is ridden. *East Retford – Wellow – Halam – Hoveringham – Gunthorpe – East Bridgford – Waltham on the Wolds – Oakham – Stamford – Castle Bytham – Bassingthorpe–Grantham*; **pages 159, 151, 144, 145, 152**.

Gloucestershire

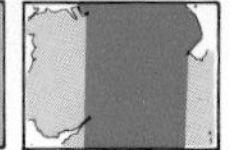

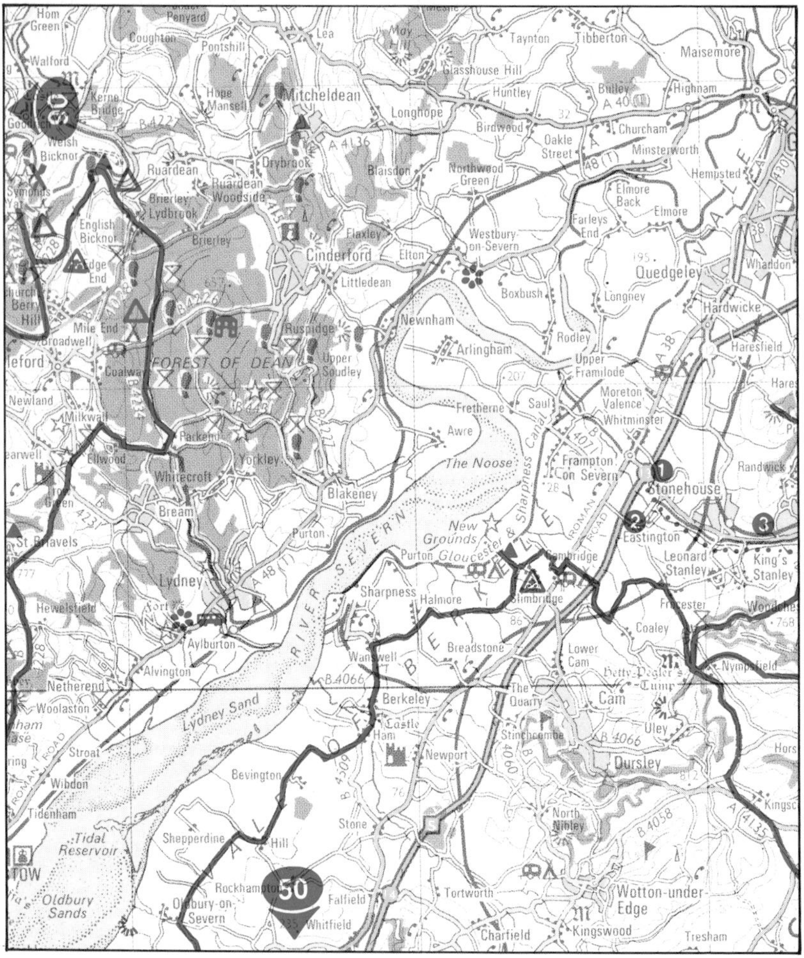

△ Climbs in the **Forest of Dean** (don't overlook the attractive forest byways); **Symonds Yat** is often over-run with tourists in summer; access to **Welsh Bicknor** youth hostel from B4228 by footpath over disused railway bridge.

🚌 **Lydney** on the Newport–Gloucester line.

✗ Cafés, pub meals at **Symonds Yat**.

⚠ Long descent from **English Bicknor** to the Wye: quiet lanes made for cycling in the **Slimbridge** area.

m **Uley**, Iron-age fort, 'Hetty Pegler's Tump'.

✱ Fine views from **Uley** and **St Briavels**.

✿ **Lydney Park**, castle and Roman temple; **Westbury** Court, water gardens.

🏛 17th-C Speech House, now a **Forest of Dean** hotel.

▲ **St Briavels** Dean (0594) 530272; **Welsh Bicknor** Dean (0594) 60300; **Slimbridge** Gloucester (045389) 275.

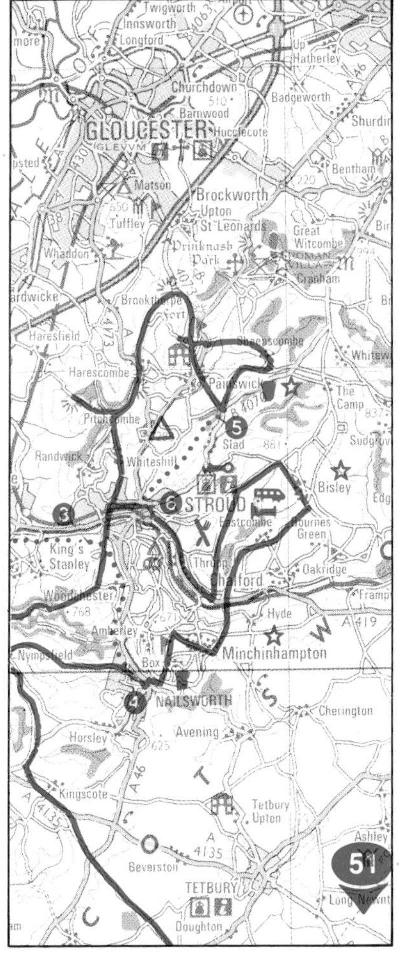

① Access to the Stroud Valleys Pedestrian/Cycle trail from car park by Ship Inn, Stroud. No access for cyclists from the bridge over the Stroud Water Canal, but there is at Ryeford, ②. No access for cyclists at the bridge, Dudbridge ③: find your way on from the Dudbridge Station car park. Access at ④, Nailsworth old station, open 1985. This useful off-highway route enables cyclists to use the level valley floors between Stroud and Nailsworth, avoiding the extremely busy main roads. The project was initiated by the Stroud Job Creation Group, a voluntary organization, and provided work for over thirty previously unemployed people, some disabled. Leaflet with details of the route from Stroud Job Creation Group, Unit F3C2, Bath Road Trading Estate, Stroud G15 3QF.

⑤ Bridleway leads off from top of hill and ⑥ bridleway access from B4070.

△ No avoiding hills in this area, but climbs are generally short and steep, or long and gentle, and in this sense the **Stroud** area is suited to cycling.

Stroud, on the Swindon–Gloucester main line. Stroud is a particularly useful centre because the town lies on the floor of one of the five interconnecting valleys here: break off riding at will to coast downhill most of the way to the station.

Limited choice, **Stroud**.

The Weighbridge, near **Nailsworth**, has plenty of character and good food; Edgemoor Inn, near Edge, above **Painswick**, good food and views.

The **W side of the circuit** gives outstanding views from the Cotswold edge over the Severn Vale.

☆ **Painswick**, **Bisley** and **Minchinhampton**, three of the most charming Cotswold stone villages in the locality.

Three bicycle shops in **Stroud**.

Stroud Downfield Hotel charges slightly above plain B & B prices.

The green woodpecker, often seen on the Stroud Valley's Cycle Trail.

Gloucestershire

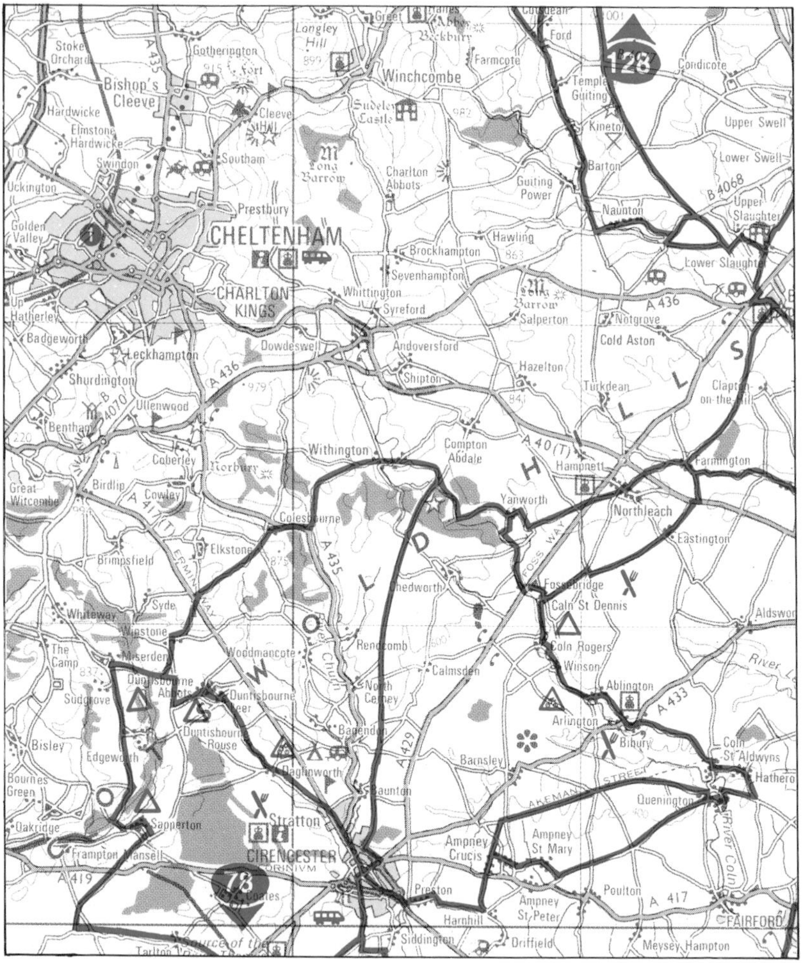

① Cheltenham–Bishop's Cleeve, proposed for 1985.

△ Undulating, but several steep hills in upper **Coln Valley**, at **Duntisbourne Abbots**, approaching **Miserden** and into **Sapperton**. Fork right at **Ford** to avoid steep climb.

🚌 **Kemble** 5 miles (8 km) SW on the A429 (Swindon–Gloucester main line) is the nearest rail access. **Cheltenham** on Birmingham–Gloucester main line.

✗ Café and pub meals at **Cirencester**, **Bibury**; pub meals **Sapperton**, **Fossebridge**.

▲ The narrow backroad through the **Coln Valley** is one of the great highlights of any Cotswold cycling expedition; lovely lane from **Daglingworth to Duntisbourne** Abbots, also **Naunton to Ford**.

▲ **Duntisbourne Abbots** Miserden (028582) 346.

Gloucestershire/Oxfordshire

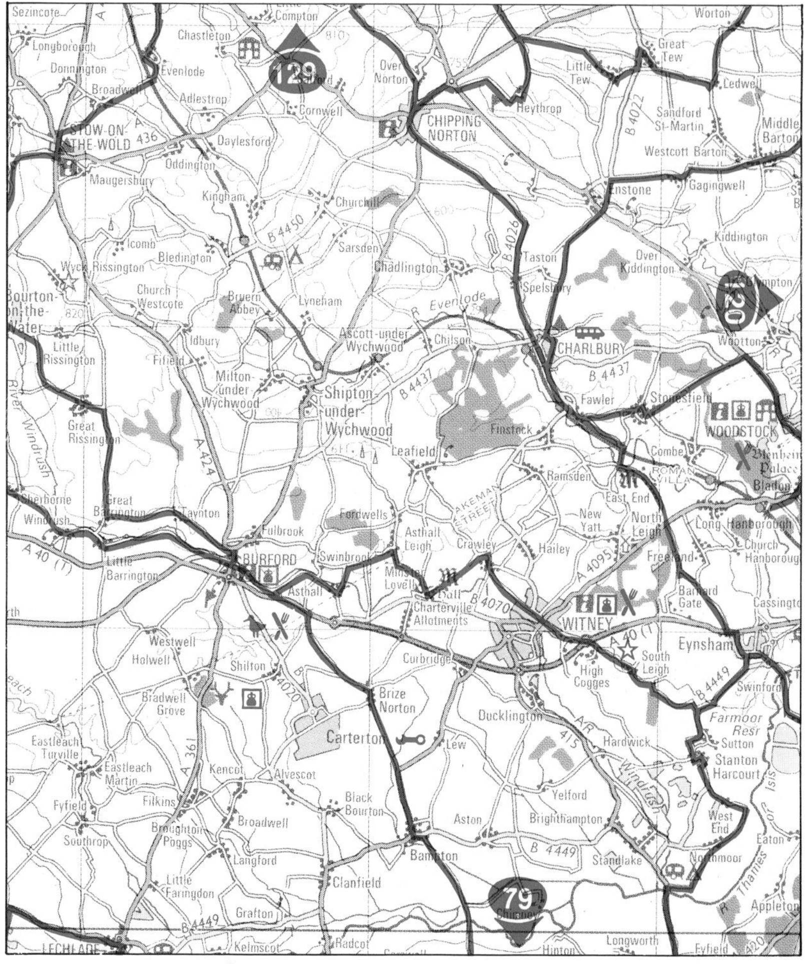

△ This is a hilly region, with a particularly long steep climb for the last 2 miles (3 km) to **Stow-on-the-Wold**.

Charlbury and other stations on the Oxford–Worcester line.

Cafés and pub meals at **Witney**, **Woodstock** and **Bourton-on-the-Water**; inns at **Burford**.

Minster **Lovell**, ruins of moated manor house; **North Leigh**, Roman villa with mosaic floor.

Woodstock, Blenheim Palace, birthplace of Winston Churchill.

Cogges Farm Museum, **Witney**; local history museum at **Burford**.

Cotswold Wildlife Park, **Bradwell Grove**.

☆ **Witney**, a wool town with a 17th-C cross and fine church.

Carterton Giles, 1 Alvescot Road.

▲ **Charlbury** 0608 810202; **Stow-on-the-Wold** 0451 30497.

Oxfordshire

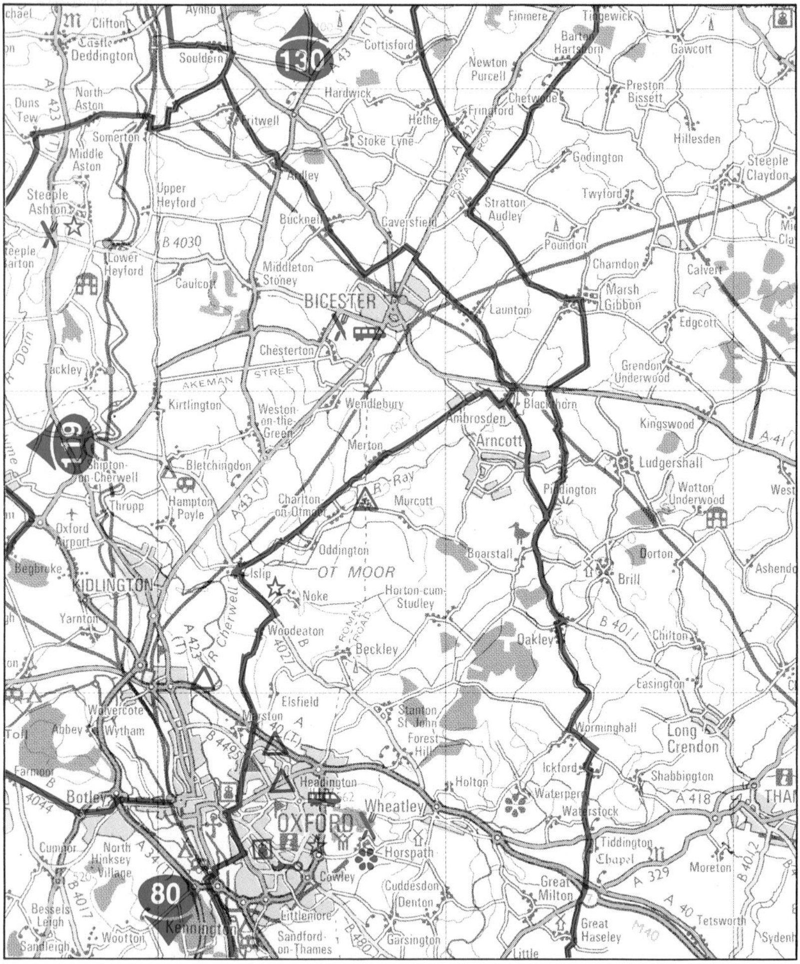

△ In and around **Oxford**, a town of cyclists, it is virtually level; fast traffic on A40, A423 – leave town via **Marston**.

Oxford 55 minutes from Paddington by InterCity train; **Bicester**, Banbury–London line.

Bicester and **Oxford**, choices.

Otmoor and its historic Seven Towns.

Botanic Gardens, **Oxford**, begun 1621.

Rousham House, S of **Steeple Aston**.

Famous art and archaeology collections at the Ashmolean Museum, **Oxford**; also (among several others), the University Museum's natural science collection.

☆ **Oxford** Christ Church Cathedral, colleges, chapels, libraries; **Brill**, a remarkably sited village; **Islip**, birthplace of Edward the Confessor.

Oxford Dentons Cycles, 294 Banbury Road; Pennyfarthing, 5 George Street.

▲ **Oxford** 0865 62997.

Buckinghamshire

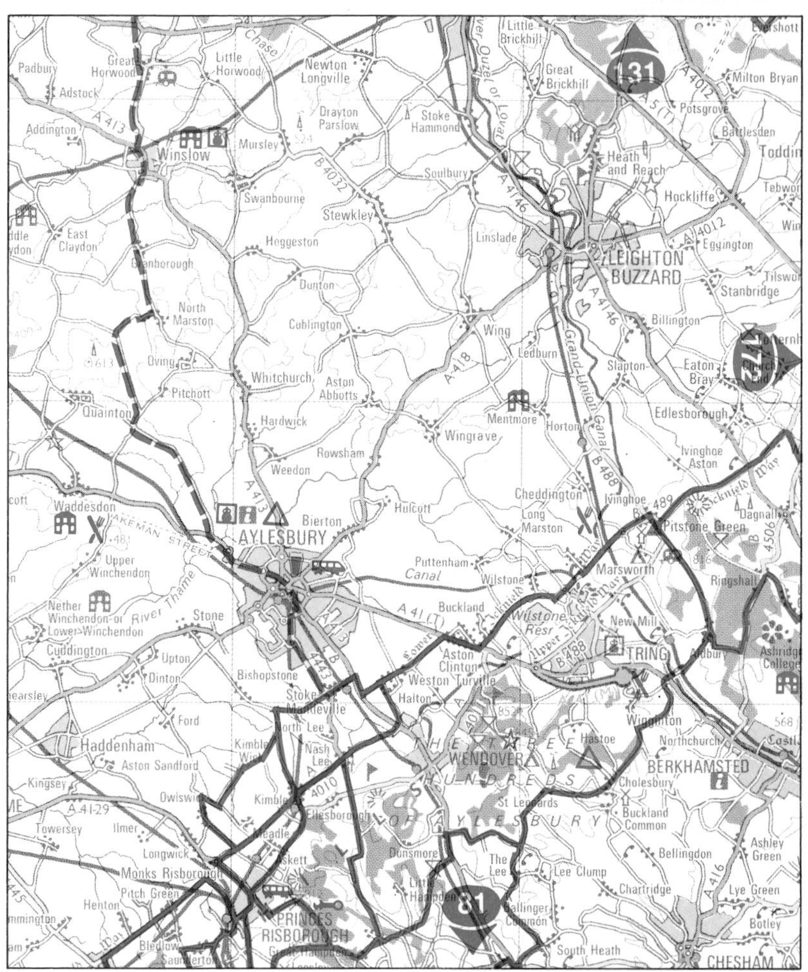

△ **Aylesbury**, county town, busy in peak hours; hard climbs in the **Chilterns**.

🚌 **Aylesbury**, **Princes Risborough**, trains from London and Birmingham.

✗ **Ivinghoe**, **Waddesdon**, **Tring**, limited choices; **Aylesbury**, choices.

🏛 Victorian mansion at **Mentmore**; **Waddesdon** Manor 18-C style aviary, deer; **Winslow** Hall, designed by Christopher Wren; **Ashridge** Park, interesting house and fine woodland walking.

▣ Florence Nightingale Museum (Crimea War), **Winslow**; Bucks County Museum, **Aylesbury**.

☆ With their lovely beech woods the **Chiltern Hills** are officially designated an Area of Outstanding Natural Beauty.

🔧 David Bolton Cycles, Market Square, **Princes Risborough**.

▲ **Ivinghoe**, Cheddington (0296) 668251.

Powys/Hereford and Worcester

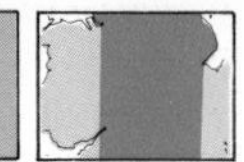

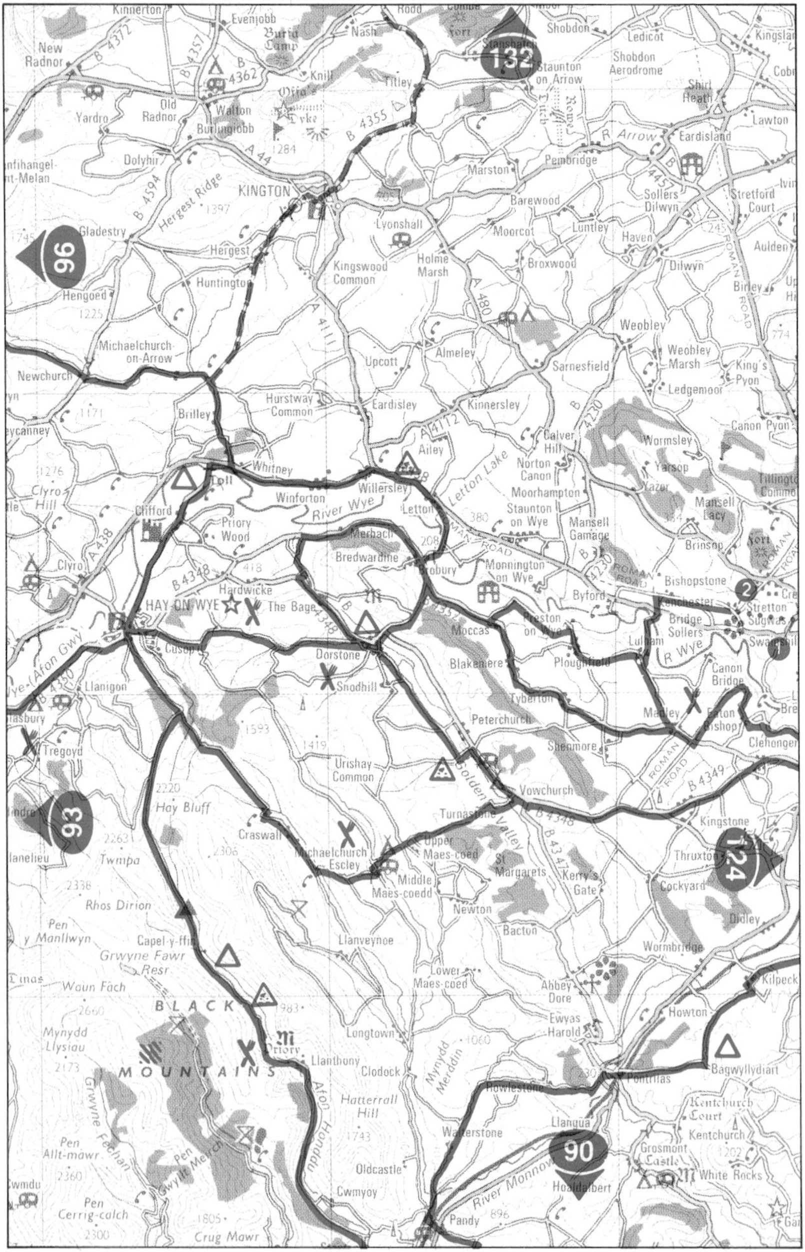

Hereford and Worcester

Upper Wye Valley

① Access to bridleway as indicated, and at ② – both easy to locate.

△ Llanthony Valley is a long climb going SE–NW, but a welcome downhill run follows from the Gospel Pass at **Capel-y-ffin** to the Wye – which in reverse direction is a steep climb on a narrow road to the Gospel Pass – take care; **Pontrilas NE** requires careful map-reading to stay on the marked lanes and avoid unnecessary hills; at **Dorstone**, approaching from E, there is a steep hill – worth the effort for the views, but to conserve energy for the Gospel Pass, use the B4348 instead; generally a demanding touring area. The toll marked near **Whitney** makes a small charge for bikes.

Glasbury, highly recommended pub, food and real ales; choices in **Hay-on-Wye**; restaurant and pub in ruins of **Llanthony Priory**; conveniently placed pubs, some with fine views at **Dorstone**, **Michaelchurch Escley**, **Eaton Bishop**.

Llanthony Valley and **Golden Valley** are the highlights of this area, but the upper Wye is very beautiful too.

Llanthony Priory, best visited out of holiday season, was founded in the 12th C. In the 15th C the monks grew tired of the harsh winter weather and built a second monastery of the same name in Gloucester. The poet Walter Savage Landor bought the ruin in 1802 with hopes of restoring it to a romantic retreat – but characteristically failed.

☆ **Hay-on-Wye**, famous for salmon fishing, and its profusion of second-hand bookshops, including world's largest.

The **Black Mountains** so-called because from the Hereford side they usually appear black. Like the Brecon Beacons from which they are separated by the Usk Valley, they are made of Old Red Sandstone, and are in the Brecon Beacons National Park.

▲ **Capel-y-ffin** Crucorney (087382) 650.

Hereford and Worcester

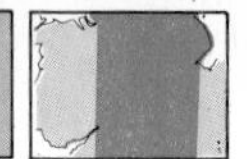

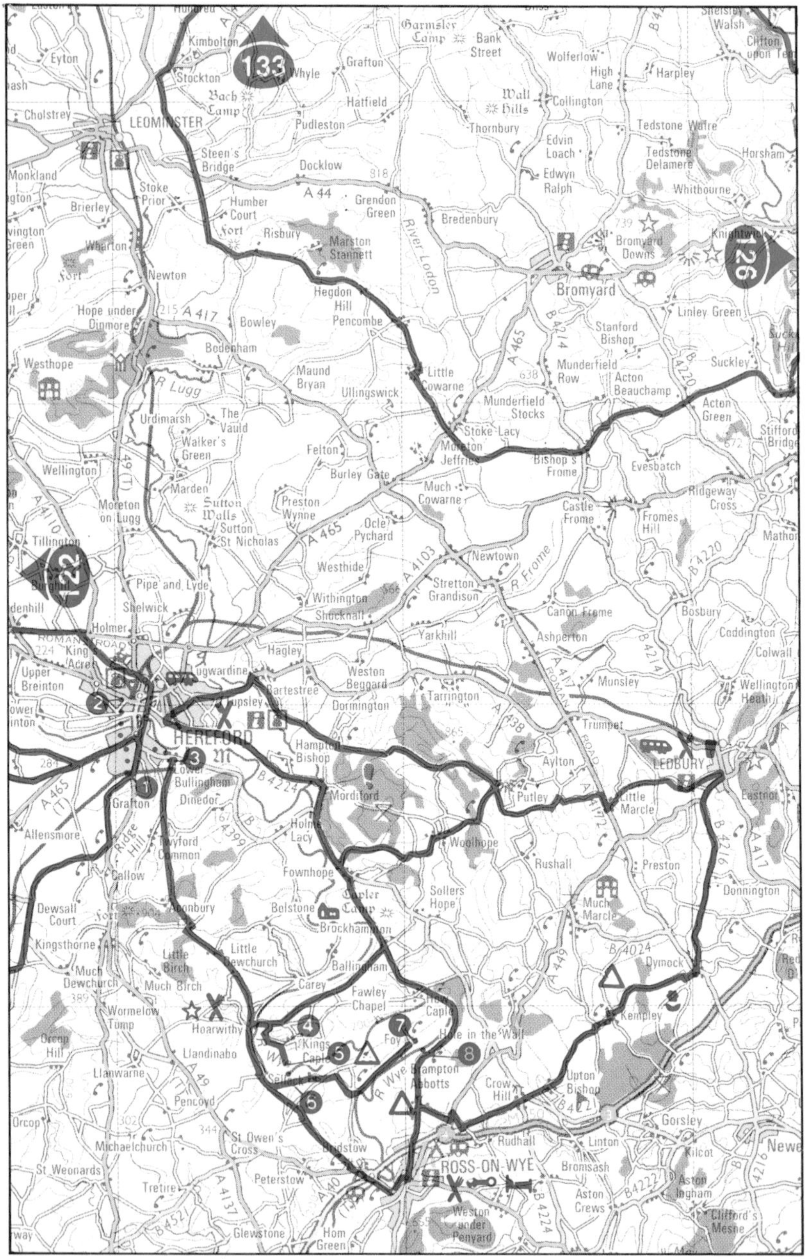

Hereford and Worcester

① Access to the Hereford cycle way system from Barton Road – ramp down near railway bridge. This disused railway line route gives easy access to the city centre, where ② the system can be joined from Belmont Road. King George's Field Route is joined ③ from Hinton Road.

△ You can continue into **Ross-on-Wye** on the marked **unclassified road**, but for a fine view of the town, situated prettily above the Wye, fork on to the A449 for the last 1½ miles (2 km) or so. It is busy – but wide. There is very little traffic on the unclassified roads over the whole of this area, but short, steep hills in the **Ledbury–Ross** area.

Hereford and **Ledbury** on the Birmingham–Hereford main line.

Hoarwithy is a fine lunch spot – choices of pub and café; choices in **Ross-on-Wye** and **Hereford**.

Ledbury The Feathers and the Talbot are genuine 16th-C inns.

Kings Caple to Brampton Abbotts – See Landranger excerpt below. Note the plaque on the S abutment of the bridge at Sellack Boat.

Brockhampton has a thatched church.

☆ **Hoarwithy** is on a particularly charming reach of the Wye.

The **Kempley** and **Dymock** area is noted for an abundance of wild daffodils in spring.

Ross-on-Wye Little & Hall, 48 Broad Street.

Radcliffe Guest House, Wye Street, **Ross-on-Wye**.

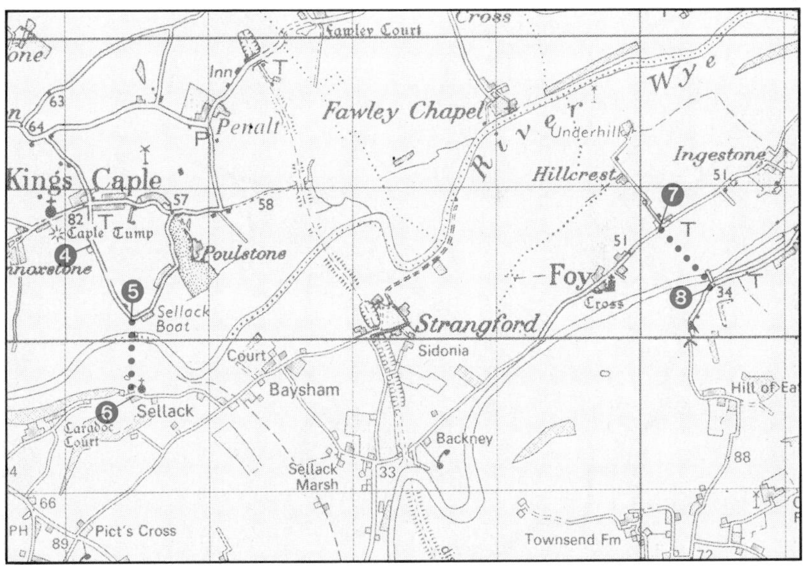

There is a delightful way to negotiate the great loop of the Wye in the Kings Caple area, but it does involve dismounting and wheeling the bike on public footpaths rather under ½ mile (0.8 km) in order to make use of two bridges. In Kings Caple ④ take the road to Sellack Boat where ⑤ a track leads to a small suspension bridge. The other side, a track leads across a field to a church, where ⑥ find unclassified road. Just over ½ mile (0.8 km) north-east of Foy, a track ⑦ leads to another bridge ⑧, with the road the other side. ⑤–⑥ and ⑦–⑧ are footpaths.

Hereford and Worcester/Gloucestershire

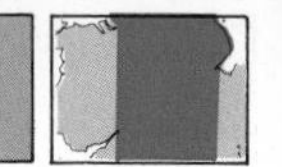

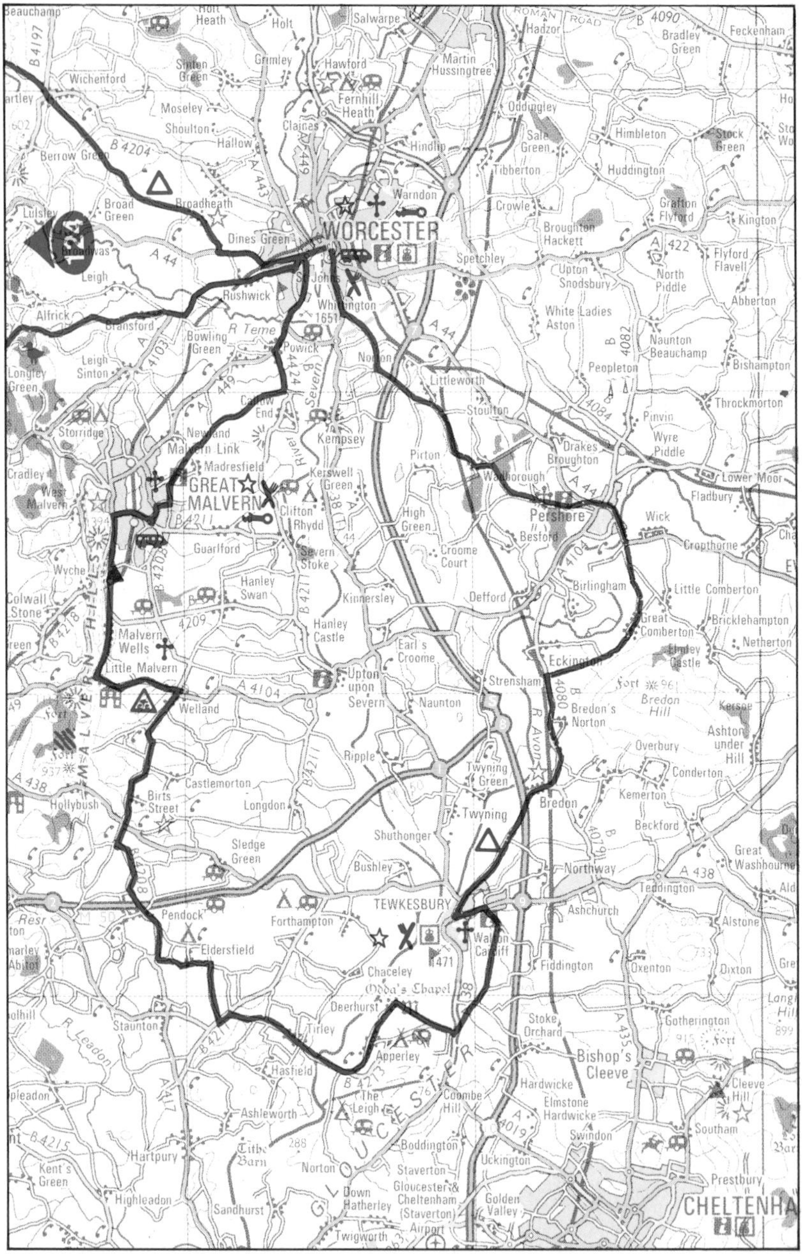

Hereford and Worcester/Gloucestershire

Tewkesbury Abbey's Central Tower is one of the most perfect examples of its kind.

△ **Worcester – Tewkesbury – Great Malvern** circuit is mostly in and around the Severn Valley – no major hills. The circuit **W of Worcester** is best ridden clockwise, to follow the Teme Valley downstream.

Worcester and **Great Malvern** on the Reading–Hereford main line, InterCity services.

Choices in **Worcester, Great Malvern** and **Tewkesbury**.

B4208 and **A4104** S of Malvern give fine views of the Malvern Hills.

Unclassified road **W of Barnsford**. The Knapp and Papermill nature reserve – birds, plants, fungi, moths and butterflies in unusual variety; circular nature trail.

☆ **Worcester**, famous for porcelain, sauce and gloves; ships motor up the Severn as far as Worcester Bridge. **Great Malvern**, chief of the chain of seven places along the Malvern Hills which share the name of Malvern, and famous for its springs. **Tewkesbury**, fine old town (interesting 16th- and 17th-C buildings) at junction of the Warwickshire Avon and the Severn.

The Malvern Hills rise impressively from the Severn Plain and provide fine walking – most of the summits easily reached by footpath.

† The Worcester – Tewkesbury – Great Malvern circuit passes several fine religious buildings: **Worcester Cathedral**, mainly early English, dates from the 13th C – superb views of the Malvern Hills from its Central Tower; **Tewkesbury's Abbey Church** ranks among the finest Norman churches in England; **Great Malvern Priory Church** has notable glass, and at **Little Malvern** the church was once part of a 12th-C priory.

Great Malvern Mycycles Leisure Sports, 271 Worcester Road, Malvern Link; **Worcester** Foggy's Bikes, 56 St Johns.

▲ **Malvern Hills** Malvern (06845) 3300.

Worcestershire/Warwickshire/Gloucestershire

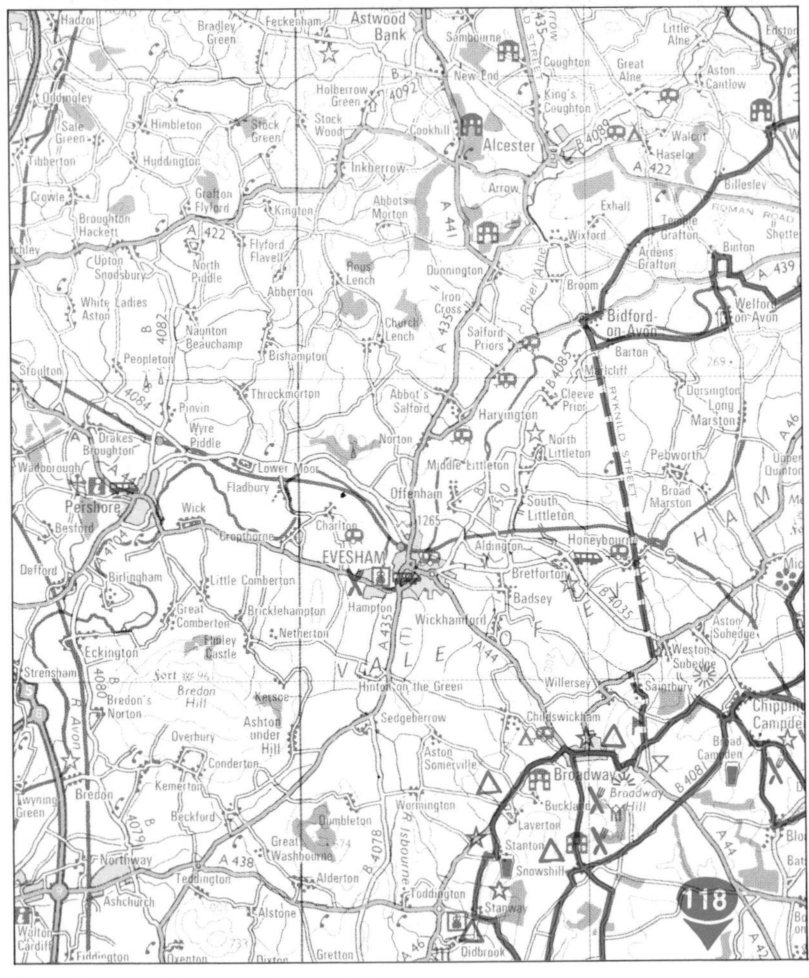

△ **North Cotswolds**: several steep hills but mostly gently undulating; the route through **Snowshill** avoids the steep climb up Fish Hill from **Broadway** – use when A46 traffic is heavy.

🚃 **Pershore**, **Evesham** and **Honeybourne** on the Worcester–Oxford line.

✗ Cafés at **Broadway, Chipping Campden, Evesham.**

🍺 At **Stanton** and **Broad Campden**.

☀ Extensive views across Vale of Evesham from 17th-C **Broadway** Tower.

🏛 **Snowshill** Manor (Nat. Trust); Ragley Hall and Coughton Court, **Alcester**.

☆ **Stanway**, tithe barn, and an impressive war memorial at crossroads; **Stanton**, 'picture book' village of Cotswold Stone; **Broadway**, famously picturesque, but many visitors in summer; **Chipping Campden**, also lovely, and less crowded, was once the market centre for Cotswold wool.

Warwickshire/Oxfordshire

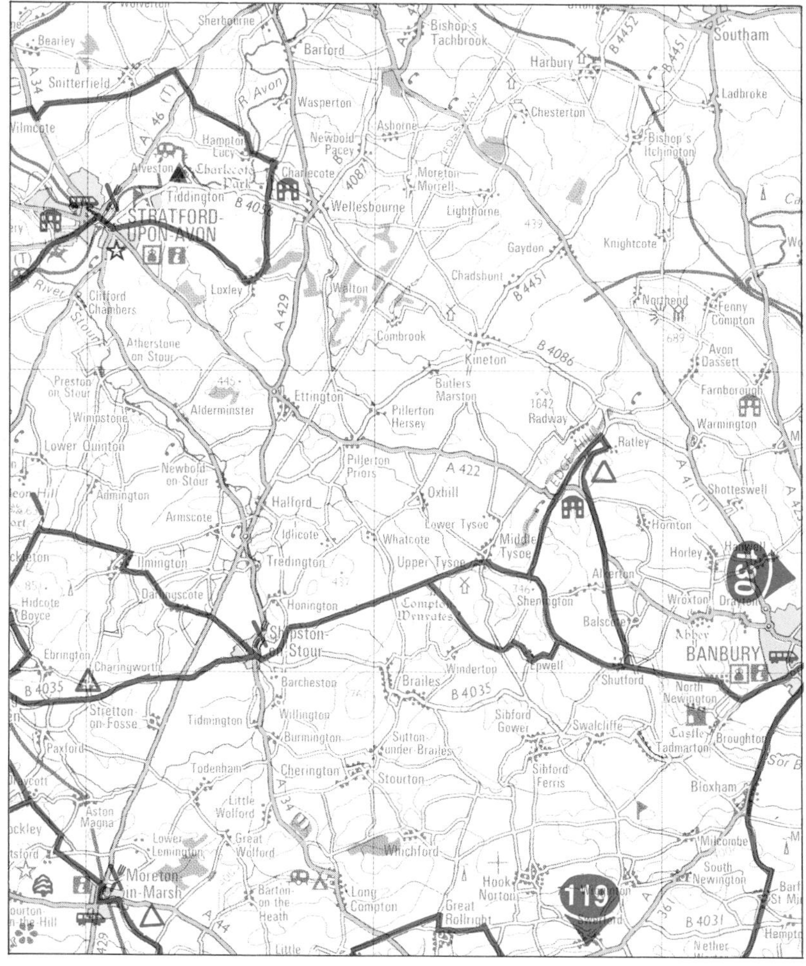

△ Climbs, particularly at **Edge Hill** and **Stretton-on-Fosse** areas. **Moreton-in-Marsh** (main street is part of Fosse Way), busy junction of A44 and A429, but peaceful backroads going N.

Moreton-in-Marsh on the Oxford–Worcester line; **Banbury** and **Stratford-upon-Avon** on the Birmingham–Oxford line.

Banbury, **Stratford**, choices; **Moreton-in-Marsh**, **Shipston-on-Stour**, cafés.

Batsford Arboretum, oriental trees and shrubs.

☆ **Stratford**, with Shakespeare's birthplace, home and memorial.

Mary Arden's House and farming museum, **Wilmcote**; Anne Hathaway's Cottage, **Shottery**; **Charlcote Park**, deer park; Upton House, **Edge Hill**, fine paintings and furniture.

Banbury Trinder, 2a/4 Broad Street.

▲ **Stratford** 0789 297093.

Northamptonshire

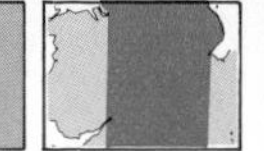

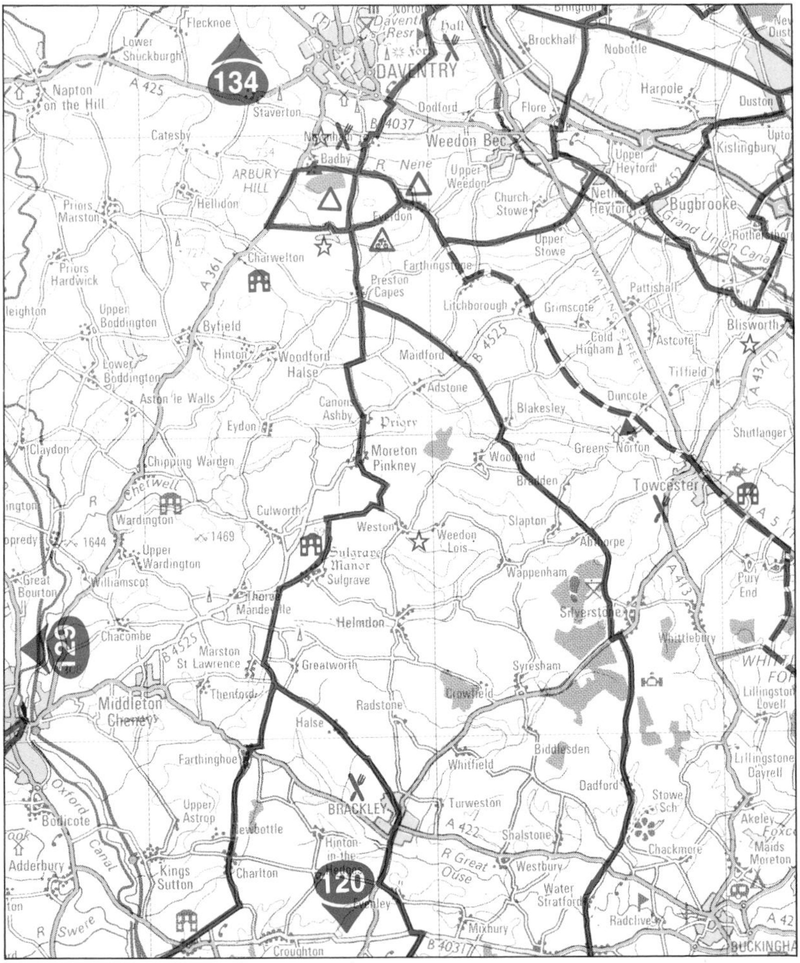

△ **Badby** area, quiet roads taking in delightful villages, hilly though few really steep gradients. Knightly Way is waymarked between **Badby** and **Greens Norton** youth hostels.

✗ Limited choices, **Towcester**, **Daventry**, **Brackley** and **Badby**.

⚠ Fine ride through **Everdon Stubs**.

🏛 **Sulgrave**: George Washington's ancestors are from this village – see the Washington Museum. Stoke Park Pavilions, **Towcester**, built in 1630 by Inigo Jones; **Charwelton**, where the River Cherwell rises in the cellar of Cherwell House.

☆ **Badby**, reputedly the most beautiful village in Northants; grave of Edith Sitwell at **Weedon Lois**; **Fawsley Park**, a deserted tudor village; **Blisworth** Canal tunnel, a scramble down steep slope to enter.

▲ **Badby**, Daventry (03272) 3883.

Northamptonshire / Bedfordshire

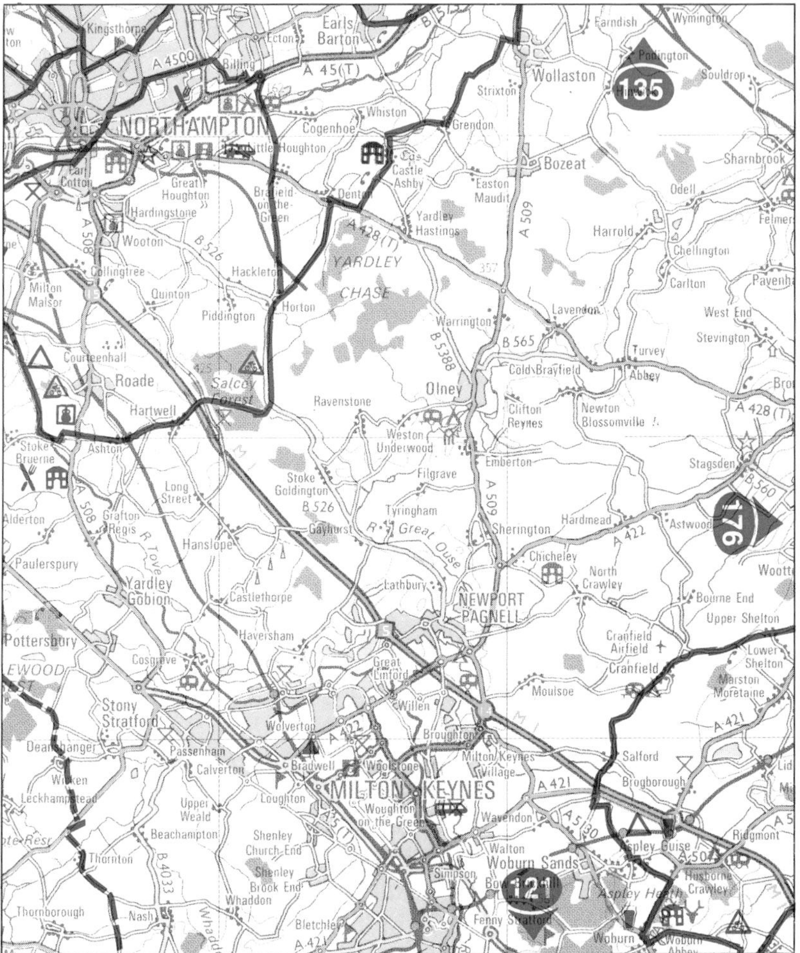

△ Avoid **Northampton's** industrial area – busy main roads; otherwise quiet, pleasant, generally level cycling; a few steep hills round **Aspley Guise**.

Northampton, **Milton Keynes**, frequent InterCity services.

Billing, **Stoke Bruerne**, cafés, pubs.

Pleasant pubs at **Aspley Guise** and **Woburn**.

Lovely woodland riding through **Salcey Forest** and **Woburn Park**; route from **Stoke Bruerne** to Blisworth runs over Blisworth Canal Tunnel.

Salcey Forest and **Hunsbury Hill**.

Castle Ashby, Elizabethan ancestral home of Marquis of Northampton; **Woburn Abbey** in deer park.

British Waterways Museum at **Stoke Bruerne**.

Northampton Reynolds, 159–161 Wellingborough Road.

▲ **Milton Keynes** 0908 310944.

Shropshire

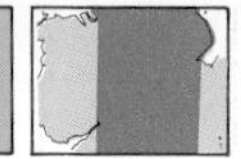

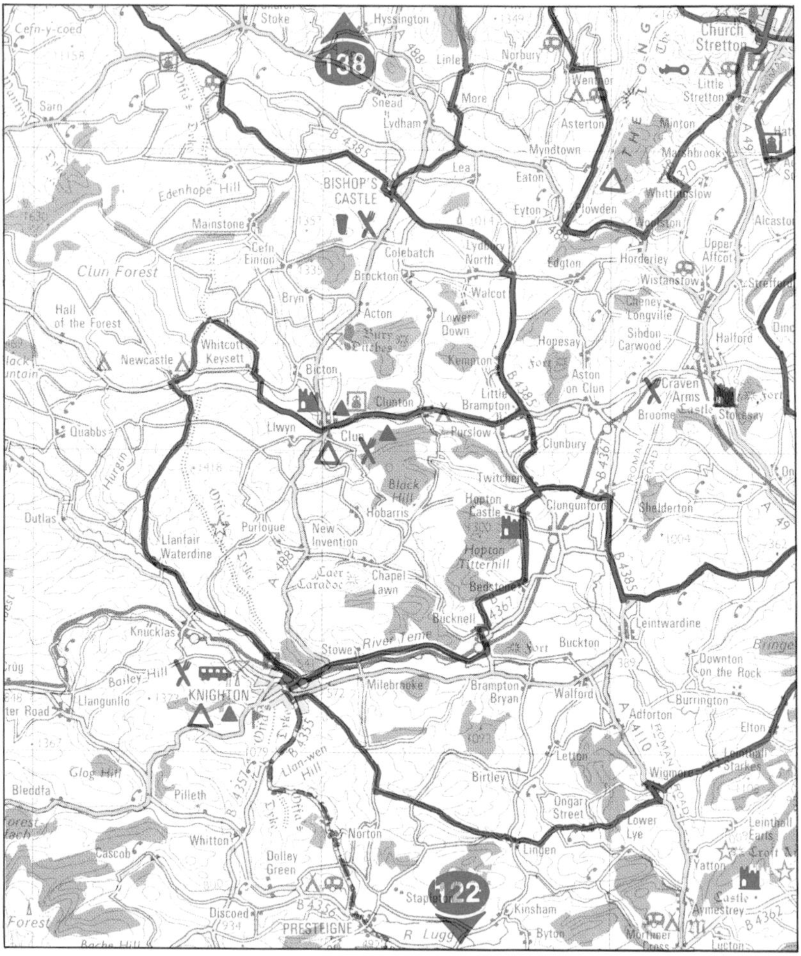

△ Hilly region: **The Long Mynd** is very steep, especially the southern end, though the flat ridge and ancient track (The Port Way) are excellent cycling – but watch for low flying gliders and falling glider tackle. **Knighton** surprisingly busy at peak times; **Clun** area, quiet lanes, mostly light traffic on B roads.

Church Stretton and other stations on Crewe–Hereford line; **Knighton** on the Shrewsbury–S Wales line.

Limited choices, **Clun**, **Knighton**, **Craven Arms**, **Bishop's Castle**.

Three Tons, with brewery, **Bishop's Castle**.

Acton Scott, working farm museum.

Castles at **Clun**, **Hopton**, **Stokesay**; **Croft Castle** is in Domesday book.

Church Stretton, Hannett, 49 High St.

▲ **Knighton** 0547 528807; **Clun Mill** (in an old water mill), Clun (05884) 582.

Shropshire/Worcestershire

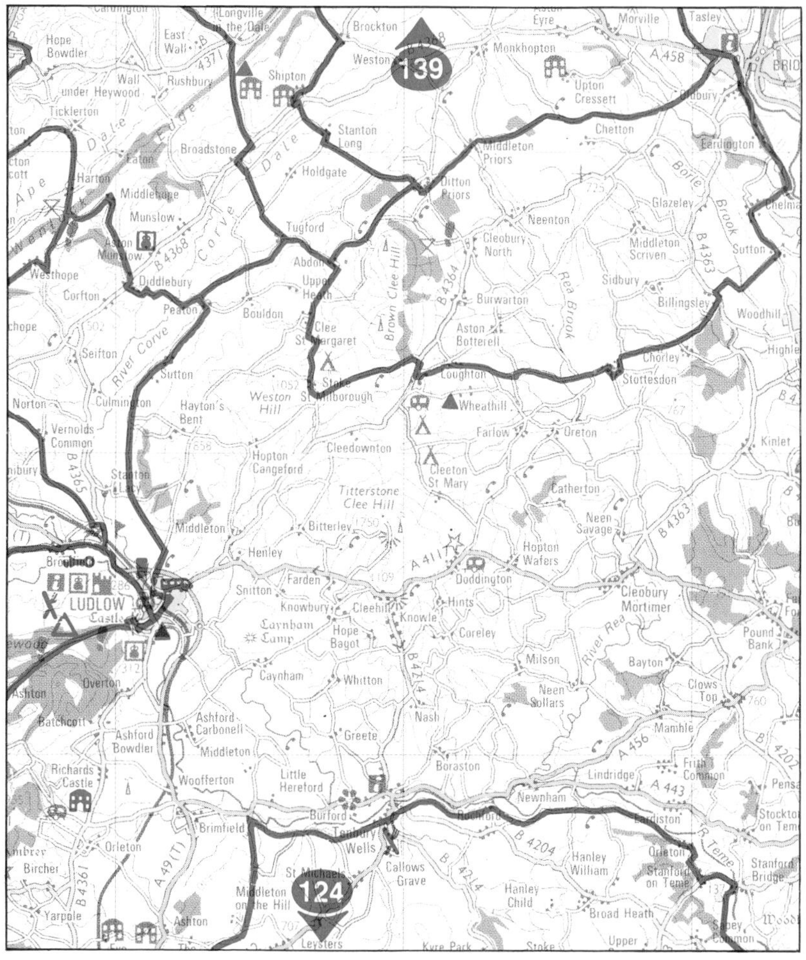

△ Hills and valleys; light traffic except **Ludlow** (quiet tourist's route into town from N is a geological trail); surrounding area, peaceful lanes.

Ludlow, on Crewe–Hereford line.

Cafés and pubs, **Ludlow** and **Tenbury Wells**.

Feathers Inn, **Ludlow**; well-placed pub at top of hill near **Wheathill** youth hostel.

☆ **Ludlow**, beautiful half-timbered houses, Norman Castle, ashes in churchyard of A. E. Houseman, author of *A Shropshire Lad*.

Country crafts museum at **Aston Munslow**; **Ludlow** museum, local finds.

Ludlow Cowdrills, 12 Old Street.

▲ **Wheathill** Burwarton (074633) 236; **Ludlow** 0584 2472; **Wilderhope**, an impressive manor house on Wenlock Edge (resident ghost), Longville (06943) 363.

Leicestershire/Northamptonshire

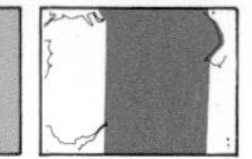

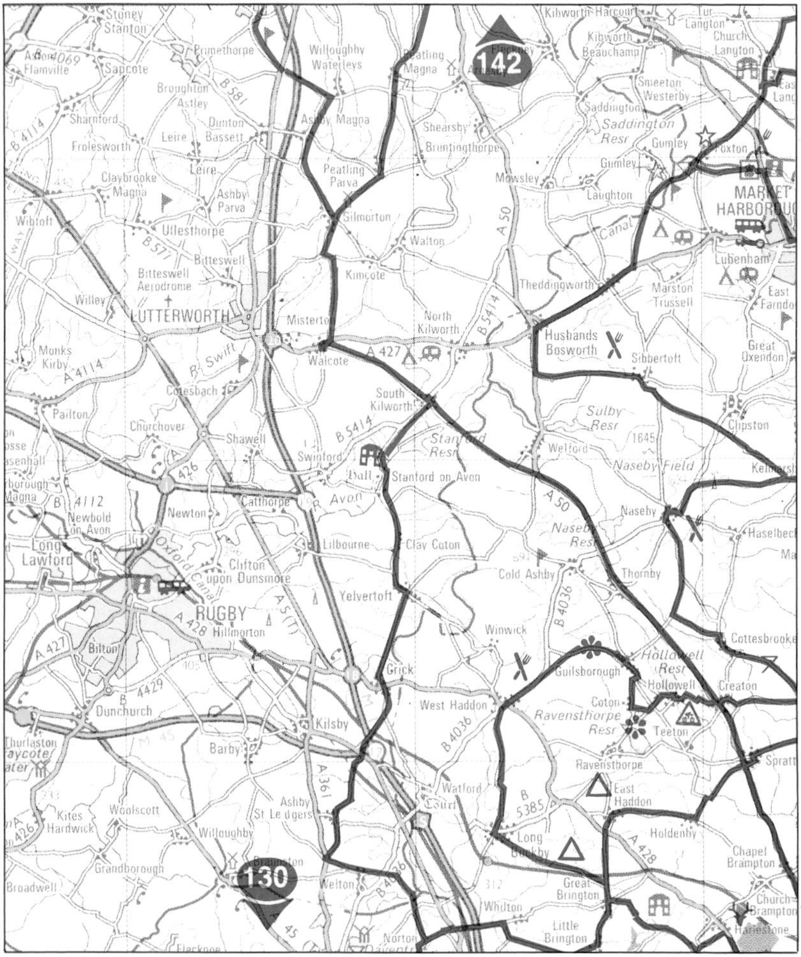

△ Road through field from **Great Brington** to **Long Buckby**.

Rugby, InterCity services; **Market Harborough** on London – Leicester line.

Cafés at Guilsborough Grange, **Husbands Bosworth** and **Foxton** Locks; pub meals at **Naseby**.

Picnic spot with view at **Cottesbrooke**.

Picturesque back roads past reservoirs at Ravensthorpe and Hollowell.

Althorpe House, home of the Spencers, near **Great Brington**; **Stanford** Hall, William and Mary house, car and motorcycle museum.

☆ **Foxton** Locks, impressive lock ladder.

Guilsborough Grange Wildlife Park, zoo and animal home; **Coton Manor**, birds/garden.

Harlestone Heath, wildlife/woodland.

Market Harborough, Halls, 12 Northampton Road.

Northamptonshire/Leicestershire

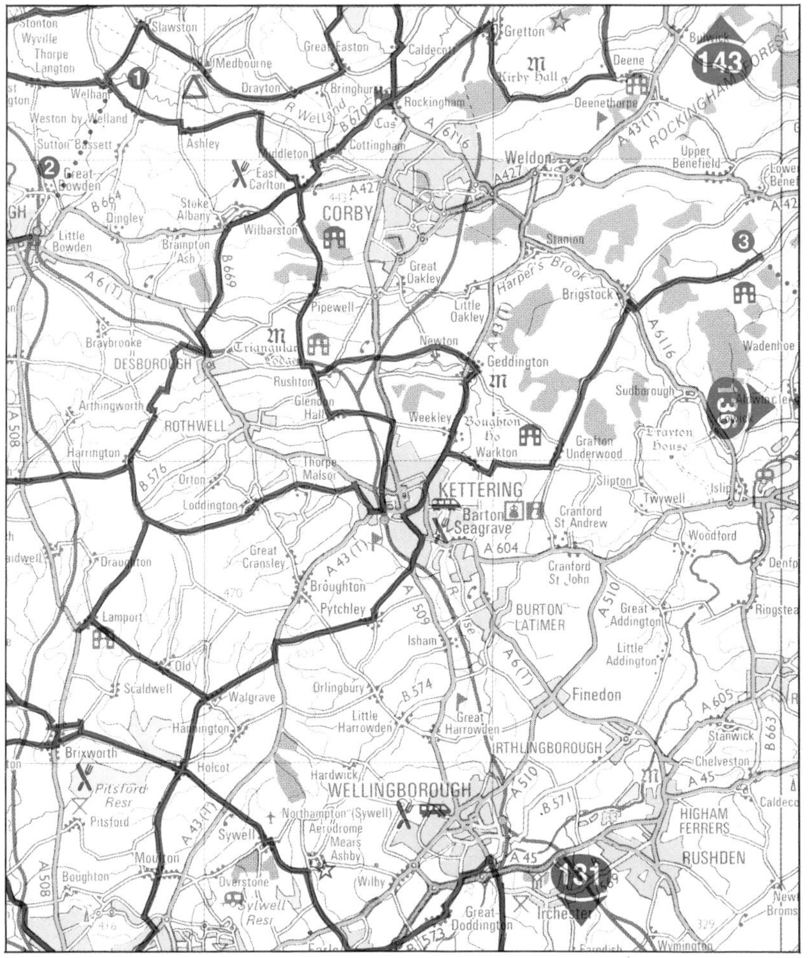

① At Welham go past church to 'No Through Road' for access to easily rideable off-highway route to ② Great Bowden.

③ Obvious access, bridleway to Pilton.

△ Climbs in **Medbourne** area.

🚂 **Kettering**, InterCity services; **Wellingborough** on London – Leicester line.

🍴 Cafés in **Brixworth**, **East Carlton** Country Park, **Wellingborough** and **Kettering**.

𝔐 Triangular lodge depicting Holy Trinity, **Rushton**; **Geddington**, best preserved Eleanor Cross in England; **Kirby Hall**, partly ruined Elizabethan mansion.

🏰 **Rockingham** Castle, towering on the hill, was built by William the Conqueror.

☆ **Mears Ashby** has Viking Wheel Cross in church; stocks, whipping post at **Gretton**.

Cambridgeshire/Northamptonshire

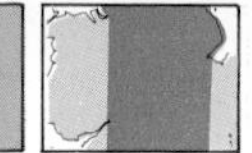

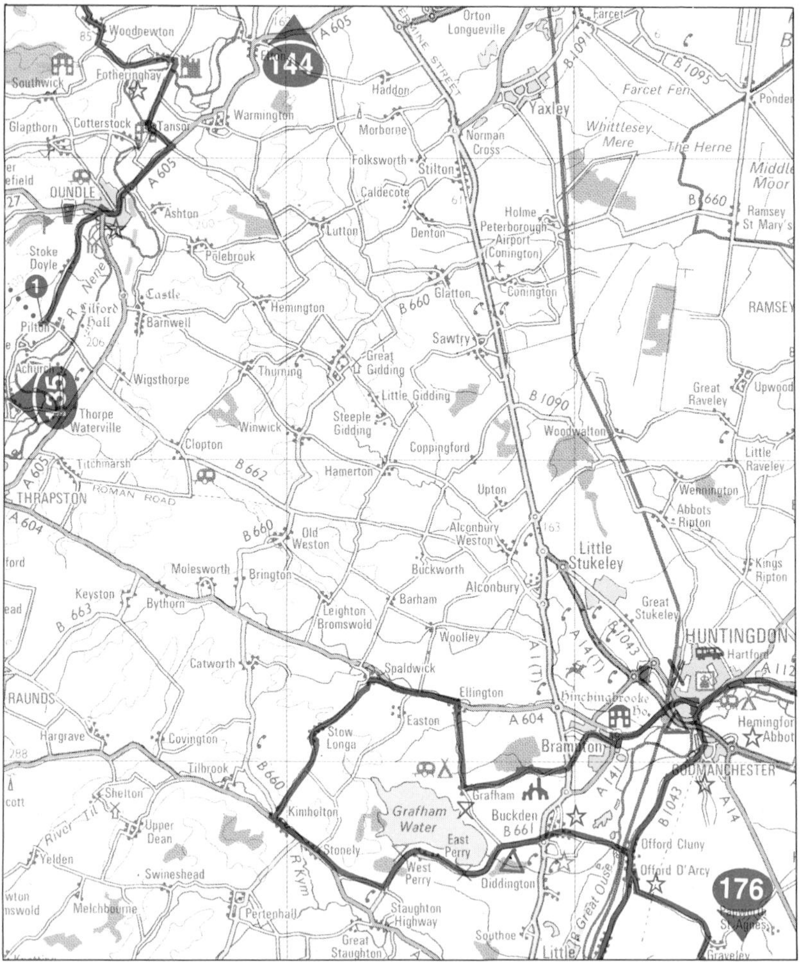

① Access to bridleway signposted at crossroads, metalled for all but the last half mile (0.8 km).

△ **Huntingdon – Hemingford Abbots**, route follows the Great Ouse River. Care crossing the A1 at **Buckden**.

Huntingdon King's Cross – Peterborough line.

Cafés, **Huntingdon**, otherwise scarce.

George Inn, **Huntingdon**; **Oundle**, White Lion Inn and Talbot Inn.

Several opportunities round **Grafham Water**, large man-made lake.

Hinchingbrooke House, 13th-C nunnery, converted to Tudor mansion.

Ruins of **Buckden** Palace.

☆ **Godmanchester**, quaint old houses, Elizabethan grammar school, old mill; **Offord Clune** and **Offord D'Arcy**, twin villages; **Oundle**, public school; **Fotheringhay**, scene of trial and execution of Mary Queen of Scots.

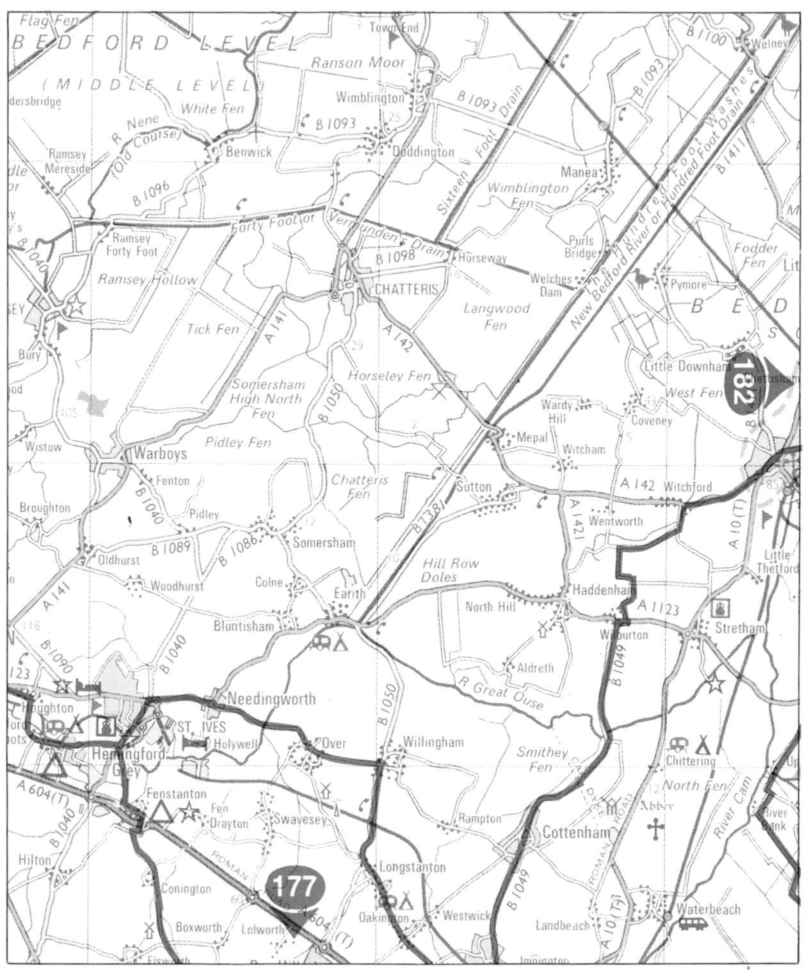

△ **Fenstanton** is bypassed and effectively cut off from traffic by the A604.

Waterbeach on the King's Lynn–Cambridge line.

Cafés and pubs at **St Ives**, scarce elsewhere.

☆ **St Ives**, where Oliver Cromwell lived for five years (statue in market place). The River Ouse is crossed by a 15th-C bridge with chapel. Cromwell's Barn is just outside the village; **Fenstanton**, home and burial place of Capability Brown, and an attractive church and clock tower; **Stretham**, 15th-C cross, old pumping house with original engine just SE; **Houghton Mill**, Cromwell's birthplace, has an intriguing old watermill, village pump and charming thatched cottages.

Camping at **Houghton** and **Chittering**.

Houghton, Millside Cottage, 9 Mill Street; **St Ives**, limited choice.

Shropshire/Powys

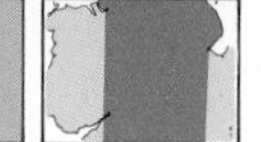

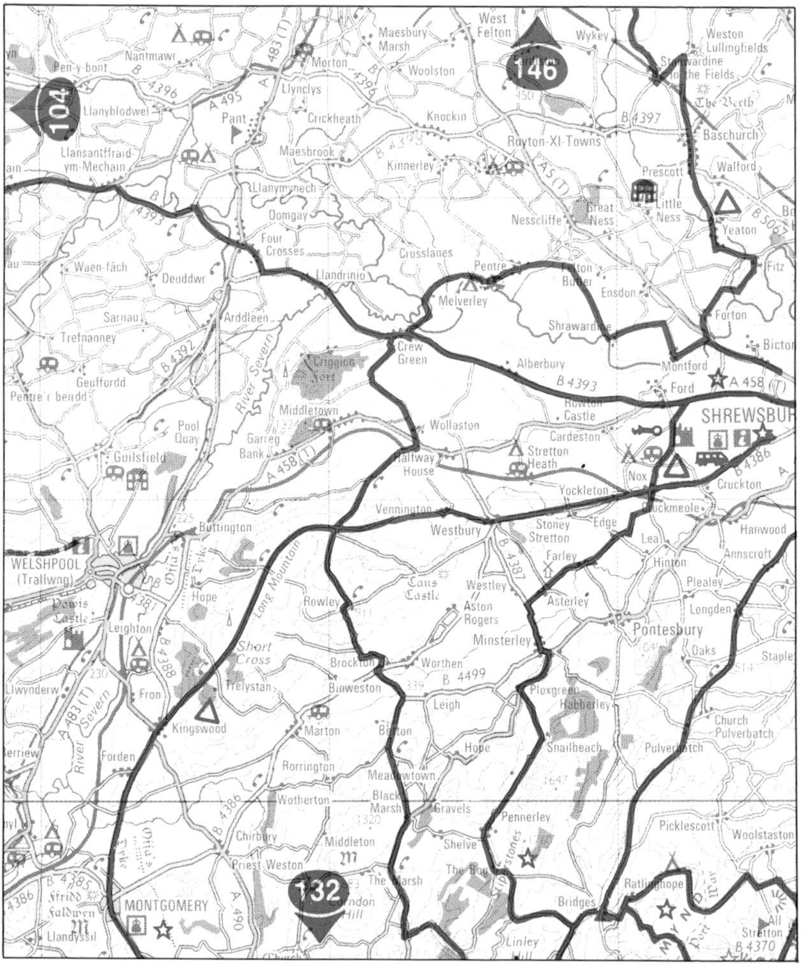

△ **Shrewsbury**, busy at peak times; **N of Shrewsbury**, moderate going; light traffic on B roads, ideal for cycling. Very hilly terrain: long and steep ascent up Long Mountain from **Kingswood**, followed by long descent.

🚌 **Shrewsbury**, InterCity services; **Welshpool** on the West Midlands line.

☆ **Shropshire Hills** is an Area of Outstanding Natural Beauty; **Stiperstones**, rocky ridge of geological interest; **Shrewsbury**, where Harry 'Hotspur' was defeated and killed: many half-timbered buildings and famous English and Welsh bridges; **Montgomery**, attractive small town with ruined castle; **Montford Bridge**, legendary escape here of Dick Turpin and Black Bess from pursuers.

🔧 **Shrewsbury** Stan Jones Cycles, Greyfriars; V. J. Cockle, 12 Milk Street.

▲ **Bridges**, Linley (058861) 656.

Shropshire

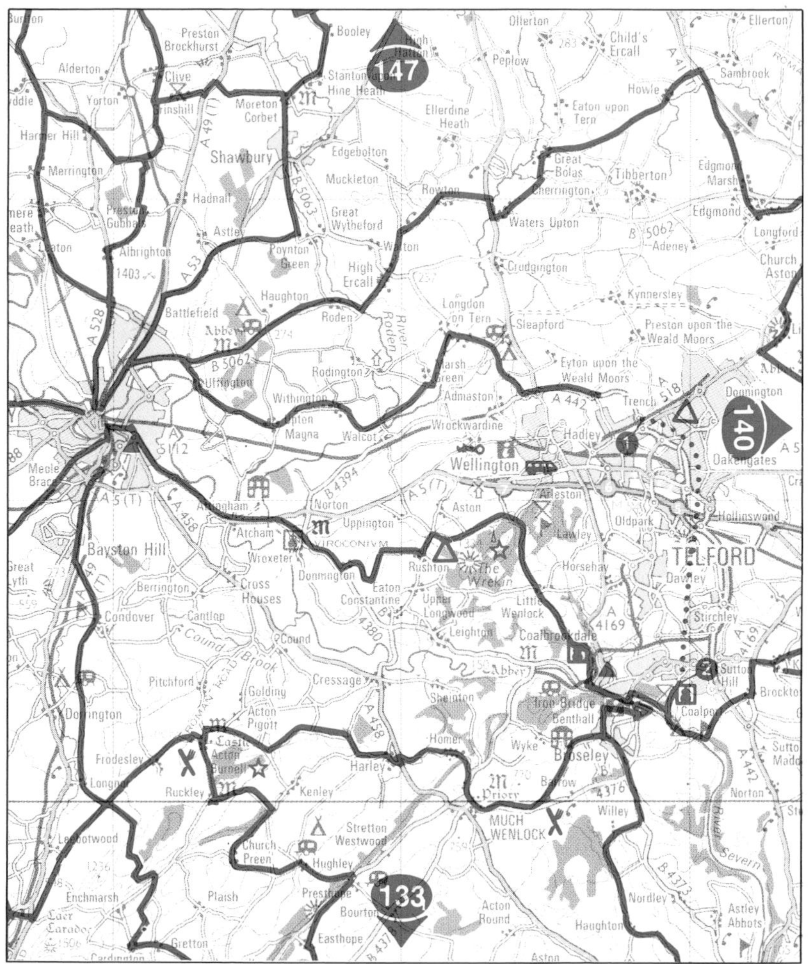

① Join the Telford Way at Trench Lock in preference to the dual carriageway, following signs across Telford to ② Coalport.

△ Steep climbs in the **Wrekin** area.

Wellington for Telford, Birmingham.

Cafés **Acton Burnell, Much Wenlock**.

Wroxeter remains of Roman town.

China Works Museum, **Coalport**; **Blists Hill** Open Air Museum; **Iron-bridge** Gorge where Abraham Darby first smelted iron and so set the scene for the Industrial Revolution.

☆ **The Wrekin**, an isolated, extinct volcano; **Acton Burnell**, simple, impressive castle ruin; remains of Shrewsbury Canal at **Uffington**, **Whithington**; **Longdon on Tern**, Thomas Telford's iron aqueduct.

Wellington Perry's, Park Street.

▲ **Shrewsbury** 0743 56397; **Iron-bridge** Gorge 095245 3281.

Shropshire/Staffordshire/West Midlands

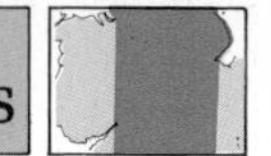

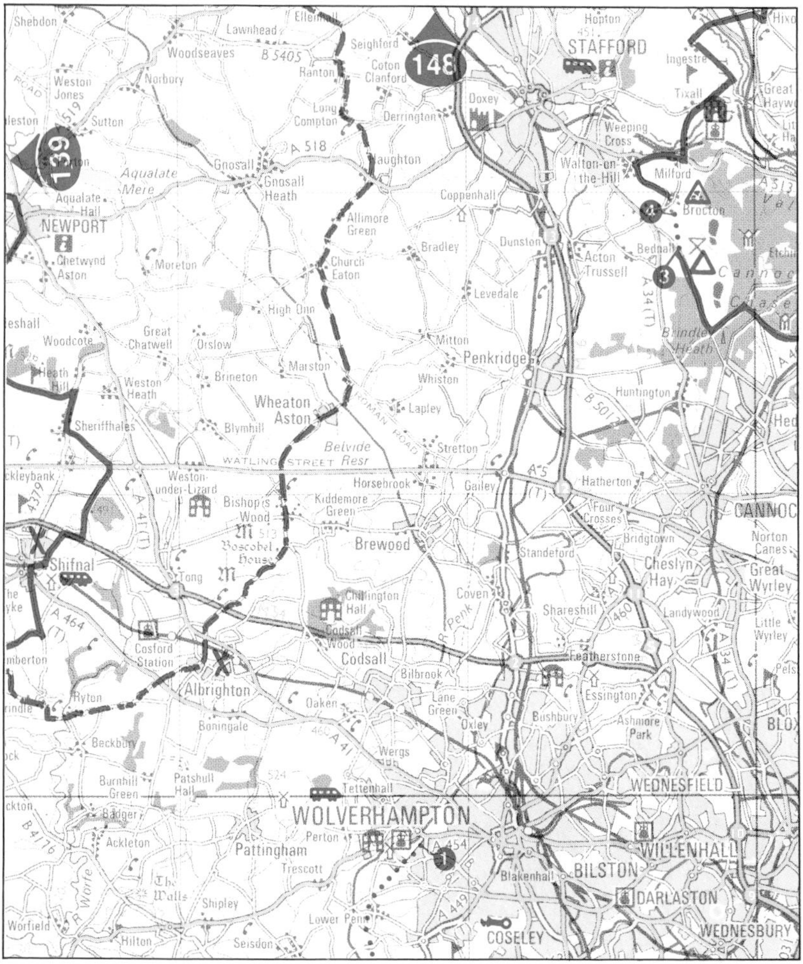

① Access to Kingswinford Branch disused railway line route from Castle Croft Road. The route continues generally SE for 10 miles (16 km) into the Birmingham suburb of Brierley Hill, where it can be joined near Fens Pool. *Details of off-highway routing in Cannock Chase, page 141.*

△ **Cannock Chase**, some steep hills.

Wolverhampton and **Shifnal** on the London–Shrewsbury main line; **Stafford** on the Birmingham–Crewe main line, InterCity services.

Limited choices, **Shifnal**, **Albrighton**.

Cannock Chase, Britain's smallest Area of Outstanding Natural Beauty, is much underestimated as a cycling area. Its bracken, heaths and pine plantations cover 7,000 acres, roamed by herds of fallow deer.

Birmingham Steve Thornhill Cycles, 506/8 Bristol Road, Selly Oak.

Staffordshire/West Midlands

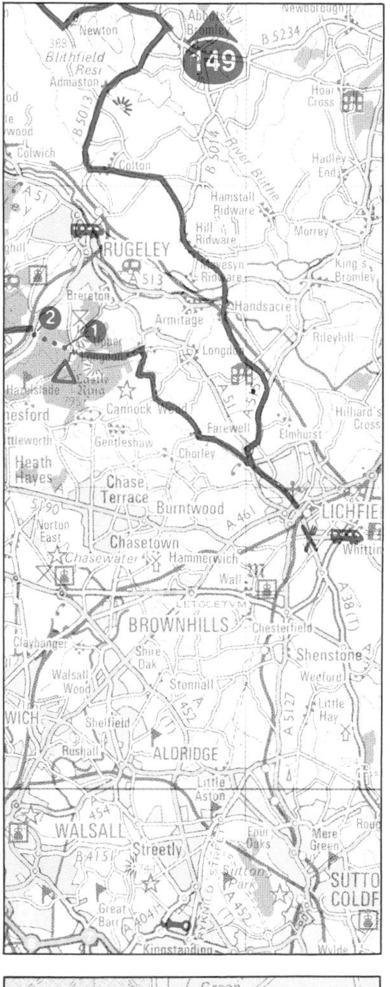

① and ②, ③, ④, access as indicated on Landranger excerpt below to off-highway routing in Cannock Chase. Marquis's Drive (in the vicinity of ②) is a forestry track with an occasionally rough surface.

△ Some steep climbs in the **Cannock Chase** area.

Lichfield and **Rugely** on the Rugby–Stafford main line.

Choices in Lichfield.

Excellent vantage point near **Brocton** on off-highway route: Welsh Border hills and Long Mynd can be seen to the W. The enormous boulder here was brought from SW Scotland by ice age glaciers. Near **Admaston** there are some fine panoramic views of Blithfield Reservoir and Cannock Chase.

Shugborough Hall, near **Tixall**: museums, gardens, riverside terraces.

Birmingham T. Moore, Wallace Road, Selly Park and Alan Richards Bike Shop, 172–178 Gravelly Lane, Erdington.

The West Bromwich Parkway is a useful cycle way in Birmingham's centre: access at Swan Lane and Colliery Road near Thomas Telford High School.

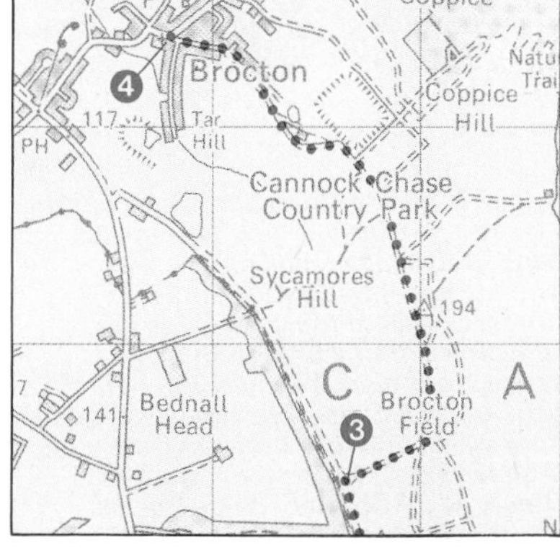

Leicestershire

Leicestershire is classic hunting country – but the fox thrives as it has always done. It lives in woods and copses. Harvest mice, by contrast, make summer nests in the corn fields or hedgerows of this predominantly agricultural area. The nest is a ball of grass or corn blades cleverly suspended from stems or twigs. Progress from stalk to stalk is assisted by the tail, used almost as a fifth limb. At 2½ inches (6½ cm) in length it is one of Britain's smallest mammals.

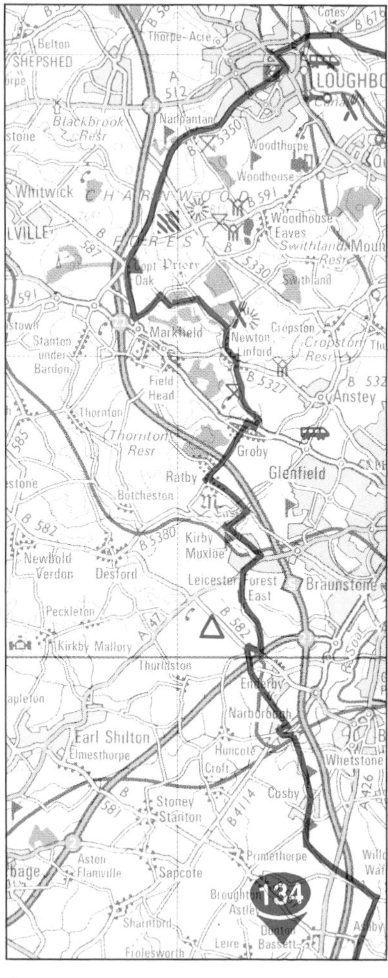

△ **Loughborough S**, all gentle riding.

🚆 **Leicester** and **Loughborough** on the London–Derby main line.

✗ Refreshments at Bradgate Park near **Newtown Linford**; choices in **Loughborough.**

⧖ **Groby**, useful picnic site.

⫽ Rugged **Charnwood Forest**.

🔧 **Loughborough** Beacon Cycles, 30 High Street.

▲ **Copt Oak** Markfield (0530) 242661.

Leicestershire

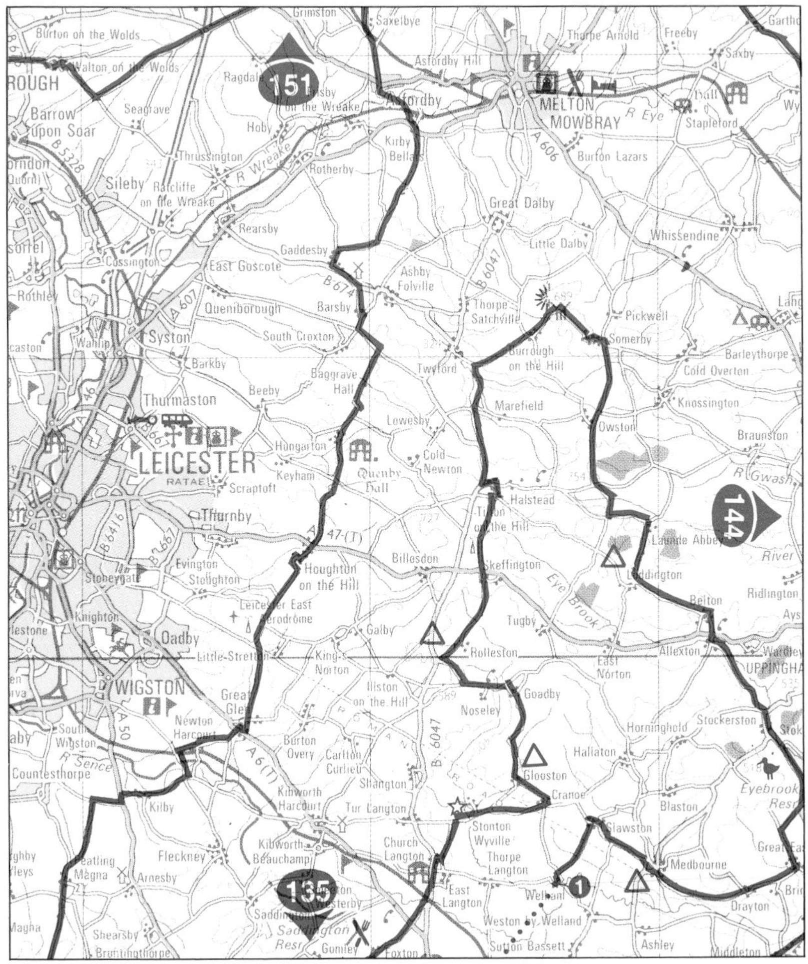

① Access to bridleway via 'No Through Road' just past church.

△ Going N from **Glooston** the road becomes gated, leading to a delightful section through parkland at **Rolleston**. Sharp right turn between **Illstone on the Hill** and Rollestone to avoid the B6047. Climbs in vicinity of **Launde Abbey**; climbs and views, **Medbourne** via Nevill Holt.

Leicester, InterCity services; **Melton Mowbray** on the Leicester–Peterborough line.

Choices at **Melton Mowbray**; pub meals, **Foxton**.

Burrough on the Hill, large Iron Age fortress, breathtaking views.

Eyebrook Reservoir, bird-watching.

Exhibits at **Melton Mowbray** Museum include Stilton cheese and pork pies.

Leicester Mottram, 286 Narborough Road.

Lincs/Leics/Northants/Cambs

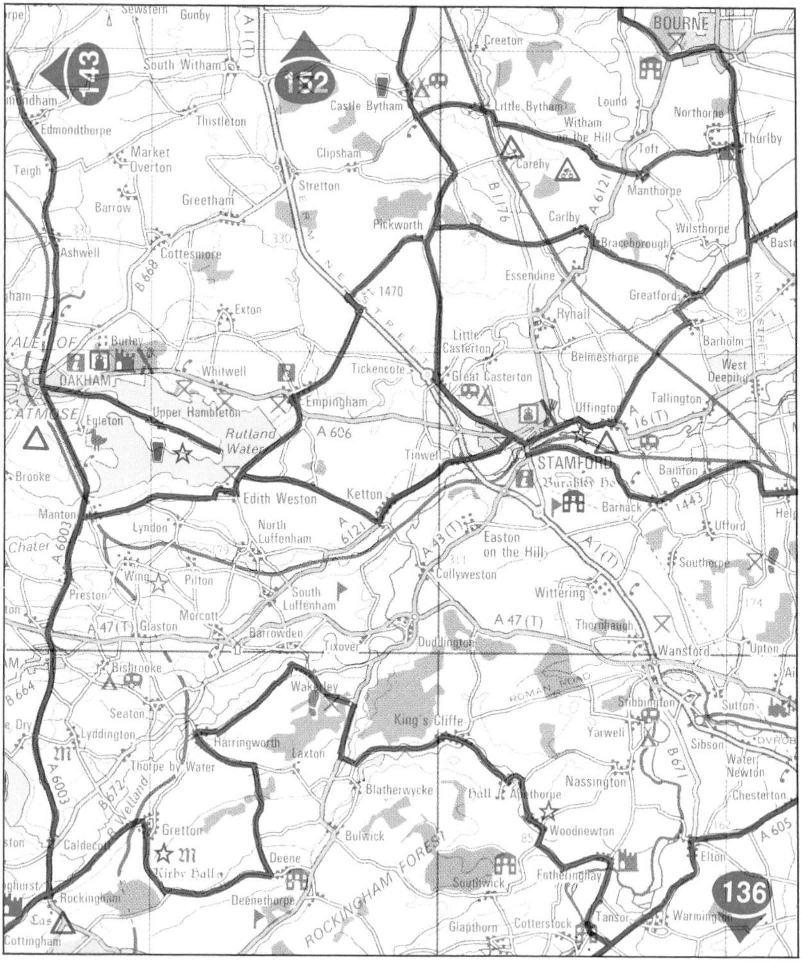

△ Climbs **Oakham to Rockingham**, but most are gentle with descents and views to compensate.

Oakham and **Stamford** on the Peterborough–Leicester line.

Stamford, Oakham, choices.

Enjoyable pubs at **Rutland Water, Castle Bytham.**

Little Bytham–Stamford area, lovely wooded scenery. **Carlby–Stamford**, idyllic cycling on quiet roads.

Oakham Castle has an intriguing horseshoe display; Dickens often visited **Rockingham** Castle.

☆ Rutland Water is a huge reservoir with a nature reserve (wildfowl and waders), water sports and nature trail; **Stamford**, a charming old town with 17th- and 18th-C buildings; see the stocks and whipping posts at **Apethorpe** and **Gretton**.

▲ **Thurlby** Bourne (0778) 425588.

Lincolnshire/Cambridgeshire

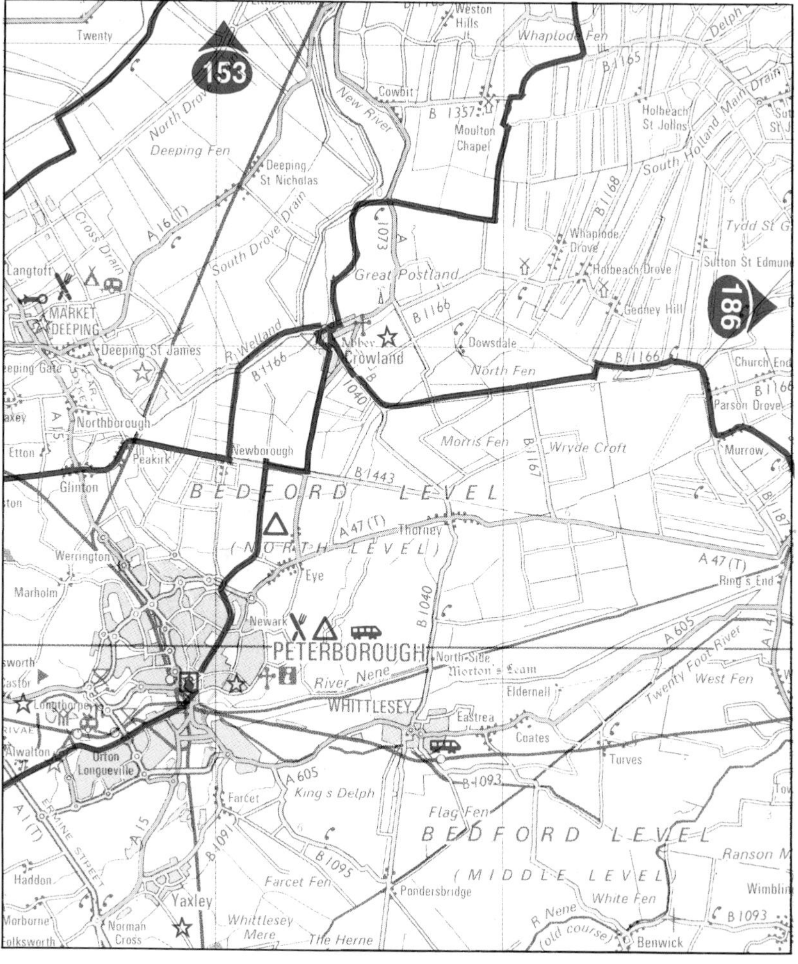

△ **Bedford Level** is fenland, truly flat. **Peterborough** is a recently developed city with heavy traffic at peak times but an extensive and successful cycle way system.

Peterborough, frequent InterCity services, King's Cross 50 minutes; **Whittlesey** on the Peterborough–Norwich line.

Choices, **Peterborough**, **Market Deeping.**

Peterborough Museum, Roman relics, many found in Whittlesey Mere.

☆ **Peterborough** grew up around the monastery founded here in the 7th C: religious and secular buildings of interest; **Longthorpe** Tower contains 14th-C murals; **Yaxley**, pretty timbered buildings; **Crowland** the 14th-C Triangular Bridge with effigy.

Deeping St James Terry Wright, 2 Horse Gate.

Shropshire/Clwyd

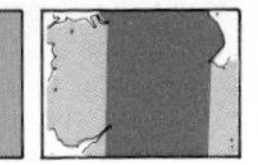

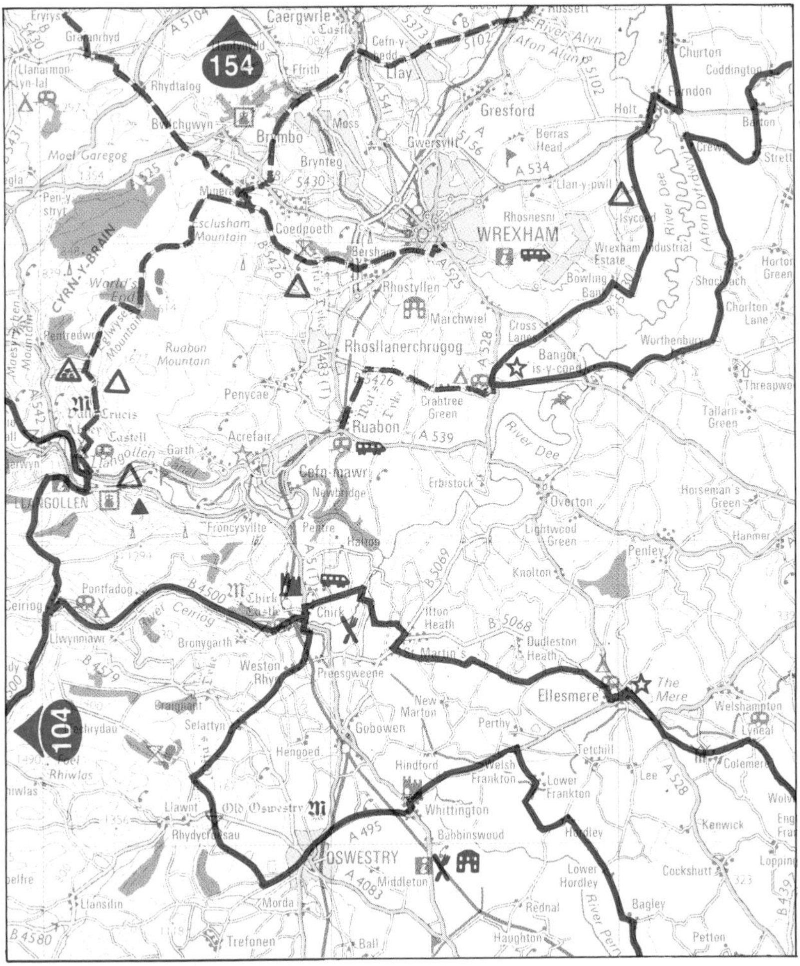

△ Road from **Llangollen** to **Ruabon** is hilly, narrow and very busy, avoid at all costs. **B5426** is acceptable, used by cycling clubs; **Holt to Bowling Bank**, quiet, well-kept roads.

🚌 Stations at **Chirk**, **Ruabon** and **Wrexham** on Chester–Shrewsbury line.

✗ **Whittington**, **Chirk**, **Oswestry**, choices.

⚠ **Llangollen to World's End**, narrow back roads through valley, mainly uphill with short steep descents.

🏛 Tyn Rhos near **Oswestry**, mansion, gardens and museum.

𝔪 **Old Oswestry**, Iron Age hill fort covers 60 acres; Valle Crucis Abbey, **Llangollen**; uninhabited **Chirk** Castle.

☆ **Ellesmere**, in Shropshire's lake district; **Bangor-is-y-coed**, unspoilt town.

🔧 **Ruabon** Cycles, Old Grammar School, Church Street.

▲ **Llangollen** 0978 860330.

Shropshire/Cheshire

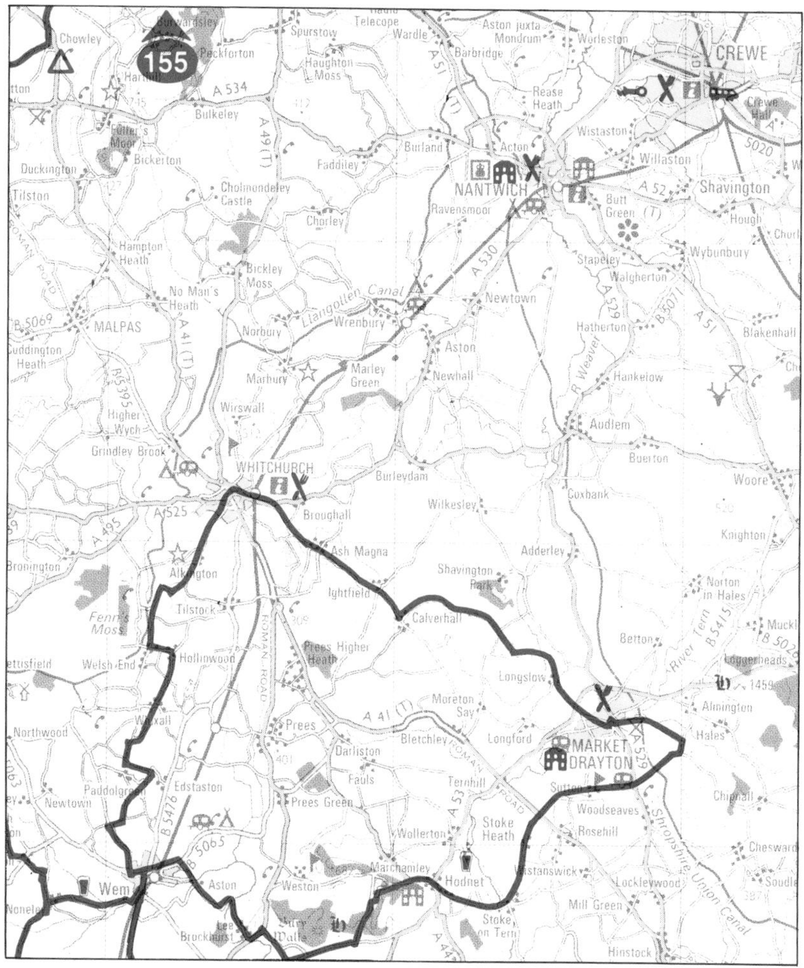

△ Mostly flat; peaceful lanes, particularly around **Stretton**.

🚂 **Crewe**, InterCity services, but subject to long closure – check with British Rail.

✕ Choices at **Whitchurch**, **Nantwich** and **Crewe**. Tea rooms, Hodnet Hall, **Market Drayton.**

🍺 Brewery at **Wem** means real ale in local pubs. The Bear Inn, **Hodnet**, has a 'banqueting hall'.

H **Loggerheads**, the site of a battle in 1459; Bury Walls, **Hopton**, site of a Civil War battle.

🏠 Dorfold Hall, **Nantwich**, is a Jacobean country house; Churche's House, **Nantwich,** a merchant's house dating from 1577; Hodnet Hall, **Market Drayton**, fine lakes and garden.

🔧 **Crewe** J. E. Williams, Edleston Road; **Market Drayton**, Beresfords, 36 Cheshire Street.

Staffordshire

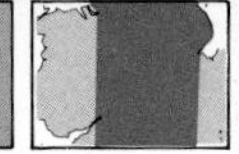

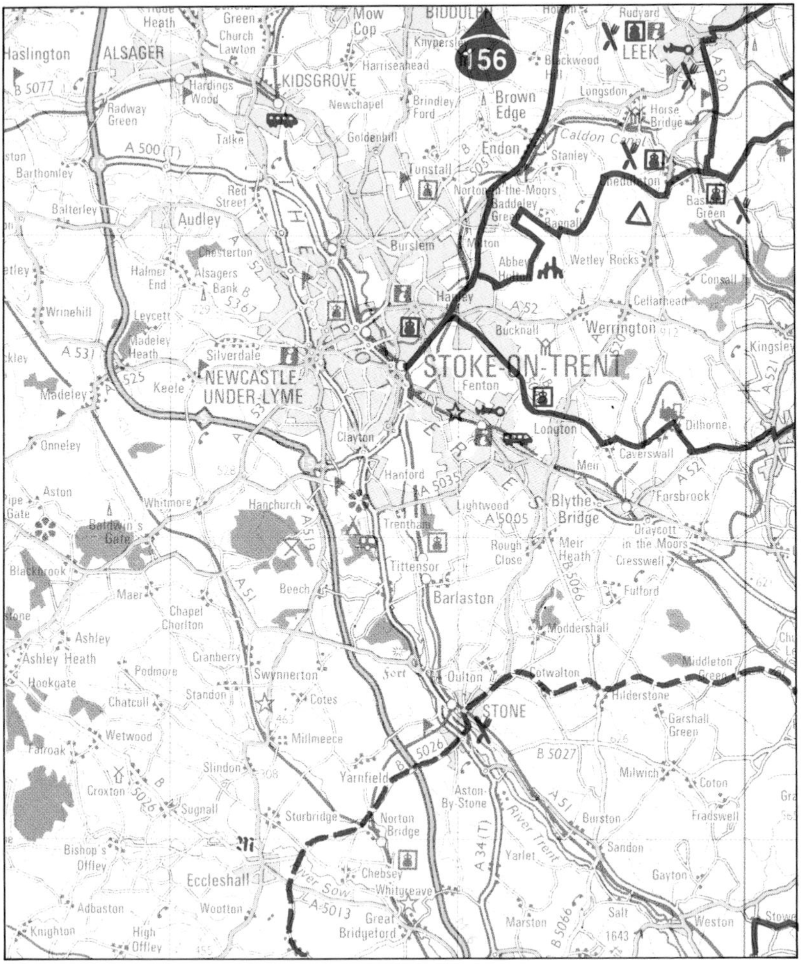

Climbs, especially in the **Leek/Stoke-on-Trent** area; latter is heavily industrial.

Stoke, InterCity services; **Kidsgrove** and other stations on the Manchester–Derby line.

Refreshments, pubs, at **Rudyard**, **Basford Green**, **Leek**, **Cheddleton** and **Stone**.

At **Eccleshall** are the remains of the castle inhabited by former bishops of **Lichfield**, and the interesting church.

Stoke, famed pottery centre.

Leek, local history museum; **Longton**, Potteries museum and interesting industrial architecture; the Spitfire Museum at **Stoke** will appeal to anyone interested in this brilliantly designed fighter; other museums at **Cheddleton** and **Basford Green.**

Leek Cycle Centre, 17 Broad Street; **Stoke** B. Rourke, 22 Waterloo Rd.

Staffordshire/Derbyshire

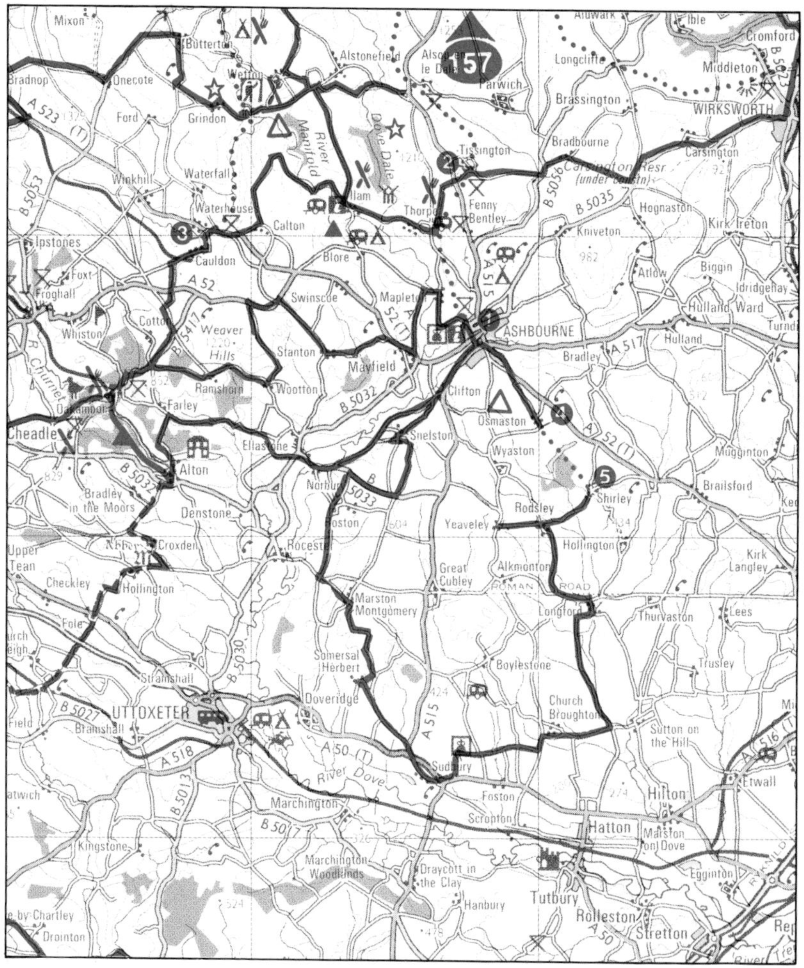

① Access to Tissington Trail at Ashbourne Cycle Hire Centre and ② Tissington.

③ Access to Manifold Railway. Path off A523 at bottom of dip.

④ Bridleway through Osmaston Park leads off at junction of roads in village. ⑤ Unclassified road (not marked on Routemaster) heads NW towards Osmaston, becoming bridleway.

△ Strenuous riding in **Peak District**; **Ashbourne** to **Sudbury**, easy gradients, quiet roads.

🚌 **Uttoxeter**, on the Derby–Stoke line.

✗ Farmhouse cafés, **Wetton**, Milldale and Wetton Mill; **Tissington**, tea room (summer); café, **Ilam** Hall; pub meals, **Butterton, Oakmoor, Cheadle.**

☆ **Dove Dale**, stepping stones; **Wetton Mill**, picturesque ford; Thors Cave near **Wetton**.

▲ **Ilam** Hall, Thorpe Cloud (033529) 212.

Nottinghamshire

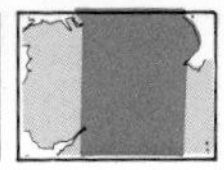

Belvoir Castle

Nottinghamshire/Lincolnshire/Leicestershire

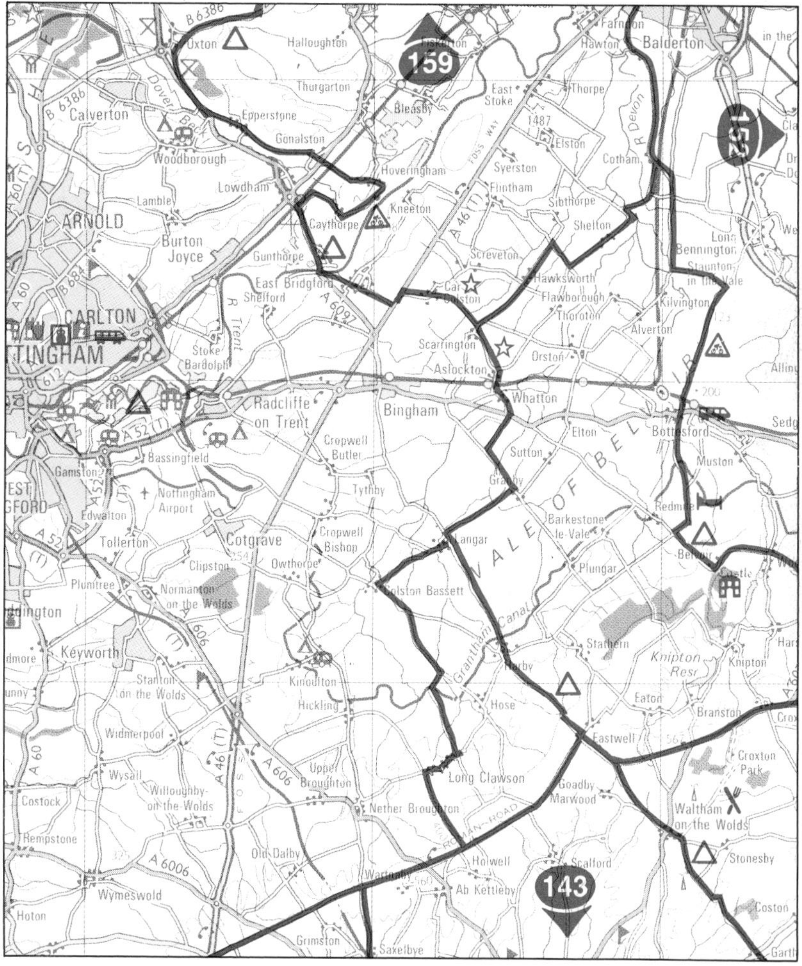

△ Severe climb into **Oxton**; little choice but to join traffic over **Gunthorpe** bridge, but escape afterwards through **East Bridgford**; stiff climb to **Belvoir**; a long pull over the **Harby** Hills; S of **Waltham on the Wolds** is a single track gated road – beware of cattle. **Nottingham** lays fair claim to be a 'cycling town', with a developing cycle way network.

Nottingham InterCity services; **Bottesford** and stations on the Grantham–Nottingham line.

Waltham on the Wolds, old pubs.

Belvoir Castle, seat of the Dukes of Rutland, views of the Vale of Belvoir, pronounced 'Beever'.

Range of museums at **Nottingham** covering industry, costume, canals and daily life.

Redmile Peacock Farm Guest House and Old Mill House.

Lincolnshire

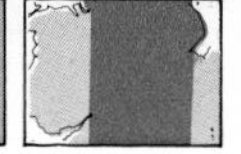

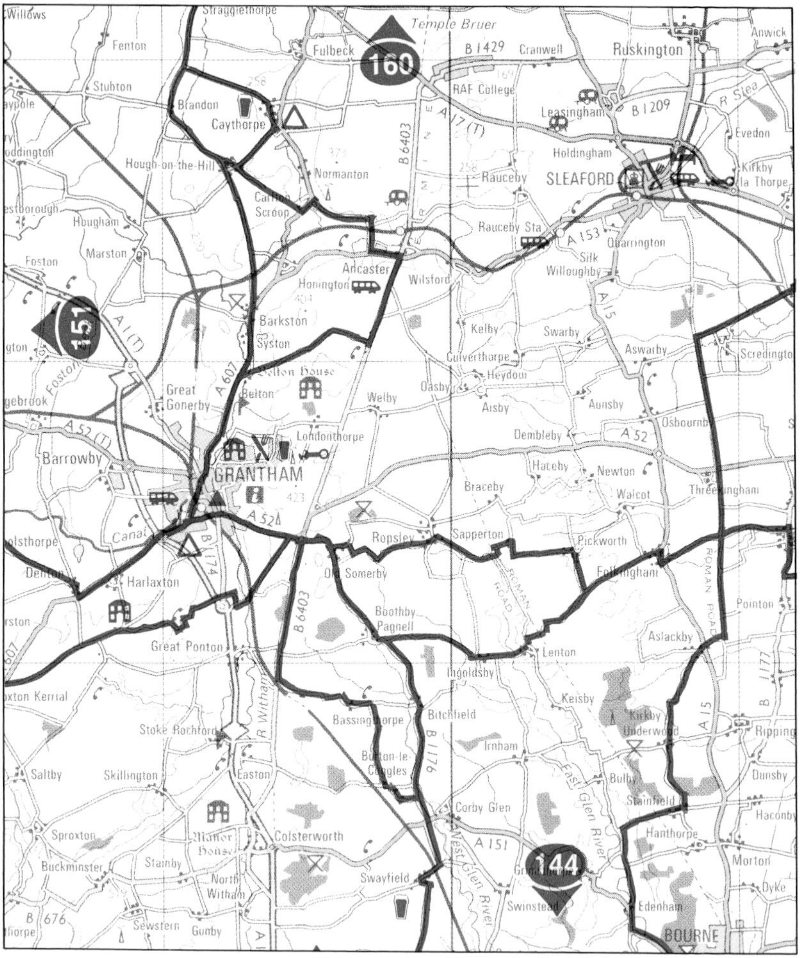

△ Long pull up A52 to get out of **Grantham**; another climb up to **Caythorpe** with long descent to **Barkston**.

🚆 **Grantham**, InterCity services and branch line to **Ancaster** and **Rauceby** and **Sleaford.**

✕ **Grantham** and **Sleaford**, choices.

🍺 Delightful looking pub at **Caythorpe** and **Swayfield**; the Angel and Royal, **Grantham**, described as England's oldest coaching inn.

🏛 **Belton** House, with magnificent landscaped park; heavily ornamental manor house at **Harlaxton**; **Grantham** House (Nat. Trust) by river.

ℌ **Grantham**, where Margaret Thatcher spent her girlhood, sometimes helping out in her father's grocery shop.

🔧 **Grantham** Don Ray Cycles, 26/27 Swinegate; **Sleaford** Nev's Cycle Centre, 52 Southgate.

▲ **Grantham** 0476 2042.

Lincolnshire

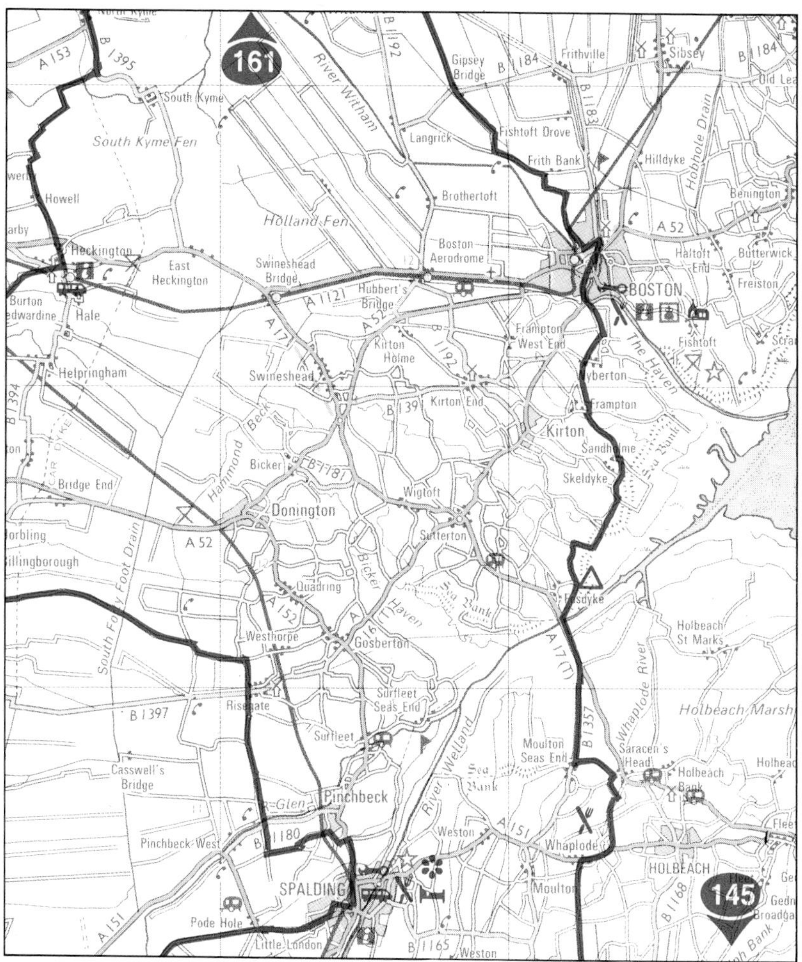

△ Exceptionally flat, straight roads, **Spalding** to **Boston**.

🚃 **Spalding**, **Heckington** and other stations on the branch lines from Grantham and Peterborough.

🍴 Choices at **Boston** and **Spalding**.

✿ Springfield Gardens, **Spalding**, is the centre of the British bulb industry: landscaped gardens, flower festivals.

⛪ At **Boston**, the church of St Botolph is one of the largest parish churches in England; the marsh and villages near Boston are noted for their fine churches; the church at **Whaplode** has some notable Norman furniture.

🔧 **Spalding** Gibbons, 112 Winsover Road; **Boston** Nev's Cycle Centre, 8 Church Street.

🛏 **Spalding** Hawices House, 34 London Road; Mrs Brown, 8 Meadow Close and Audrey's Residencia, 14 Welland Place, London Road.

Clwyd/Cheshire

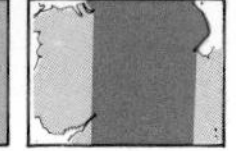

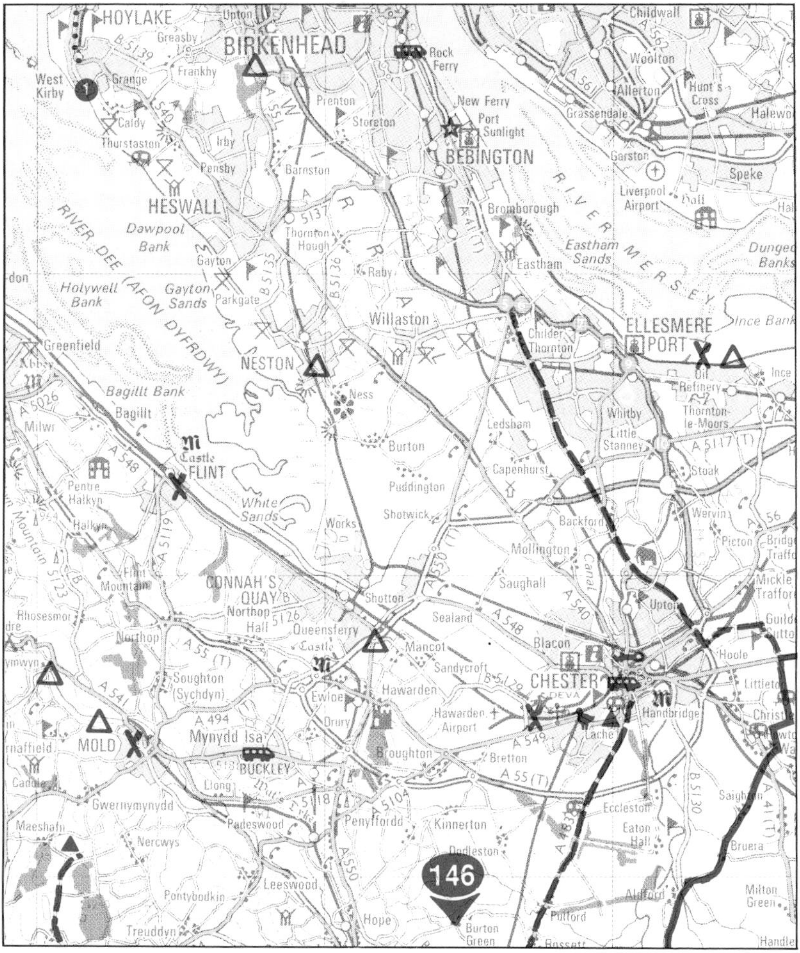

① Access to North Wirral promenades routes, awaiting approval.

△ **Birkenhead** region industrial and busy; miscellaneous off-highway opportunities to avoid traffic, **Queensferry**, **Neston** and **Ellesmere Port**, also **Mold** and **Rhydymwyn.**

[train] **Chester**, InterCity services; **Birkenhead** to Liverpool ferry, cyclists prohibited in peak hours.

✗ **Flint, Mold, Ellesmere Port, Chester**.

[castle] **Ewloe** Castle; **Flint** Castle; Roman amphitheatre at **Chester**.

☆ **Chester**, ancient city walls, medieval timber 'galleried' houses, cathedral; **Port Sunlight**, village for soap workers, gardens.

[cycle hire] **Chester** Cycle and Pram Centre, Upper Northgate Street.

▲ **Chester** 0244 671097; **Maeshafn**, Llanferres (035285) 320, on shoulder of Moel Findeg.

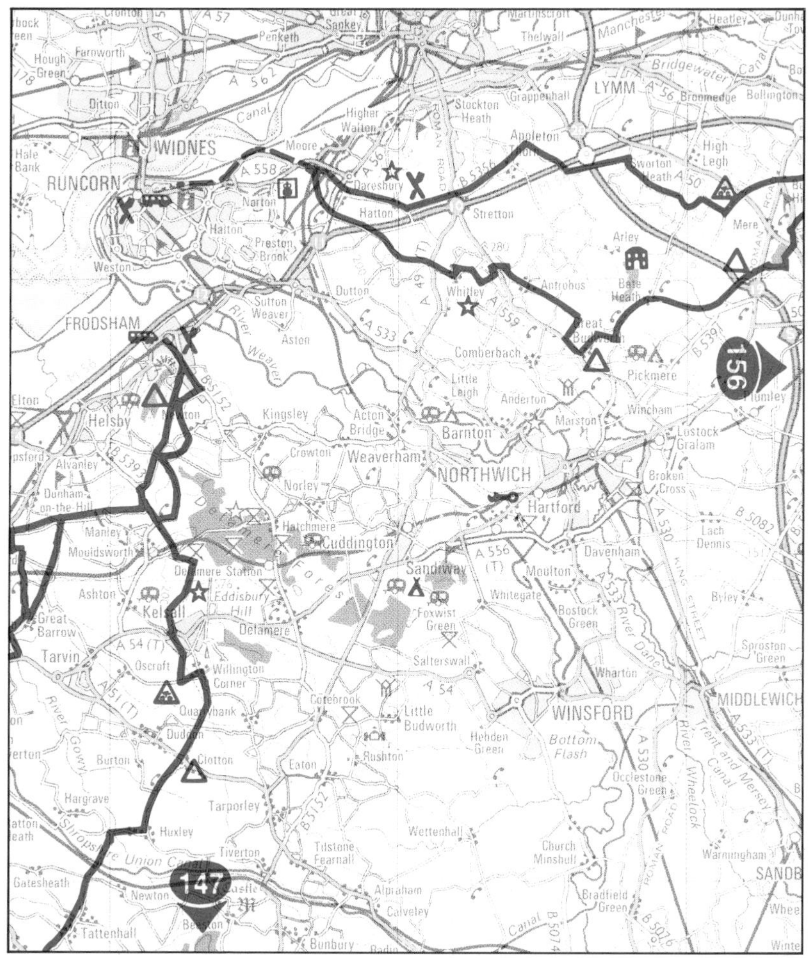

△ Steady but gentle climb out of **Frodsham** giving excellent views of beautiful Delamere Forest. Don't be put off by tree-lined hills in **Clotton** area, no need to climb most of them; beware cobbled roads in historic **Great Budworth**. Walk bike across junction near **Mere** to avoid busy roundabout.

🚆 **Runcorn**, **Frodsham** and stations on Liverpool–Leeds line.

✗ At **Daresbury**, **Runcorn**, **Frodsham**.

▲ **Appleton Thorn** E, ideal cycling roads: smooth, flat and quiet; **Frodsham–Tattenhall**, beautiful flat ride.

🏛 **Arley** Hall, 14th-C house, splendid gardens.

☆ **Daresbury**, birthplace of Lewis Carroll; popular fishing spot at **Higher Whitley**; Kelborrow castle, high on **Eddisbury Hill**.

⛺ Camping in **Delamere Forest**.

🔧 **Northwich** J. Gee, 136–40 Witton St.

Cheshire

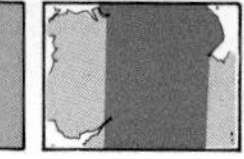

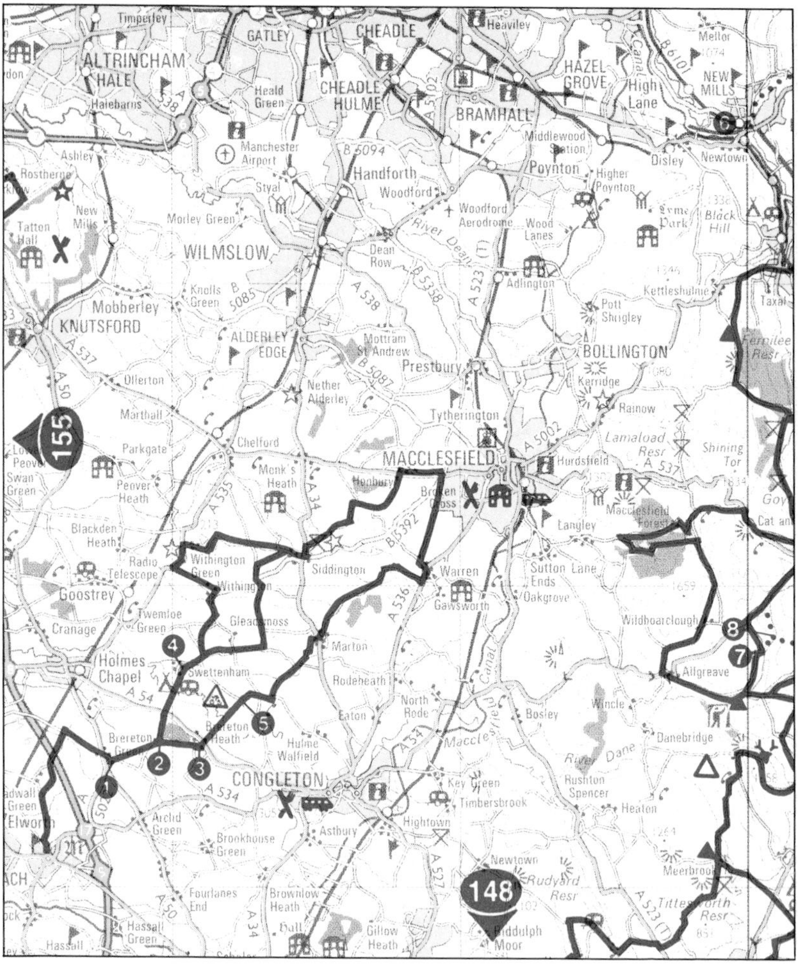

① to ⑤ routing in Brereton Green area not shown on Routemaster mapping.

⑥ Access to Sett Valley Trail, River Bridge, New Mills.

⑦ Rough track leads to packhorse bridge ⑧ over River Dane, from which bridleway climbs steeply NW to A54 or rough track to A53.

△ Steep climbs into Peak District.

🚃 **Macclesfield** on the Manchester–Sheffield line.

✗ Choices at **Macclesfield**, **Congleton**; café at **Tatton Hall**.

⚠ Deserted lanes, **Breretons** area.

☆ **Rostherne** Mere, attractive lake, wildfowl; **Rostherne** church has rare gate in the churchyard.

🏛 Several fine houses in the **Macclesfield** area, notably Gawsworth Hall, Adlington Hall and Capesthorne.

▲ Peak hostels via YHA Regional Office, Matlock 0629 4666.

Derbyshire/Staffordshire

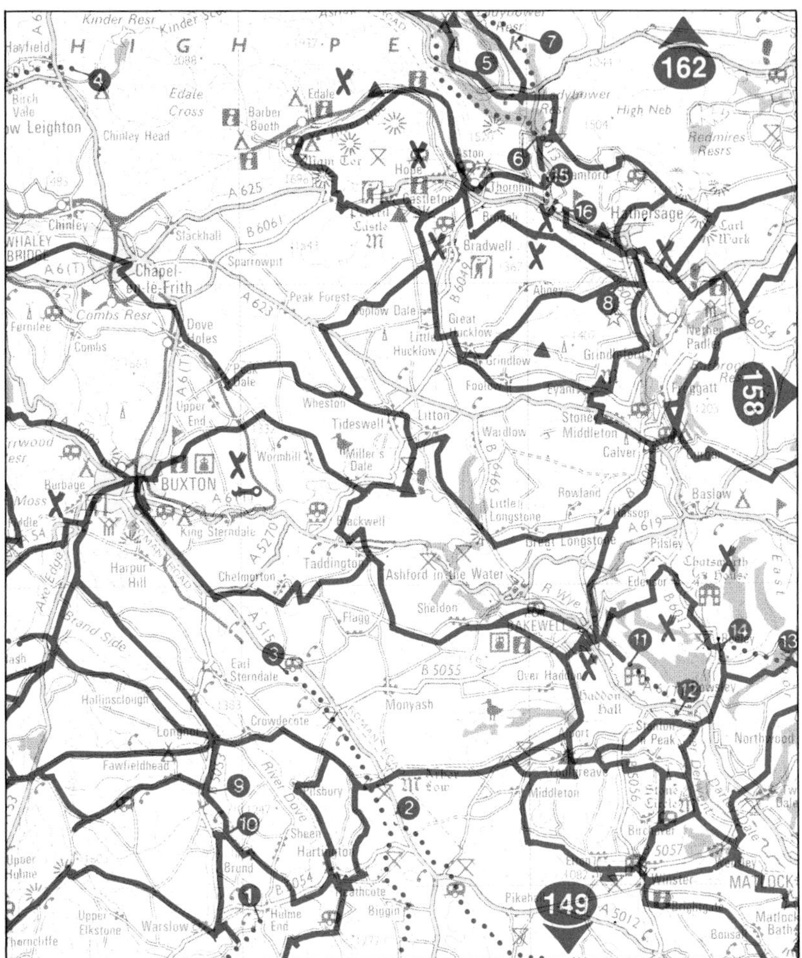

① Access to Manifold Railway Path.

② Parsley Hay Cycle Hire Centre. ③ Sparklow Inn.

④ Sett Valley Trail, Hayfield church.

⑤ Unclassified road along Ladybower Reservoir, cyclists/walkers only on Sundays; cycle hire.

⑥ On W side of Yorkshire Bridge use waterworks drive then forest track. ⑦ Track and waterworks drive E side.

⑧ Road not shown on Routemaster leads off from Highlow Hall entrance.

⑨ and ⑩ road not on Routemaster.

⑪ and ⑫ bridleway easily located.

⑬ Stony road leads to Beeley lodge ⑭, entrance to Chatsworth Park.

⑮ Bridleway leads off from close to railway bridge and ⑯ A6013.

Cafés as marked.

Buxton Hemshall Ltd, 42 High Street.

▲ Bookings via YHA Regional Office, Matlock 0629 4666.

Derbyshire/Nottinghamshire/S Yorkshire

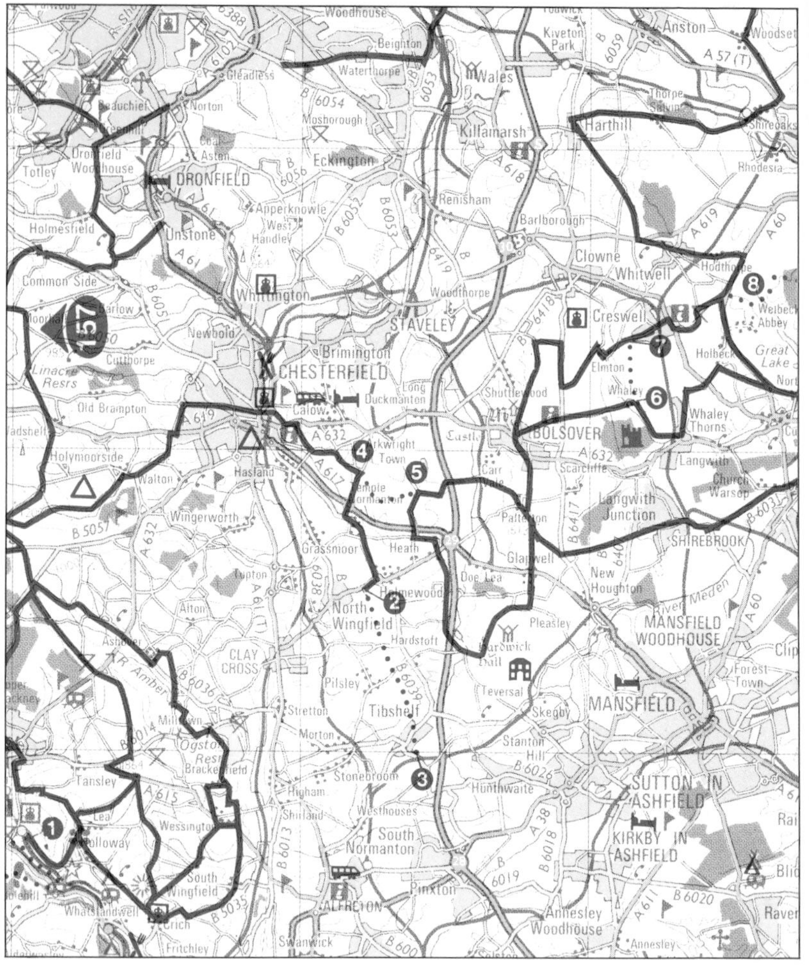

① Access to Cromford Canal and High Peak Trail near Cromford Station.

② Tibshelf Trail off A6175 and ③ at remaining railway bridge.

④ and ⑤ bridleway as indicated, also ⑥ and ⑦.

⑧ **Welbeck** estate road easily located.

△ Heavy traffic, **Mansfield** and A617 flyover, **Chesterfield**; climbs up to and into Peak District, **W from Chesterfield**.

Chesterfield, Alfreton, InterCity services.

Chesterfield and **Crich**, choices.

Hardwick Hall (Nat. Trust) famous Tudor house.

Revolution House, **Old Whittington**; Peacock Heritage Centre, **Chesterfield**; museum and caves at **Creswell** Crags; **Crich** Tramway Museum.

Bolsover Castle.

Marriotts, 18 South St., **Chesterfield.**

Nottinghamshire

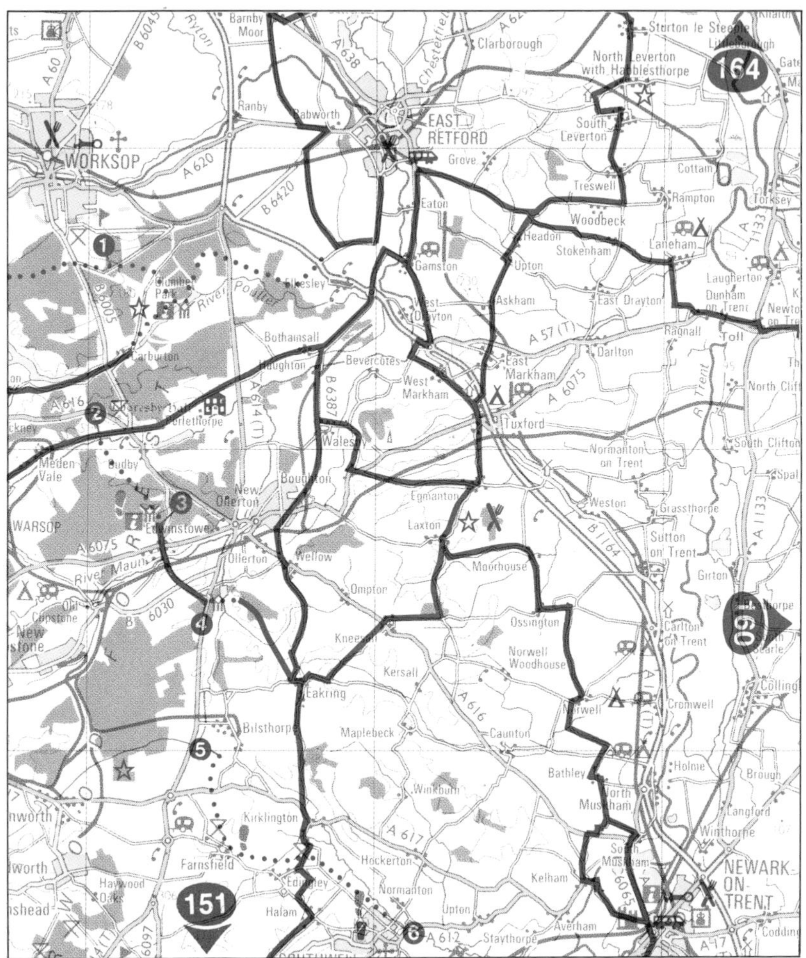

① Clumber Park permits cyclists (no charge); large scale maps available at cycle hire centre.

② and ③ bridleways through Sherwood Forest Country Park.

④ At Rufford Abbey walk through grounds to join lane to Eakring.

⑤ Access to Southwell Trail at the old station, Bilsthorpe and ⑥ Hockerton Road, Southwell.

🚃 **East Retford**, **Newark-on-Trent**, InterCity services.

🍴 Choices at **East Retford**, **Worksop**, **Laxton**, **Newark**.

☆ **Sherwood Forest** Park, with the 1,400-year-old Major Oak; **Clumber Park**, chapel, lake, woods; **Laxton**, Saxon farming system has been intriguingly re-created.

▲ Camp sites **as marked**.

🔑 **Newark** Marriotts, 16a Appleton Gate; **Worksop** Columbia Cycles, Kilton Rd.

Lincolnshire

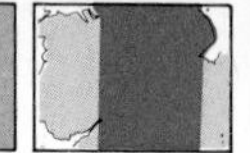

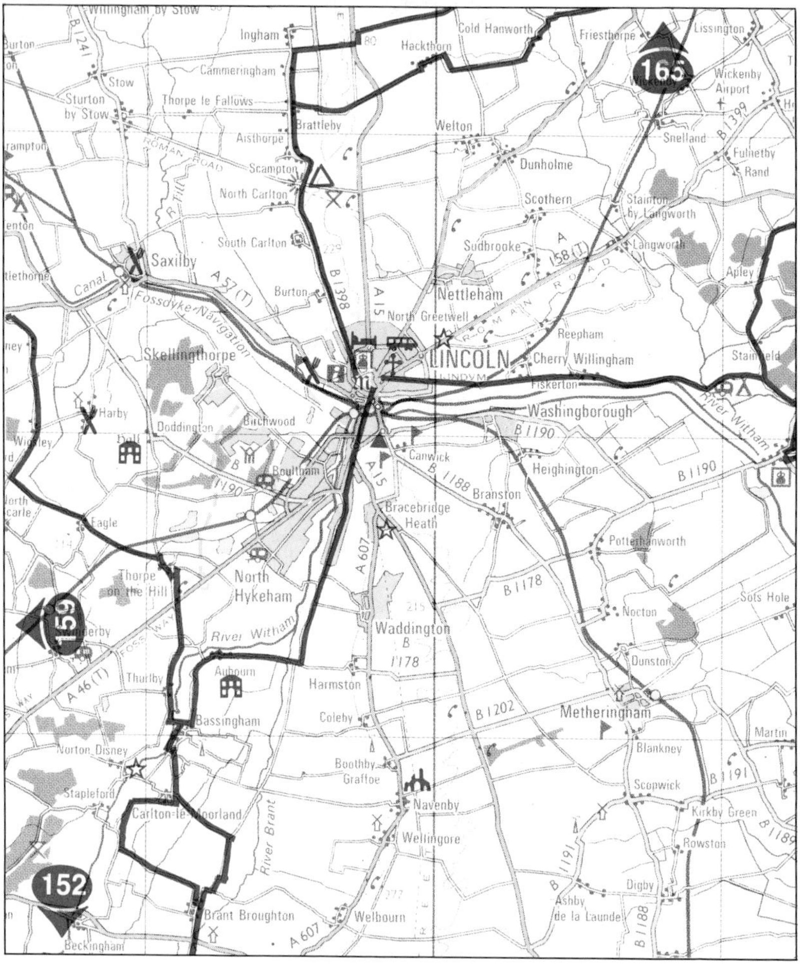

△ A generally flat area broken by the central line of the Lincolnshire Cliff, a **low ridge** giving good views; busy A roads.

🚌 **Lincoln** and other stations on the Sheffield–Leeds line.

✗ Limited choices, **Harby**, **Saxilby**; Stokes High Bridge Cafe on the Norman bridge, **Lincoln**.

☆ Historic **Lincoln**, with Newport Arch (Roman), Jew's House (Norman) and the Bishop's Palace; church at **Norton Disney** has monuments to Walt Disney's forbears; on **Bracebridge Heath** are the ruins of Dunston Pillar, the first land lighthouse.

✝ Beautiful medieval **Lincoln** Cathedral.

𝔪 **Lincoln** Castle, founded by William I.

Somerton Castle remains, **Navenby**.

Doddington Hall, Elizabethan Manor; 16th-C house at **Aubourn**.

▲ **Lincoln** 0522 22076.

Lincolnshire

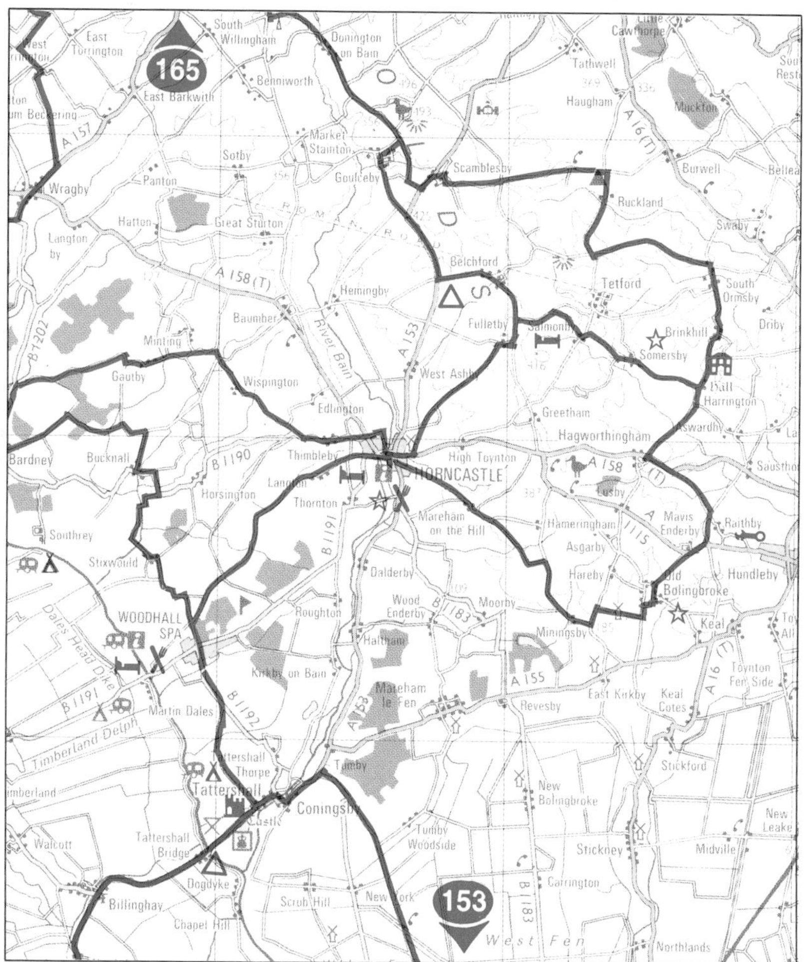

△ Tattershall area, part of **The Fens**, very flat, watch crosswinds. Lincolnshire Wolds (**Horncastle** area), fine touring, worth short climbs for views.

✗ Tea House in the Woods, Spa Grounds, **Woodhall Spa**; **Horncastle**, limited choice.

☆ **Somersby**, birthplace of Tennyson; **Horncastle**, partly preserved Roman walls and **St Mary's Church** with its Civil War artefacts. **Old Bolingbroke**, 18th-C village, birthplace of Henry IV.

Harrington Hall, setting for Tennyson's *Maud*.

Five-storey, fortified **Tattershall** Castle, notable for 15-C brickwork.

Spilsby (name just off map) W. Elley, George Hotel Yard.

Tattershall, **Martin Dales**, **Southrey**.

Horncastle, Cross Keys Inn; **Salmonby**, The Red Lion, High Street; **Woodhall Spa**, Dunns Guest House.

South Yorkshire

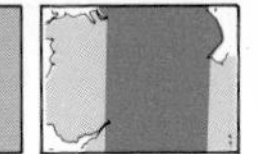

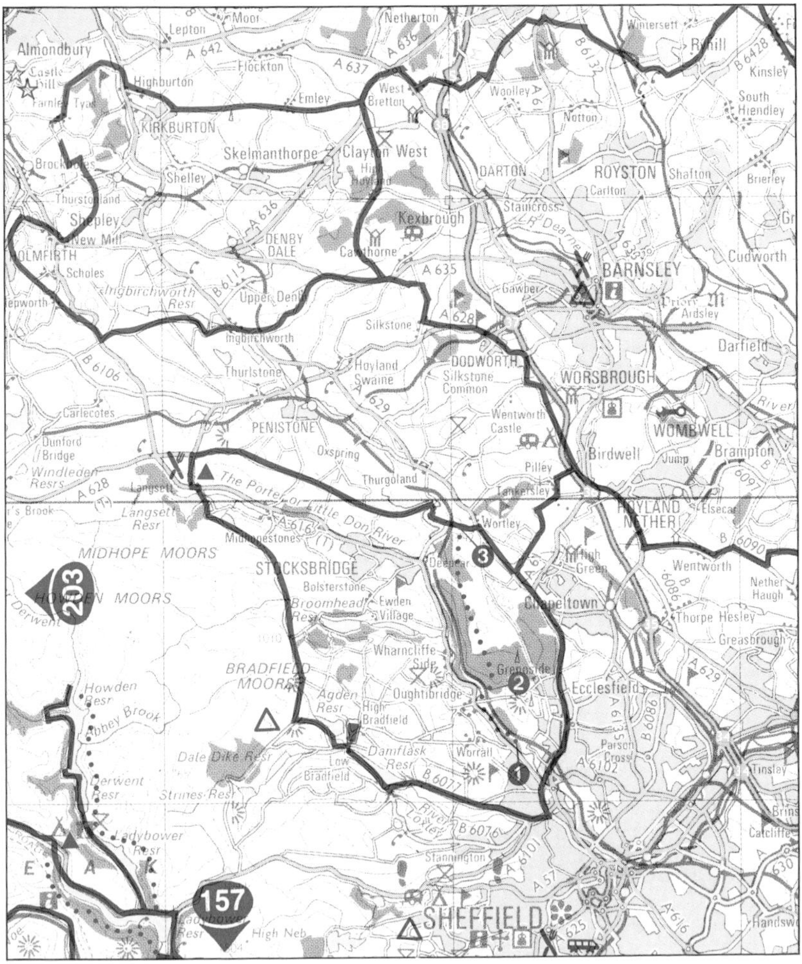

① Cul-de-sac off A61 at Wadsley Bridge between railway and river gives access to Beeley Woods and Wharncliffe Wood off-highway route. ② Oughtibridge–Grenoside road either side of railway and ③ B6088 just E of railway.

△ Access to **Peak District** from **Sheffield** involves long climbs, busy roads. Shortish climb gives access along a ridge at **Bradfield**. Heavy traffic: **Sheffield** and **Barnsley**.

🚆 **Sheffield**, frequent InterCity services.

✕ **Barnsley**, **Sheffield**, choices; **Langsett**, popular cyclist's café; pub overlooking Damflask reservoir between **High** and **Low Bradfield**.

☆ **Castle Hill**, early Iron Age camp.

🔧 Allens Cycle Centre, 23 Barnsley Road, **Wombwell**. (Easy repairs, **Hagg Farm** hostel.)

▲ **Langsett**, Barnsley (0226) 762445; **Hagg Farm** Hope Valley (0433) 51594.

South Yorkshire

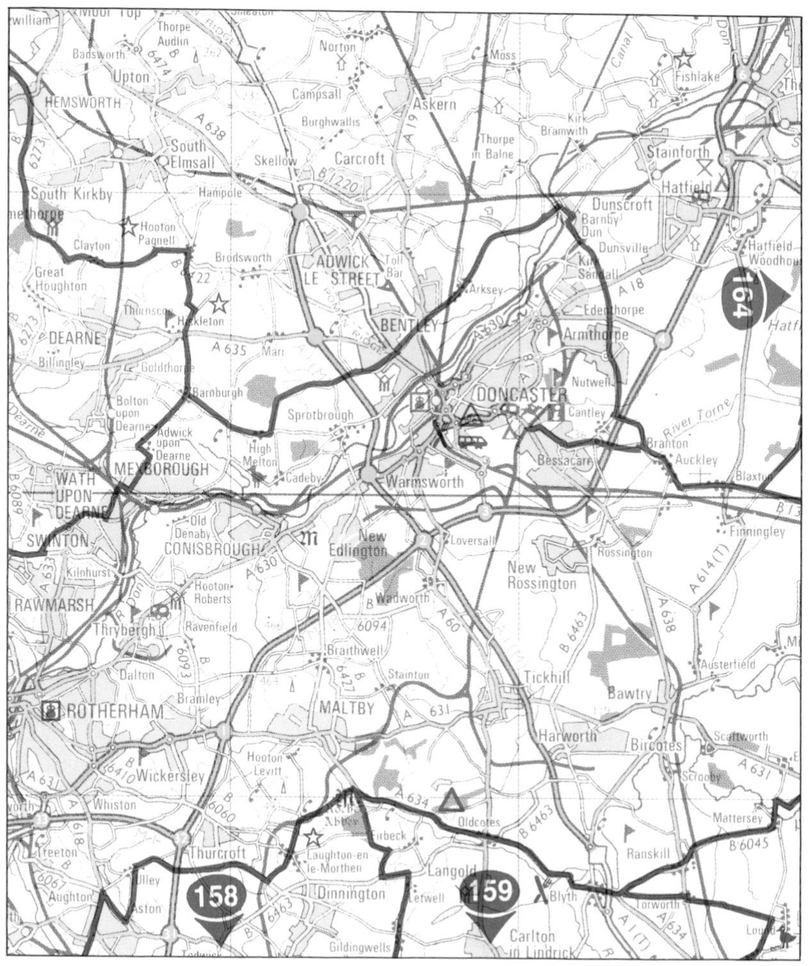

△ **A634** generally quiet; **Doncaster** is a town of cyclists, very flat. Generally easy to avoid industrial areas.

Doncaster, InterCity services.

Blyth, useful café; choices **Doncaster**.

Hare and Hounds, **Fishlake**.

Roche Abbey, ruins with grounds landscaped by Capability Brown, public footpath running round; Norman castle remains at **Conisbrough**.

Wetlands bird sanctuary at **Lound**.

Rotherham's museum and art gallery in an 18th-C building at Clifton Park.

☆ **Hooton Pagnell**, giant musical box in belfry of church plays different tunes every three hours; **Hickleton**, real skulls on lych gate; **Fishlake**, carvings on church; **Laughton en le Morthen**, attractive village, church with pre-Norman Conquest N doorway.

H. O. Smith, 63/65 Copley Road, **Doncaster**.

Lincolnshire/Humberside/Nottinghamshire

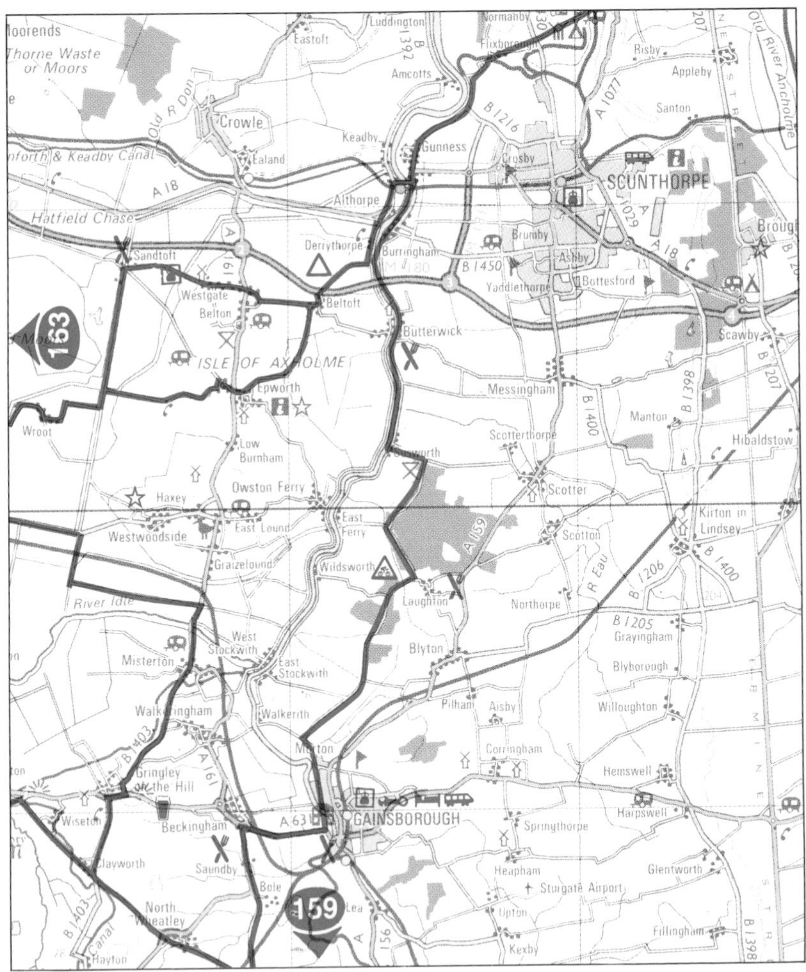

△ Mostly flat.

🚌 **Gainsborough** (two stations) and **Scunthorpe** on the Doncaster–Barnetby branch line.

✗ **Sandtoft** garden centre; Riverdale Riding Stables, **Butterwick**; Alan's Café, **Saundby**; choices at **Gainsborough**.

🍺 Good pub at **Gringley on the Hill**.

⚠ Lovely cycling in **Laughton** Forest.

▣ **Sandtoft** Transport Museum, buses, trams and trolley buses under restoration; **Gainsborough** Old Hall, 15th-C manor with medieval kitchen; **Scunthorpe** museum, art gallery.

☆ **Epworth**: the Old Rectory, birthplace of John and Charles Wesley, restored 1957, oldest Methodist shrine; **Broughton**, 11th-C Saxon tower on church; **Haxey**, 14th-C medieval strip cultivation in evidence.

🔧 Cycle Centre, Church Street, **Gainsborough**.

Lincolnshire/Humberside

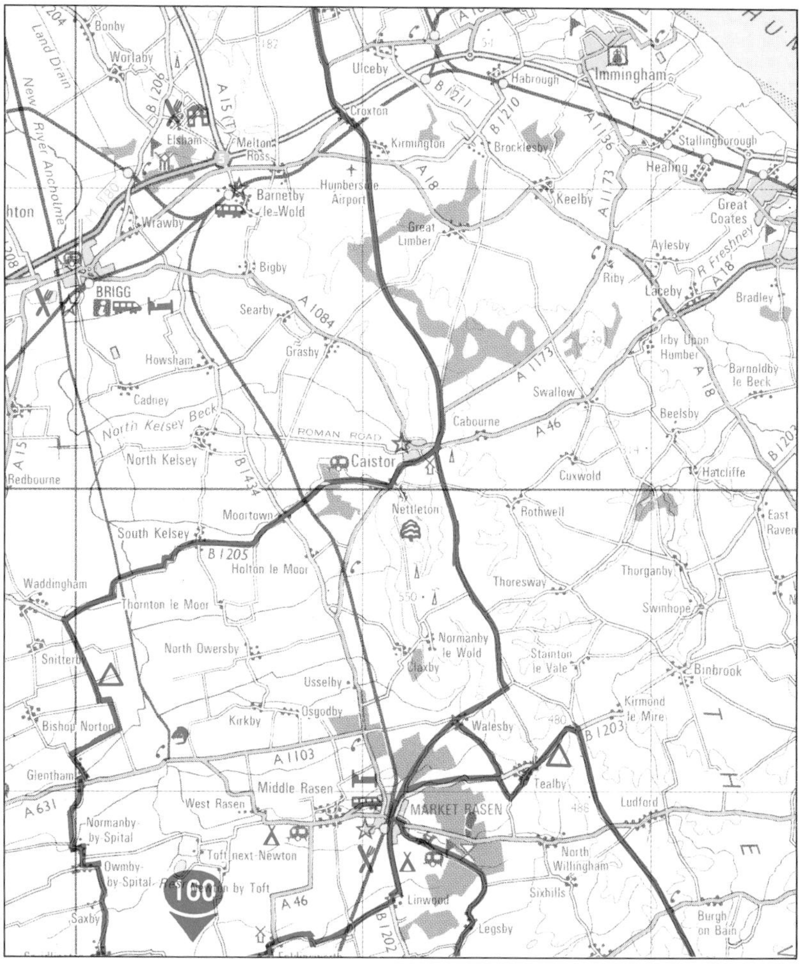

△ Mainly level cycling to **west**; Lincolnshire Wolds rising to east above **Market Rasen** are moderately hilly.

Barnetby, Brigg and other stations on the East Retford–Grimsby line.

Choices at **Market Rasen**, **Brigg**; Sunday only, **Elsham** Country Park.

☆ Traces of Roman and earlier occupation at **Market Rasen**; Pelham's Pillar on Wolds above **Caistor** commemorates plantations by Earl of Yarborough, 1840; late Norman church with leaden font, **Barnetby**; the market town of **Brigg** prospered with fen drainage.

Elsham Hall, country park, lakes, wild gardens, nature trails, waterfowl, blacksmith, pottery and crafts centre.

Woodland Trust conservation work, **Nettleton** Wood.

Middle Rasen and **Market Rasen.**

Hotels, B & B, **Brigg**; **Market Rasen**, Limes Cottage, Gainsborough Road.

ROUGHAM 2
GEDDING 2
BEYTON

5

EAST ANGLIA

Three gears is adequate to explore the whole of this region. Suffolk has a few bumps, but remains easy enough; Norfolk is easier still: don't be misled by the locals who call the slightest rise a 'hill'. The Fens, roughly north and north-east from Cambridge, are the largest area of flat land in the country; Essex, Hertfordshire and Bedfordshire are rarely demanding.

The only catch is the wind: it can blow unobstructed over great tracts of land, slowing you down to a crawl, or boosting your progress to exhilarating speeds. The prevailing wind direction, as over the whole British Isles, is from the south-west, but beware, too, of easterly and north-easterly winds, blowing in direct from Siberia, bitterly cold and dispiriting.

There are few major towns in this region, and the villages are often compact and sleepy; the landscape itself has a correspondingly remote atmosphere. In Suffolk you will find a relatively intimate pattern of enclosed fields and woodland; in Norfolk a much grander landscape, dominated by the huge, much-changing skies which the painters of the Norwich school prized so much.

Over the whole region, a dense network of lanes makes avoiding main roads, often frighteningly busy, an easy task. Unspoilt countryside, within easy reach of London, is easier to find here than anywhere. It is a region made for cycling – even a relatively large portion of the towns now have cycleway facilities.

Selected tours

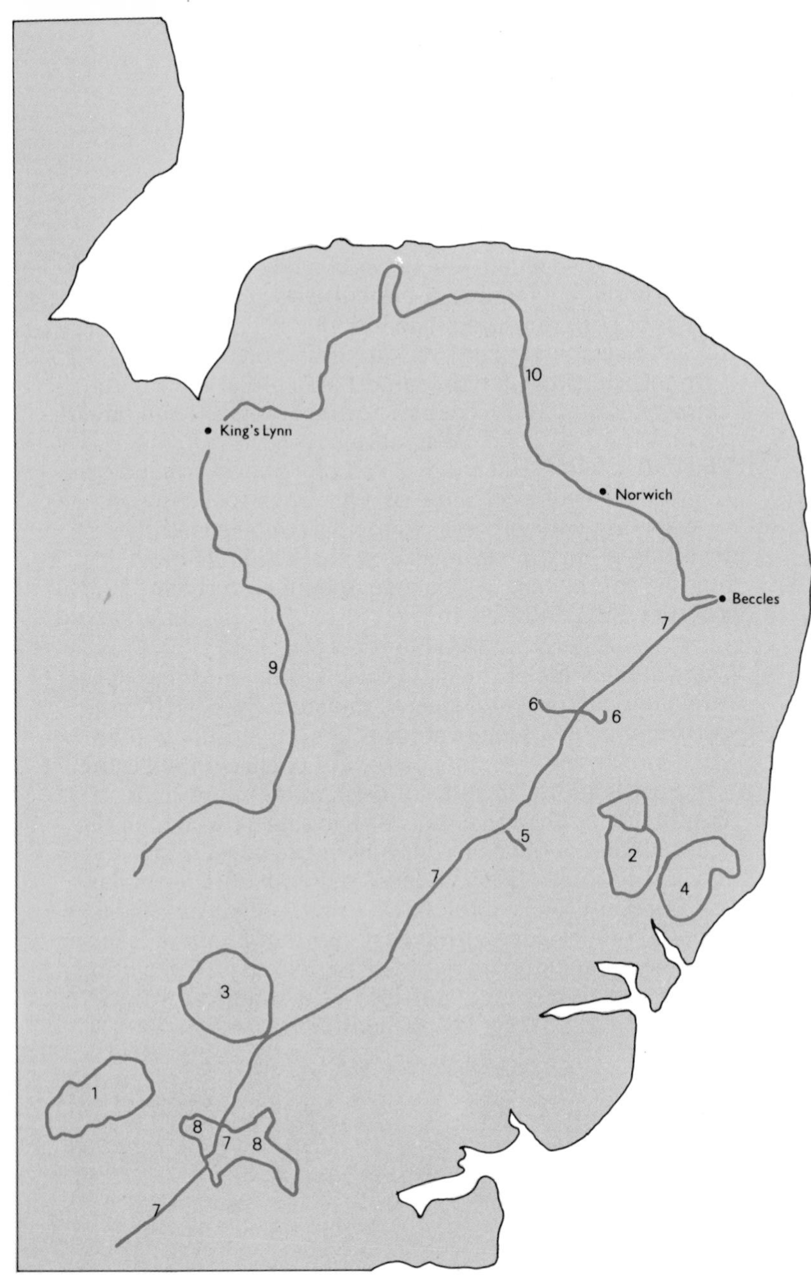

Selected tours

A cross-section of the tours in this region, showing typical rides which can be put together from the route network in a range of localities; further details **pages 170–1**.

Day rides

Two-day tours

Three days or longer

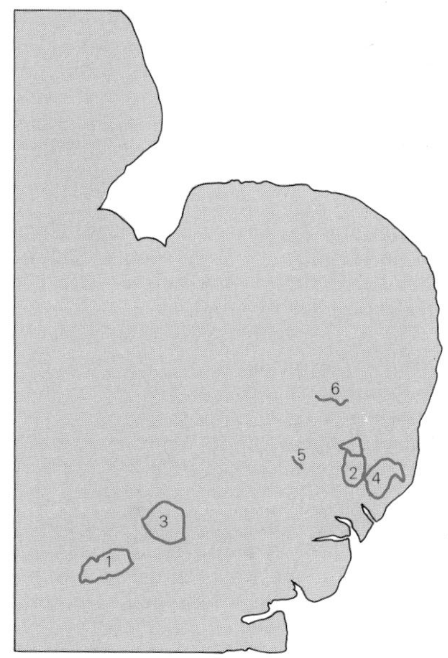

Day rides

1 Hertfordshire lanes, west from Bishop's Stortford, about 37 miles (59 km). Large portions of Hertfordshire are built up, but this is a pleasant rural area with a sprinkling of picturesque villages. *Bishop's Stortford – Sacombe – Bishop's Stortford;* **page 173.**

2 South-east Suffolk, Framlingham, Saxtead Mill and Debenham, about 40 miles (64 km). A fine introduction to the joys of riding Suffolk lanes. Here, even trunk roads carry less through traffic than A and B roads in other parts of the country. Very easy cycling (though the country is not actually flat), hence the comparatively high day's mileage, which can be shortened to 32 miles (51 km). *Woodbridge – Wickham Market – Letheringham – Framlingham – Cretingham–Woodbridge, with the option to shorten the route by leaving out the Debenham loop, cutting from Easton to Cretingham;* **page 180.**

3 North-west Essex, Thaxted, Finchingfield and Ashdon, about 34 miles (54 km).

Selected tours

Through one of the most beautiful parts of Essex, wandering along backroads in rolling countryside. Saffron Walden is a lovely old town and an ideal starting point. *Saffron Walden–Finchingfield – Castle Camps – Saffron Walden;* **pages 174, 178.**

4 East Suffolk, Orford and Snape, about 37 miles (59 km). Easy, family cycling, largely through forest, and so useful in poor weather. Though near the coast, little is seen of it unless diversions are made. *Woodbridge – Orford – Blaxhall – Woodbridge;* **pages 180, 181.**

5 Four isolated Suffolk churches, centred on Stowmarket, about 20 miles (32 km). A meandering route designed to visit some interesting churches in remarkable settings: an introduction to Suffolk's great heritage of churches. *Stowmarket – Gipping – Needham Market – Buxhall–Stowmarket;* **page 179.**

6 Norfolk–Suffolk border, attractive villages east from Diss, about 34 miles (54 km). An interesting ride, with several excellent pubs along the way, in remote countryside, and a few welcome undulations. *Diss – Hoxne – Syleham – Wingfield – Stradbroke – Laxfield – Brockdish – Pulham Market – Shimpling–Diss;* **page 184.**

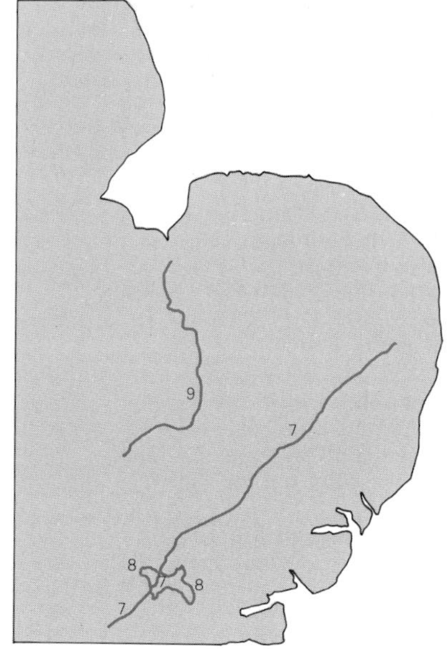

Two-day tours

7 Epping to Beccles, a ride out of London into East Anglia, about 120 miles (192 km). A long, relatively straight ride, designed to be ridden north-eastwards, but perfectly feasible in the reverse direction. There is scarcely a slope, and cyclists wanting a challenge could complete it in a long day, returning by train; but most will enjoy it more as a weekend away, or a longer holiday. Strategically placed stations on the route offer chances to shorten the journey. *Epping–The Rodings – Great Dunmow – Wethersfield – Sudbury – Hoxne – Bungay – Beccles;* **pages 173, 174, 179, 184, 185.**

8 Hatfield Forest and The Rodings, about 50 miles (80 km). Peaceful, often meandering cycling on quiet backroads close to London. An easy family ride, with no hills of consequence, which could be completed in a day, even by a group, given an early start. *Chelmsford – Felsted – Bran End – High Roding – Hatfield Broad Oak–Beauchamp Roding – Good Easter–Chelmsford;* **page 174.**

Selected tours

9 Cambridge to King's Lynn, 56 miles (90 km). Don't be put off this ride by the knowledge that the direct route from Cambridge to north Norfolk is boring, and a nightmare of fast, heavy traffic. This indirect route keeps largely to the Fenland 'Shore', where a succession of beautiful churches was built with the profits reaped from the rich arable country. Rail access at either end. *Cambridge – Newmarket – Feltwell – King's Lynn*; **pages 177, 178, 182, 186.**

Three days or longer

10 Beccles to King's Lynn, about 110 miles (176 km). This is a superb introduction to the many facets of Norfolk. It wanders through some attractive and interesting villages, and almost entirely avoids the north Norfolk coast road, which is narrow, exposed and especially busy at holiday times. Rail access at either end. *Beccles – Thwaite St Mary – Norwich – Reepham – Holt – Field Dalling – Great Walsingham – Holkham Estate Road – Burnham Thorpe – Burnham Market – Fring – Castle Rising–King's Lynn*; **pages 185, 189, 192, 191, 190.**

Bedfordshire/Hertfordshire

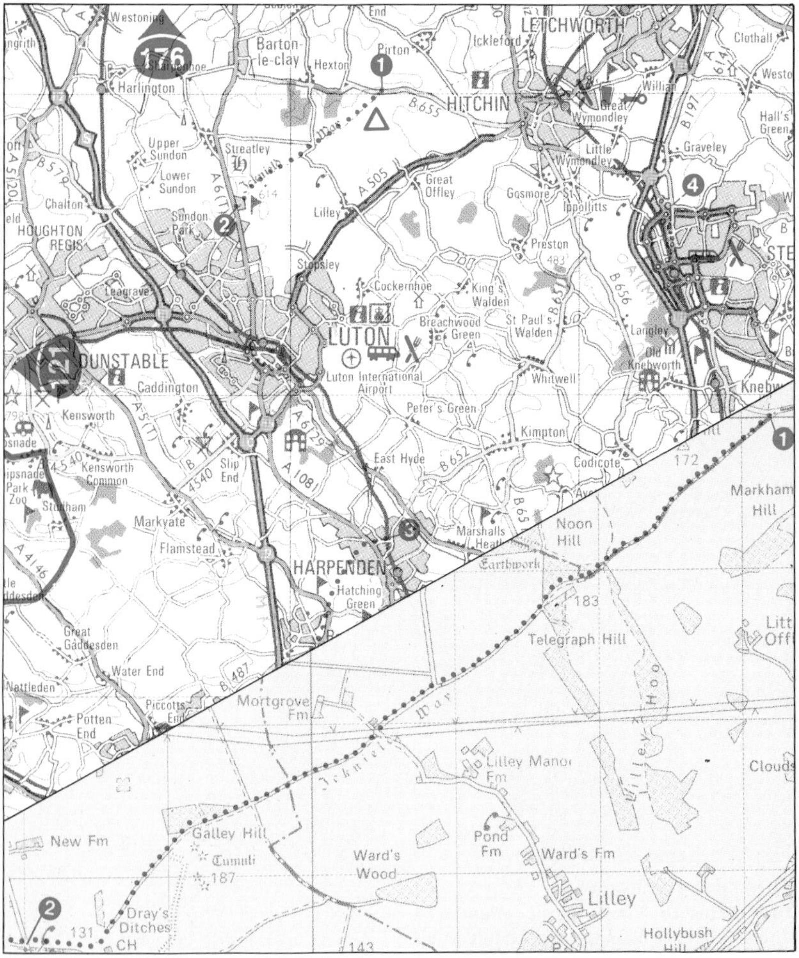

① Access to the Icknield Way about 1 mile (1.6 km) E of Pegsdon (not on map) and ② from the A6 about 4 miles (6.4 km) N of Luton town centre.

③ Access to the Harpenden–Hemel Hempstead disused railway line (Nicky Line) in Clarence Road off the A6 and (not on map) in Eggfield Road, Hemel Hempstead.

④ Stevenage has extensive cycle routing.

△ **The Icknield Way** goes over Telegraph Hill, one of the few significant climbs in the area; surface badly eroded in parts.

Luton on the London–Leicester main line; **Stevenage** on the London–Peterborough main line, both with frequent InterCity services.

Choices at **Luton, Stevenage, Hitchin**.

Hitchin is a fairly unspoiled market-town with several old inns.

Hitchin Frost 94/95 Walsworth Road.

Hertfordshire / Essex

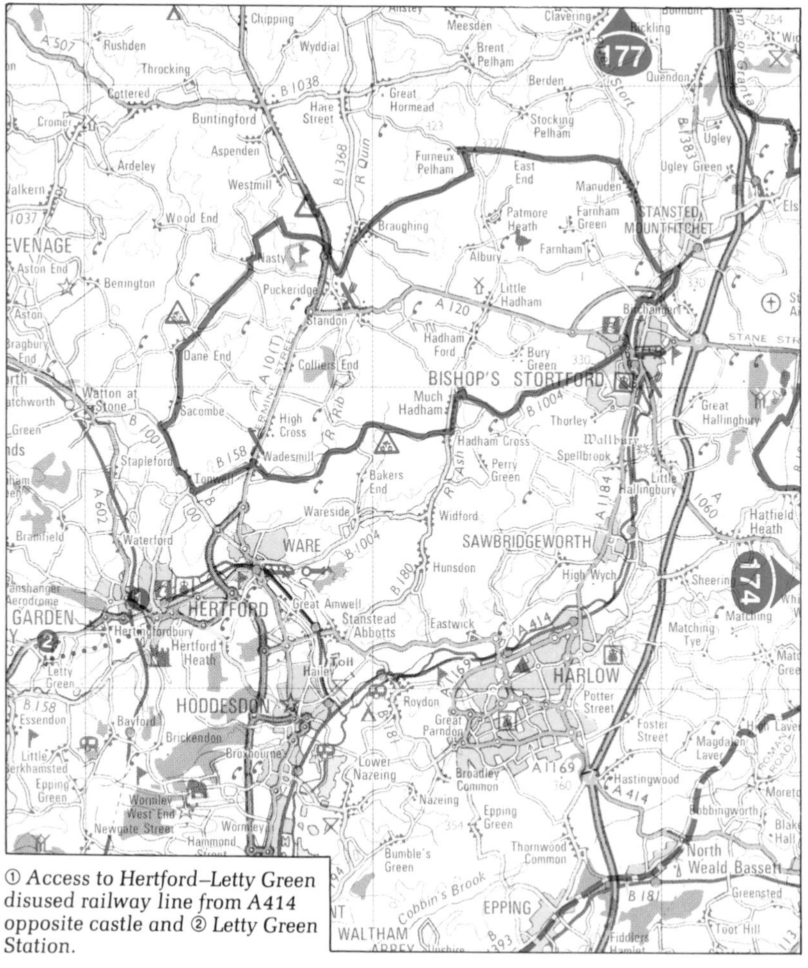

① *Access to Hertford–Letty Green disused railway line from A414 opposite castle and* ② *Letty Green Station.*

△ A few gradual climbs, but overall very easy; open countryside **west of Bishop's Stortford** easily explored on quiet lanes.

Regular service to **Bishop's Stortford** on London–Cambridge InterCity route; occasional services to **Ware** from Liverpool Street.

Bishop's Stortford, choices; pub meals at **Much Hadham**, **Wadesmill**, and **Puckeridge**.

The circuit follows mainly quiet back roads, the best of which are from **Much Hadham** to **Wadesmill**, and from **Sacombe** to **Westmill.**

The old vicarage in **Bishop's Stortford** is a museum associated with the 19th-C statesman Cecil Rhodes.

☆ To the east of **Hoddesdon**, the riverside Lea Valley Regional Park.

Ware, Highways Cycles, 1 New Road.

▲ **Harlow** 0279 21702.

Essex

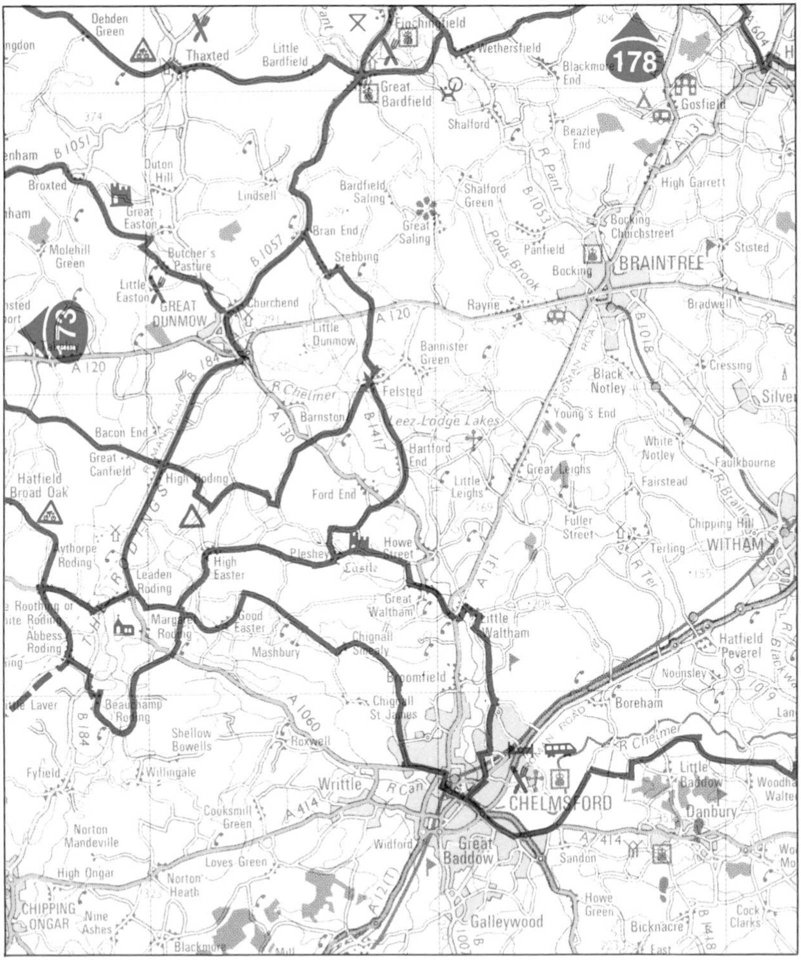

△ Generally easy cycling with no hills of consequence and exceptionally little traffic on the unclassified roads.

Frequent service to **Chelmsford** on the London–Norwich InterCity line.

Chelmsford, choices; pub meals and café at **Great Dunmow**; pub meals at **Thaxted** and **Finchingfield.**

The lane through **Debden Green** to **Thaxted** and beyond is delightful; good cycling in **Hatfield Forest**.

Pleshey village is enclosed in an earthen rampart with a huge motte and bailey on the south side; motte and bailey castle at **Great Easton.**

Several fine churches in **The Rodings**, a group of tiny picturesque villages in the valley of the River Roding.

Finchingfield has a fine green.

Great Bardfield, revived local crafts.

B & B **Chelmsford**, Tanuda Hotel, New London Road.

Essex

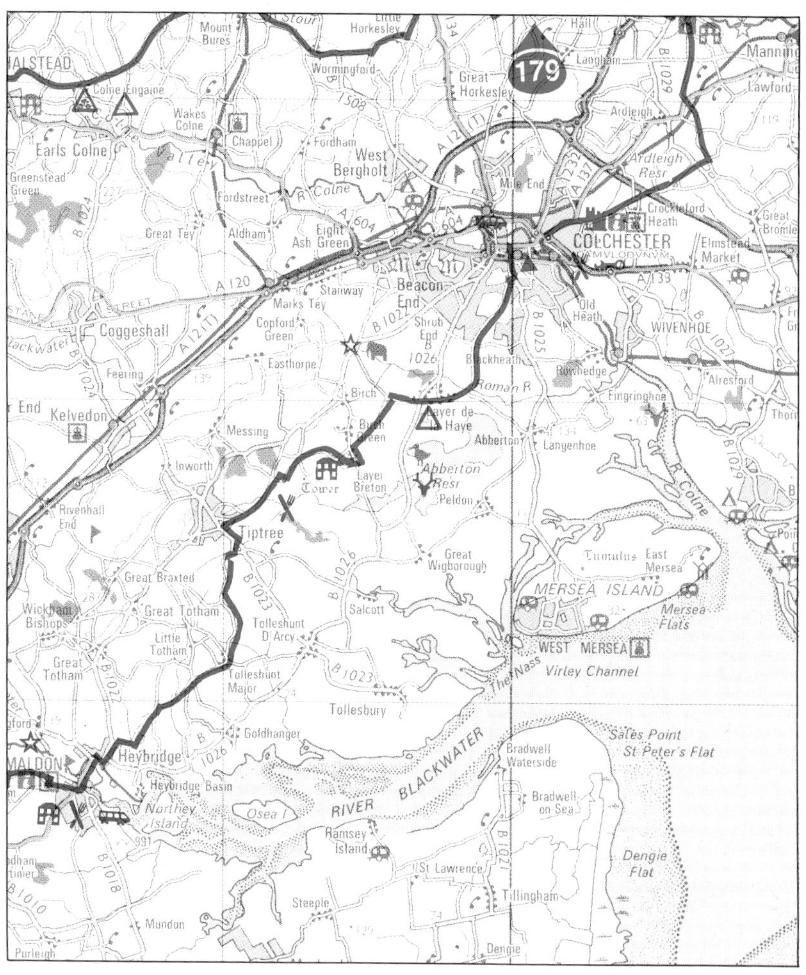

- △ **Saffron Walden–Colchester** generally flat; undulations in the **Colne Valley.**
- Frequent InterCity services to **Colchester** from London Liverpool Street.
- **Colchester**, choices; **Tiptree, Maldon**, limited choices.
- Pleasant cycling in the **Colne Valley.**
- **Colchester** was stormed in AD 62 by Boadicea; it has a Norman castle with a museum; the city walls are best seen on the western side.
- ☆ **Maldon**, on the River Blackwater, a picturesque port and yachting resort.
- Beeleigh Abbey, 1 mile (1.6 km) west of **Maldon** by footpath, is a 16th-C house; Layer Marney Hall (near **Layer Breton**) is 13th-C.
- ☆ Zoo at Stanway Hall near **Layer-de-la-Haye.**
- Wildlife at **Abberton** Reservoir.
- **Colchester** Cycle Store, St John Street.
- ▲ **Colchester** 0206 867982.

Bedfordshire/Cambridgeshire

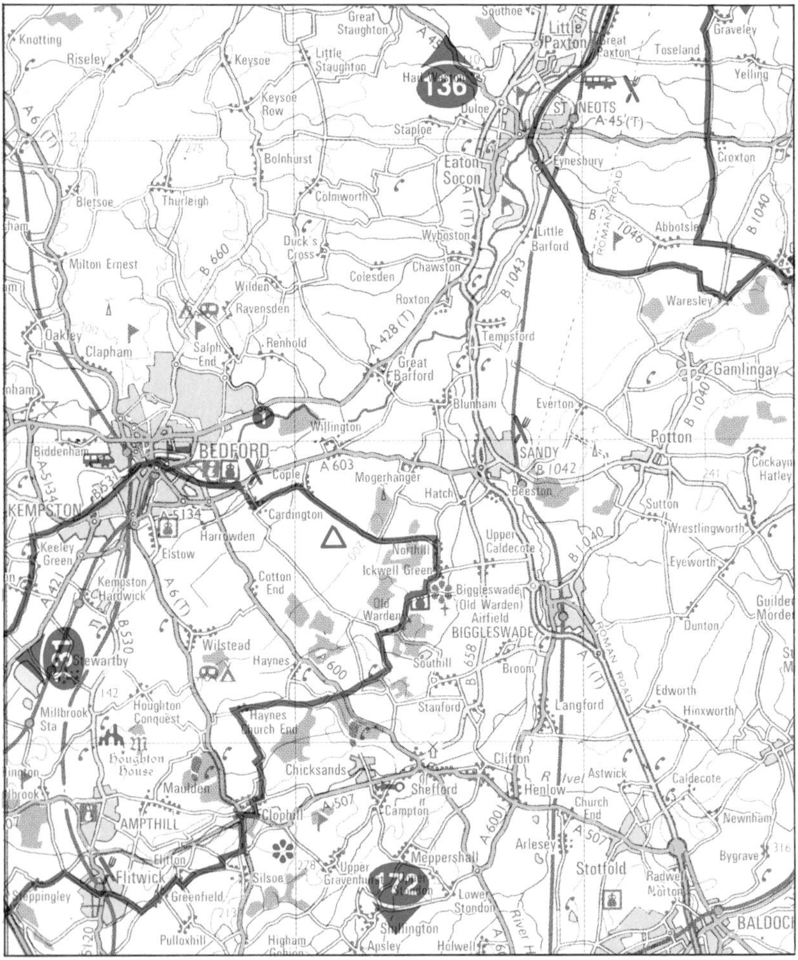

① Bedfordshire has an extensive cycle way system.

△ Though less flat than other areas of East Anglia, the going is easy overall; very little traffic on **country lanes.**

Frequent InterCity services, **Bedford**; regular services, **St Neots**.

Choices at **Bedford**; **St Neots**, **Sandy** and **Flitwick**, limited choices.

Houghton House, built in 1600 from designs by Inigo Jones.

Silsoe gardens feature one of the few 17th-C Dutch canal gardens.

Bedford Museum, also Bunyan Museum and boating on the Ouse; **Old Warden** The Shuttleworth Trust Museum displays historic aircraft dating from 1909, bicycles dating from 1868, and engines/cars from 1895.

Shefford Whitbread, 4 N. Bridge St.

B & B **Bedford**, Malanda, 75 Goldington Avenue.

Cambridgeshire / Hertfordshire

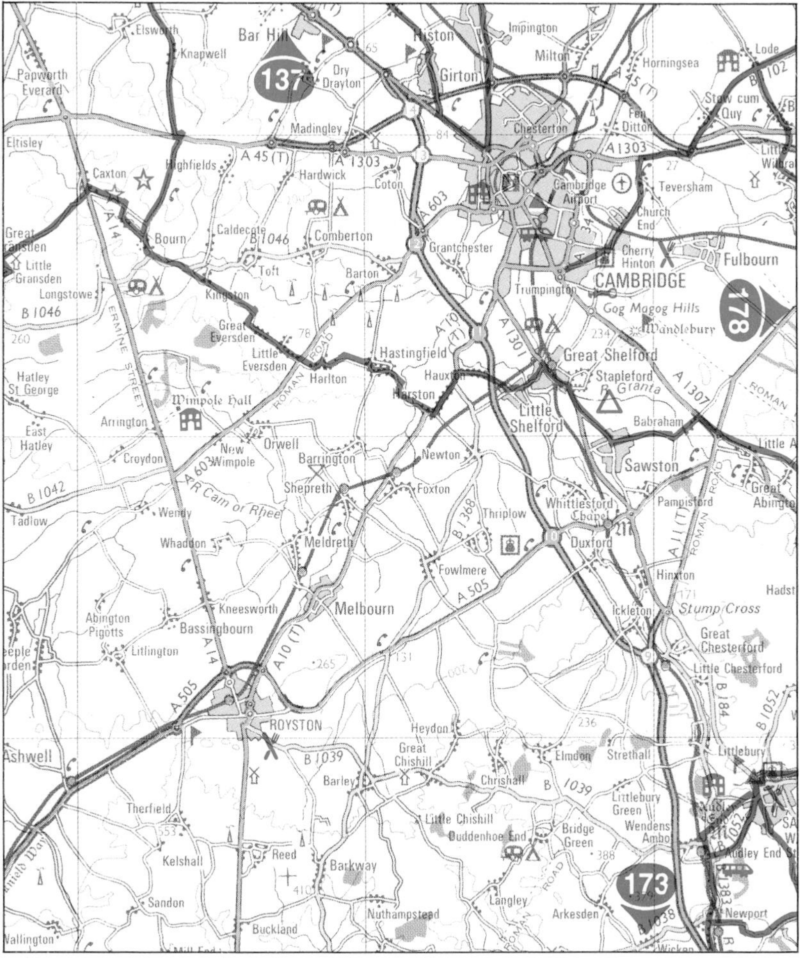

△ Peaceful cycling, though **Great Shelford** to **Sawston** is built up; the **Gog Magog Hills** to north of the marked route rise to all of 222 feet (68 m).

Frequent trains to **Cambridge** on London–King's Lynn InterCity route; many stop at **Audley End**.

Cambridge, choices; **Royston**, limited choices; pub meals and café at **Saffron Walden.**

☆ **Caxton**, reputedly the oldest windmill in England (closed for repairs 1984).

Audley End House, palatial Jacobean mansion and park; comparable is **Wimpole Hall** (Nat. Trust) – approach from the A603; the best buildings in **Cambridge**, a city of cyclists, are along the 'Backs' from King's College to Magdalene College.

Cambridge, Hayward, Laundress Lane.

▲ **Cambridge** 0223 354601.

Suffolk/Essex/Cambridgeshire

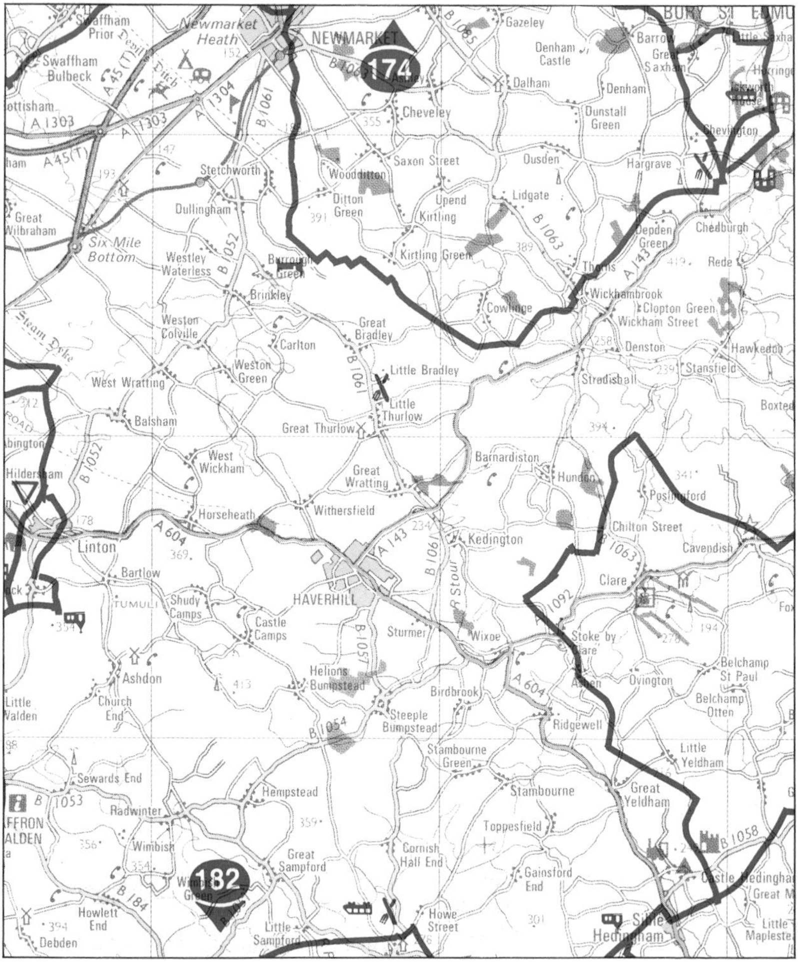

△ The route follows quiet byroads through gently undulating countryside with no really steep hills and few long climbs, though one through **Poslingford**.

Frequent services to **Newmarket** on the Cambridge–Ipswich line.

Newmarket, choices; **Haverhill**, limited choices.

Great Maplestead has one of the five round churches in England, built by the Knights Hospitallers.

Denston has perhaps the loveliest small church in Suffolk; at **Swaffham Prior** there are twin churches in the same churchyard.

Purton Green Farmhouse, **Stansfield**, is an aisled hall, probably 14th-C, the oldest timber-framed building in Europe.

B & B **Steeple Bumpstead**, 24 Water Lane.

Suffolk

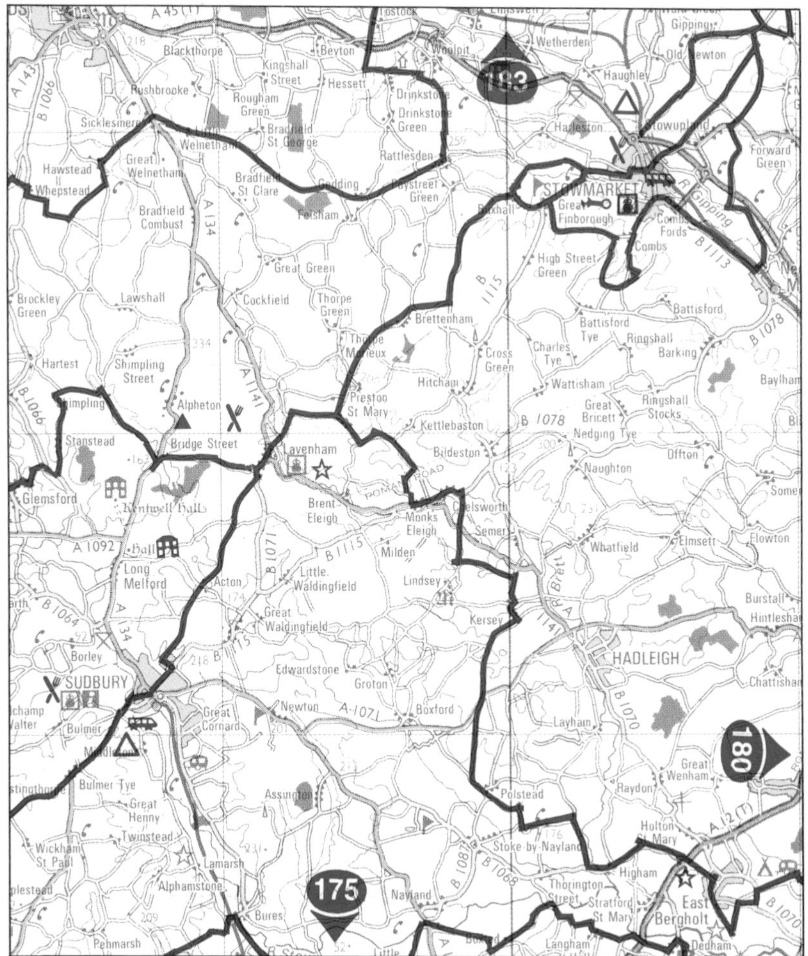

△ The **A131 approaching Sudbury** can become badly congested; particular care needed when crossing the **A45**.

🚌 **Sudbury**, regular services on line from Colchester; **Stowmarket**, frequent InterCity service on London–Norwich route.

✗ **Sudbury**, **Stowmarket**, choices; **Lavenham**, limited choices.

▣ **Stowmarket**, museum of rural life.

☆ **Long Melford**, with its 16th-C Hall and one of the most splendid perpendicular churches in the country; **Lavenham**, picturesque and unspoiled Saxon village, museum of local life; **East Bergholt**, birthplace of Constable – his paintings immortalize the Stour district.

🔧 **Stowmarket**, Not Just Bikes, 31 Stowupland Road.

▲ **Alpheton**, Cockfield Green (0284) 828297.

Suffolk

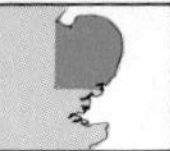

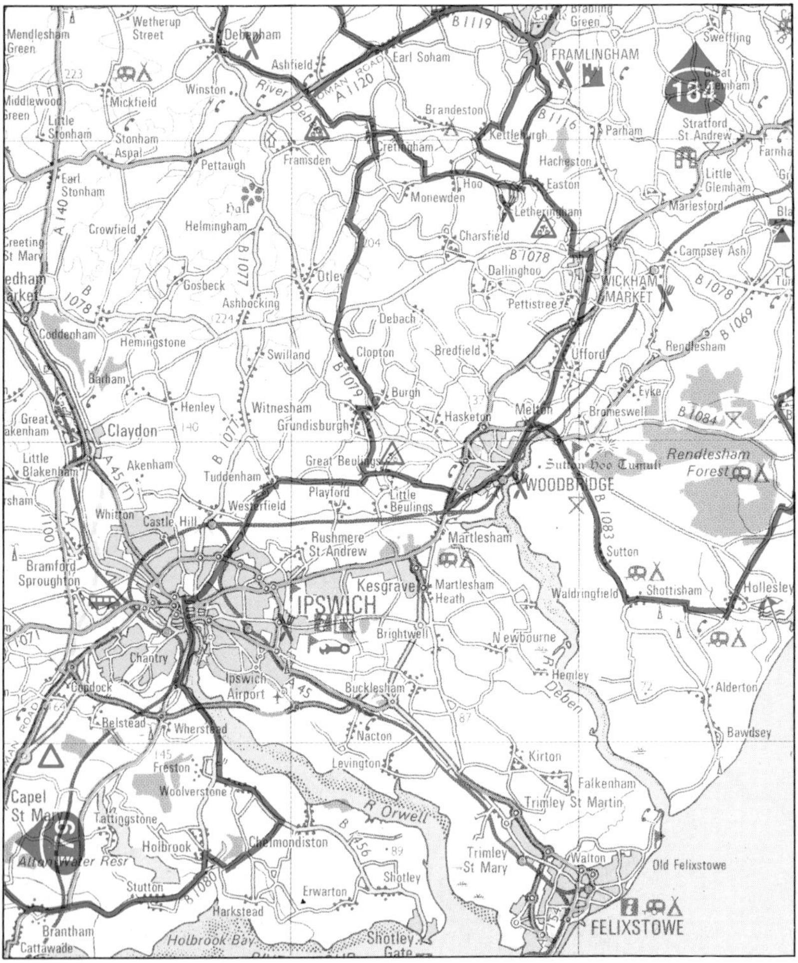

△ Apart from the busy **A12**, even the trunk roads carry less through traffic than most A and B roads.

Frequent InterCity service to **Ipswich** on the London–Norwich line.

Ipswich, choices; pub meals and cafés at **Woodbridge**, **Framlingham** and **Debenham**; pub meals at **Wickham Market** and **Saxtead Green**; tea rooms at **Letheringham** Mill.

Best cycling is through the Deben Valley from **Wickham Market** to **Kettleburgh**, and on lanes from **Debenham** to **Cretingham** and from **Grundisburgh** to **Woodbridge.**

Site of the **Sutton Hoo** Saxon ship burial.

Framlingham Castle, with moat and 13 towers.

Ipswich, Jacobi's Cycles, 74/6 Norwich Road.

▲ **Blaxhall**, Snape (07288) 206.

Suffolk

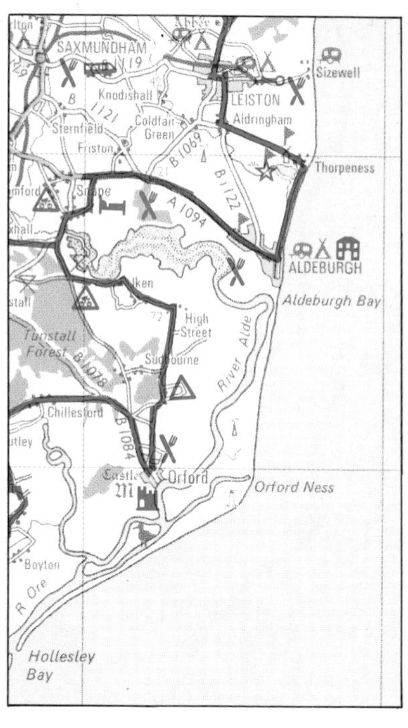

- Exceptionally peaceful and flat; the route is often through **forest**, and although this is a coastal region, little is seen of the shore itself.
- Regular service to **Saxmundham** on Ipswich–Lowestoft line.
- **Saxmundham**, **Leiston**, **Aldeburgh**, limited choices; cafés and pub meals at **Orford**, in village and at quay; tea rooms at **Snape**.
- Best cycling is on the byway from Orford to Snape via **Iken**, and from **Snape** to Campsey Ash.
- Unclassified road from **Hollesley** leads to beach at Shingle Street (4 miles (6.5 km) return).
- Picturesque **Orford** has a massive 12th-C castle keep which forms an 18-sided polygon.
- **Thorpeness**, a seaside village beloved by generations of holidaymakers.
- **Aldeburgh**, Moot Hall amid encroaching shingle.
- **Leiston**, Nunns, 100 High Street.
- B & B **Snape**, Rose Villa, The Street.

The elegant bar-tailed godwit, a wader of the east Suffolk wetlands.

Cambridgeshire/Suffolk/Norfolk

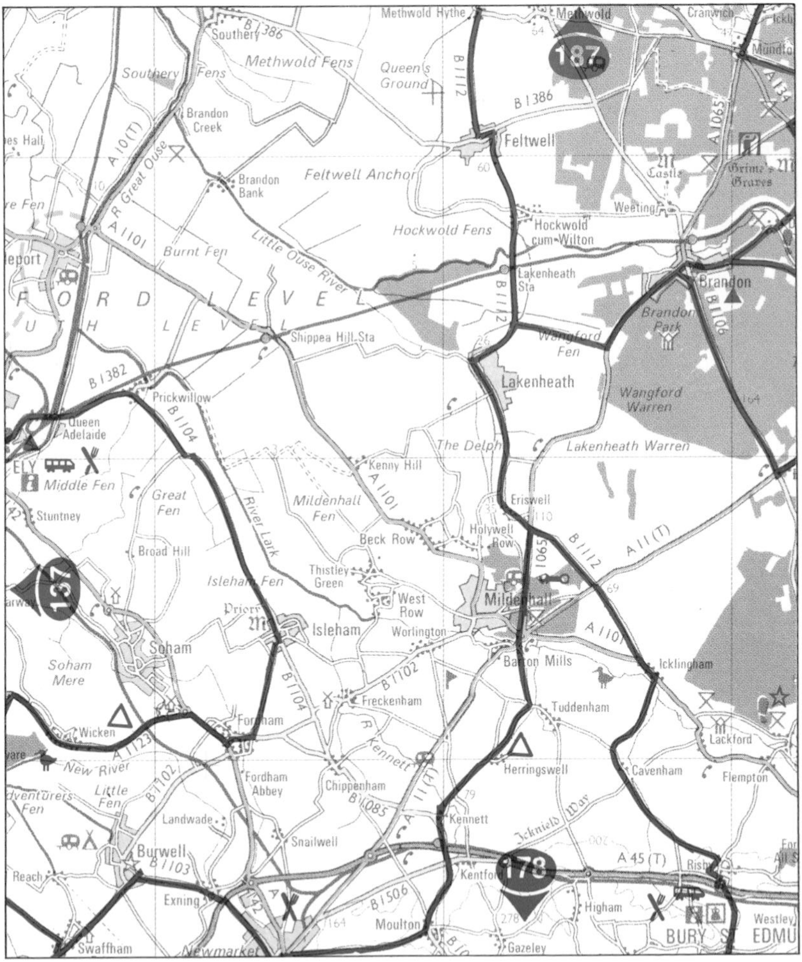

△ Virtually flat; traffic may be fast on the narrow **A1123**; mostly quiet lanes, for example **between Tuddenham and Herringswell**.

🚌 **Newmarket** (name not on this map), **Bury St Edmunds**, regular service on Cambridge–King's Lynn route, infrequent service on Ely–Norwich line.

✗ **Ely, Newmarket, Bury St Edmunds.**

Grime's Graves, prehistoric flint mines with shafts and galleries open.

Wicken Fen (Nat. Trust), the oldest nature reserve in Britain.

† **Ely**, one of the great cathedrals.

☆ **West Stow** Anglo-Saxon village.

Mildenhall, Morley's, 32a High Street.

▲ **Ely**, only open July 22–Sept 1 – bookings up to July 25 to YHA Regional Office, 40 Calver Street East, Colchester, otherwise to St Mary's Street, Colchester; **Brandon** Thetford (0842) 812075.

Norfolk/Suffolk

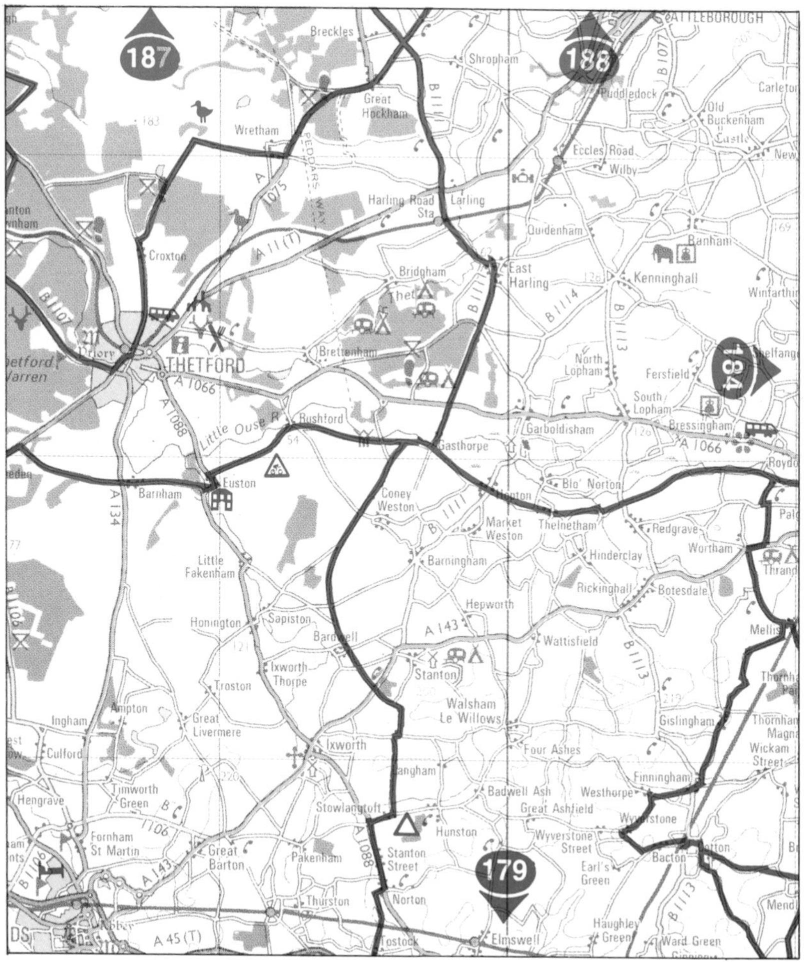

△ Virtually flat; **A1088** may be busy.

Diss, frequent service on London–Norwich InterCity route; infrequent service to **Thetford** and other stations on Birmingham–Norwich line.

Thetford, limited choices.

Thetford, scanty remains of three medieval religious houses; fine castle mound.

17th-C **Euston Hall** gave its name to Euston Station, built on London property owned by the Dukes of Grafton, former owners of the Hall.

East Wretham, fine nature reserve.

Thetford Forest (and Lakenheath Warren – see page 182), nature trail: red squirrels, deer, golden pheasants.

Route follows **Little Ouse River**; **S of Thetford** route passes through Breckland, heath with firs and small meres.

B & B **Bury St Edmunds**, The Lilacs, 18 Horsecroft Road.

Norfolk/Suffolk

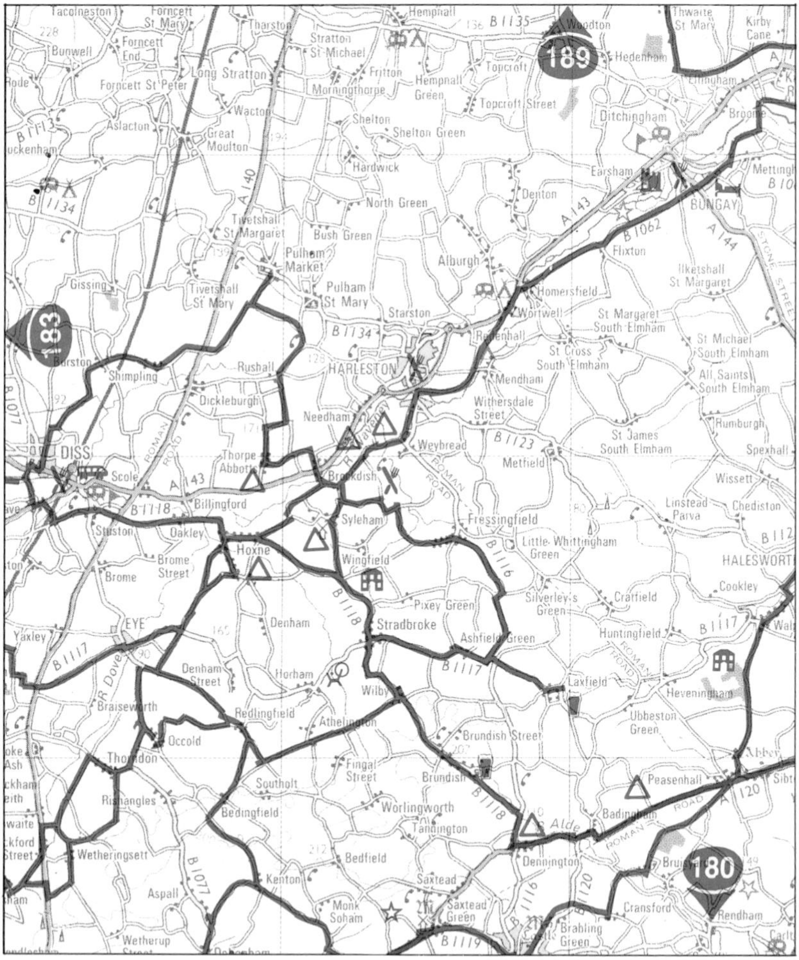

△ A virtually flat area except for steep climbs E into **Hoxne**, S into **Dennington**, E out of **Badingham**; undulations S of the **River Waveney** are greater than N of it; potholes between **Syleham** and **Wingfield**; lorries on **A143**.

Diss, frequent InterCity service on Norwich–Ipswich line.

Diss, **Harleston**, **Bungay**, limited choices; cooked meals at the Greyhound, **Brockdish**.

The Crown, **Brundish**, garden; local Adnams beer, King's Head, **Laxfield.**

Heveningham Hall is 18th C; 14th-C **Wingfield** College, open Sundays in summer.

Castle ruins at **Bungay.**

Pottery (open) on right of **Stradbroke–Wilby** road.

☆ Working windmill, **Saxtead Green**.

B & B M. Sheppard, 22 Quayes Lane, **Bungay**.

Norfolk / Suffolk

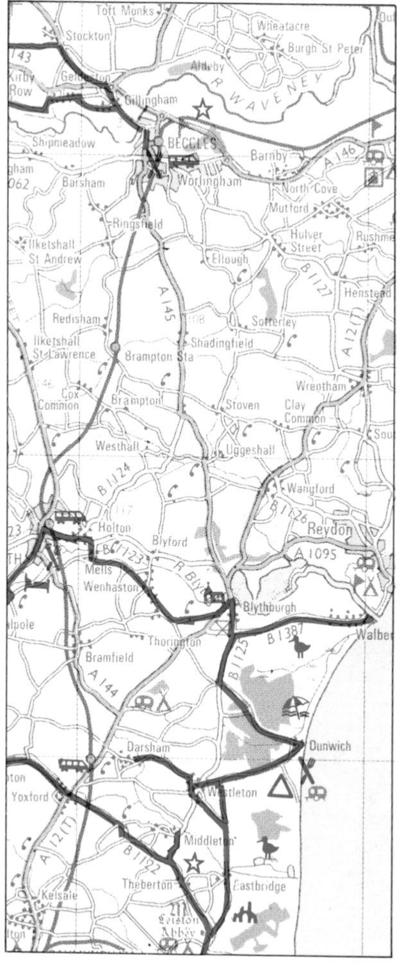

△ **Dunwich** crowded in summer.

Beccles, Halesworth, Darsham on the Ipswich–Lowestoft line: occasional services, though frequent in late afternoons.

Beccles, Halesworth, limited choices; **Beccles** is noted for its crayfish. The Ship, **Dunwich**, serves meals.

Dunwich, beach rather gravelly, but still a pleasant place to swim.

☆ **Beccles**, sailing and angling on the River Waveney.

Famous RSPB bird reserve at Minsmere near **Theberton**, a wild marsh and reed habitat extending over a large area; one of Britain's finest coastal National Nature Reserves at **Walberswick.**

Leiston Abbey, 12th-C ruins.

B & B, **Halesworth**, Fen-Way, School Lane.

Above, the bearded tit, inhabitant of the coastal marshlands and reedbeds at Walberswick.

Left, hen harrier, one of the winter highlights of Walberswick, quartering the reeds, wings slightly raised during the long glides it takes between lazy flapping.

Norfolk/Cambridgeshire

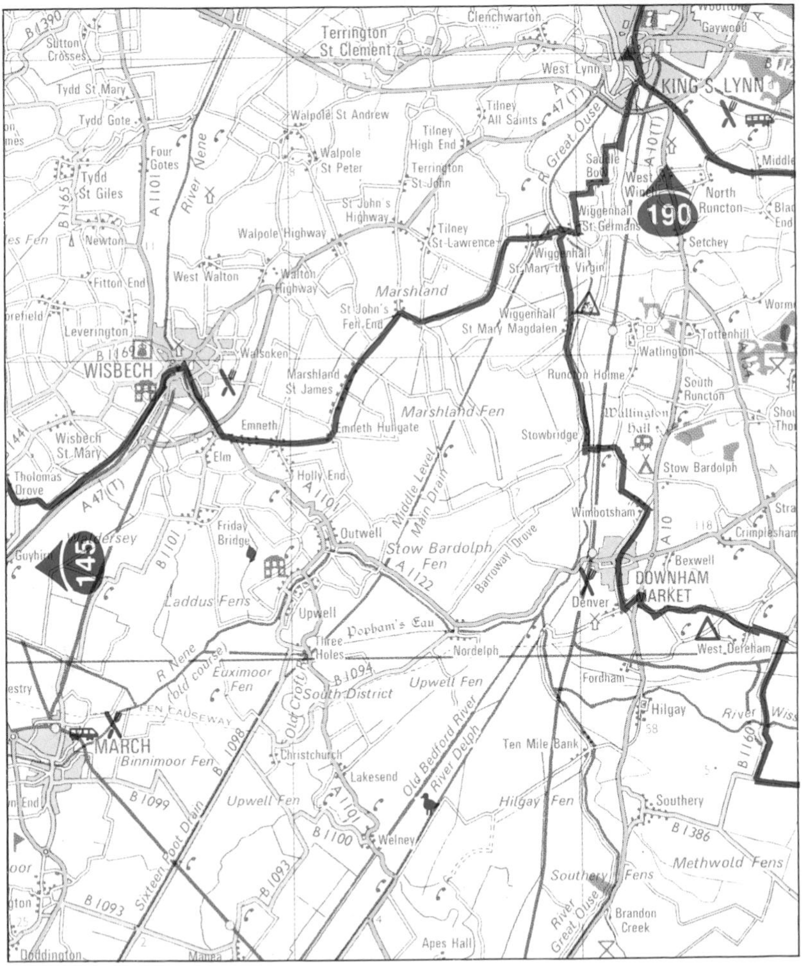

△ Virtually flat; **King's Lynn** busy in summer; careful map-reading required on the twisting route **between Denver and Methwold Hythe**.

🚌 **King's Lynn** and other stations on the London–King's Lynn line, regular services; frequent service to **March** on the Ely–Peterborough line.

✗ **King's Lynn**, **Wisbech**, **March** and **Downham Market**, choices.

⚠ Pleasant route alongside the **Great Ouse River**, on Fen shoreline. An inspiring feature of cycling in Norfolk is its ever-changing skies.

🐦 Detour to **Welney Wildlife Refuge** next to the Ouse Washes, one of the great areas in Europe for wildfowl, with hides, observatory, floodlighting (closed June–July).

🏛 **King's Lynn** is a town of fine buildings ranging from the 14th to 19th C.

▲ **King's Lynn** 0553 2461.

Norfolk

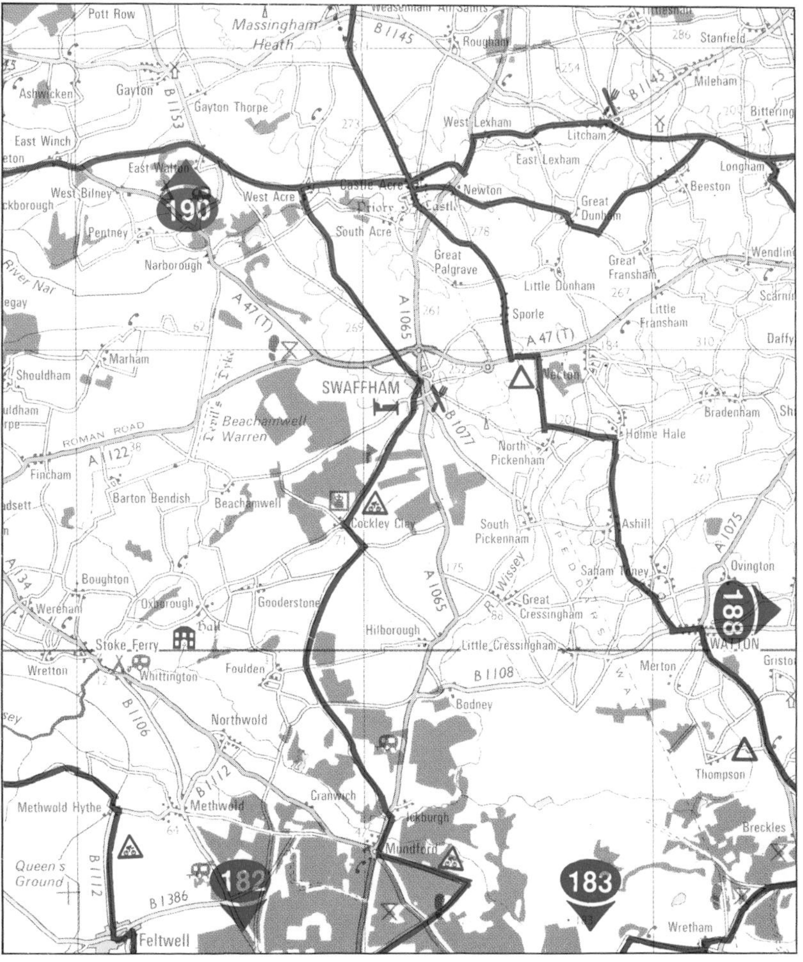

① Access to Peddars Way at the obvious right bend in the Roman road between Castle Acre and Great Massingham: track well-signposted, easy to follow.

△ Little traffic, but care needed when crossing the **A47**; unpaved parts of **Peddars Way** can be heavy going.

Nearest **station** is Downham Market, page 186, frequent service on the Cambridge–King's Lynn line; or Wymondham, page 188.

Swaffham, limited choices.

Higher ground comes as a welcome change **S of Methwold Hythe** ('Hythe' meant landing place – on the Fen shoreline).

Oxborough Hall (Nat. Trust), 15th-C moated mansion with 80-foot (24-m) gatehouse; grounds with woodland walk.

B & B **Swaffham**, Purbeck House, Whitsands Road.

Norfolk/Suffolk

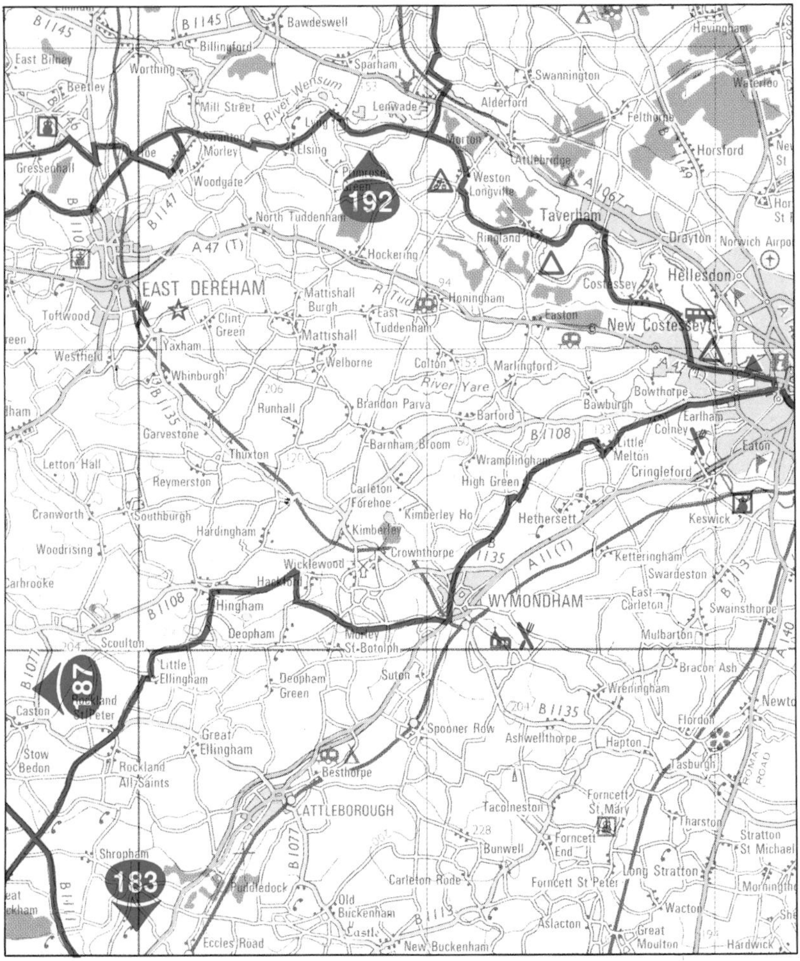

△ Gentle undulations through Ringland Hills **S of the A1067**, otherwise flat; busy short stretch on **A47** W of Norwich.

🚆 **Norwich**, frequent InterCity service on Liverpool St–Norwich route; regular services, **Wymondham** on the Norwich–Ely line.

✗ **Norwich**, choices; **East Dereham**, **Wymondham**, limited choices.

▣ **Gressenhall**, Rural Life Museum; **Norwich**, fine collection of Norfolk school paintings.

⚠ Valley of the River Wensum, **Lyng to Ringland**, with steep wooded cliffs.

⛪ **Wymondham** (pronounced 'Windham') has one of the finest churches in Norfolk.

☆ **East Dereham**, tomb of the 18th-C poet William Cowper, who wrote the famous ballad of John Gilpin's ride.

▲ **Norwich** 0603 27647.

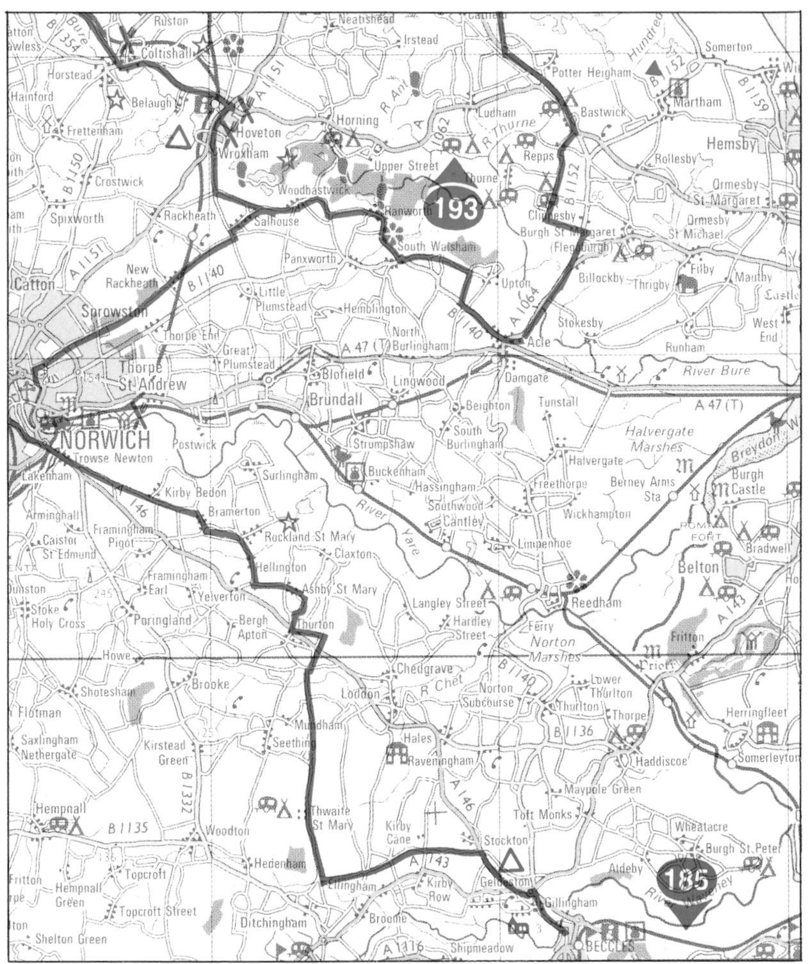

△ Virtually flat and mostly clear of traffic except for **A416 near Beccles**; **Wroxham** and **Hoveton** busy in summer.

Norwich, frequent InterCity service; further choices on lines from Norwich to Lowestoft, Yarmouth and Cromer.

Norwich, Wroxham, Coltishall.

☆ The Broads are shallow lagoons and long expanses of reed and fen; **Wroxham Broad** is 'Queen of the Broads'; Neatishead gives glimpses of Barton Broad; Wroxham–Hoveton is the centre for boat hire and river trips; much wildfowl in the reed beds of **Rockland Broad. Coltishall** is a boating and angling centre with a picturesque lock; **Belaugh**, picturesque green, boats and peace.

Gillingham is pure early-Norman.

Norwich, Kirby, 5 St Benedicts Street.

▲ **Martham**, Great Yarmouth (0493) 740430.

Norfolk

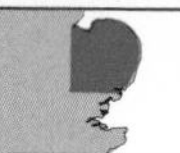

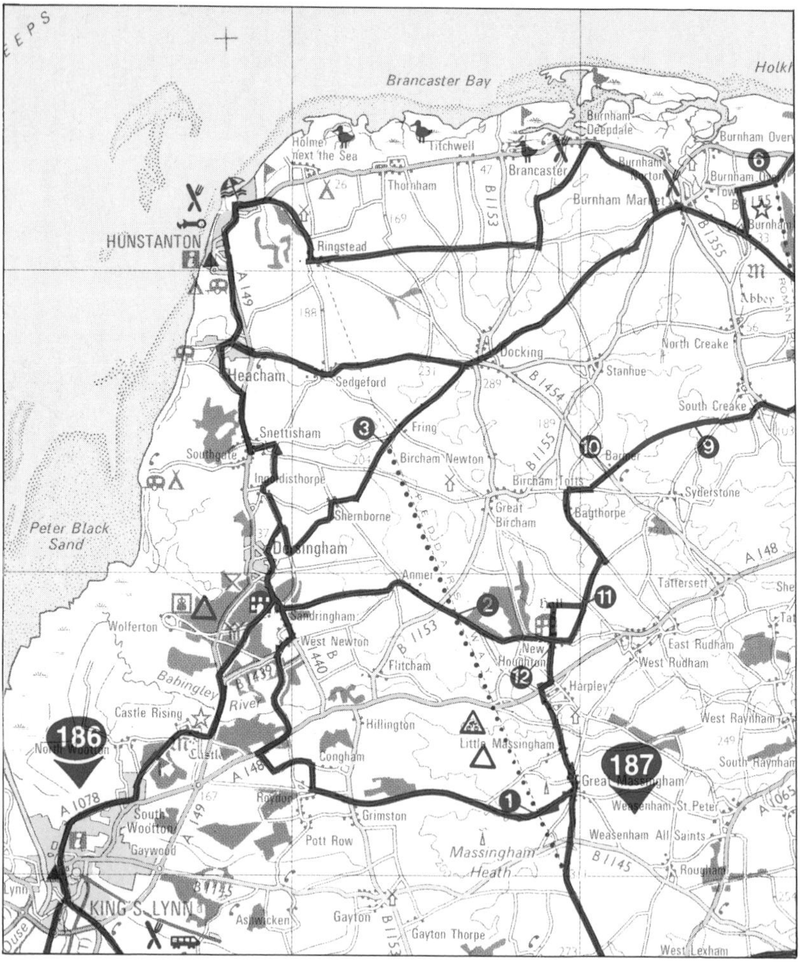

△ Avoid the **A419** between King's Lynn and Sandringham.

Regular InterCity services to King's Lynn from London.

Choices at **King's Lynn**; pub meals and restaurant in **Hunstanton**; good local fish at **Burnham Market, Brancaster**.

Peddars Way gives a fine feeling of isolation in sections away from roads.

☆ Admiral Nelson was born at **Burnham Thorpe**.

Hunstanton and E, sandy beach.

Here is some of the best birdwatching in Europe: 30 miles (48 km) that include **Titchwell Marsh, Brancaster** and **Holme Nature Reserves**.

Sandringham House, a residence of the Royal Family, cycling on some roads through estate.

Hunstanton, Crown, 92 Westgate.

▲ **Hunstanton** 04853 2061; **King's Lynn** 0553 2461.

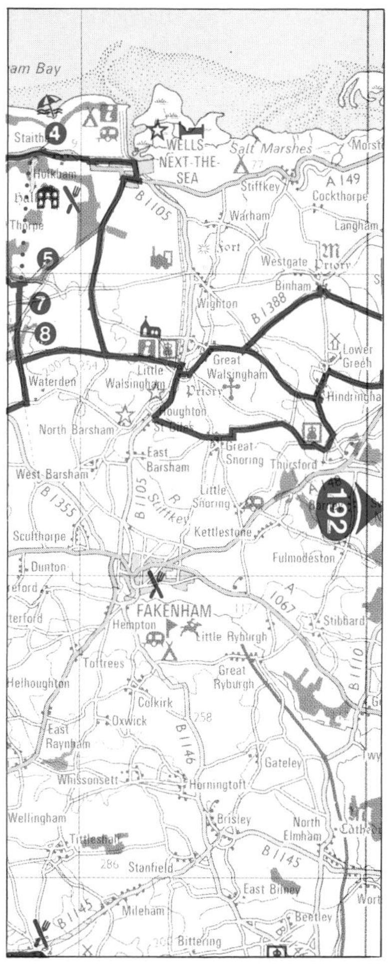

① ②, ③ and other intersections with roads give access to Peddars Way. From ③ NE the Way becomes a footpath rather than a bridleway – no right of way for cyclists, do dismount and push. Unpaved sections make for heavy going, but this 'unofficial' long distance path is fine cycling.

④ By courtesy of Lord Coke of Holkham Hall, Holkham estate roads may be used by cyclists. ④ marks the main entrance (North Drive), conspicuous on the coast road; open 9–6 on weekdays and, by the side gate, at weekends. The south entrance, ⑤, is open 9–6 on weekdays only. The west entrance, ⑥, is open 9–6 on weekdays only. Please keep strictly to the tarmac estate roads, easily followed.

If going S from ⑤, make for the triumphal arch. At ⑦ cross the unclassified road as indicated (if cycling N, make for the obelisk). At ⑧ the tarmac road indicated by the green line (but not by the Routemaster mapping) is easily located. ⑨ indicates another tarmac lane not shown by Routemaster mapping: access obvious from Bloodgate Hill SW of South Creake. No problems route-finding between ⑨ and ⑫ – road leads straight ahead (ignore crossing tracks). ⑩ is easily located at Barmer – telephone box close by. ⑪ marks a further tarmac lane, unsignposted, but obvious at the crossroads indicated by Routemaster. At ⑫, a crossing of lanes, turn left if cycling the route N–S, or right if vice-versa. ⑫ marks access to a tarmac lane along the Houghton Hall estate boundary. Houghton has restricted opening times; ring Tourist Information, Norwich, 0603 20679.

△ Not really seaside riding as a saltmarsh plain stretches out in front.

Café at **Litcham**; **Wells**, **Fakenham**, limited choices; the Globe Inn, **Wells**, is pleasant to sit outside.

The shrines at **Little Walsingham** have attracted pilgrims for centuries.

Holkham Gap, on the coast opposite **Holkham**, is a wide, windswept beach with pine-studded dunes reached by a formal drive; sandy beach extending W from **Wells-next-the-Sea**.

Holkham Hall, the huge white brick house of the Earls of Leicester.

☆ At **Wells** a steam train takes passengers a mile to the beach; whelks are boiled in sheds at E end of quay.

B & B **Wells**, Arch House, 50 Mill Road.

Norfolk

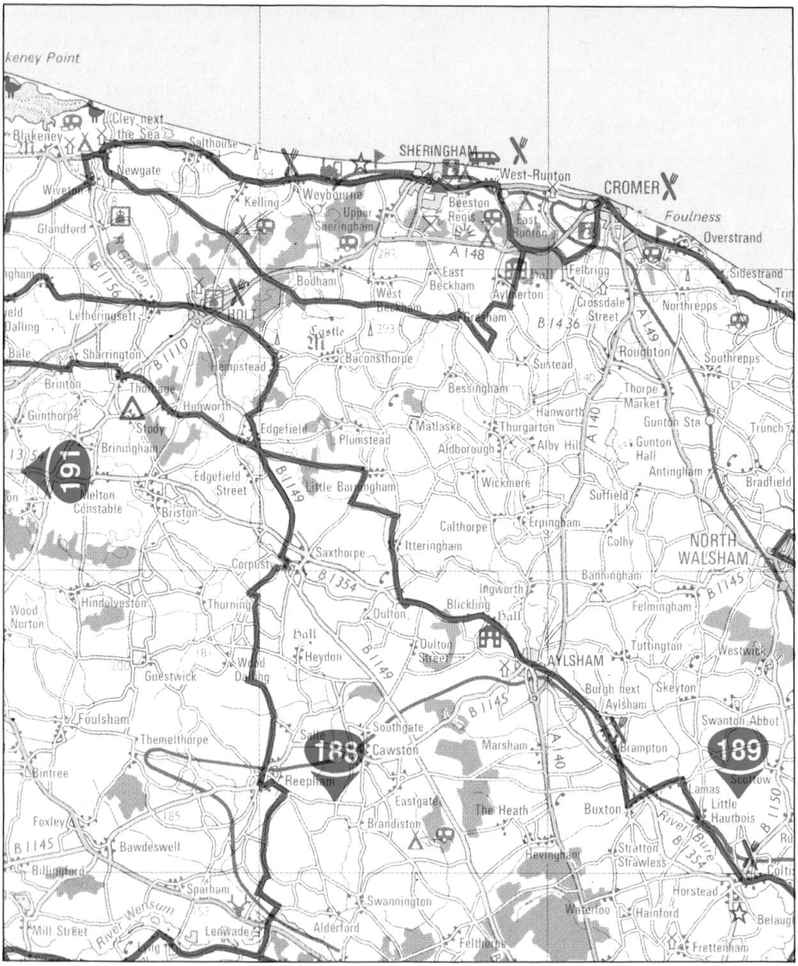

△ The narrow, winding coastal road often carries fast traffic with swaying caravans; the cyclist who braves it in winter should be prepared for cold conditions (weather: Norwich 0603 8091); gradients easy (with a few exceptions, for example **Stody** and **Hunworth**).

🚂 **Sheringham**, infrequent service on line from Norwich.

✗ Restaurant at **Weybourne**; **Sheringham**, **Cromer**, **Holt**, **Aylsham**, limited choices.

🏛 **Blickling Hall** in 4,500-acre park.

🐦 The Norfolk Naturalists' Trust reserve at **Cley** is the most famous bird sanctuary in Britain; nature reserve at **Blakeney Point**, with wildlife trips by motor boat.

☆ Steam train from **Sheringham** to Weybourne.

▲ **Sheringham** 0263 823215.

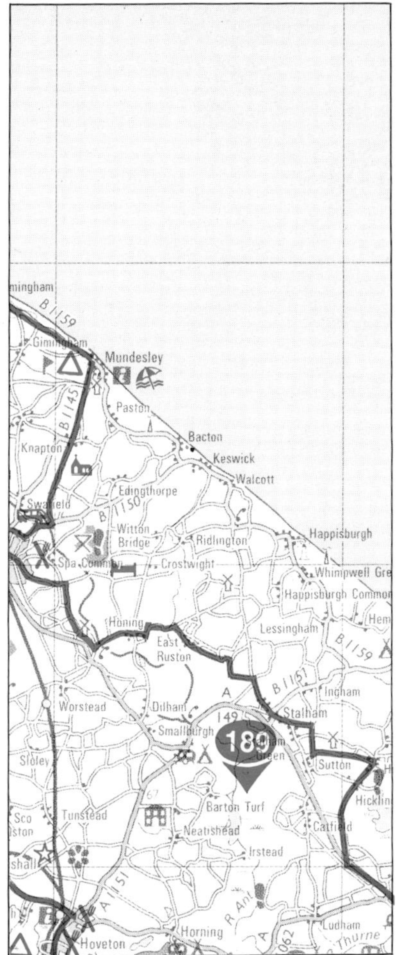

△ **Coast road** narrow and busy, otherwise straightforward, flat cycling.

Regular services to **North Walsham** (see page 192) on Norwich–Sheringham line.

Hoveton, North Walsham, choices.

Mundesley, seaside resort with fine sands, cliffs and visitor attractions.

Knapton church has a double hammerbeam roof.

B & B **Witton**, Old Rectory.

Blicking Hall, with its mellow brick gables and pinnacles. The four corner turrets with lead caps are distinctive; the showpiece of the interior is the Gallery's magnificent ceiling. Anne Boleyn spent her childhood in a previous house on the site.

6

NORTHERN ENGLAND

This region contains three of the great upland areas of England – arguably *the* three greatest: the Lake District, the Pennines and the North York Moors. A fourth upland area, the Yorkshire Wolds, north of the Humber, is hilly, but not on the same scale.

The beauties and characteristics of the first three are endlessly talked and written about, and the fourth generally less so; either way, this does not much help the cyclist who has never toured the region before. He, or she, wants some kind of perspective on their relative difficulty.

Heading the league, unquestionably deserving the category of extremely strenuous, is the Lake District. The climbs are many, very long and very steep, and the off-highway riding, grand as it may be, is generally as rough as rough can be.

Next come the Pennines – covering several touring areas – and on this scale best categorized as plain strenuous. At their southern end is the northern part of the Peak District – High Peak – where the climbs come rapid and steep if you ride against the 'grain' of the hills. North from the Peak District, the term 'Pennines' encompasses the South Pennines, the Dales and the North Pennines. You cannot tour them without climbing, more or less continuously, but on the whole the slopes are long but gradual, or steep but short.

By contrast, the North York Moors are merely hard work. Once up on the plateau, there is plenty of ridge riding, or flat valley-floor cycling to compensate for the initial effort.

Bottom of the league are, of course, the Yorkshire Wolds: small, gently contoured chalk hills, with plenty of easy valley riding to offset steepish climbs to the tops.

Selected tours

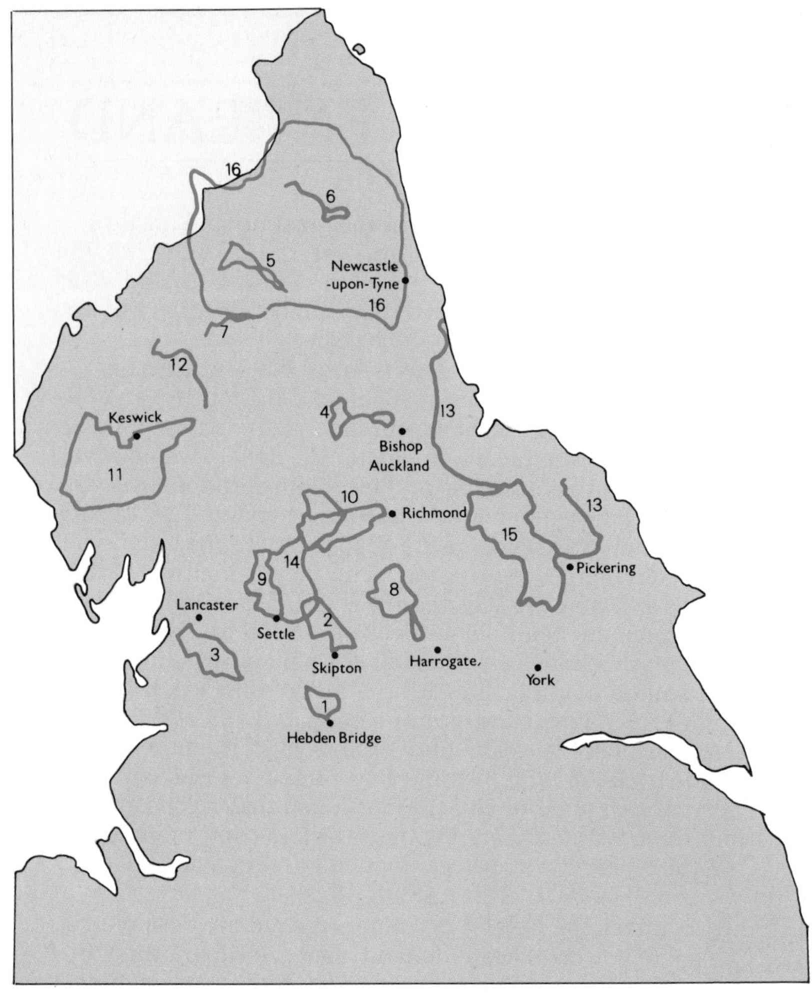

A cross-section of the tours in this region, showing typical rides that can be put together from the route network in a range of localities; **details pages 197–9**.

Day rides

1 Wycoller and Howarth
2 The Dales – Skipton and Grassington
3 Trough of Bowland
4 Durham Moors
5 Kielder Reservoir
6 Coquetdale
7 Hadrian's Wall

Two-day tours

8 The Dales from Harrogate
9 The Three Peaks
10 The Dales from Richmond
11 Lake District
12 The Eden Valley

Selected tours

Three days or longer

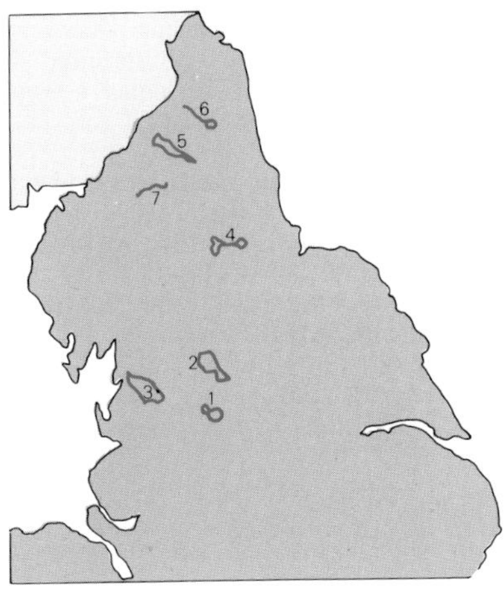

Day rides

1 Wycoller and Howarth, South Pennines moorlands and ravines, about 30 miles (48 km). A strenuous ride, but the scenery is majestic. *Hebden Bridge–Trawden–Haworth–Hebden Bridge*; **pages 206, 207**.

2 The Dales – Skipton and Grassington, about 45 miles (72 km). Superb Yorkshire Dales country and several of the major visitor attractions. *Skipton – Bolton Abbey – Grassington – Arncliffe – Malham Cove – Rylstone – Skipton*; **pages 206, 207, 214, 215**.

3 Trough of Bowland, SE from Lancaster, about 40 miles (64 km). A combination of quiet country lanes and wild fell country, a strenuous day. *Lancaster–Glasson Dock Cycle Way – Street – Chipping – Syket – Lee–Lancaster*; **pages 204, 205**.

4 Durham Moors W from Bishop Auckland into the Hamsterley Forest area, about 40 miles (64 km). A hard day, best tackled anti-clockwise to get longest downhill runs. *Bishop Auckland–Hamsterley – Wolsingham – Eggleston – Hamsterley–Bishop Auckland*; **pages 235, 236**.

5 Kielder Reservoir, Northumberland, about 38 miles (61 km). No really strenuous climbs on this circuit of the reservoir; a fine, solitary forestry road down the N side. *Bellingham – Kielder – Falstone–Bellingham*; **pages 238, 239**.

6 Coquetdale, Northumberland, about 45 miles (72 km). This is one of the most remote valleys in the north of England, its head buried in the Cheviot Hills. The outward journey is a gradual climb, but the return is mostly freewheeling – a demanding, but rewarding family expedition. Access by rail is unfortunately not easy. *Rothbury–Holystone–upper Coquetdale – Alwinton – Warton – Rothbury*; **page 242**.

7 Hadrian's Wall, selected features between Brampton and Bardon Mill Stations, about 20 miles (32 km). A specialized tour taking in several major features of the Roman wall, quite easily ridden in a day, with stops, and returning by train. *Brampton Station – Tilsland – Greenhead–Bardon Mill*; **page 238**.

Selected tours

Two-day tours

8 The Dales from Harrogate, about 55 miles (88 km). One of the best days out on a bike from this north Yorkshire town, penetrating well into the eastern Pennines; very hilly, with spectacular views: for preference ride clockwise. *Harrogate – Wilsill – Lofthouse – Masham – Winksley – Fountains Abbey – Shaw Mills–Harrogate*; **pages 208, 218.**

9 The Three Peaks – Whernside, Ingleborough and Pen-y-ghent, about 60 miles (96 km). Classic Yorkshire, but removed from the most popular haunts such as Malham and Wharfedale, this circuit takes in some of the bleakest, and grandest Pennine scenery. Well served with youth hostels, pubs, hotels and real ale. *Settle–Ingleton–Dent–Horton in Ribblesdale–Settle*; **page 214.**

10 The Dales from Richmond, about 60 miles (96 km). A very hilly ride through some of the wildest parts of Yorkshire, visiting two of the loveliest dales. *Richmond – Reeth – Tan Hill – Thwaite – Hawes – Castle Bolton – Richmond*; **pages 218, 214, 215.**

11 Lake District, centred on Penrith, about 104 miles (166 km). A punishing tour, only for the fit; those seeking a sporting challenge might make it in one day. It takes in six of the great Lake District passes, and a large portion of the finest scenery. Extend it to three days or more – accommodation is plentiful. *Penrith – Kirkstone Pass – Ambleside – Little Langdale – Wrynose Pass – Hardknott Pass – Eskdale Green – Gosforth – Ennerdale Bridge – Cockermouth – Braithwaite – Buttermere – Rosthwaite – Keswick – Scales – Penrith*; **pages 224, 226, 227, 232.**

12 The Eden Valley, Carlisle to Penrith, 40 miles (64 km). A useful family weekend in this otherwise demanding region, or an energetic day out. Gradients are not difficult, and the Eden Valley has relatively gentle, attractive scenery, with fine views. Main line railway stations at either end. *Penrith – Lazonby – Armathwaite – Durdar–Dalston–Penrith*; **pages 233, 234.**

Selected tours

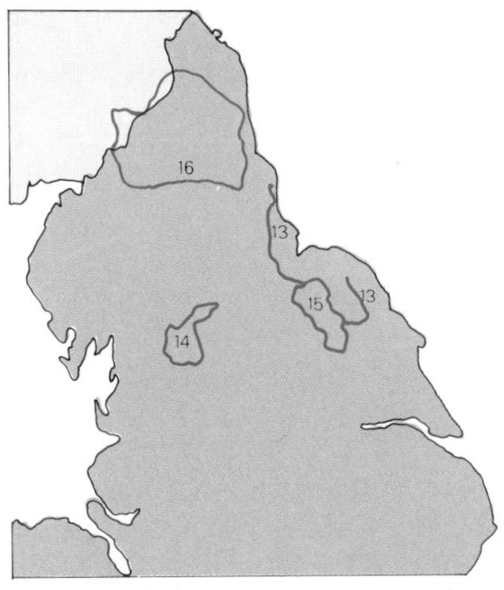

Three days or longer

13 Whitby to Newcastle-upon-Tyne, about 110 miles (176 km). A trip of fascinating contrasts: the bleak grandeur of the North York Moors; some of England's highest sea cliffs; the lush farming land of County Durham and industrial villages built around the coalmining industry, and finally, industrial Tyne and Wear. Rail access at either end. *Whitby–Robin Hood's Bay – Scarborough – Pickering – Lastingham – Castleton – Great Ayton – Eaglescliffe – Houghton-le-Spring – Sunderland – South Shields – Newcastle-upon-Tyne*; **pages 222, 223, 237, 240, 241**.

14 Yorkshire Dales Circuit, based on Settle, about 120 miles (192 km). This is a figure of eight shaped route in the northwestern Dales, giving a choice of the full 120 miles, with 7,500 feet (2,286 m) of climbing, or a shorter route of 90 miles (144 km) with 4,400 feet (1,341 m) of climbing. The roads chosen are relatively traffic-free, even in peak holiday season. The super-fit could do the longer route in two days, but there are sufficient attractions along the way to make the tour last a week. *Settle – Clapham – Ingleton – Dent – Hardrow (option to shorten route by cutting from here to Hawes) – Thwaite – Muker – Reeth – Askrigg – Hawes – Oughtershaw – Buckden – Kettlewell – Arncliffe – Malham–Settle*; **pages 214, 215**.

15 North York Moors from Malton, about 95 miles (152 km). The northern half of the route is very hilly, but taken at the right pace, this could be a family ride. The route takes in Farndale, famous for its wild daffodils in early April. The moors are at their best in late summer, when the heather is in bloom. *Kirby Misperton – Wrelton – Lastingham – Westerdale – Kildale – Great Broughton – Osmotherley – Rievaulx – Helmsley – Hovingham – Terrington – Kirkham – Norton–Kirby Misperton*; **pages 210, 211, 222, 220**.

16 Northumberland, based on Newcastle-upon-Tyne, and penetrating N of the Border, about 180 miles (288 km). Hard climbs and some of the most deserted roads in England. An introduction to many of the county's beauties, and visitor attractions. *Newcastle – Greenhead – Hawick – Kirk Yetholm – Wooler – Alnwick – Amble-by-Sea – Newcastle*; **pages 240, 238, 239, 241**, rest of route in Scotland section.

S Lancashire / Merseyside / Gtr Manchester

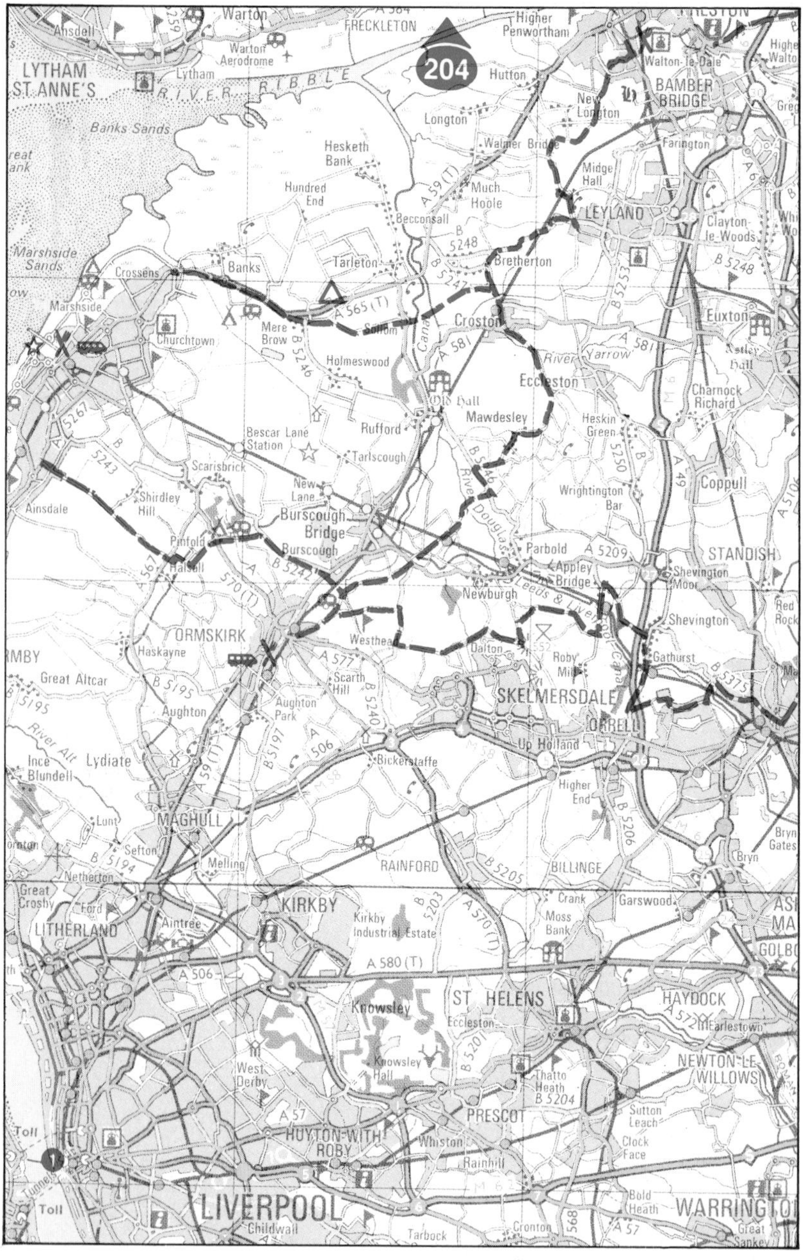

Warton
FRECKLETON
Higher Penwortham
Ansdell
Warton Aerodrome
204
Hutton
LYTHAM ST ANNE'S
Lytham
RIVER RIBBLE
Walton-le-Dale
BAMBER BRIDGE
New Longton
Longton
Banks Sands
Walmer Bridge
Farington
Hesketh Bank
Midge Hall
Hundred End
Much Hoole
LEYLAND
Clayton-le-Woods
Becconsall
Marshside Sands
Banks
Tarleton
Bretherton
Crossens
Marshside
Mere Brow
Sollom
Croston
Euxton
Churchtown
Holmeswood
River Yarrow
Astley Hall
Eccleston
Charnock Richard
Old Hall
Mawdesley
Rufford
Heskin Green
Bescar Lane Station
Tarlscough
Scarisbrick
Coppull
Shirdley Hill
New Lane
Wrightington Bar
Ainsdale
Burscough Bridge
Burscough
Pinfold
Parbold
STANDISH
Halsall
Appley Bridge
Shevington Moor
Newburgh
Leeds & Liverpool Canal
Shevington
River Douglas
ORMSKIRK
Westhead
Dalton
Roby Mill
Gathurst
Haskayne
Scarth Hill
SKELMERSDALE
Great Altcar
ORRELL
Aughton Park
Aughton
Up Holland
River Alt
Lydiate
Bickerstaffe
Ince Blundell
Higher End
MAGHULL
Lunt
Sefton
Bryn Gates
Netherton
Melling
RAINFORD
Bryn
BILLINGE
Great Crosby
Crank
Garswood
Ford
KIRKBY
Moss Bank
LITHERLAND
Aintree
Kirkby Industrial Estate
ST HELENS
HAYDOCK
Knowsley
Eccleston
Earlestown
West Derby
Knowsley Hall
NEWTON-LE-WILLOWS
Thatto Heath
PRESCOT
Sutton Leach
HUYTON-WITH-ROBY
Whiston
Clock Face
Rainhill
Toll
Tunnels
LIVERPOOL
Childwall
Bold Heath
WARRINGTON
Tarbock
Cronton
Great Sankey

S Lancashire/Merseyside/Greater Manchester

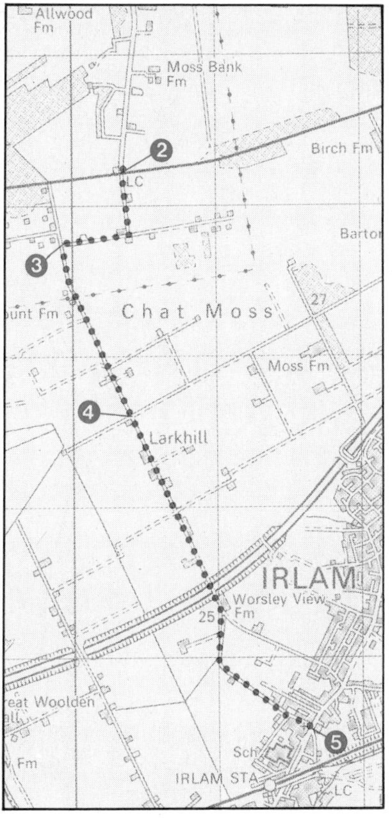

① The local council is considering changing by-laws to permit cycling along the promenades from Seacombe Ferry Landing Stage all the way via Hilbre Point to West Kirby (promenade ramp) on the Dee Estuary (not on map).

② Access to this useful N–S route, avoiding industrial areas, at the level crossing. From here to ③ the surface is in part broken brick – bumpy. From ③ to ⑤ the surface improves. At ⑤ join the busy A57 for an unavoidable 1½ mile (2.5 km) linking section to ⑥ 'Bob's Ferry' over the Ship Canal. (Operating hours: Mon–Fri 5.30 am–11 pm; Sat and Sun 6.30 am–11 pm; small charge for bikes.) Bob's Lane connects the N side of the ferry with the A57. ⑦ Access from A6144 at Partington.

⑧ This right turn is easy to miss: the road to Sollom leads off 50 yards (45 m) after a Methodist chapel.

△ The **A565** has cycle paths, but the marked alternative is pleasanter.

🚂 **Southport** (name off map) and **Ormskirk** on branch lines from Liverpool.

ℌ N of White Stake, near **New Longton**, read the plaque on this former workhouse (right of road).

✕ Choices **Southport**, **Ormskirk**, **Preston**.

🔧 **Blackburn** Warlands, 20 King Street.

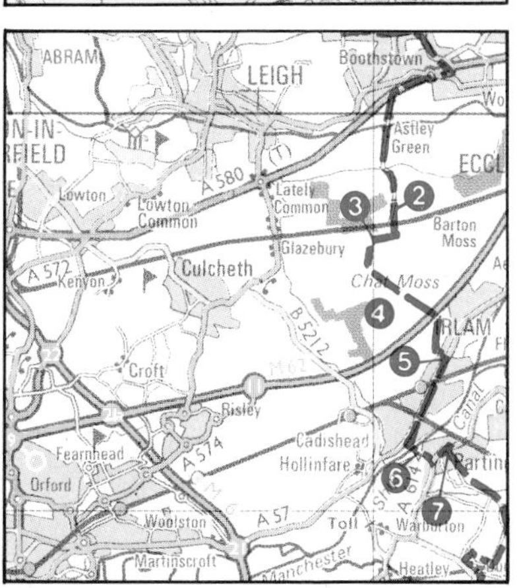

Greater Manchester / West Yorkshire / North Derby

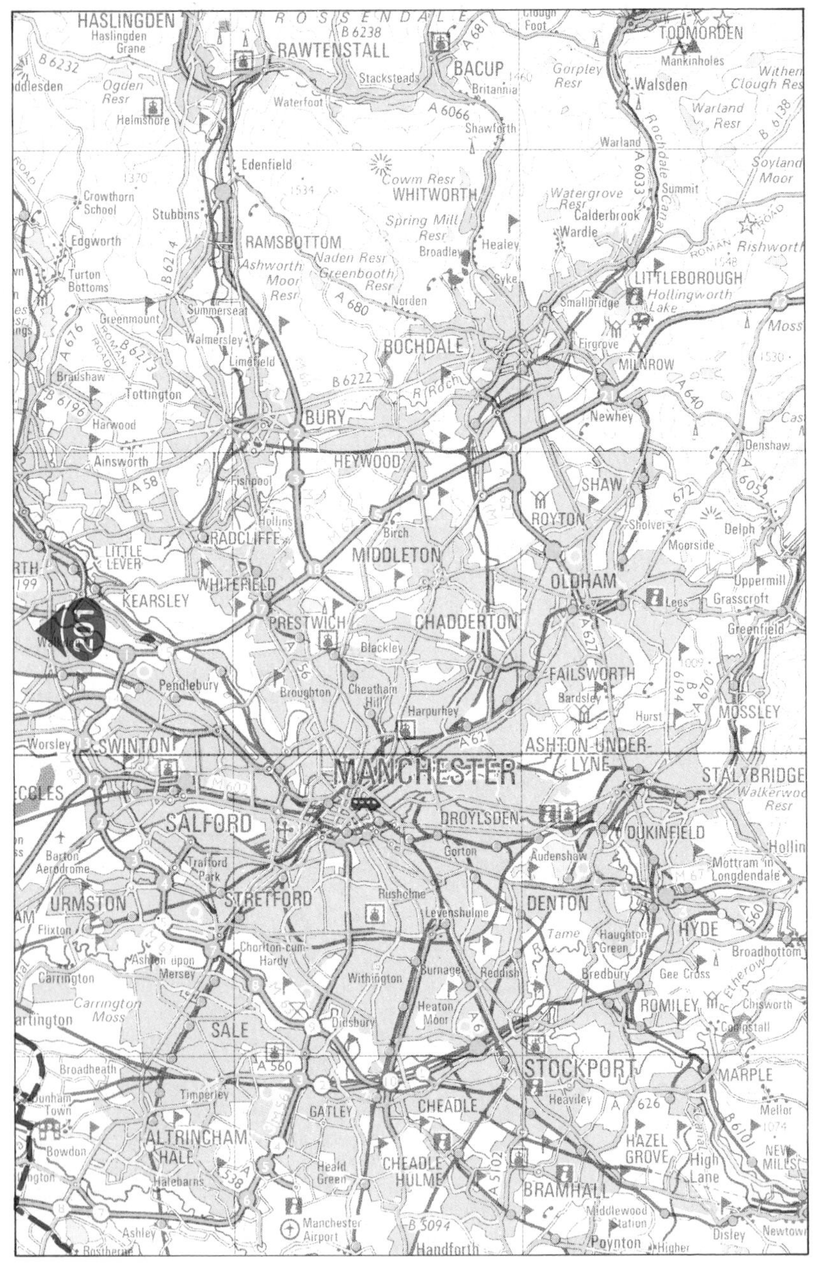

Greater Manchester / West Yorkshire / North Derby

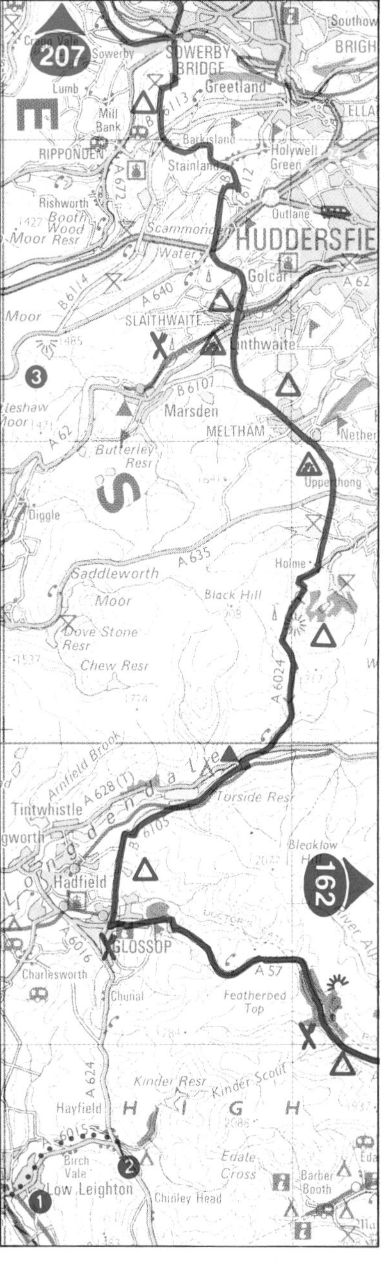

① Access to the Sett Valley Trail disused railway line route at River Bridge, New Mills and ② Hayfield church.

③ Access here to the Pennine Way long-distance path. This official long distance path, the first such route to be established, was opened in 1965. It is well waymarked, easy to leave or join at the numerous places where it crosses roads BUT: only parts are bridleway – study Landranger Sheets 74, 80, 86, 91, 98, 103, 109 and 110 for details; the going is extremely rough and strenuous overall, only for well-equipped adventure cyclists; much of the route is over high, desolate terrain with acute visibility problems in poor weather – take note of the warnings given on page 13. This S part of the Way is not nearly so popular with rough-stuffers as the N sections. An interesting account of the Pennine Way is in *Long Walks* by Adam Nicolson (Pan).

△ Heavy climbs up Snake Pass, **E of Kinder Scout**, exposed road; climb **N of Glossop**, then undulating; very steep climb to summit of Holme Moss, **S of Holme**; 1½ mile (2.5 km) climb N of Meltham; steep twisting climb N of **Slaithwaite**, climb **Stainland– Barkisland** and **S of Sowerby Bridge**. Snake Pass is one of the most formidable Pennine crossings, often snowbound in winter.

🚆 **Manchester** and **Huddersfield**, InterCity services.

🍴 Cafés at **Glossop**, **Slaithwaite**; pub meals at Snake Inn, below Snake Pass, **E of Kinder Scout**.

⛰ Plenty of exhilarating downhill stretches, for example into **Meltham** and **Slaithwaite**.

☀ Superb views on descent from Snake Pass, **E of Kinder Scout**.

▲ **Crowden-in-Longdendale** Glossop (04574) 2135, in former railwaymen's cottages, in remote part of Peak District National Park, YHA membership not necessary.

Lancashire

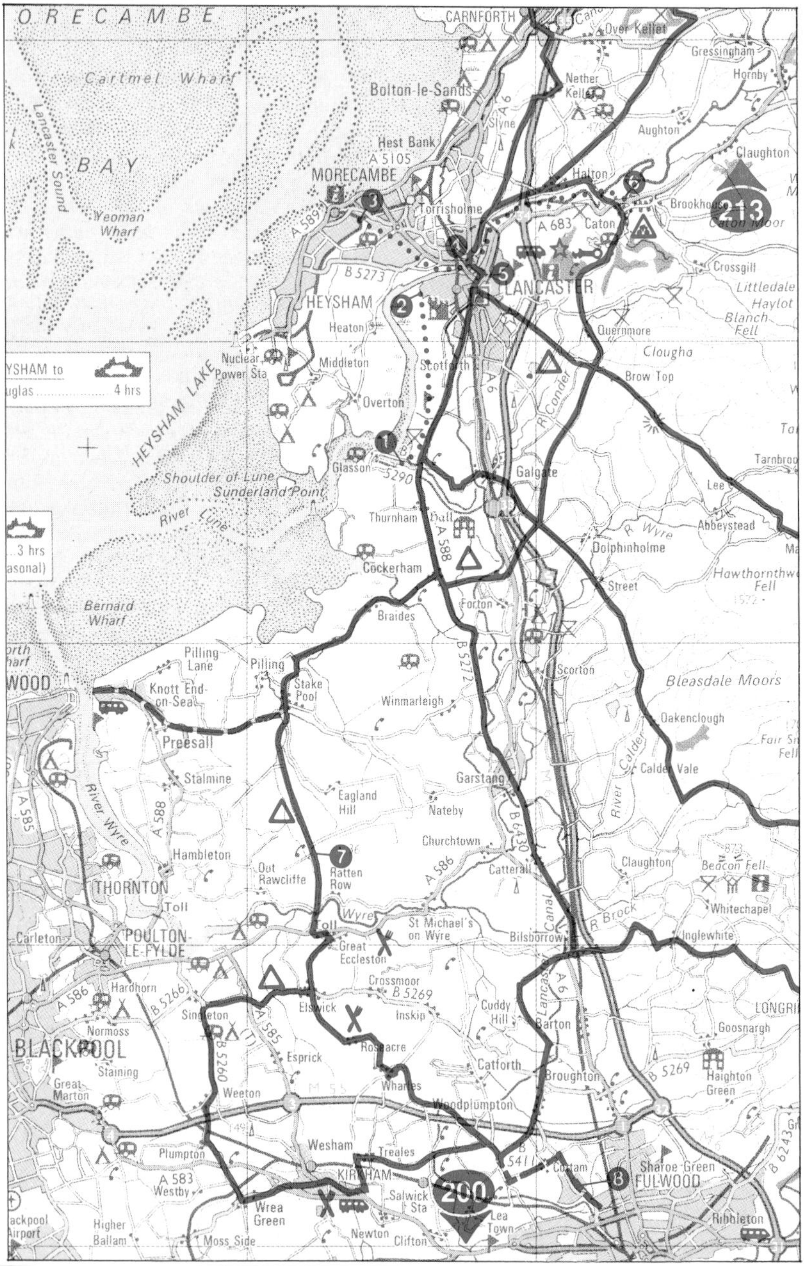

MORECAMBE BAY
Cartmel Wharf
Lancaster Sound
Yeoman Wharf
CARNFORTH
Over Kellet
Gressingham
Hornby
Nether Kellet
Bolton-le-Sands
Slyne
Aughton
Hest Bank
A 5105
Claughton
MORECAMBE
Halton
Torrisholme
Brookhouse
213
Caton Moor
A 589
A 683
Caton
Crossgill
B 5273
LANCASTER
Littledale
Haylot
HEYSHAM
Blanch Fell
Heaton
Quernmore
Clougha
HEYSHAM to Douglas ... 4 hrs
Nuclear Power Sta
Middleton
Scotforth
Brow Top
HEYSHAM LAKE
Overton
A 6
R. Conder
Glasson
B 5290
Galgate
Tarnbrook
Shoulder of Lune
Sunderland Point
Lee
River Lune
Thurnham
Hall
Abbeystead
A 588
R. Wyre
Dolphinholme
...3 hrs (seasonal)
Cockerham
Street
Hawthornthwaite Fell
Bernard Wharf
Forton
Braides
North Wharf
Pilling Lane
Pilling
FLEETWOOD
Stake Pool
Scorton
Bleasdale Moors
Knott End-on-Sea
B 5272
Winmarleigh
Oakenclough
Preesall
Fair Snape Fell
Stalmine
River Wyre
Calder Vale
A 588
River Calder
Garstang
Eagland Hill
Nateby
A 585
B 6430
Churchtown
Hambleton
Claughton
Beacon Fell
Out Rawcliffe
Ratten Row
A 586
Catterall
THORNTON
Toll
Whitechapel
Wyre
Carleton
POULTON-LE-FYLDE
Toll
St Michael's on Wyre
Bilsborrow
R. Brock
Inglewhite
Great Eccleston
Crossmoor
B 5269
Hardhorn
A 586
B 5266
Cuddy Hill
Lancaster Canal
LONGRIDGE
Singleton
Elswick
Inskip
Barton
Goosnargh
Normoss
A 585
BLACKPOOL
B 5260
Esprick
Roseacre
Catforth
Staining
Broughton
B 5269
Haighton Green
Great Marton
Weeton
M 55
Wharles
Woodplumpton
Wesham
Treales
B 5411
Plumpton
A 583
Westby
KIRKHAM
Cottam
Sharoe Green
FULWOOD
Wrea Green
200
Salwick Sta
Blackpool Airport
Higher Ballam
Lea Town
Ribbleton
Moss Side
Newton
Clifton
B 6243

Lancashire

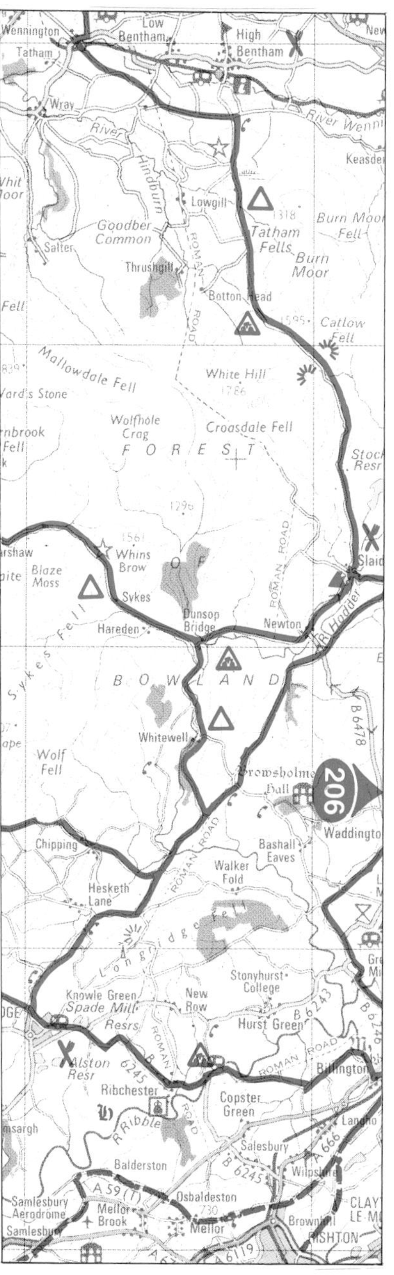

① Access to Glasson Dock Railway Path at Glasson Dock and ② bridleway at extreme end of New Quay Road.

③ Access to Morecambe–Lancaster Railway Path by level crossing at rail junction for Keysham branch line and ④ Greyhound Bridge.

⑤ Access to Lancaster–Bull's Neck section of River Lune Cycle Way at S side of Greyhound Bridge and ⑥ Bull's Neck picnic site off A683 about ¼ mile (0.4 km) E of Brookhouse. ① to ② and ⑤ to ⑥ together form the River Lune Recreational Footpaths and Cycle Ways – leaflet available.

⑦ The North Lancashire Cycle Way, fully signposted is 130 miles (208 km) of carefully devised cycling mainly on quiet unclassified roads. Several stretches of the bridleway are included. Ride it clockwise to avoid struggling into a south-westerly. The North Lancashire Cycle Way links with Cumbria Cycle Way (page 212).

⑧ Cycle Way under construction will run 1½ miles (2.5 km) in and out of Preston.

△ Climbs all through **Bowland** sections: **N of Sykes** and **E of M6 at Lancaster**; elsewhere generally level, especially **Preston–Lancaster** via Stake Pool. The **B5269/5266** carry heavy traffic in and out of Blackpool on bank holidays.

Preston and **Lancaster** on the Carlisle main line, InterCity services; **Kirkham** on the Preston–Blackpool main line: ferry connecting **Fleetwood with Knott End-on-Sea** accepts bicycles.

Cafés at **Great Eccleston**, **Elswick**, **Kirkham**, **Longridge**, **Slaidburn**, **High Bentham**.

The **Ribble** and **Lune Valleys** are excellent cycling country, deserving exploration. The **Forest of Bowland** is superb country; **Bowland Fells**, bleak but beautiful moorland.

Ribchester was a Roman fort.

Lancaster The Cycle Shop, 1 Westbourne Road.

▲ **Slaidburn** 02006 656.

Lancashire / West Yorkshire

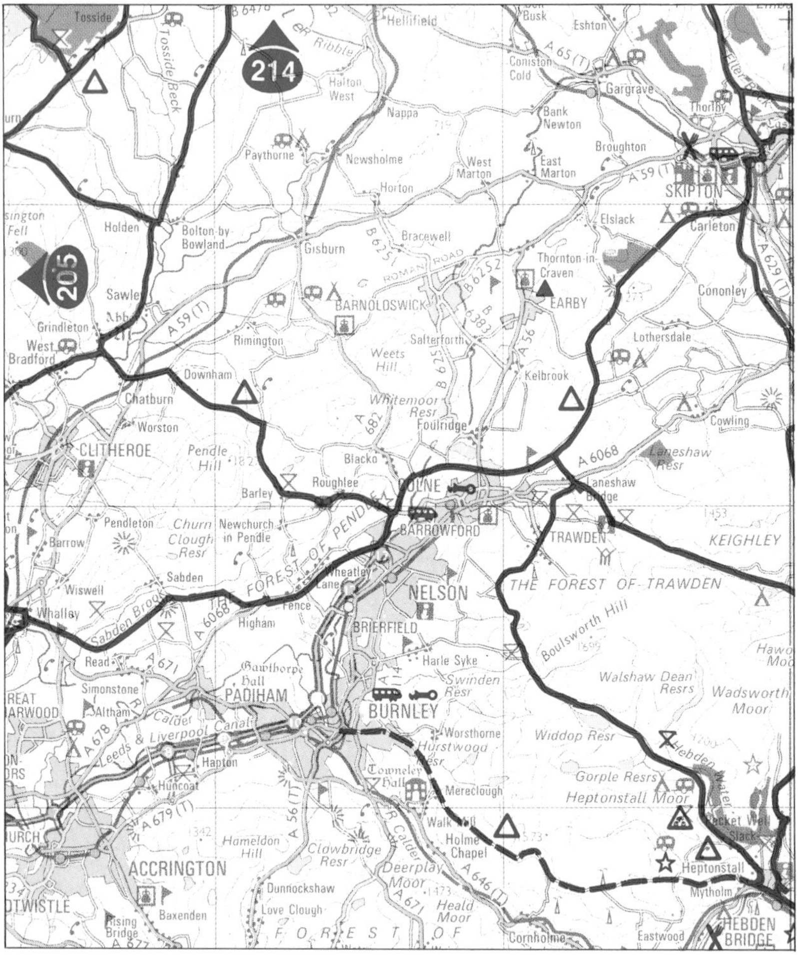

△ Avoiding main roads means climbs SW of **Tosside**, from **Chatburn** to **Barrowford**, **Colne – Skipton** and **Burnley – Hebden Bridge**; Hebden Bridge – Trawden – Haworth circuit extremely strenuous with major climbs **NW from Hebden** and **SW from Oxenhope**; **Ilkley–Beamsley**, a gradual climb.

🚃 **Burnley** and **Colne** on the Preston–Colne branch line; **Keighley** and **Skipton** on the Bradford – Barrow branch line; **Ilkley** on the Leeds–Ilkley branch line.

✕ Choices (cafés and pub meals) at **Hebden Bridge**, **Skipton**, **Haworth** and **Ilkley**; tea rooms in Cavendish Pavilion, **Bolton Abbey**; opportunities scarce on wilder parts of routing.

🍺 The Withens, **N of Illingworth** on Worley Moor, Yorkshire's highest pub.

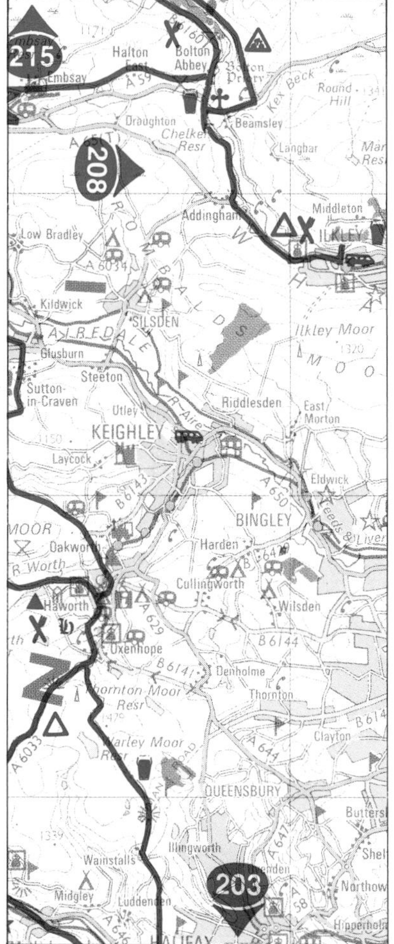

Bolton Abbey

⚠ Despite the effort, the climb **NW from Heptonstall** is exhilarating; **Ilkley NW through Bolton** is delightful, improving as it progresses through Wharfedale.

☆ **Hebden Bridge**, 'capital' of the South Pennines area, its double-decker houses stacked above each other on the hillsides to minimize wasted space; **Heptonstall**, the focal point of the former weaving community hereabouts, ruins of 13th-C church in graveyard of 19th-C church; 17th-C grammar school contains museum, open at weekends.

✝ **Bolton Abbey** – properly Bolton Priory – the nave of whose church has been used as a parish church since about 1170. This and ruined parts of the former priory are beautifully sited near the River Wharfe. Nearby Bolton Hall belongs to the Duke of Devonshire.

⧖ Black Dean, **E of Gorple Reservoirs**, is a picturesque valley with a stream running through and a choice of picnic places.

Haworth, a place of pilgrimage for fans of the Brontë family. The three Brontë sisters and their brother were brought up here by their father, the vicar, from 1820. The once gloomy parsonage is now a museum. Charlotte and Emily are buried in the churchyard. A track leads across the moors to Far Withens, thought to be the model for Wuthering Heights – the Earnshaws' home high up on the wild moors in Emily Brontë's famous novel.

Burnley Bob Whittaker Cycles, 2/4 Queen Victoria Road; **Colne** Hargreaves, 20 Dockray Street.

▲ **Haworth** 0535 42234; **Earby** Burnley (0282) 842349.

North Yorkshire

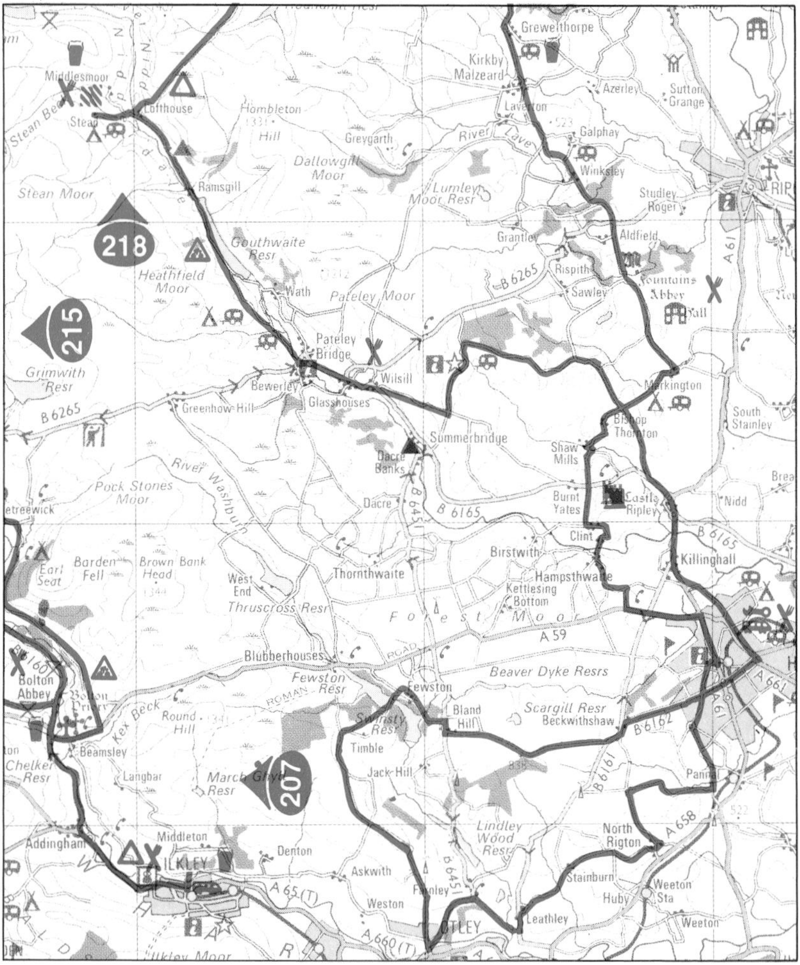

Hard climbs throughout, typically **NE from Lofthouse**; **Ilkley–Bolton Abbey** details, page 206.

Harrogate, on the main line from Leeds.

Choices **Harrogate**, **Pateley Bridge**; cafés at **Fountains Abbey** and **Stean**.

Unspoiled pub at **Middlesmoor**, but it involves a climb.

Outstanding **Yorkshire Dales** scenery over whole area.

Detour to **Stean** for remarkable walks under overhanging limestone ravine.

Fountains Abbey, one of the largest monasteries in England and perhaps the most beautifully situated; impressive portions remain intact. Nearby is Jacobean Fountains Hall.

Tudor **Ripley** Castle.

Harrogate A. Pockington, 1 Wedderburn Road.

Dacre Banks Harrogate (0423) 780431.

Fountains Abbey

North Yorkshire

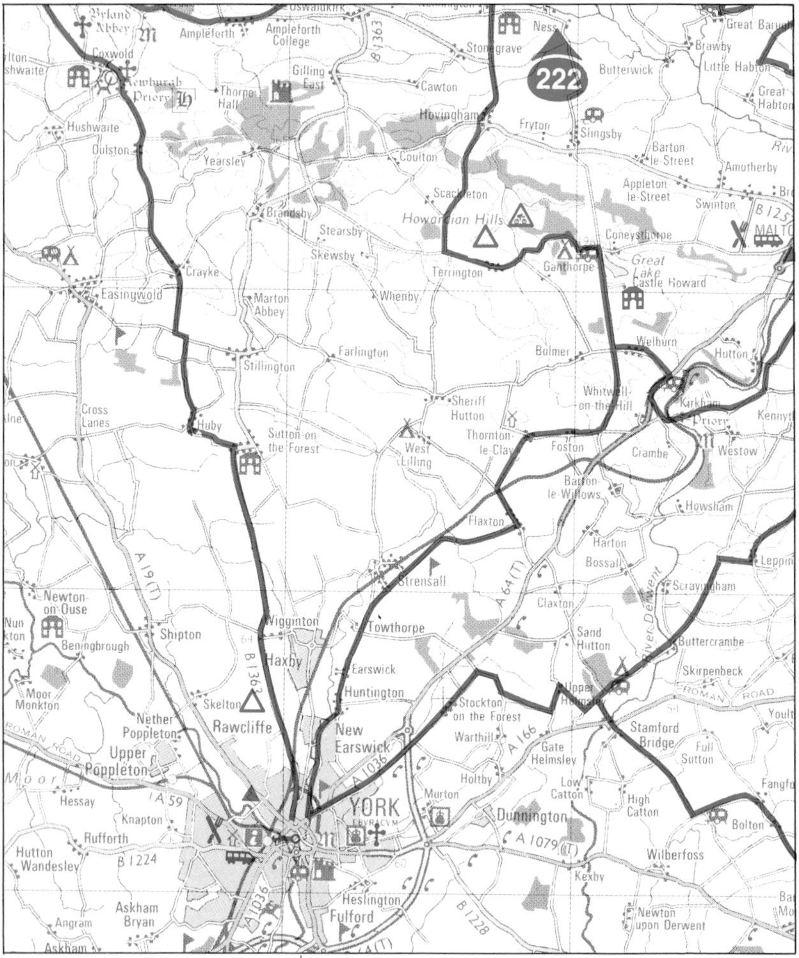

△ Mostly flat, with the exception of the **Howardian Hills**; **B1363** traffic light.

Frequent services to **York** on the InterCity route from London; regular services to **Malton** on the York–Scarborough InterCity route.

Choices, **York**, **Malton**.

Through the **Howardian Hills**, with views of the moors.

Castle Howard, the famous and resplendent 18th-C house by Vanbrugh – paintings, gallery of costume, furniture, outbuildings, 69-acre lake.

✝ **York**, with its Minster, one of the finest cathedrals in England, and its medieval City Walls; **Byland Abbey**, a 12th-c Cistercian foundation.

The headless body of Oliver Cromwell is reputed to be preserved by his descendants at **Newburgh Priory**.

York Cycleworks, 18 Lawrence St.

▲ **York** 0904 53147; **Malton** 0653 2077.

North Yorkshire

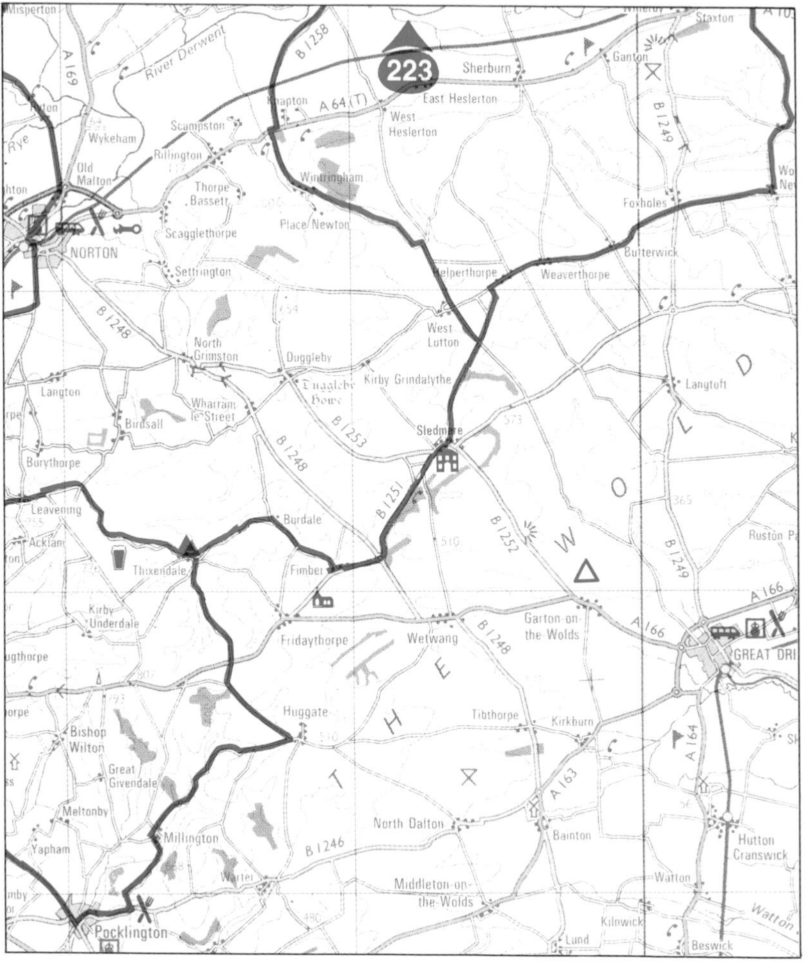

△ The Wolds are moderately strenuous in parts, generally rising to around 500 feet (152 m) above sea level, but be prepared for bitter winds coming off the North Sea. The highest point of the hills is more than 800 feet (244 m) above sea level at Garrowby Top.

Regular service to Malton (**Norton**) on the York–Scarborough InterCity route; occasional service to **Great Driffield** on the Hull–Scarborough branch line.

Norton, Great Driffield, limited choices; bar food at Feathers Hotel, **Pocklington**.

Hand-pumped ales at Cross Keys, **Thixendale**.

Driffield has a private museum of the area's archaeology; Roman items at **Malton**.

Malton D. H. Reed, St. Leonard's Vicarage.

▲ **Thixendale** Driffield (0377) 88238.

Cumbria

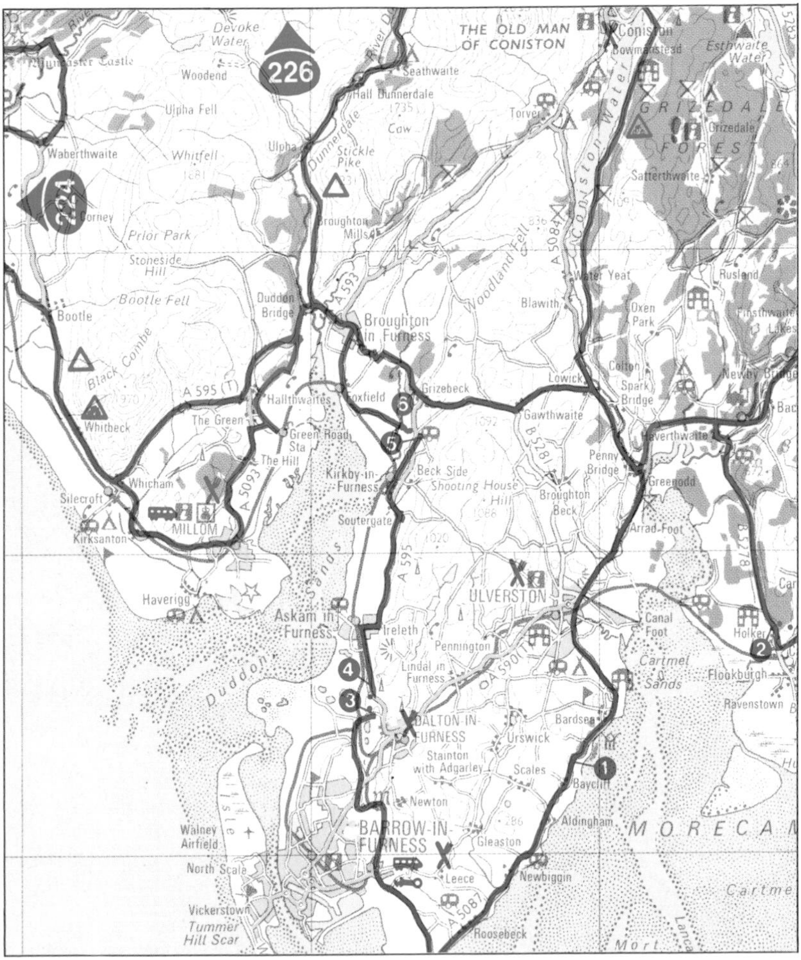

① The Cumbria Cycle Way is a circular route around the entire county. Cyclists do not find it as well signposted as the North Lancashire Cycle Way, but the Cumbria Cycling Club, who devised the route, say that it can be quite easily followed using their descriptive leaflet in conjunction with the waymarks. ②, ③, ④, ⑤ and ⑥ are sections using bridleways, easily located. Prevailing wind: south-westerly.

△ **W half of the Cumbria Cycle Way** is mainly coastal, reasonably level, but it uses a section of the busy A595; **Duddon Bridge–Seathwaite**, hilly.

🚆 **Barrow-in-Furness**, **Millom** and stations on Lancaster–Carlisle line.

X Choices in **centres as marked**.

🔧 **Barrow** Cumbria Cycles, 27 Aisdale Road.

▲ **Hawkshead** 09666 293.

Cumbria/Lancashire

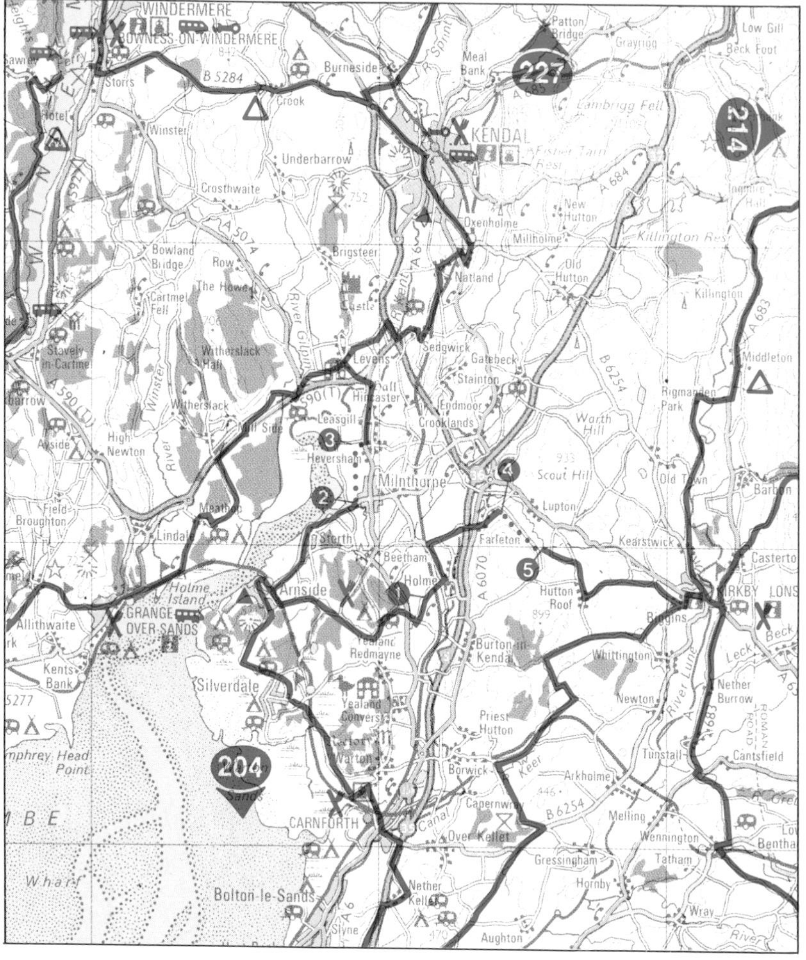

① The North Lancashire and Cumbria Cycle Ways share a common route between Arnside and Kirkby Lonsdale. Details of former see page 205; of latter see opposite; ②, ③, ④ and ⑤ mark bridleway sections.

△ The **E half of the Cumbria Cycle Way** winds through Pennine dales, reasonably level, but expect climbs.

Grange-over-Sands and other stations on the Lancaster–Carlisle branch line; **Windermere**, **Kendal** and other stations on the Oxenholme–Windermere branch line; ferries (bike accepted) connect **Bowness-on-Windermere**, **Sawrey** and **Lakeside**.

Kendal Brucies Bike Shop, 187, Highgate; **Windermere** Renta-camp Leisurehire, Station buildings. Both offer repairs and hire.

▲ **Arnside** 0524 761781; **Kendal** 0539 24066.

North Yorkshire/Cumbria/Yorkshire Dales

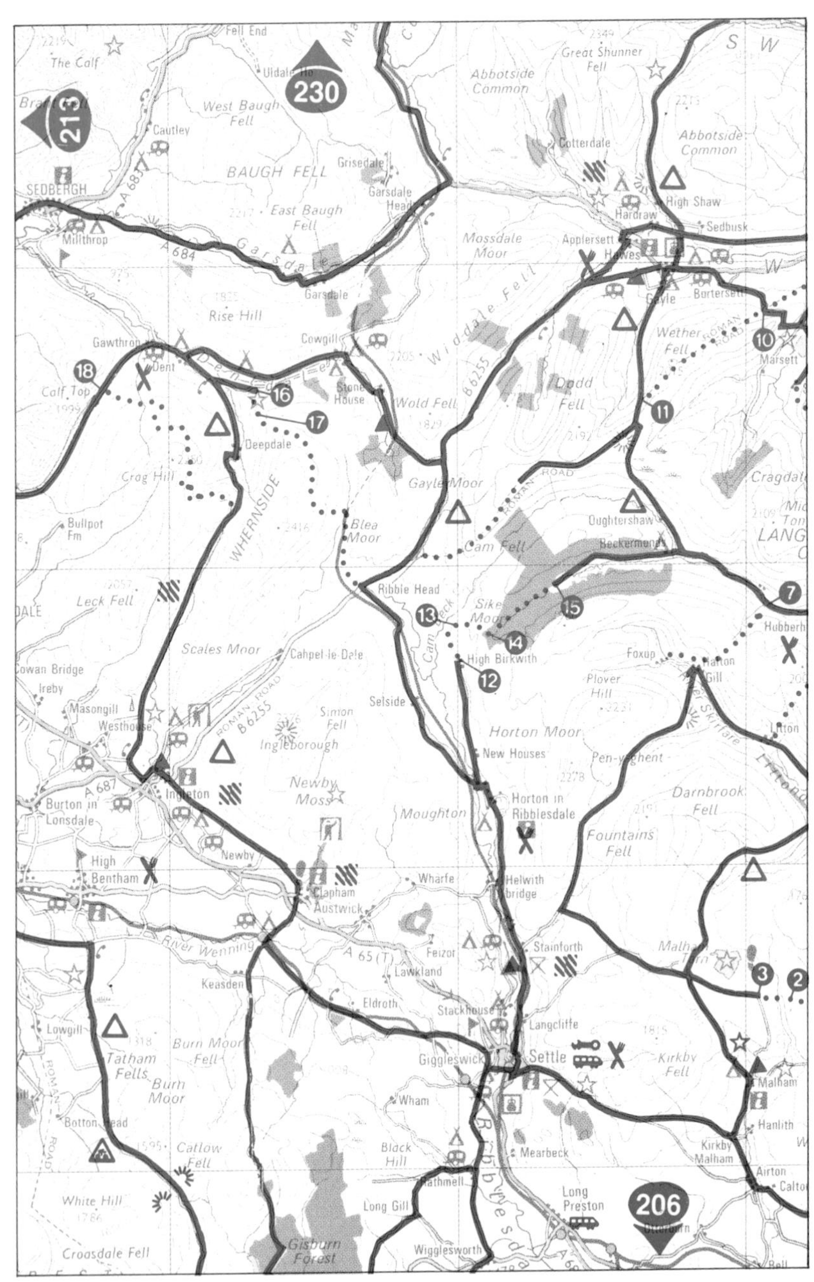

North Yorkshire/Cumbria/Yorkshire Dales

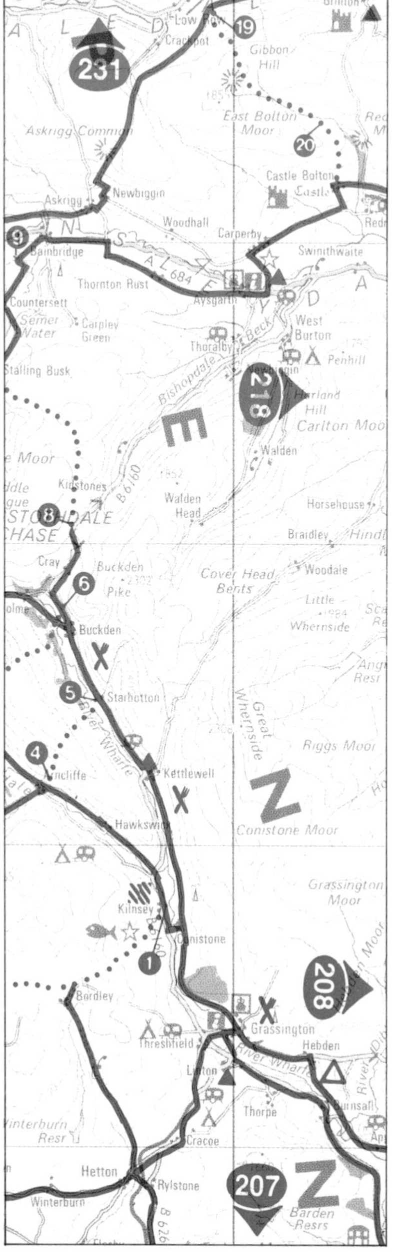

① to ⑳ details see pages 216–17.

△ **Gayle Moor**, unfenced road, beware of sheep; **Arncliffe–Malham**, gated road, be prepared to dismount and open/close gates; extremely hard climb to summit of Fleet Moss Pass, **N from Oughtershaw**; take care on steep descent into **Gayle/Hawes**; gated road S of **Dent**; **B6255** is fast, but with little traffic; steep climbing at times **N of High Shaw** to Butter Tubs Pass; **Burnsall–Grassington**, climbs; across **Tatham Fells**, part of the North Lancashire Cycle Way, details page 205.

🚆 **Settle** and **Long Preston** on the Bradford–Carlisle branch line.

✕ Choices of cafés and pubs at **Hawes, Grassington, Settle, Dent, Kettlewell**; pub meals at **Buckden, Hubberholme, Horton in Ribblesdale.**

⛰ The Yorkshire Dales – green valleys winding down from the moorland heights of the Pennines – wonderful, if strenuous, cycling touring.

☆ **Malham** Cove, with its 300-foot (90-m) limestone face.

Besides Malham Cove, there are impressive natural features all over the area: two waterfalls; walks from **Ingleton** (stout footwear required); **Stainforth** Force; access to **Hardraw** Force, the highest waterfall above ground in England, is from the Green Dragon Inn (note sign above doorway to gentleman's lavatory); Gaping Gill, 3 miles (5 km) from **Clapham** has a 240-foot (73-m) fall; Yordas Cave, in the woods above the **Ingleton–Dent unclassified road**, the third largest cavern in Britain; **Kilnsey** Crag, a famous overhanging rock climb.

🔧 **Settle** Settle Cycles, Dukes Street.

▲ **Grinton Lodge** Richmond (0748) 84206; **Hawes** 09697 368; **Aysgarth** Falls 09693 260; **Dentdale** Dent (05875) 251; **Ingleton** 0468 41444; **Kettlewell** 075676 232; **Stainforth** Settle (07292) 3577; **Linton** Grassington (0756) 752400; **Malham** Airton (07293) 321.

North Yorkshire/Cumbria/Yorkshire Dales

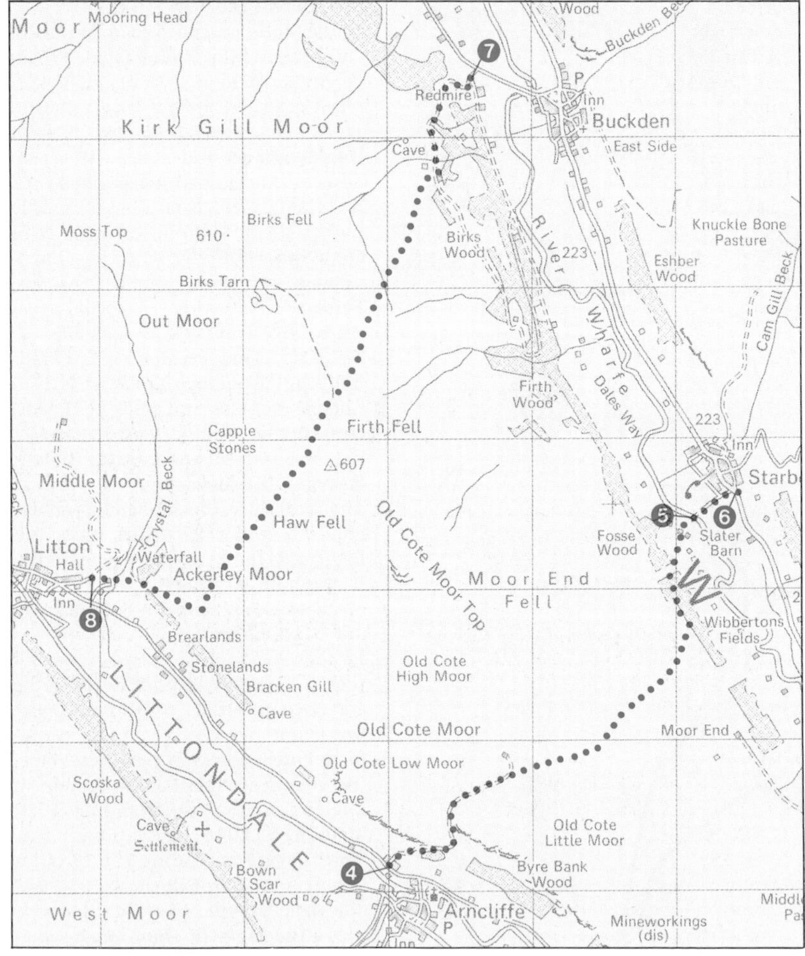

The Yorkshire Dales are a rough-stuffing paradise. To see how this off-highway routing links in with the other routing in the area, see pages 214–15.

① To locate Mastiles Lane, a true 'green road', go past the inn at Kilnsey, past the quarry and up the hill. The Lane is easily followed to ② the ford on the Gordale Beck (footbridge nearby if in flood). It joins unclassified road ③ at Street Gate, N of Malham.

④ NW of Arncliffe a signposted track leads steeply upwards past a house and on to the moor. Pass to right of derelict farm to ladderstile at summit. Follow track down to scarp overlooking Wharfedale and left through woods to ⑤ footbridge over river and a long, rough lane to Starbotton.

⑥ Track signposted Litton; on the open moor, posts mark the route to the ladderstile at the summit. Take care on steep descent to cross ford to emerge in Litton by the Queen's Arms.

⑦ A track signposted Halton Gill leads off from the hamlet of Raisgill. It is broad and easily followed to Horsehead Gate at the summit, and down a steep, winding descent to Halton Gill.

⑧ Leaving Buckden by the Aysgarth road look for stony track continuing over cattle grid at summit of climb, where road turns right. Follow track, climbing steeply to plateau of Stake Moss. From the plateau the track is rideable throughout, but take care on steep drop to metalled lane above Stalling Busk.

⑨ About 1 mile (1.5 km) after leaving Bainbridge on the Countersett Road, where the road turns left, the track of a Roman road leads straight on. It is broad and straight, crossing the Buttersett/Countersett road ⑩ and continuing to the road on Fleet Moss ⑪. Turn left here and in about ½ mile (0.8 km), where the road turns left, continue straight on with the Roman road, still metalled. Join the Pennine Way at Kidhow Gate. Carry on, through another gate, after which the metalling ends. Continue, ignoring Pennine Way turn to Gearstones.

⑫ Where the road ends at High Birkwith, go up track and turn right ⑬ at Old Ing Farm. Soon go left ⑭ up a rough limestone forestry road through Langstrothdale. At High Green Field Farm ⑮ the track leaves forest and joins a fairly well surfaced road.

⑯ Leave Dent by the unclassified road following the S side of Dentdale, going SE, and ignore the right turn to Ingleton. Take the next right and in a few yards the track ⑰ leading left round the N flank of Whernside. It drops to cross the railway S of Bleamoor Tunnel and runs down E side of railway to Ribblehead.

⑱ Leave Dent heading NW, forking left at Gawthrop and up steep hill. At top of Barbondale, just over the summit, take track to left which winds round to summit of Dent–Ingleton road on White Shaw Moss.

As rough stuff goes, this is a first-class surface, but it will deteriorate after rain.

⑲ A track leads off SE from the unclassified road on the S side of the River Swale, W of Grinton, signposted Castle Bolton. Follow it up to the summit, past old mine shaft and down Ape Dale to shooting lodge ⑳. Turn right past lodge, over hill, and down to Castle Bolton.

North Yorkshire

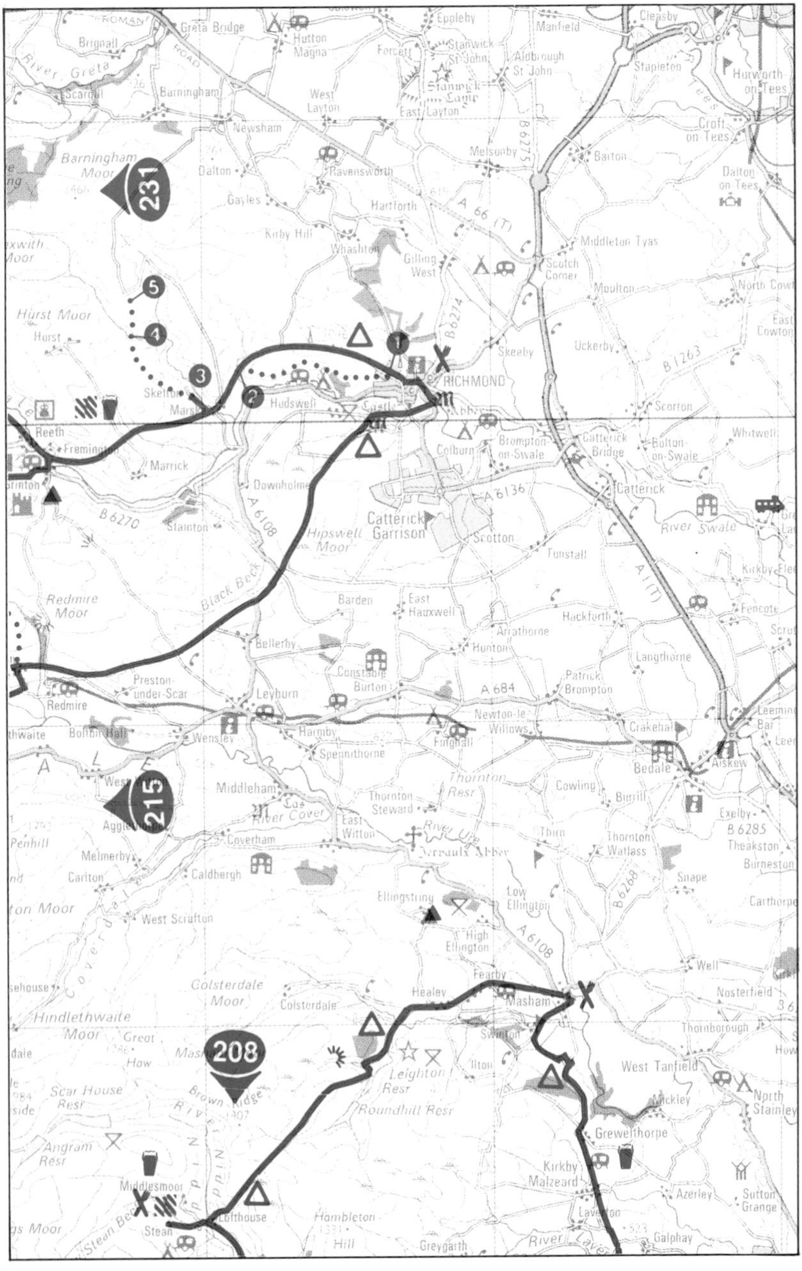

Greta Bridge
Hutton Magna
Eppleby
Manfield
Cleasby
Brignall
River Greta
Forcett
Stanwick St John
Aldbrough St John
Stapleton
Hurworth-on-Tees
Scargill
Barningham
West Layton
Stanwick Camp
East Layton
Newsham
B 6275
Croft-on-Tees
Barningham Moor
Dalton
Ravensworth
Melsonby
Barton
Dalton-on-Tees
231
Gayles
Hartforth
A 66 (T)
Kirby Hill
Whashton
Middleton Tyas
Gilling West
Scotch Corner
Hurst Moor
Hurst
Moulton
North Cowton
East Cowton
B 6274
Skeeby
Uckerby
B 1263
RICHMOND
Skelton
Marske
Hudswell
Castle
Scorton
Reeth
Fremington
Brompton-on-Swale
Catterick Bridge
Bolton-on-Swale
Whitwell
Marrick
Colburn
Downholme
Catterick
A 6136
B 6270
Stainton
A 6108
Catterick Garrison
Hipswell Moor
Scotton
River Swale
Tunstall
A 1 (T)
Black Beck
Redmire Moor
Barden
East Hauxwell
Hackforth
Arrathorne
Hunton
Bellerby
Langthorne
Constable Burton
Patrick Brompton
Preston-under-Scar
Leyburn
A 684
Redmire
Newton-le-Willows
Crakehall
Leeming Bar
Bolton Hall
Wensley
Harmby
Finghall
Spennithorne
Bedale
Aiskew
Middleham
Thornton Resr
Cowling
Burrill
West Witton
215
Aggleforth
Thornton Steward
Cas
River Cover
East Witton
Exelby
B 6285
Penhill
Coverham
River Ure
Thirn
Thornton Watlass
Theakston
Melmerby
Jervaulx Abbey
Burneston
Carlton
Caldbergh
Snape
B 6268
Ellingstring
Low Ellington
Carthorpe
West Scrafton
High Ellington
A 6108
Well
Fearby
Healey
Colsterdale Moor
Colsterdale
Masham
Nosterfield
Hindlethwaite Moor
Great How
Swinton
Thornborough
208
Leighton Resr
Ilton
West Tanfield
Scar House Resr
Brown Ridge
Roundhill Resr
Mickley
North Stainley
Grewelthorpe
Angram Resr
Kirkby Malzeard
Middlesmoor
Azerley
Sutton Grange
Lofthouse
Hambleton Hill
Laverton
Stean
Greygarth
River Laver
Galphay

North Yorkshire

① Take A6108 W out of Richmond; at the left bend on the outskirts fork right; climb hill and where road ends in track continue through woods and on to open ground below Whitcliffe Scar. Pass Applegarth Farm and continue to unclassified road ② about 1 mile (1.5 km) NE of Marske.

③ After Skelton Hall take the track which forks left, up steep hill, through gate on to moor. It is easily followed round the scarp, then drops steeply to ④ Helwith Farm. Carry on up the lane to join unclassified road ⑤.

△ All the routing marked is strenuous, with, typically, long climbs W from **Richmond** and SW/SE from **Masham**.

Nearest station at Northallerton, about 5 miles (8 km) SE on the **B6271** – York–Newcastle main line.

Choices **Richmond** and **Masham**.

Richmond

The pubs at **Reeth** and **Grewelthorpe** are useful stopping places.

Spectacular views, for example E down on to the Vale of York from road **above Leighton Reservoir**.

B6270 at Reeth Swaledale, with the River Swale rushing through, is one of the wildest and most beautiful Dales.

Richmond is picturesque market town; Norman Castle on edge of precipice above River Swale, Georgian theatre, and on the river bank outside the town, Easby Abbey, founded 1155, in a beautiful situation.

▲ **Grinton Lodge**, details page 215; **Ellingstring** Bedale (0677) 60303, July, Aug and Sept only – write at other times to YHA Yorks Region, 96 Main Street, Bingley.

North Yorkshire

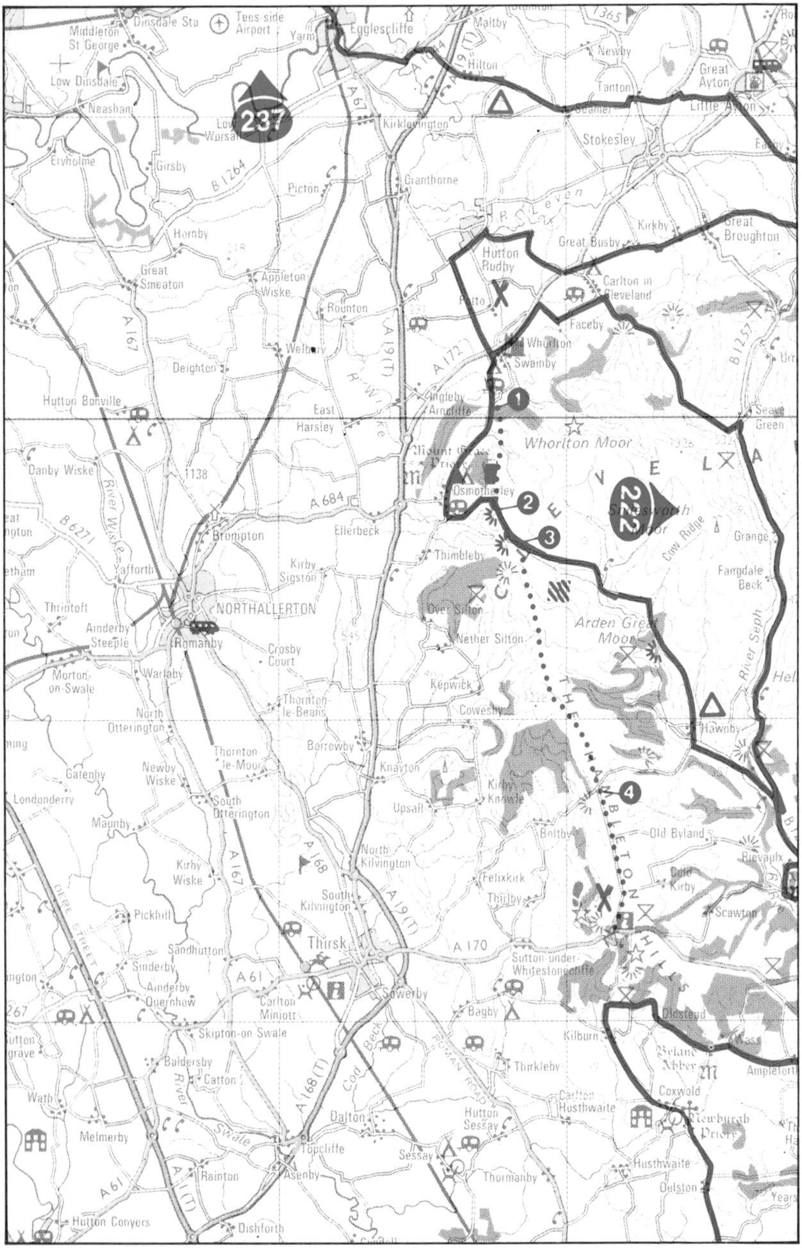

Middleton St George
Dinsdale Sta
Tees-side Airport
Yarm
Egglescliffe
Maltby
Newby
Hilton
Great Ayton
Tanton
Low Dinsdale
Neasham
Seamer
Little Ayton
237
Low Worsall
Kirklevington
Stokesley
A 67
A 1044
A 19(T)
Eryholme
Girsby
B 1264
Picton
Crathorne
R Leven
Kirkby
Great Broughton
Great Busby
Hornby
Hutton Rudby
Great Smeaton
Appleton Wiske
Carlton in Cleveland
Potto
Rounton
Faceby
Whorlton
Swainby
B 1257
A 167
Welbury
A 172
R Wiske
Deighton
Ingleby Arncliffe
Hutton Bonville
East Harsley
Seave Green
Whorlton Moor
Danby Wiske
1138
Mount Grace Priory
C L E V E L A N D
Osmotherley
A 684
222
Snilesworth Moor
Cow Ridge
Grange
B 6271
River Wiske
Brompton
Ellerbeck
Thimbleby
Yafforth
Kirby Sigston
Fangdale Beck
Thrintoft
Ainderby Steeple
NORTHALLERTON
Romanby
Over Silton
Arden Great Moor
Nether Silton
Crosby Court
River Seph
Morton-on-Swale
Warlaby
Kepwick
North Otterington
Thornton-le-Beans
Cowesby
Hawnby
THE HAMBLETON HILLS
Borrowby
Thornton le-Moor
Gatenby
Newby Wiske
Knayton
Kirby Knowle
Londonderry
South Otterington
Upsall
Maunby
Boltby
Old Byland
Rievaulx
North Kilvington
A 168
A 167
Felixkirk
Cold Kirby
Kirby Wiske
South Kilvington
Thirlby
Scawton
DERE STREET
Pickhill
A 19(T)
Thirsk
Sandhutton
A 170
Sinderby
Sutton-under-Whitestonecliffe
A 61
Ainderby Quernhow
Carlton Miniott
Sowerby
Bagby
Skipton-on-Swale
Oldstead
Kilburn
Wass
Baldersby
Byland Abbey
Ampleforth
River Swale
Catton
Thirkleby
Cod Beck
ROMAN ROAD
A 168(T)
Wath
Coxwold
Carlton Husthwaite
Newburgh Priory
Dalton
Hutton Sessay
Melmerby
Topcliffe
Sessay
Husthwaite
A 1(T)
Rainton
Asenby
Thormanby
Oulston
A 61
Hutton Conyers
Dishforth

Rievaulx Abbey

① At the old quarries join track leading S over Osmotherley Moor. Join unclassified road ② at Slape Stones; continue S on road and in about 1 mile (1.5 km) continue straight on with track ③ following the Cleveland Way over the Hambleton Hills to ④ road above Boltby. Carry straight on using unclassified road to reach Sutton Bank.

△ Severe climbs through Cleveland Hills/North York Moors, for example N out of **Hawnby**; climb going **E from Hilton**.

Northallerton and **Thirsk** on the York–Newcastle main line; **Great Ayton** on the Middlesbrough–Whitby branch line.

Limited choices **Hutton Rudby**; tea/refreshments from mobile canteen in car park on Sutton Bank, **E of Sutton-under-Whitestonecliffe** on the A170, summer weekends; otherwise opportunities scarce. Useful pub at **Osmotherley**. Several inns in the area have the incomparable Theakston's Old Peculiar on tap.

Fine views over North York Moors and Vale of York, **SE of Osmotherley** and on **Arden Great Moor**.

The Moors are at their best in late summer when the heather is in bloom. Getting up on to the Moor is hard work, but the tops are relatively flat and provide fine, if energetic walking. The **Cleveland Way** (see ③ above) has some superb cliff-edge sections – but beware of sea frets – banks of fog which roll suddenly inland.

Rievaulx The ruin is as lovely as its wooded valley setting. The monastery was destroyed during Henry VIII's dissolution of the monasteries.

▲ **Osmotherley** 060983 575.

North Yorkshire

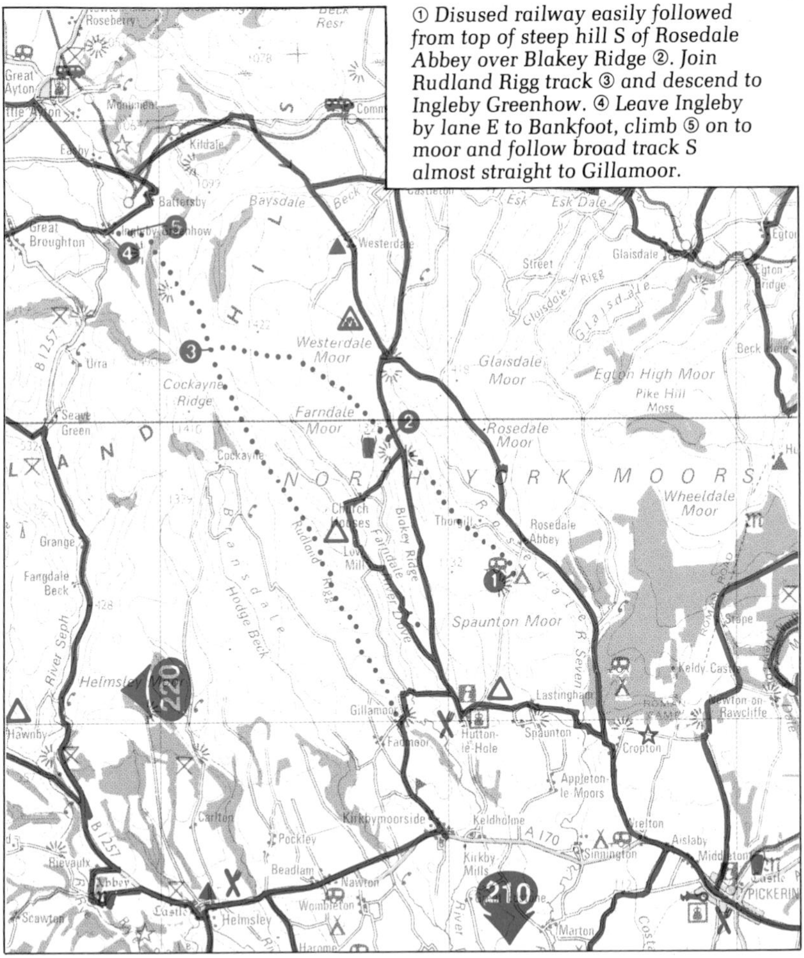

① Disused railway easily followed from top of steep hill S of Rosedale Abbey over Blakey Ridge ②. Join Rudland Rigg track ③ and descend to Ingleby Greenhow. ④ Leave Ingleby by lane E to Bankfoot, climb ⑤ on to moor and follow broad track S almost straight to Gillamoor.

△ The bleak beauty of the North York Moors is at its best in August when the heather is in flower; the Moors form a plateau which is quite flat on top, but there are steep climbs up to it, for example **Pickering–Hutton-le-Hole** and on to **Farndale Moor**.

🚆 Infrequent services, **Commondale** and other stations on the Whitby–Middlesbrough branch line.

✗ **Pickering**, choices; **Helmsley**, limited choices. Tearooms and evening meals in pub at **Hutton-le-Hole**.

🍺 Pubs are open all day Monday in **Pickering** (market day); pub near summit of **Farndale Moor**.

⛰ The route **through the Moors** offers numerous extensive views as marked.

☆ Roman camps near **Cropton**.

🔧 **Pickering** W. Best, Hungate.

▲ **Helmsley** 0493 70433; **Westerdale Hall** Castleton (Yorks.) (02876) 469.

North Yorkshire

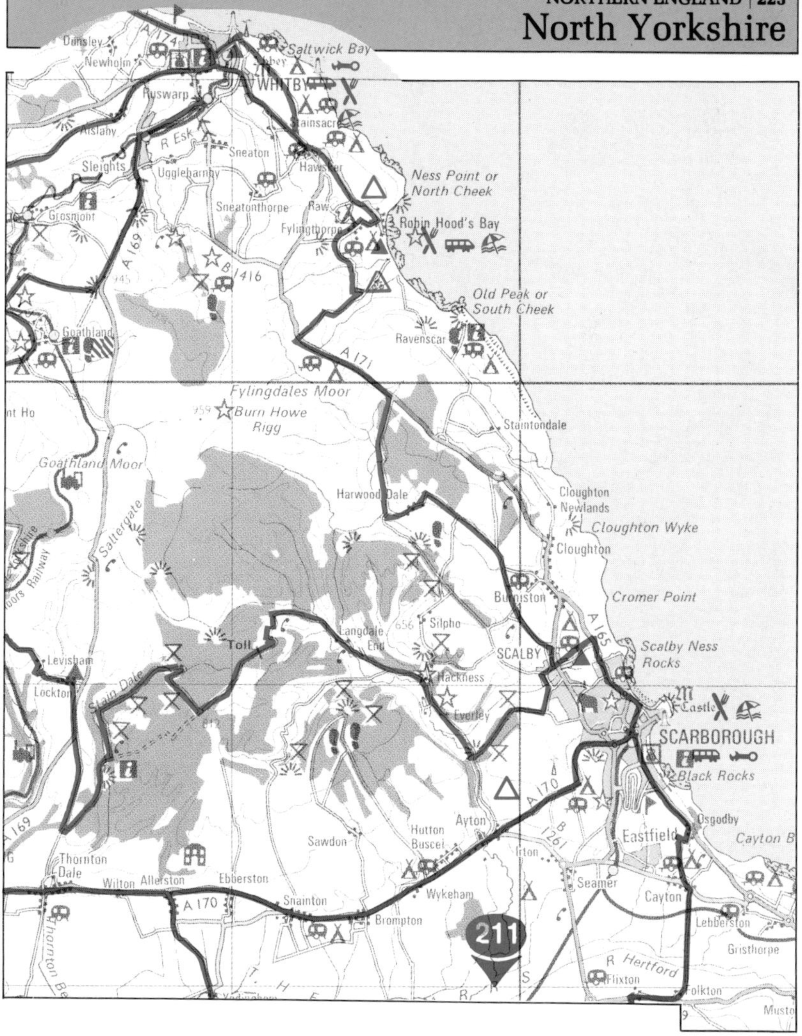

△ Mostly strenuous, with hard climbs up to the moors: a spectacular descent into **Robin Hood's Bay**, then a lung-bursting ascent to the main road; the **A170 near Scarborough** is busy on summer weekends and bank holidays.

Frequent service to **Scarborough** on the InterCity route from York; the Middlesbrough–**Whitby** line can claim to be British Rail's most beautiful.

Scarborough, **Whitby**, choices; **Robin Hood's Bay**, limited choices.

Some of England's highest sea cliffs, in the **Robin Hood's Bay** area.

Scarborough (two sandy bays); **Whitby** (via lift); **Robin Hood's Bay**.

Waterfalls at **Goathland**.

Scarborough Len Raine, 25 Victoria Road; **Whitby** Blenkeys, 6 Flowergate.

▲ **Scarborough** 0723 361176; **Whitby** 0947 602878; **Boggle Hole** Whitby (0947) 880352.

Cumbria

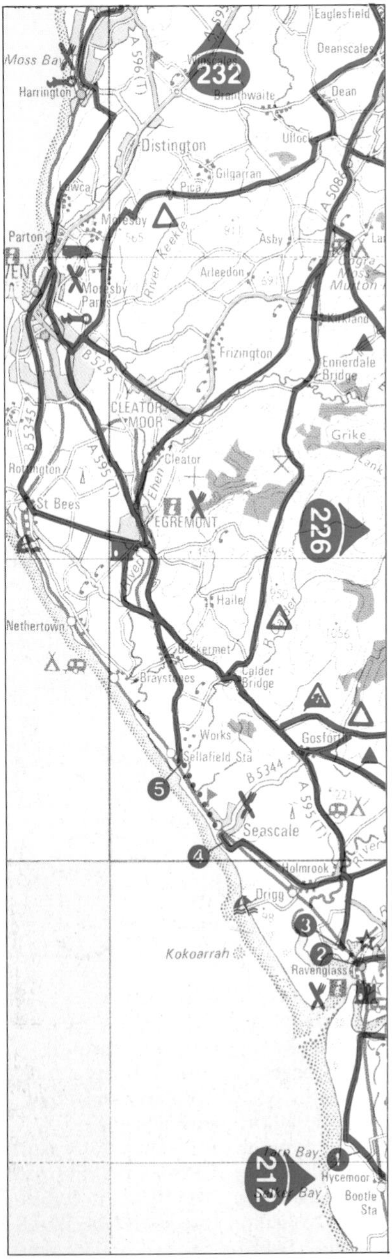

① The Cumbria Cycle Way (details page 212) is not fully signposted, but with help from the leaflet available, route-finding is not difficult. ②–③ is track; ④–⑤ is cinder track on beach side of railway.

△ Except for coastal routing, severe climbs, for example **Calder Bridge to Ennerdale Bridge, E from Moresby, inland from Gosforth**.

Whitehaven (name not all on map) and other stations on the Cumbria coast line.

Choices **Whitehaven**, **Workington** (name off map) and **Egremont**; limited choices, **Seascale** and **Ravenglass**.

Unclassified road **N of Gosforth** leads E up **Wasdale** to a fine ride along the edge of Wast Water with superb views.

Beaches S of **St Bees** and at **Drigg**.

☆ The **Ravenglass** and Eskdale railway, a small-gauge line up the Rivers Mite and Esk to Eskdale Green and Dalegarth, 13 mile (21 km) round trip, summer only.

Muncaster Castle **off A595 E of Ravenglass**, Elizabethan features, 16th-c–17th-c furniture, grounds, bird garden, garden centre; **Egremont** Castle ruins.

Whitehaven Arnstrong Cycles, 51 Roper Street and Mark Taylor, 21 King Street; **Workington** cycle hire from Lakes Leisure, The Old School, Siddick.

▲ Near by on Wast Water and Ennerdale Water – see page 226.

Opposite, Ambleside in the heart of the Lake District – see page 227.

Cumbria

For details of off-highway routing on this map, see pages 228–229

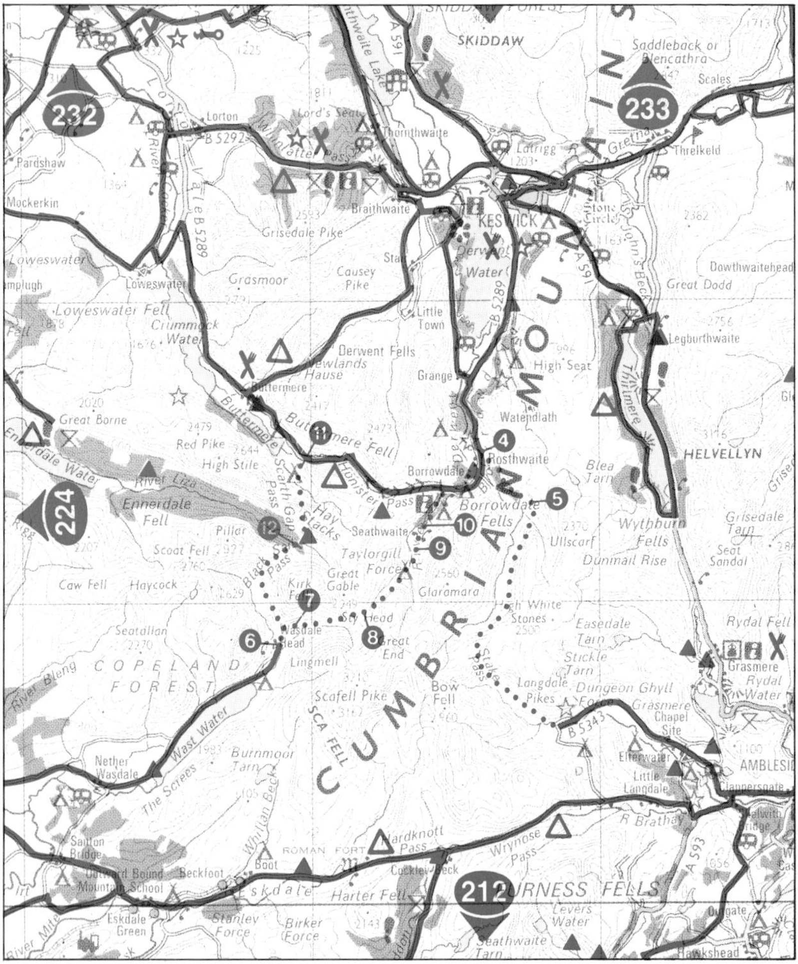

△ Touring for the fit. Standing out from many punishing climbs are the great passes: **Wrynose, Hardknott, Whinlatter, Newlands** and **Honister**. Take care on the forest road by **Ennerdale Water**. At peak times use the **unclassified road on the W side of Thirlmere** in preference to the A591.

✗ Choices **Cockermouth, Keswick, Grasmere**; refreshments, **Whinlatter Visitor Centre, Buttermere** and, in season, Dodd Wood, foot of **Skiddaw**.

⛰ Adjectives to describe this central area of the Lake District have long ago been used up, but cyclists will find the twisting road down **Borrowdale** particularly exhilarating.

☆ **Keswick** boat trips; Seatoller Information Centre at foot of **Honister Pass**.

▲ Eighteen hostels on this map alone – bookings via Regional Office, Windermere 09662 2301/2.

Cumbria

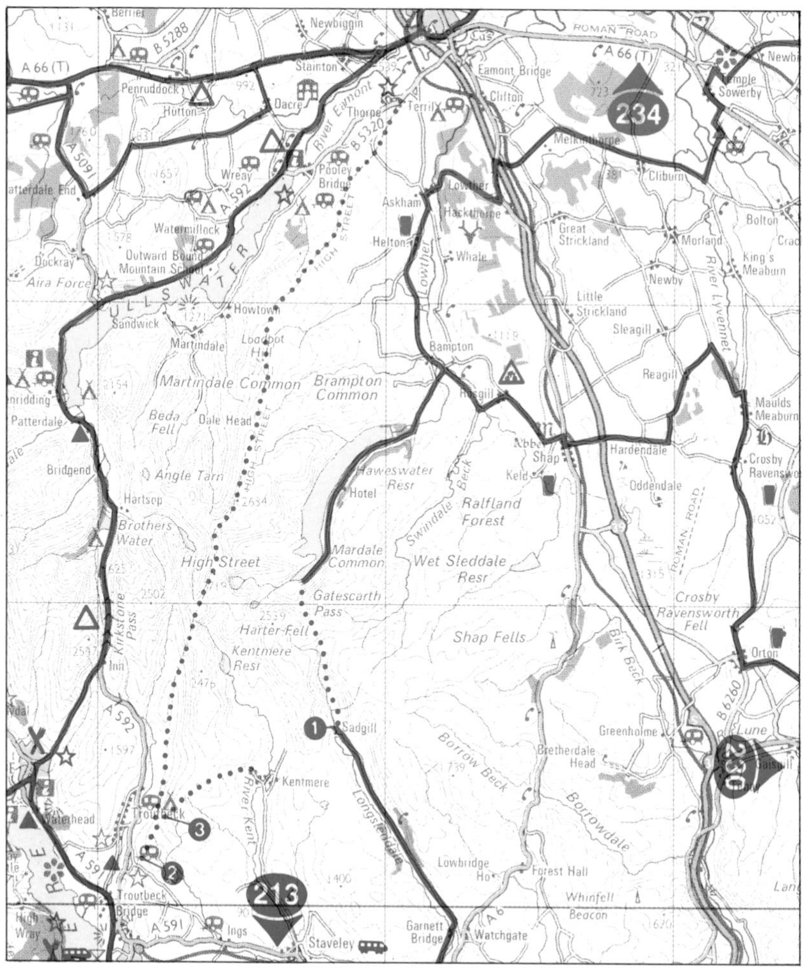

△ **Kirkstone** Pass, a punishing climb; **Pooley Bridge to Penrith**, hilly; **A66**, though a busy access road at peak times, is superb riding through magnificent scenery.

🚌 **Staveley** and **Windermere** (name not on map), on the Oxenholme–Windermere branch line.

✗ Choices **Windermere**, **Ambleside**, **Penrith** (name not on map).

🍺 Useful pubs at **Askham, Shap, Crosby Ravensworth** and **Orton**.

▲ **Temple Sowerby–Orton** covers the E fringes of the Lake District, still fine touring with excellent views E and W.

☆ Boat trips on **Ullswater** – a few cycles allowed as freight. **Windermere** and **Ambleside**, Lake District centres crowded in summer; boat trips.

ℌ **Crosby Ravensworth** A grave in the churchyard has a CTC badge on it.

▲ See comment on page 226.

Cumbria

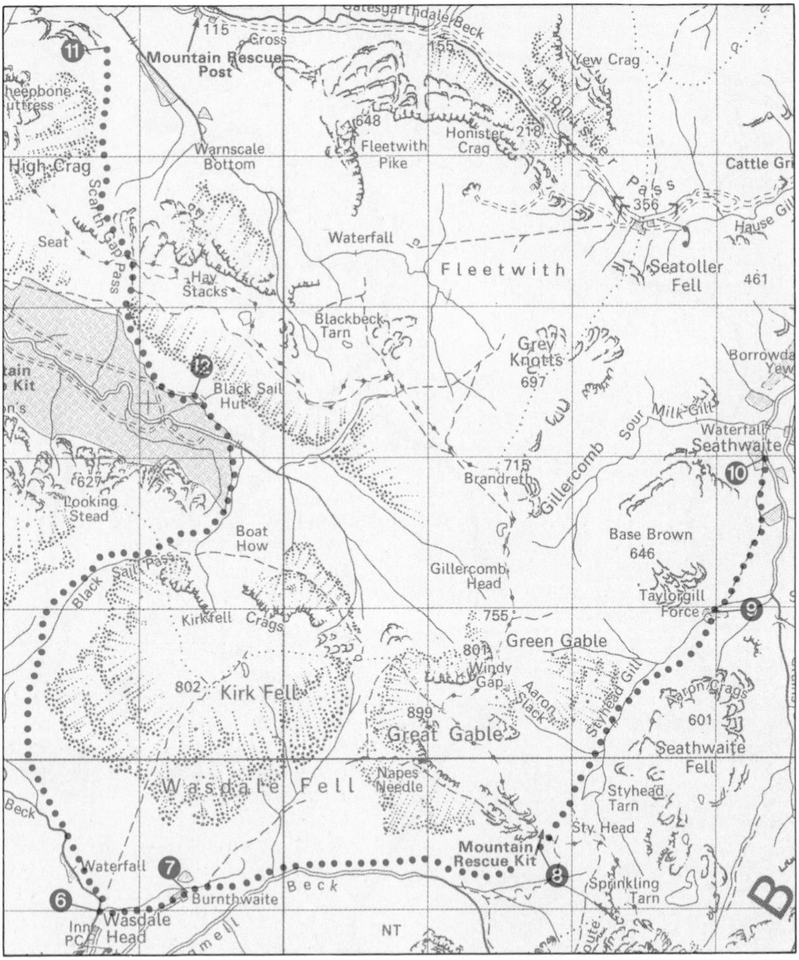

The opportunities for **off-highway riding in the Lake District** are plenty, but expect conditions as rough as, if not rougher than any upland area of Britain. In addition, the weather is extremely changeable; do not attempt any of this routing without large-scale maps or having rung the daily recorded weather forecast on Windermere 09662 5151. All the routing below requires a great deal of pushing and carrying the bike, and some sections of track will be barely passable. **The numerals are featured on the Routemaster mapping, pages 226–227**.

① (Gatescarth Pass) From Sadgill continue up track, over the pass and down to road along Haweswater.

② (Garburn Pass) On the A592 S of Troutbeck Church follow the track E through Howe and then swing NE up

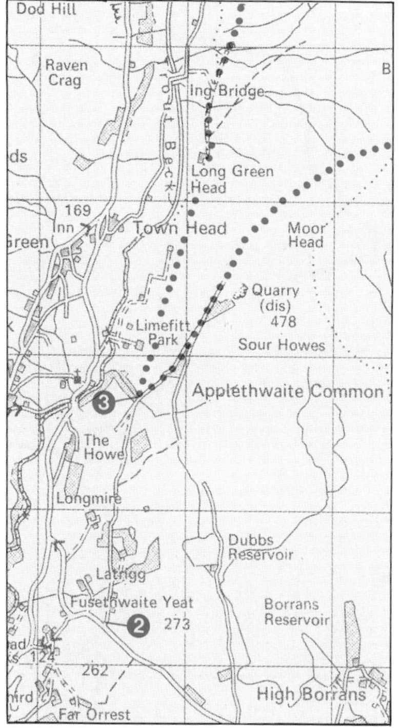

the fellside. Go through the pass and drop to Kentmere.

③ (Roman Road) From Howe turn left and continue N up the right side of Trout Beck and Hagg Gill. Take the footbridge over Hagg Gill to the left bank and continue with the Roman Road, easily followed along High Street Ridge down to the B5320 S of Penrith.

④ (Stake Pass) Leave Rosthwaite by lane

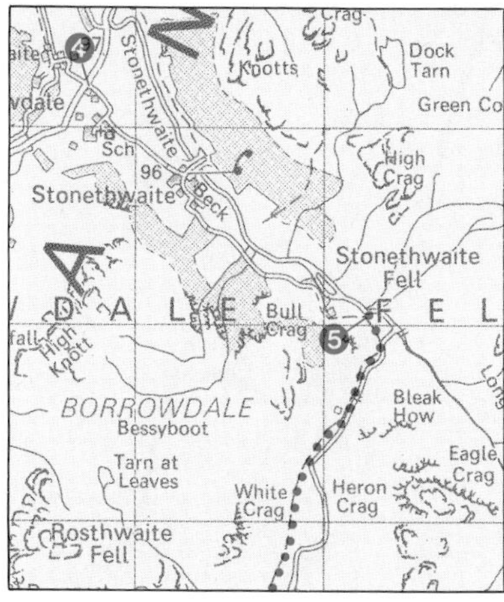

going S, and continue ⑤, along left bank of Langstath Beck. Go through pass and drop down zig-zag track to Mickleden and road into Langdale.

⑥ (Sty Head Pass) Leave Wasdale Green by track past house and little church to ⑦ Burnthwaite Farm. Go through farm via gates on to grass track, which becomes stony and lifts steeply over flank of Great Gable to summit cairn and mountain rescue box ⑧. Continue on left of Sty Head Tarn down to Stockley Bridge ⑨ and down track to Seathwaite ⑩. Continue on lane to Seatoller at foot of Honister Pass.

⑪ (Scarth Gap) Leave Buttermere at SE end of lake by Gatescarth Farm. Cross field and footbridge. Follow track up fellside below Hay Stacks and drop to edge of forest to join Ennerdale forestry road W of Black Sail Youth Hostel ⑫. From Black Sail Youth Hostel it is possible to turn right over the beck and go uphill by a forestry fence, following a steep rough track to the summit (detours possible to make the going easier). The drop to Gatherstone Beck and Mosedale is long and rough, the final stretch passing an old packhorse bridge and Wasdale Head Hotel to reach Wasdale Green ⑥.

Cumbria/Durham

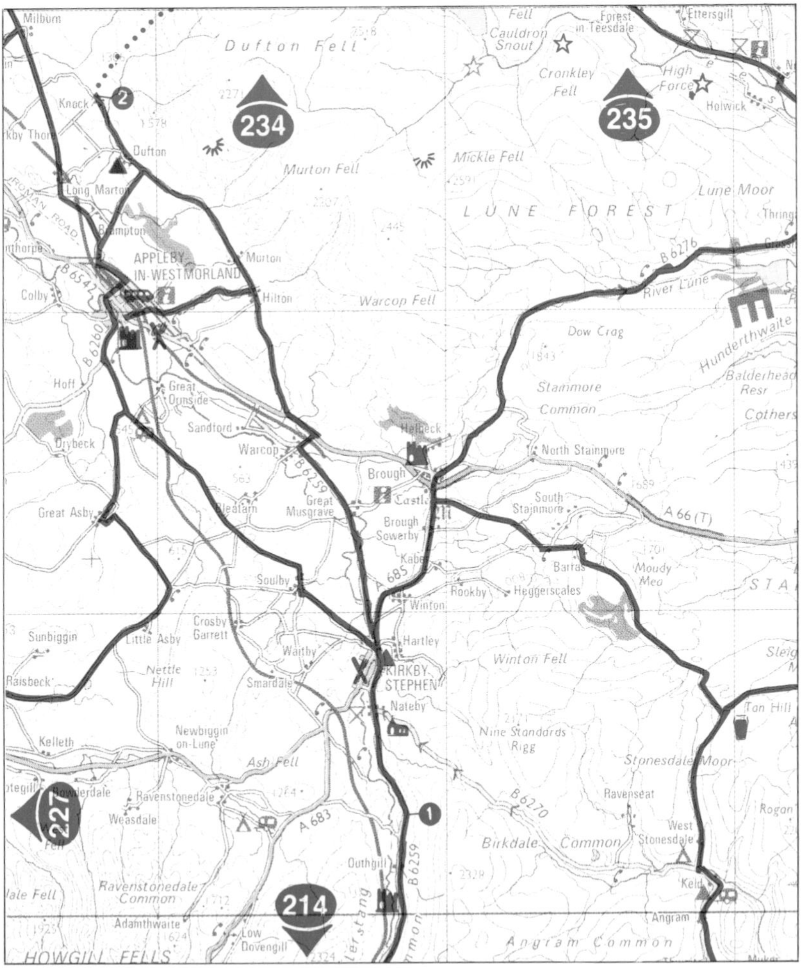

① The North Lancashire Cycle Way, details page 205.

② This bridleway section of the Pennine Way gives a dramatic and strenuous Pennine crossing to Garrigill (page 234), but it must be ridden from the other (clockwise) direction for maximum effect: the last four miles (6·5 km) down to Knock is free-wheeling.

△ Severe climbs throughout, typically **Arkengarthdale–Healaugh**.

🚌 Infrequent service to **Appleby-in-Westmorland** on the Leeds–Carlisle branch line.

✗ **Appleby, Kirkby Stephen, Startforth**, limited choices.

🍺 **Tan Hill** Inn, the highest pub in England – 1,730 foot (527 m).

✻ The huge, impressive natural amphitheatre of High Cup Nick, between **Murton and Dufton Fells**, is a stren-

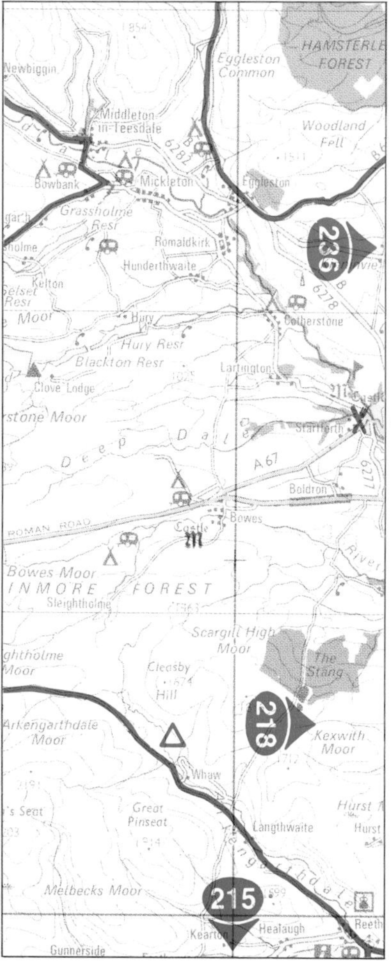

uous 5-mile (8-km) walk E along the Pennine Way from Dufton. The Way is a bridleway here, and rough-stuffers use it to cross to Langdon Beck, but it is not a right of way for cyclists the whole distance; extremely strenuous, only for best weather conditions. **Mickle Fell**, 2,591 feet (790 m), offers amazing views.

☆ **High Force** waterfall is as dramatic as any in England.

The market town of **Appleby-in-Westmorland** has a castle with a collection of rare breed animals; Pendragon Castle (not marked on map), **S of Outhgill** between road and river; ruined 12th-c castle at **Brough**.

Remains of Roman fort and Norman castle, **Bowes**.

Kirkby Stephen's church has an interesting medieval stone showing Satan in bonds.

▲ **Dufton** Appleby (0930) 51236; **Kirkby Stephen** (0930) 71793; Baldersdale (near **Startforth**) Teesdale (0833) 50629.

High Force

Cumbria

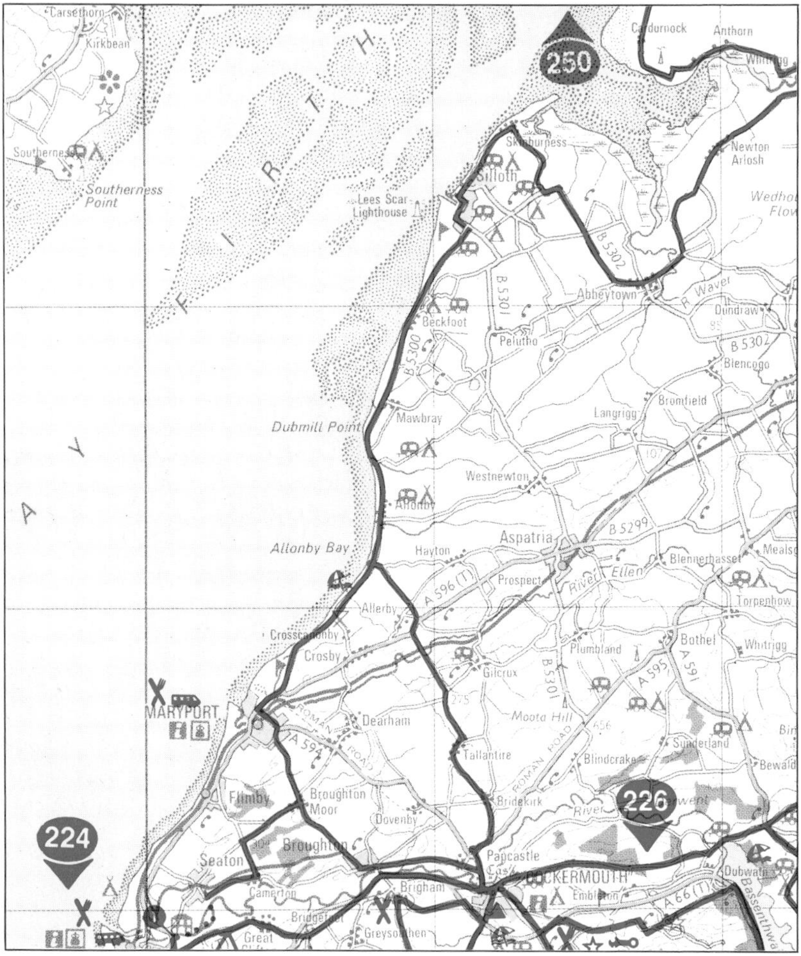

① Cumbria Cycle Way, details page 212. This is a footpath and bridleway section along the River Derwent shown on a large-scale map excerpt in the official leaflet.

△ Intermittent climbs on all the routing except the **A66**, which is relatively level and quiet. A large number of bends – ride single file at all times.

Workington, **Maryport** and other stations on the Cumbria coast line.

Choices **Cockermouth**, **Workington**, **Maryport**; limited choices, **Brigham**.

Swimming in **Bassenthwaite Lake** and in the Cocker and Derwent at **Cockermouth**; extensive beach **N from Maryport**.

☆ **Cockermouth**, birthplace of Wordsworth, is a useful touring centre.

Cockermouth Cycle shop in Market Place.

▲ **Cockermouth** 0900 822561.

Cumbria

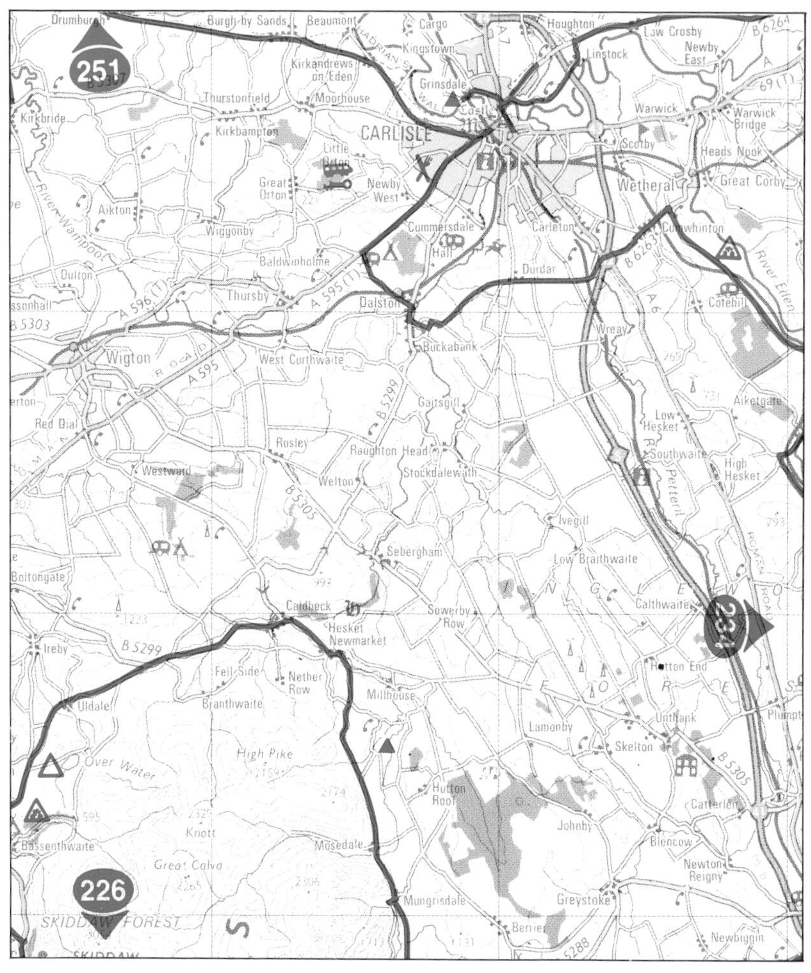

△ Moderate to strenuous climbs round **Skiddaw Forest** circuit.

Six great railway lines meet at **Carlisle**; the main lines from Inverness and London; the Cumbria coast line and the trans-Pennine line from Newcastle upon Tyne; and the branch lines through SW Scotland from Glasgow and along the Pennines from Bradford and Leeds.

Choices, **Carlisle**.

Fine riding through the **Eden** Valley and views on the **Skiddaw** circuit.

John Peel, hero of the hunting song, was a local man and his grave is in the churchyard at **Caldbeck**.

Carlisle Border Cycles, 133 Lowther Street; cycle hire from T. P. Bell, 18–22 Abbey Street.

▲ **Carlisle** (0228) 23934; Carrock Fell (near **Hesket Newmarket**) Caldbeck (06998) 325.

Cumbria

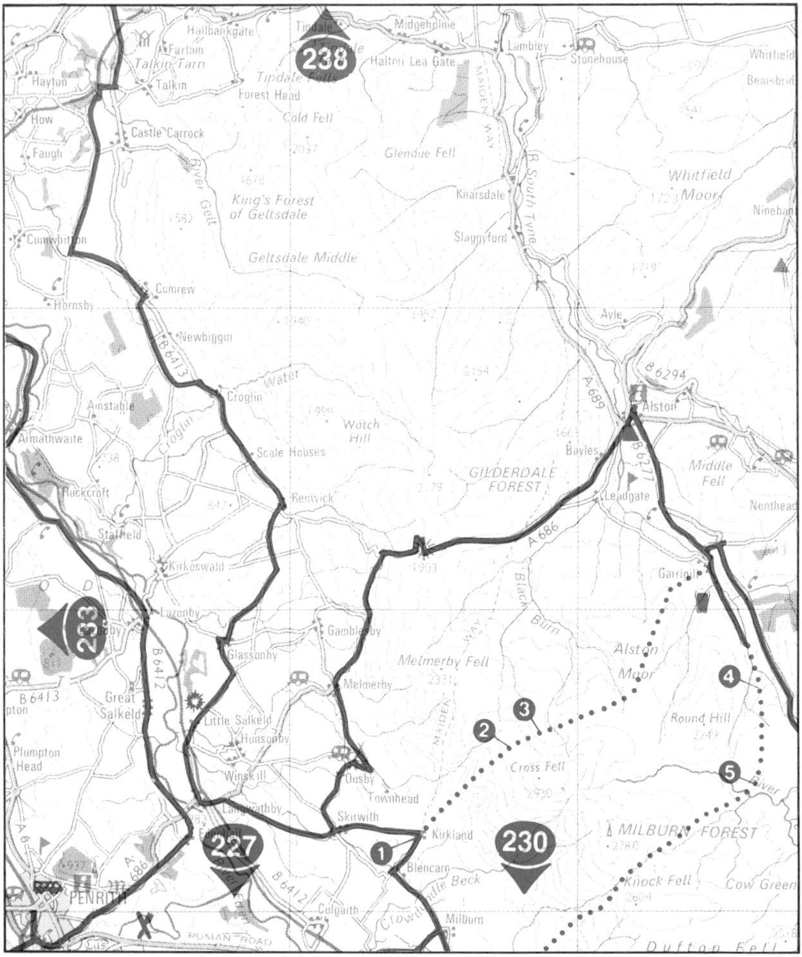

① Corpse Road to Garrigill. ② Where rough road turns sharp left, keep straight on with rough grass track – follow cairns. ③ From Greg's Hut follow Pennine Way to Garrigill.

④ Continue on track. ⑤ At Road End Bridge do not cross to Moor House but follow N bank of river on old mine road. Note pylons of weather station on Great Dun Fell and cross skyline ½ mile (0.8 km) S of pylons where small brick building can be seen; join road to weather station; downhill now to Knock. *Both routes are spectacular, severely strenuous; attempt only if fit, in first-rate visibility, properly equipped (page 11). Ride clockwise.*

Penrith on the Preston–Carlisle route.

Choices at **Penrith**.

The George and Dragon, **Garrigill**.

Long Meg near **Little Salkeld**.

▲ **Alston** 0498 81509.

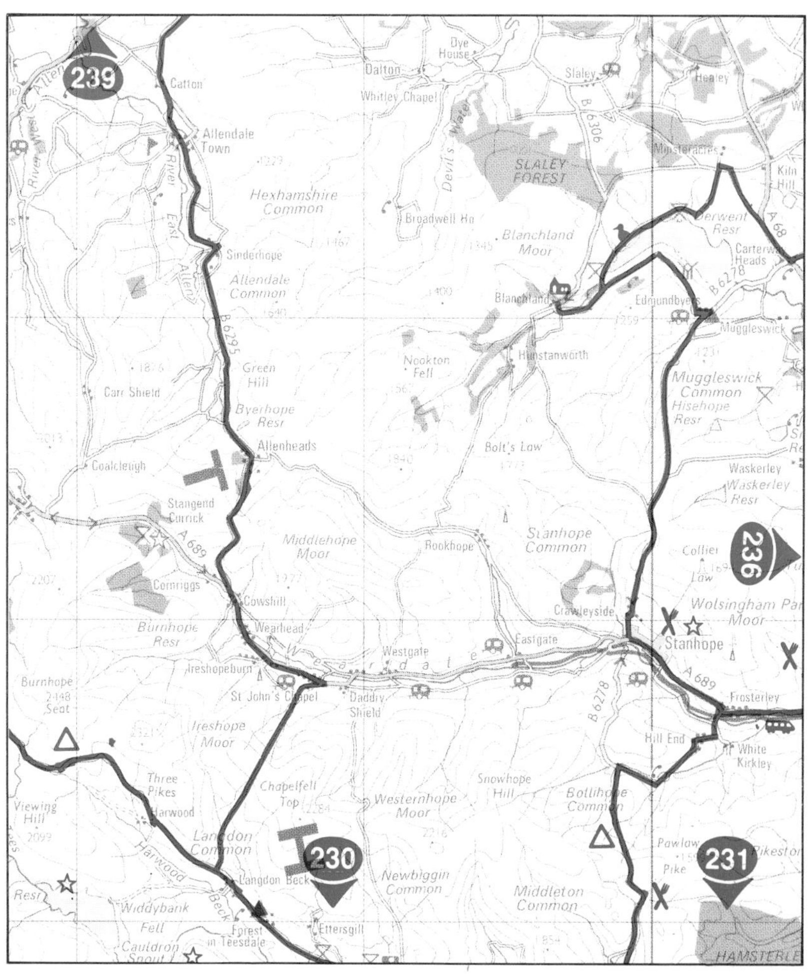

△ Both **B roads** are very hilly, but the B6277 in particular is an exhilarating road, with surprisingly little traffic. The route from Stanhope past **Pawlaw Pike** is best tackled N–S.

🚌 Nearest is Bishop Auckland, page 236.

🍴 **Stanhope**, limited choices; meals at the Grey Bull, **Wolsingham** (name partly off map); bar snacks at the Three Tunns near **Eggleston**, S of Pawlaw.

⛪ **Blanchland's** church contains 12-C remains and the village square was part of an 18th-C model village.

🐦 **Derwent Reservoir** nature reserve.

☆ **Stanhope**, in the midst of this quarrying area, is a useful centre for walks on the moors; just S of Cow Green reservoir (reached by footpath over Widdybank Fell) is the dramatic Cauldron Snout – a series of waterfalls created by the River Tees.

▲ **Langdon Beck** Teesdale (0833) 22228.

Durham/Cleveland

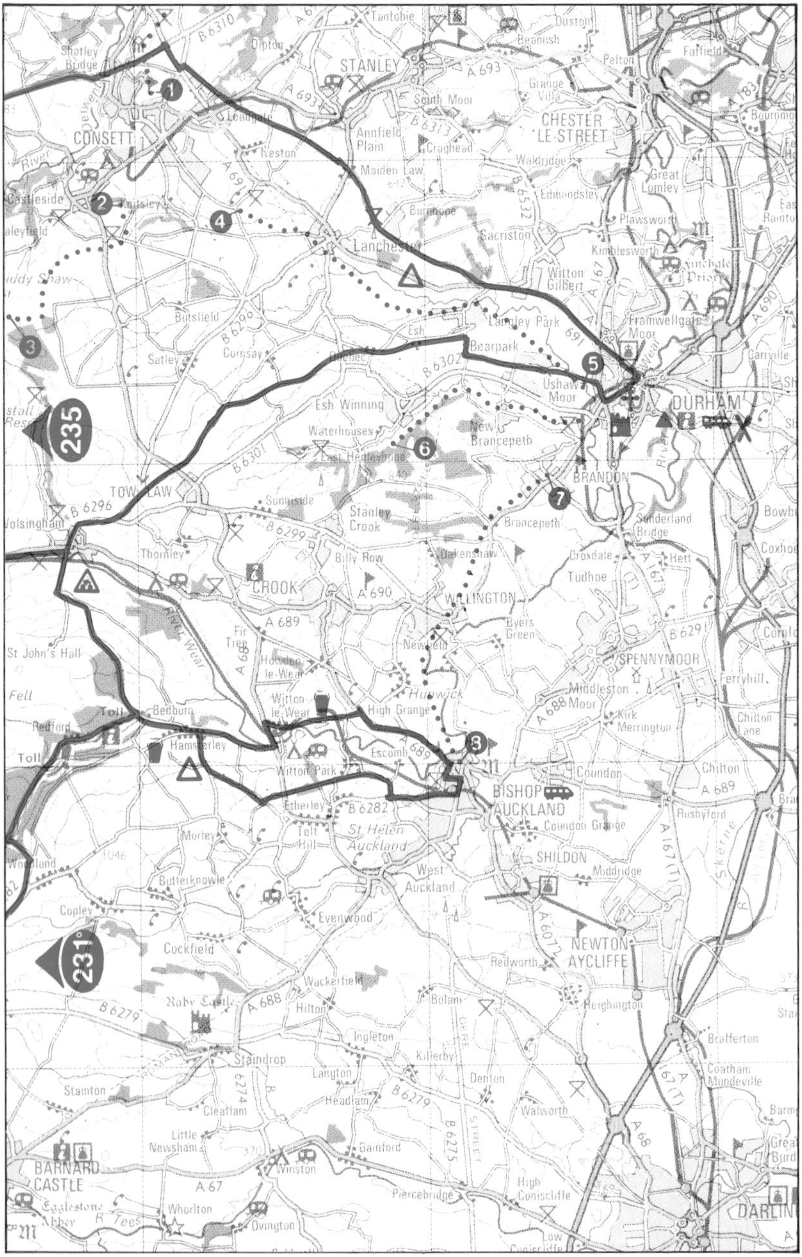

235

231

Durham/Cleveland

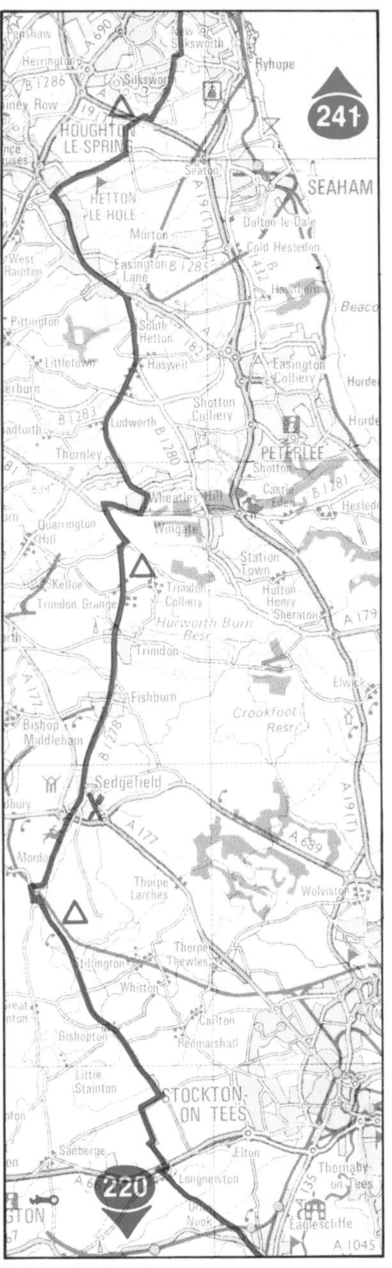

① Access to disused railway line route through Derwent Walk Country Park opposite hospitals in Consett.

② Access to Waskerley Way, a rough moorland route, at Hown's Gill viaduct and ③ Waskerley.

④ Access to Lanchester Way disused railway line route down from Harbuch Cottages and ⑤ Baxter Wood bridleway.

⑥ Deerness Walkway from B6302 E of Broom and at Waterhouses.

⑦ Access to Brandon and Bishop Auckland Walkway (disused railway line route) at viaduct and ⑧ Brandon playing fields.

△ **Longnewton–Sedgefield** is undulating; **Sedgefield** N becomes a mixture of mining villages and rural riding; severe climbs going **W from Bishop Auckland** and **Durham**; climb over low range of hills **N from Houghton-le-Spring**.

Bishop Auckland on the Darlington–Bishop Auckland branch line; **Durham** on the Darlington–Newcastle main line.

Plentiful choices in Durham; choices in **Sedgefield**.

Witton-le-Wear and **Hamsterley**.

The **E side of the Pennines** here are known as the Durham Moors, and they offer some breath-taking scenery.

✕ Picnic site at **Burnhope**, fine views.

† **Durham**, dramatically sited above the Wear, with its cathedral, one of the largest in England. Dr. Johnson described the interior as one of 'rocky solidity', perhaps a misleading description for such an impressive church interior. The great circular columns have a remarkable amount of zig-zag or chevron patterning cut into them.

Durham Castle, founded by William the Conqueror in 1072.

Darlington Peter Rippon Cycles, 29 High Northgate.

▲ **Durham** Booking to YHA Regional Office, Durham 0385 42588 or Guisborough 0287 35831.

Northumberland/Cumbria

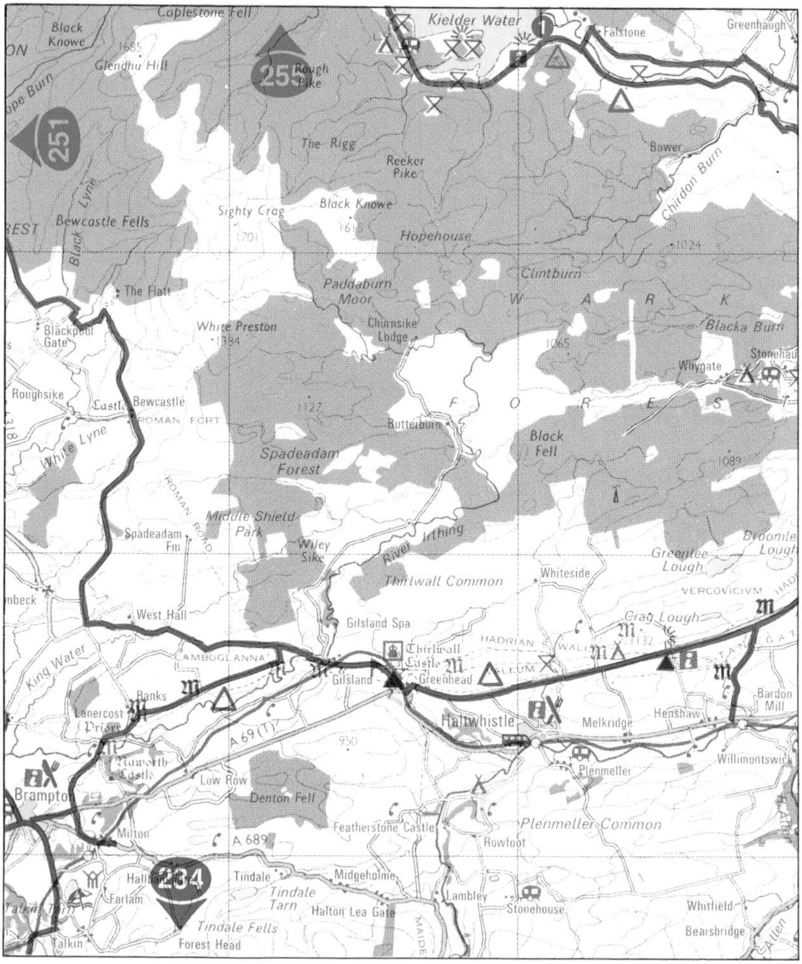

① Forestry track leading along the N side of Kielder Reservoir; mostly rideable, though unsurfaced beyond Gowanburn Farm; surface improves at Kielder Dam.

△ The unclassified road **following Hadrian's Wall** E is peaceful; **B6318** is steep uphill at first; **Falstone E** is narrow and hilly.

Infrequent services to **Haltwhistle** and other stations on the Newcastle–Carlisle branch line.

Haltwhistle, **Brampton**, limited choices.

Falstone–Bellingham is outstanding; **N side of Kielder Reservoir** remote.

Bathing in **Talkin** Tarn.

𝔪 This is the most interesting section of the 73-mile (117-km) Hadrian's Wall.

▲ **Greenhead** Gilsland (06972) 401; Once Brewed (N of **Henshaw**) Bardon Mill (04984) 360.

Northumberland

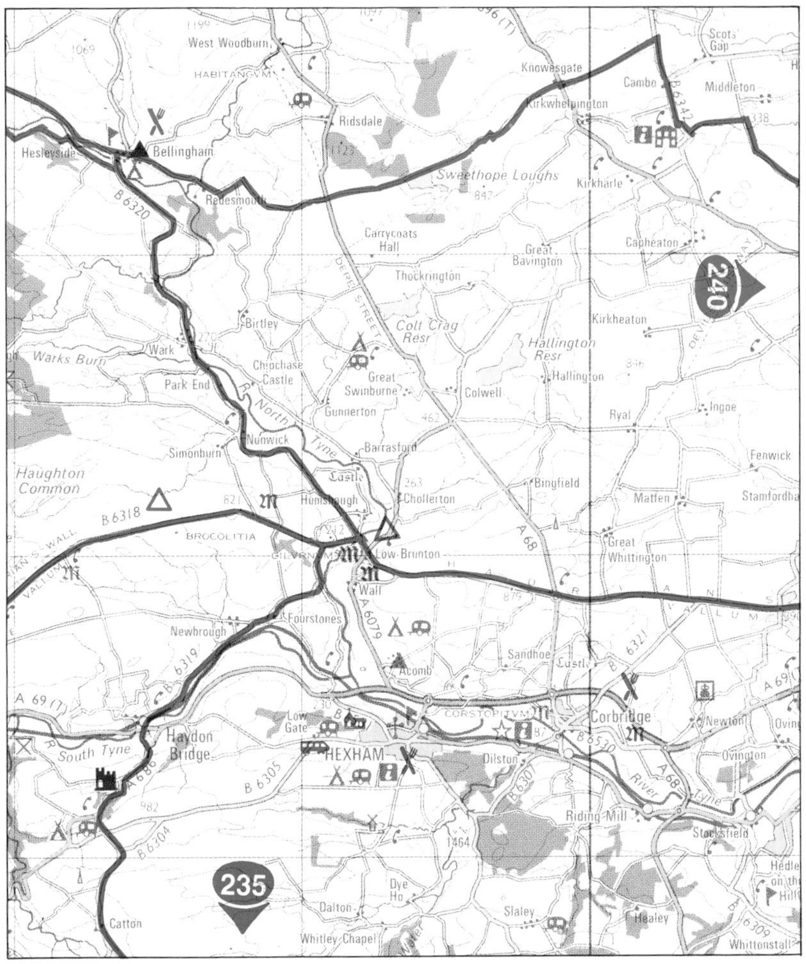

△ Gentle hills on the **B6318**, surprisingly quiet for a classified road; delays at **Low Brunton** on single-track bridge with traffic lights.

🚐 Infrequent service to **Hexham** on the Newcastle upon Tyne to Carlisle branch line.

✗ **Hexham**, **Corbridge**, choices; pub meals and café at **Bellingham**.

⛪ **Hexham**, exceptionally interesting church with 8th-C Acca Cross, Saxon Bishop's Chair and 7th-C crypt.

𝔐 **Hadrian's Wall** reaches its northernmost point at Limestone Corner and the *vallum* or rampart is clearly visible here; rewarding sights include Chesters Fort and Museum (marked **'Cilurium'**), **Corbridge** Fortress and **Brunton** Turret.

🏰 Langley Castle (marked but not named on **A686**) is 14th C.

▲ **Bellingham** 0660 20313.

Tyne and Wear

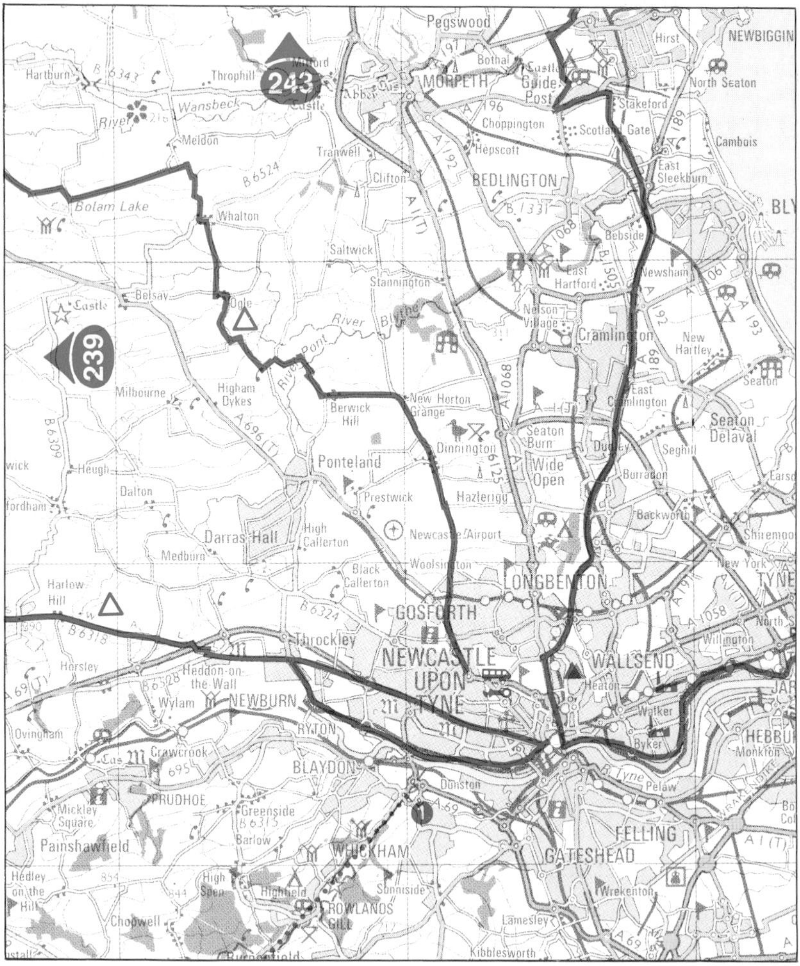

① Access to Derwent Walk Country Park disused railway route at River Tyne and Derwent Haugh.

△ Moderate climbs W and NW **out of Newcastle upon Tyne**.

Newcastle, on the York–Edinburgh main line, InterCity services, also on the Carlisle–Middlesbrough branch line: the **South Shields–North Shields ferry** accepts bikes.

Attractive road through **Whitburn**.

South Shields has a long, sandy beach.

There is some easy and pleasant walking along the cliffs from **Marsden Bay**, with the added attraction of seeing some interesting sea birds. The chief attraction is Marsden Rock, an isolated stack which provides nesting sites for kittiwakes, fulmars and cormorants. The rock itself is immediately adjacent to the Marsden Grotton public house in Marsden Bay, and from here it is

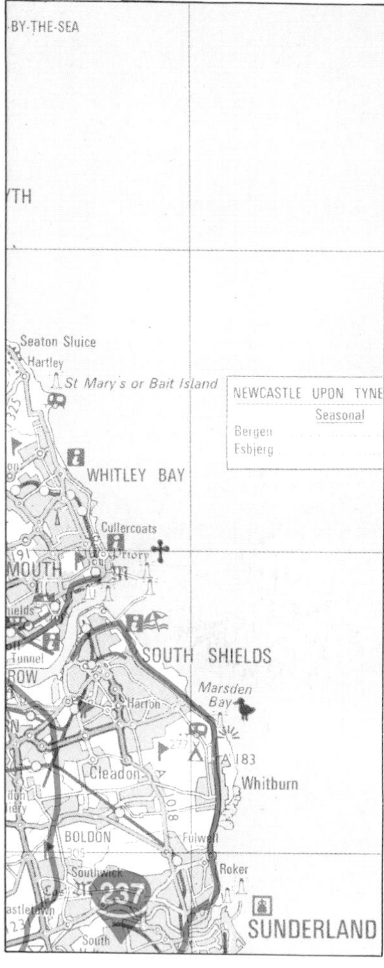

simple to follow the cliff path SE about a mile (1.5 km) to the lighthouse, or NW 2 miles (3 km) to Trow Point.

The fish quay at **Tynemouth** makes an absorbing visit, and the sights and sounds of the shipyards at **Wallsend** and **Walker** should not be overlooked.

Ruins of **Tynemouth** Priory and Castle.

Newcastle Denton Cycles, 177 Westgate Road.

Newcastle 0632 812570.

Kittiwake colonies, such as on Marsden Rock, can be spectacular, with the birds' grassy nests attached to the sheer cliff face. No problem in identifying the cormorant, a large, rather prehistoric looking bird which may stand with its wings outstretched, drying in the wind.

Northumberland

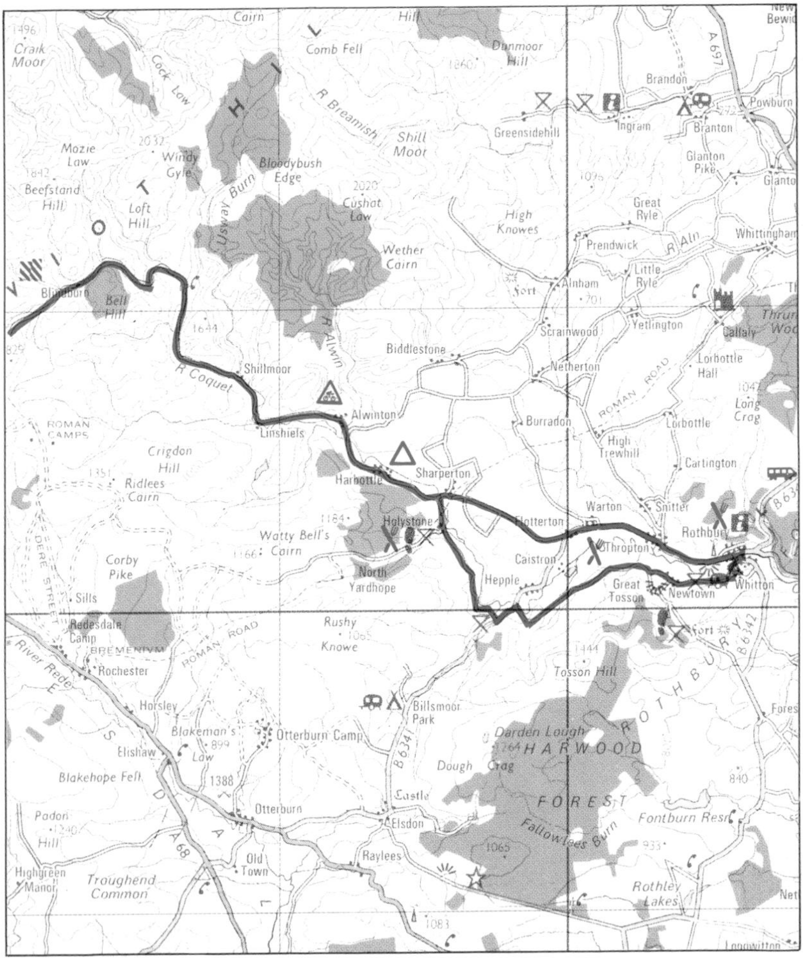

△ It is a gradual climb NW up Coquetdale along the river **Coquet**, but expect a few short, steep hills whether riding up the dale or down. The road twists and turns, crossing and re-crossing the river.

Nearest is Acklington, 16 miles (26 km) E of **Rothbury** – see page 243.

The scenery is lovely whichever way this secluded valley is ridden – but the **return ride to Rothbury** on a falling gradient is cycling at its best.

Pub meals and cafés in **Rothbury**; pub meals at **Holystone** and **Thropton**; advisable to carry food and drink if riding to the end of the Dale.

Fine views through the whole tour.

The road carries on to within a mile (1.5 km) of **the border**, which can be reached from Mackendon Farm by footpath only (restricted access, firing range).

Northumberland

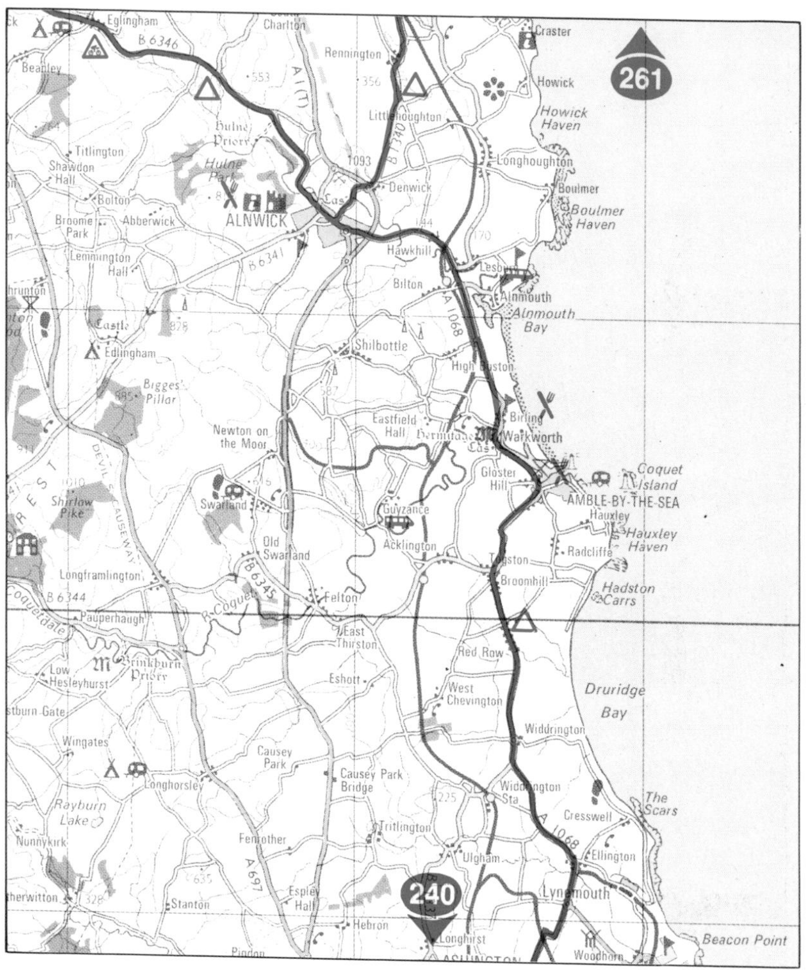

△ **Ellington–Alnwick** variable; increasingly hard climbs **N and NW from Alnwick**.

Alnmouth, **Acklington** and other stations on the Newcastle–Edinburgh main line.

Choices Alnwick and **Amble-by-the-Sea**; limited choice, **Warkworth**.

Inland from Alnwick, some of the most remote roads in England.

Alnwick (pronounced 'Annick') is a charming walled town dominated by the castle, main seat of the Dukes of Northumberland – the Percys – guardians of the border in times past and still practically private princes in their own right. The castle is much restored, but an interesting example of medieval fortification; on view inside are Percy treasures and paintings.

Warkworth Castle is a fine ruin, and worth a visit.

7
SCOTLAND

The highways and byways of Scotland – like the Scottish character itself – can be deceptive. A cycling tour north of the Border needs careful planning.

Distances indicated by a glance at the map can be particularly misleading, for roads often twist around lochs or through mountain passes, making the journey much longer than the map's scale can reveal. Similarly, distances between villages, and thus food supplies, can be larger than anywhere else in the country, so fill your panniers and carry emergency rations.

Gradients are another source of deception. Here, in the British Isles' greatest tracts of uplands, a significant share of climbs are long and gentle, within the capabilities of family groups.

On the other hand, road surfaces, particularly at higher altitudes, can be pitted and rough, the result of frost damage. Then again, there are some appalling road surfaces in some of the towns.

If you are visiting Scotland for a holiday, you will probably want to make use of the train service. Oban, for instance, terminus of the line via Crianlarich from Glasgow, gives access to vast tracts of wonderful West Highlands touring; cycling there from, say, south of Glasgow, could be a waste of holiday time.

In the least populous mountain areas, the road network can amount to nothing more than A or B roads, many of them single track, with room for passing only at selected wide points. Most are far more deserted than any country lane elsewhere, and because there are so few of them, reading smaller scale maps such as Routemaster becomes relatively effortless.

Don't overlook the possibility of island-hopping, but again, plan carefully. There are many privately-owned ferry services besides the ones indicated on the maps: a list is published in the CTC handbook.

Selected tours

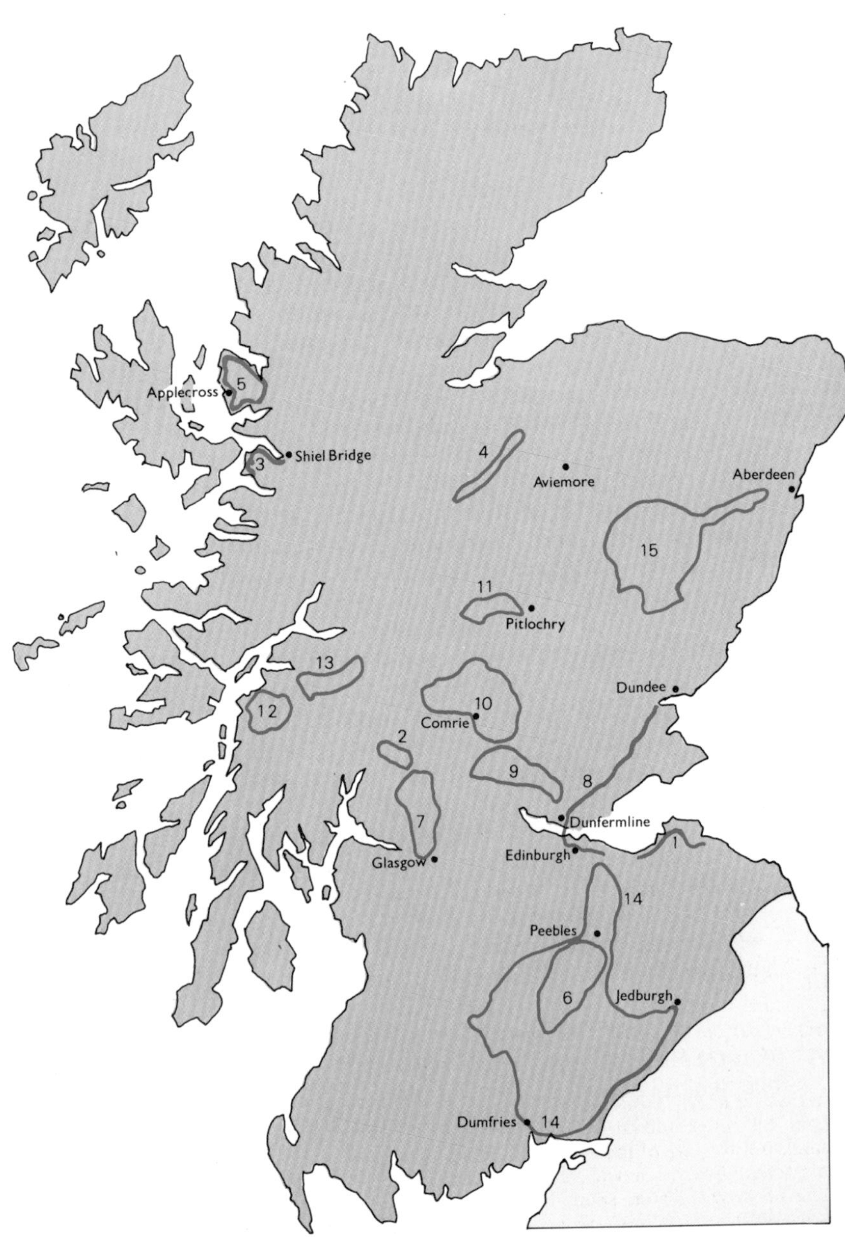

Selected tours

A cross-section of the tours in this region, showing typical rides that can be put together from the route network in a range of localities; details pages 247–9.

Day rides
1 Edinburgh to Dunbar
2 Loch Katrine and the Trossachs
3 Sandaig
4 Carrbridge and Newtonmore
5 The Applecross Round

Two-day tours
6 Borders
7 North of Glasgow
8 Edinburgh to Dundee
9 Ochil Hills
10 Loch Tay
11 Loch Tummel and Glen Errochty
12 Oban and Loch Awe
13 Glen Kinglass

Three days or longer
14 Borders and Southern Uplands
15 Aberdeen, Ballater and Glen Doll

Day rides
1 Edinburgh to Dunbar, about 45 miles (72 km). Mostly easy riding, much of it right beside the Firth of Forth. Regular rail links between Dunbar and Edinburgh. *Edinburgh–Musselburgh–North Berwick – East Linton – Stenton – Pitcox–Dunbar (last two places not on mapping, but route easy to identify)*; **pages 264, 265**.

2 Loch Katrine and the Trossachs, with Aberfoyle as a base, about 30 miles (48 km). One of the loveliest parts of Central Scotland, but off-highway routing enables the cyclist to escape most of the traffic; gradients vary from easy to severe. *Aberfoyle – Kinlochard – Stronachlachar – Strath Gartney – Bochastle–Callander*; **page 269**.

3 Saindaig, in the Kyle of Lochalsh area, about 30 miles (48 km). A chance to search out the site of the cottage at Sandaig where Gavin Maxwell, author of *A Ring of Bright Water*, spent his happy years with the otters. *Shiel Bridge–Gleneig – Eilanreach – Arnisdale and return with a diversion up to Dun Grugaig*; **page 296**.

4 Carrbridge and Newtonmore, a circuit in the Cairngorms region, also taking in Aviemore, about 60 miles (96 km). This is a long day's ride, but it offers dramatic mountain scenery while keeping mostly to level valley floors. *Newtonmore – Ruthven – Coylumbridge – Nethy Bridge – Carrbridge – Aviemore – Kingussie – Newtonmore*; **pages 291, 300**.

5 The Applecross Round, a circuit of Applecross Forest, in the Loch Torridon area of the Western Highlands, about 45 miles (72 km). One of the most exciting rides in the west of Scotland, involving a ride over the grim Pass of the Cattle, with its severe gradients and hairpin bends. The road is surfaced throughout. Allow a full day and do not attempt in poor visibility. *Shieldaig – Fearnmore – Applecross – Shieldaig*; **page 302**.

Selected tours

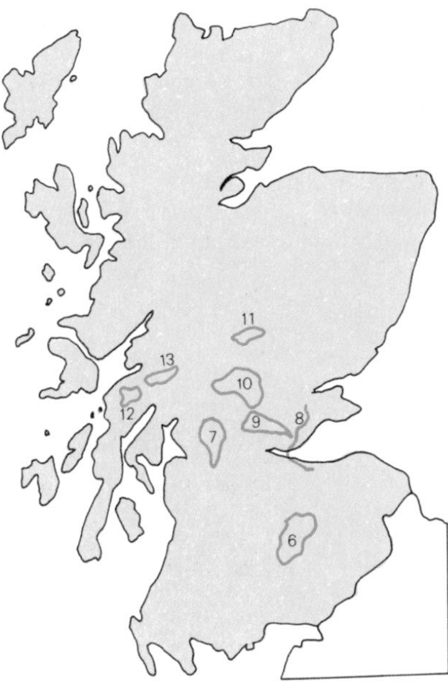

Two-day tours

6 Borders, based on Peebles and Moffatt, about 88 miles (141 km). The route starts at Carstairs Junction, making access from Glasgow, Edinburgh and the north of England particularly easy. It takes in some of the finest Borders scenery, with plenty of rugged mountain views, and is strenuous in parts, a challenging single day's ride, but a comfortable weekend. The route is mainly on A and B roads, but they are as quiet as unclassified roads elsewhere in the country. *Carstairs–Peebles – Mountbenger – Moffat – Broughton – Biggar – Carstairs*; **pages 256, 257, 253**.

7 North of Glasgow, taking in the Campsie Fells, Achray Forest and Loch Katrine, about 80 miles (128 km). Much of the route is on A roads, but they carry little traffic. The scenery is varied – hills and lochs – and there is plenty of historical interest, all within easy reach of Scotland's largest conurbation. *Clydebank (Temple) – Mugdock – Aberfoyle – Stronachlachar – Off-highway route along Loch Katrine N shore–Aberfoyle–Glasgow, with an alternative route back to Glasgow via Fintry and Lennoxtown*; **pages 263, 269, 270**.

8 Edinburgh to Dundee, about 60 miles (96 km). Varied scenery through Fife and along the Tay estuary, possible as a single day, but more comfortable as two. *Edinburgh – Queensferry – Inverkeithing – Kelty – Leslie – Falkland – Newburgh – Wormit – Dundee*; **pages 272, 273, 275**.

9 Ochil Hills, about 75 miles (120 km). Takes in the best of these hills, with plenty of steep ascents. *Dollar–Hill End – Drum – Glendevon – Gleneagles – Braco – Doune – Bridge of Allan – Menstrie – Devonside – Dollar*; **p. 272**.

10 Loch Tay, and Loch Earn, a circuit which can be based on Stirling, about 90 miles (144 km). The rugged mountain scenery around Loch Tay contrasts with the sleepy flat region of the Earn Valley between Crieff and Auchterarder. Strenuous in parts, but could be ridden in a day by the fit sporting cyclist. *Stirling – Muirtown – Fowlis Wester – Buchanty – Amulree – Kenmore – Killin – Lochearnhead – Comrie – Braco – Stirling*; **pages 270, 271, 272, 274, 278, 287**.

11 Loch Tummel and Glen Errochty, in the Blair Atholl area, about 50 miles (80 km). There is plenty to see on this tour – from the spectacular Bruar Falls to Blair Castle, seat of the Duke of Atholl, and so it is suggested as a two-day ride. Superb mountain views and plenty of places for picnicking. *Pitlochry–Blair Atholl – Trinafour – Kinloch Rannoch – Foss – Portnacraig – Pitlochry*; **p. 287**.

12 Oban and Loch Awe, about 44 miles (70 km). Spectacular West Highland scenery, hard climbs, and plenty of 'wild' camping places – a pity to cram into one day. *Oban – Kilmelford – Kilchrenan – Taynuilt – Oban*; **page 276.**

13 Glen Kinglass, with access from Bridge of Orchy Station, about 50 miles (80 km). This tour involves about 20 miles (32 km) of off-highway routing. One section of track in Glen Kinglass is rather rough and may involve some wheeling – but the route is still suitable overall for a conventional touring bike. There is a conveniently placed camp site at Bridge of Awe. The scenery here in the heart of the West Highlands needs no qualification. *Bridge of Orchy Station–track along Glen Kinglass – Bridge of Awe–Pass of Brander–Strath of Orchy–Glen Orchy*; **pages 276, 277**.

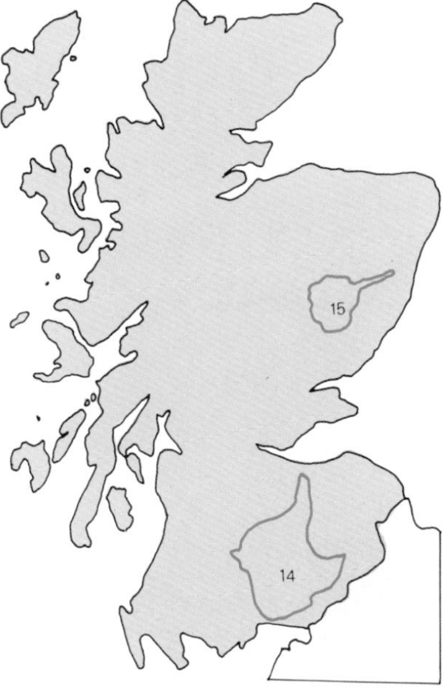

Three days or longer

14 Borders and Southern Uplands, about 110 miles (176 km). A fine tour for anyone with time to take in the best of the Southern Uplands and Borders. Six days would be a sensible time to allow, but the energetic could of course manage it quicker: the riding is a mixture of strenuous hill country and undulating roads. Could be shortened by returning on the train from Dumfries if Edinburgh is the starting point. *Edinburgh – Innerleithen – Crossleg – Hawick – Jedburgh – Newcastleton – Langholm – Annan – Dumfries – Sanquhar – Abington – Biggar – Penicuik – Edinburgh*; **pages 264, 258, 254, 255, 259, 251, 250, 252, 256, 257**.

15 Aberdeen, Ballater and Glen Doll, about 136 miles (218 km). A challenging tour, ideal for a long weekend, and for those who enjoy a sense of achievement. There are plenty of heavy climbs, and some off-highway routing (not all rideable, but no carrying is necessary). Memorable views and a first-class introduction to Deeside and the wild country to the south. *Aberdeen – Strachan – Ballater – Glen Doll – Dykehead – Fettercairn – Bridge of Dye – Woodlands – Aberdeen*; **pages 294, 295, 281, 293**.

Dumfries and Galloway

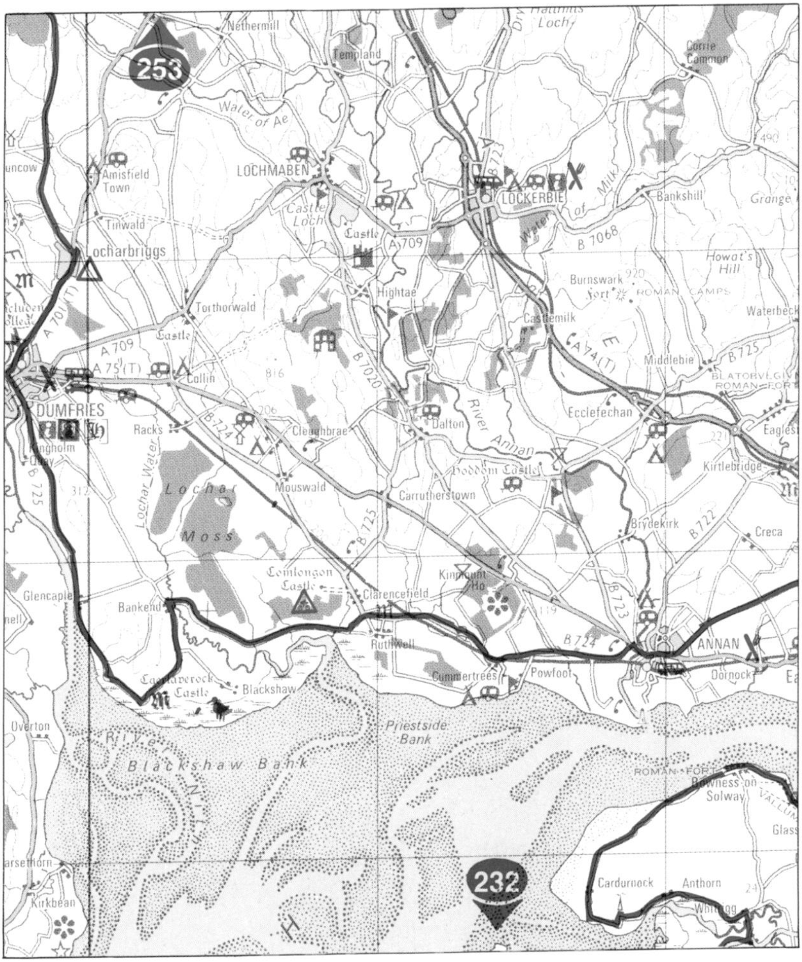

- △ **Dumfries–Locharbriggs**, short stretch of trunk road, traffic at peak periods.
- **Lockerbie**, on the London–Carlisle–Glasgow InterCity route; **Annan** and **Dumfries** on the Carlisle–Glasgow branch line.
- Good pub food at the Queensberry Arms, **Annan**: limited choices, **Dumfries, Lockerbie**.
- Pleasant, level riding, **Dumfries–Annan**.
- Sea and shore birds, **Blackshaw Bank**.
- Moated **Caerlaverack Castle**; Greyfriars Monastery, **Dumfries**.
- **Dumfries's** Museum has archaeology and folk exhibits.
- **Dumfries** Burns' House is kept as a museum to Scotland's national poet; Burns family mausoleum in St. Michael's churchyard.
- **Dumfries** Cycles, 25 Glasgow Street and Kirkpatrick Cycles, 13 Queen St.

Dumfries and Galloway/Cumbria/Borders

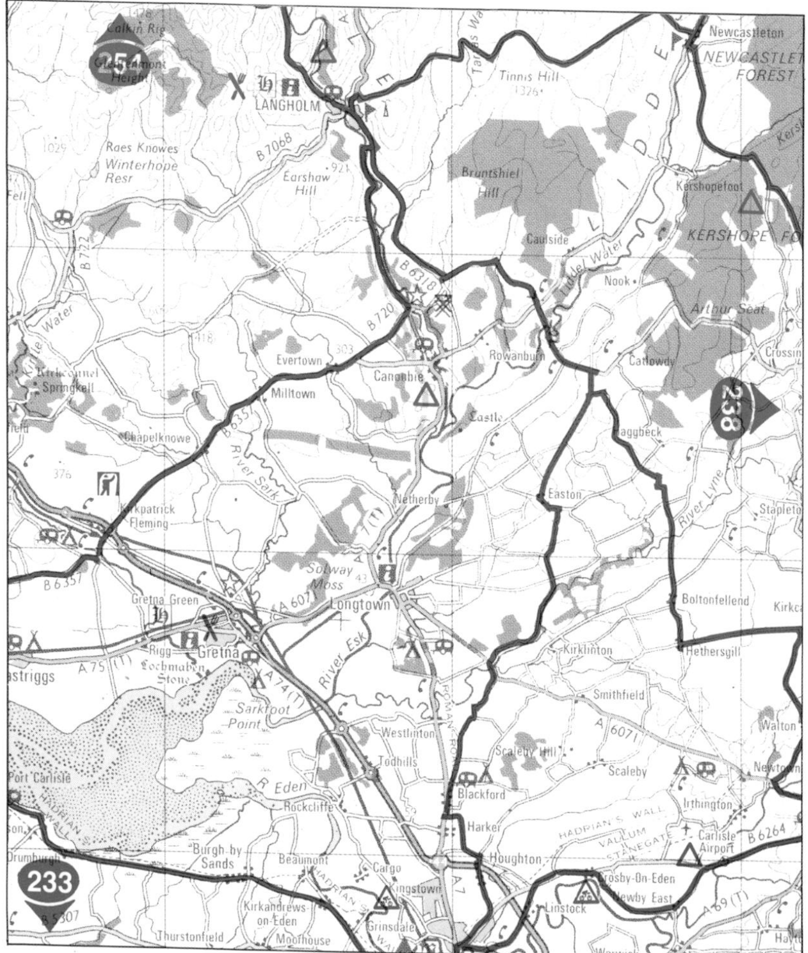

△ Climb through narrow gorge, **N from Langholm**; steep hills, **Kershope Forest** and **Canonbie** areas; **B6264** is busy where it runs close to Carlisle Airport.

Carlisle (name off map) on the London–Edinburgh InterCity route.

Pub meals and cafés at **Langholm**; limited choices, **Gretna**.

Around **Grinsdale** is an excellent touring area; from **Burgh by Sands** to **Low Crosby**, the road follows roughly the line of Hadrian's Wall.

Robert the Bruce's Cave at **Kirkpatrick-Fleming**.

Langholm is a beautifully situated little town where the forbears of Neil Armstrong, first man on the moon, once lived. The monument on the hilltop commemorates General John Malcolm.

Pleasant site on banks of **River Esk**.

▲ **Carlisle** 0228 23934.

Dumfries and Galloway/Strathclyde

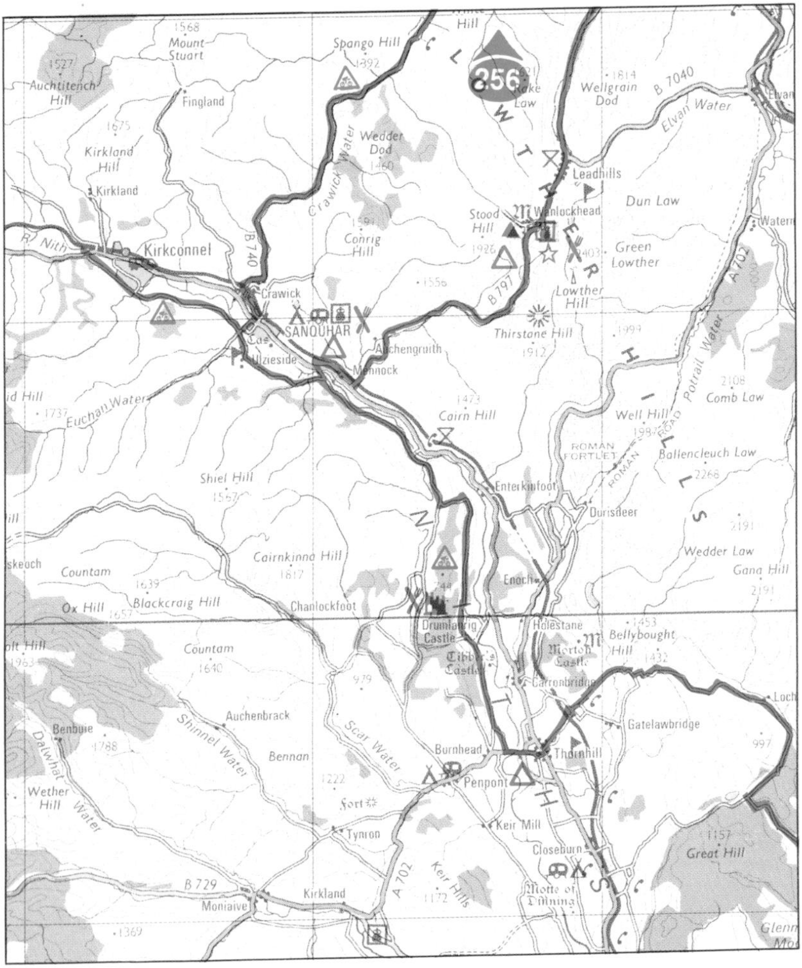

Hill
1568
Mount Stuart
Spango Hill
1392
256
Rake Law
1814
Wellgrain Dod
B 7040
Elvan Water
1527
Auchtitench Hill
Fingland
1675
Kirkland Hill
Kirkland
Wedder Dod
1460
Crawick Water
LOWTHER HILLS
Leadhills
Dun Law
Stood Hill
Wanlockhead
1591
Conrig Hill
B 740
R. Nith
Kirkconnel
Crawick
SANQUHAR
Cas.
Ulzieside
Auchengruith
Mennock
B 797
1556
2403
Green Lowther
Lowther Hill
Thirstone Hill
1912
1999
A 702
Potrail Water
2108
Comb Law
1737
Euchan Water
1473
Cairn Hill
Well Hill
ROMAN FORTLET
ROMAN ROAD
Ballencleuch Law
2268
Shiel Hill
1567
Enterkinfoot
Durisdeer
2191
Wedder Law
Gana Hill
Cairnkinna Hill
1817
Countam
1639
Ox Hill
1657
Blackcraig Hill
Chanlockfoot
744
Enoch
Drumlanrig Castle
Holestane
1453
Bellybought Hill
1432
Morton Castle
Tibbers Castle
Carronbridge
Countam
1640
979
Auchenbrack
Shinnel Water
Scar Water
Gatelawbridge
Benbuie
1788
Dalwhat Water
Bennan
Burnhead
Thornhill
997
Penpont
Wether Hill
1222
Fort
Tynron
Keir Mill
Closeburn
1157
Great Hill
B 729
A 702
Keir Hills
1172
Motte of Dinning
Moniaive
Kirkland
1369

△ Steep climb up glen to **Wanlockhead**; twisting hills round **Sanquhar**. Check map carefully at **Penpont** road junction.

🚌 **Kirkconnel** on Glasgow–Carlisle line.

✗ Limited choices, **Wanlockhead** and **Sanquhar**; teas at **Drumlanrig Castle**.

⛰ Lovely scenery on road from **Spango Bridge**. Traffic-free road runs parallel to main **A76**, from **Kirkconnel–Burnhead** past castles and through woodlands, excellent surface.

🏰 **Drumlanrig Castle**, 17th C.

☆ **Wanlockhead** at 1,380 feet (421 m) is highest village in Scotland. **Leadhills** Church has the gravestone of 137-year-old resident.

🏛 Mining Museum and lead mine open to the public at **Wanlockhead**.

▲ **Wanlockhead** No telephone; apply in writing to the Warden, Lotus Lodge, Biggar, Lanarkshire.

Dumfries and Galloway/Borders

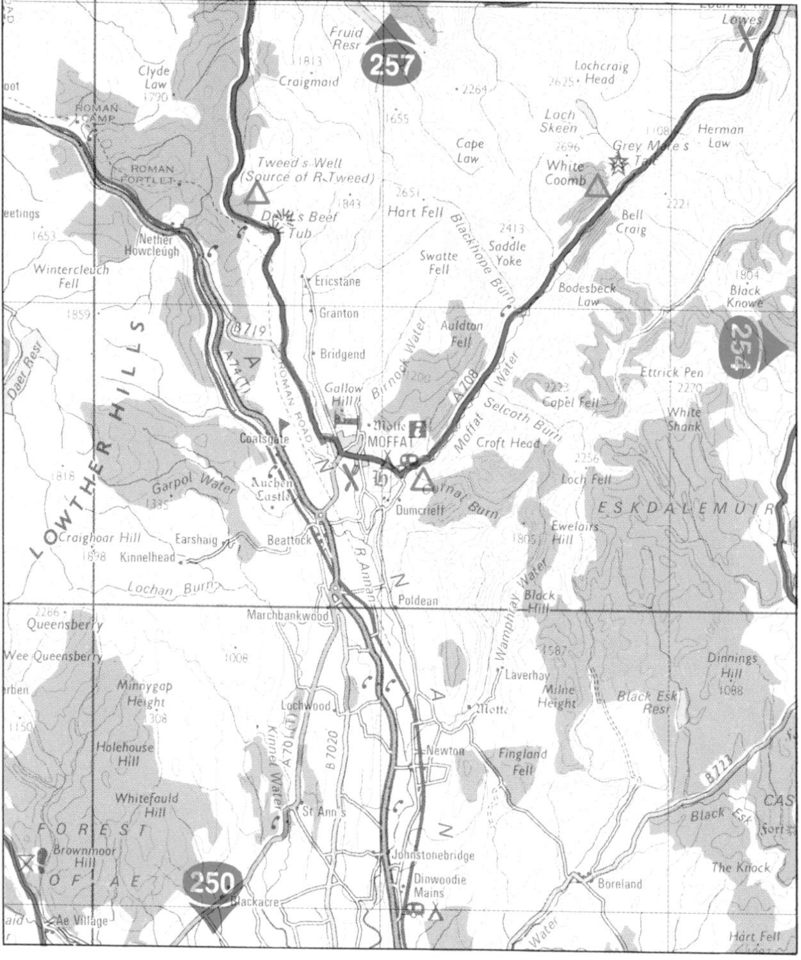

△ Steep climbs, particularly **Herman Law** and above **Devil's Beef Tub**; narrow, hilly road leads to **Grey Mare's Tail** (the short, steep path up the waterfall can be treacherous if wet or in poor visibility); winding ascent from **Moffat**, busy with tourist traffic in high season.

✗ **Moffat**, choices; café and inn on shore of **St Mary's** Loch, NE of Herman Law on the A708.

☆ **Grey Mare's Tail** is a spectacular waterfall plunging 200 feet (60 m) into Moffat Water. The source of the River Tweed is at nearby Tweed's Well.

Devil's Beef Tub is a huge natural hollow (fine views), once a renowned hiding place for stolen cattle.

Moffat was once a small-time spa town, with miraculous cures claimed on behalf of its sulphur springs.

Plenty of guest-houses in **Moffat**.

Borders

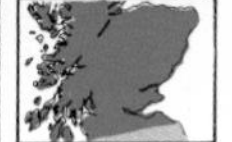

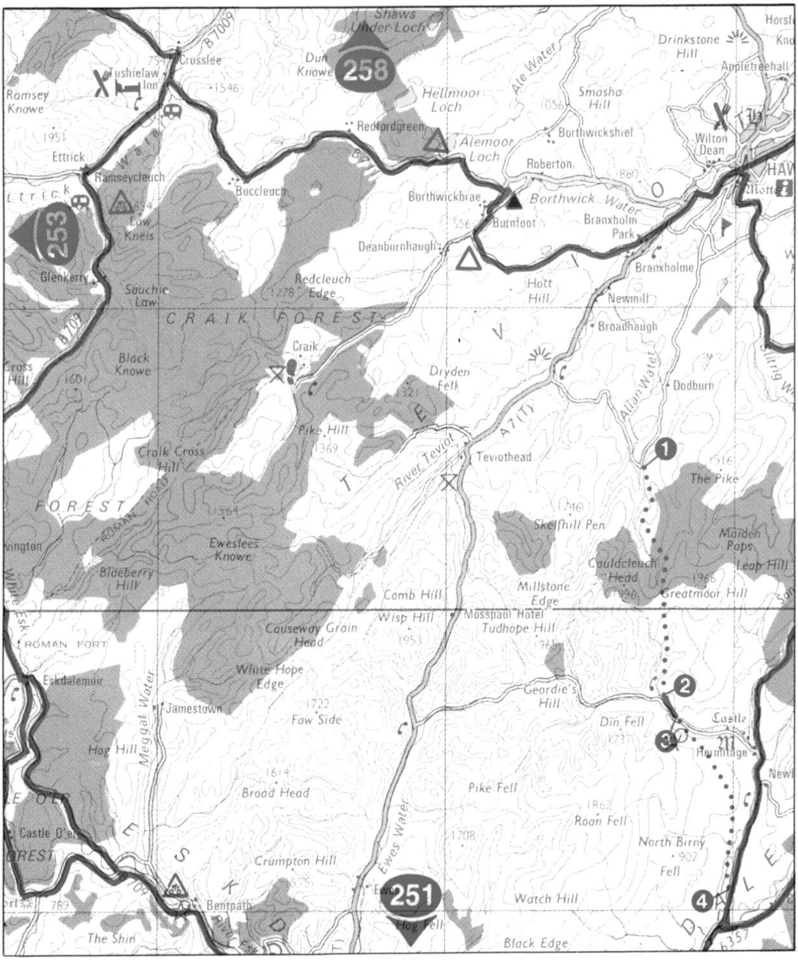

① Access to the Thieves Road at Priesthaugh. Continue S, past Priesthaugh Burn, over Swire How, down to Braidley Hope and the road ② along Hermitage Water. A few hundred yards downstream ③ turn S at Dinley on the Thief Sike track to Redheugh ④.

△ Intermittent climbs, for example on the **B711 E of Alemoor Loch** and the unclassified road **S of Burnfoot**.

✗ The **Tushielaw Inn** is something of an oasis in these parts, a fine pub serving meals; choices, **Hawick**.

⛺ Some delightful riverside riding, for example through **Eskdale**; an exciting forest descent to the **Ettrick** Valley.

Hawick, now a centre of the Scottish textile industry, was destroyed by the English in 1570.

At **Tushielaw Inn**.

▲ **Snoot**, Roberton, Hawick, Roxburghshire TD9 7LY.

Borders

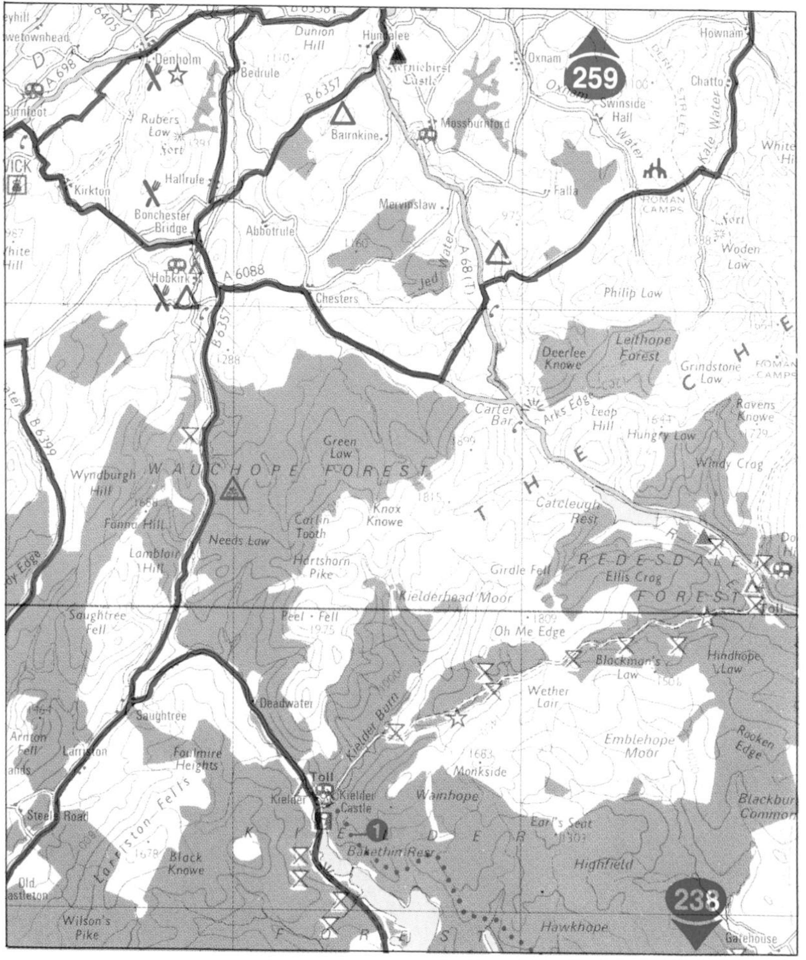

① Details of off-highway route on NE bank of Kielder Reservoir, plus other back-up information, page 238.

△ Climbs, notably on the **B6357 SW from Hundalee** and the unclassified road **NE from the A68**. The **unclassified road through Hobkirk** avoids climbing, and traffic, on the A6088.

✗ Pub meals at **Denholm** and **Hobkirk**; local cheese at **Bonchester Bridge**.

▲ Fine riding through **Wauchope Forest**, 145,000 acres of forest and moor, mostly S of the border.

☆ **Denholm** is a pleasant stopping-place with a large village green.

'**Roman Camps**', and the remains of many castles in this region are a reminder of continual garrisoning, possession and repossession of the border country in times past.

▲ **Ferniehurst Castle**, a spectacular setting. Jedburgh (08356) 3398.

Strathclyde/Borders

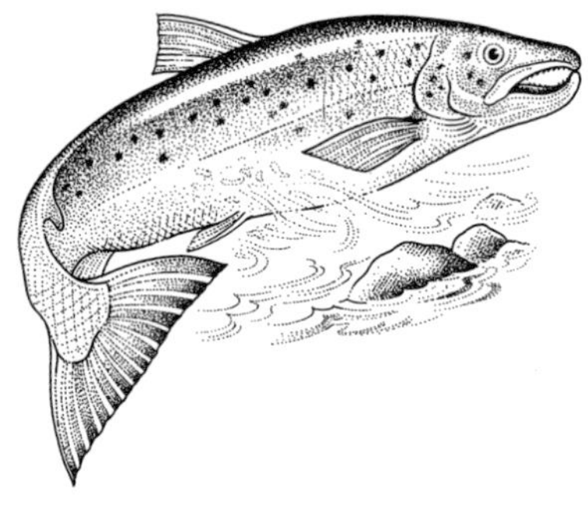

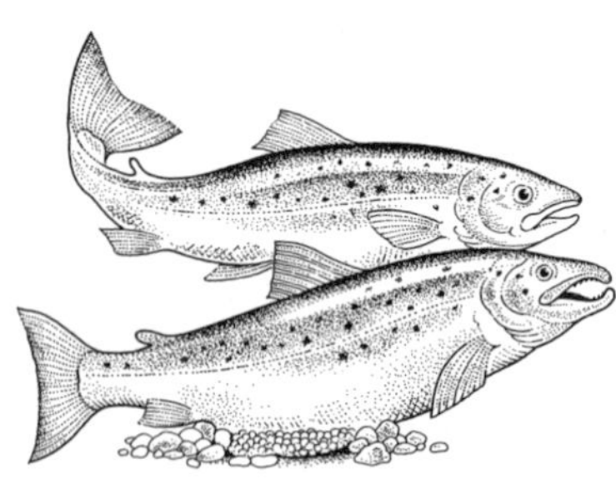

Salmon, undisputed king of Scotland's lochs, rivers and burns: the fish may ascend to an upland stream as high as 3,000 feet (914 m) above sea level in order to spawn, leaping up several waterfalls on the way. Then it creates a shallow scrape on the stream or river bed in which the eggs are laid and fertilized.

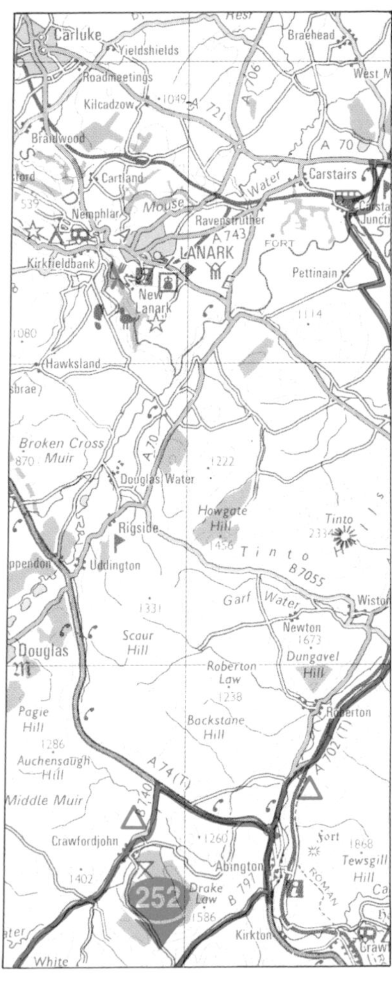

① Manor Head Pass, very severe.

△ Flat except for steep climb eastwards from **Talla Reservoir**, and climb to hill fort from **Broughton**; **B740** is hilly.

Regular services to **Carstairs** on the InterCity route from Carlisle to Glasgow or Edinburgh.

Lanark, choices; **Biggar**, **Carnwath**, limited choices.

The road from **Tweedsmuir to Cappercleuch** is truly desolate.

Strathclyde/Borders

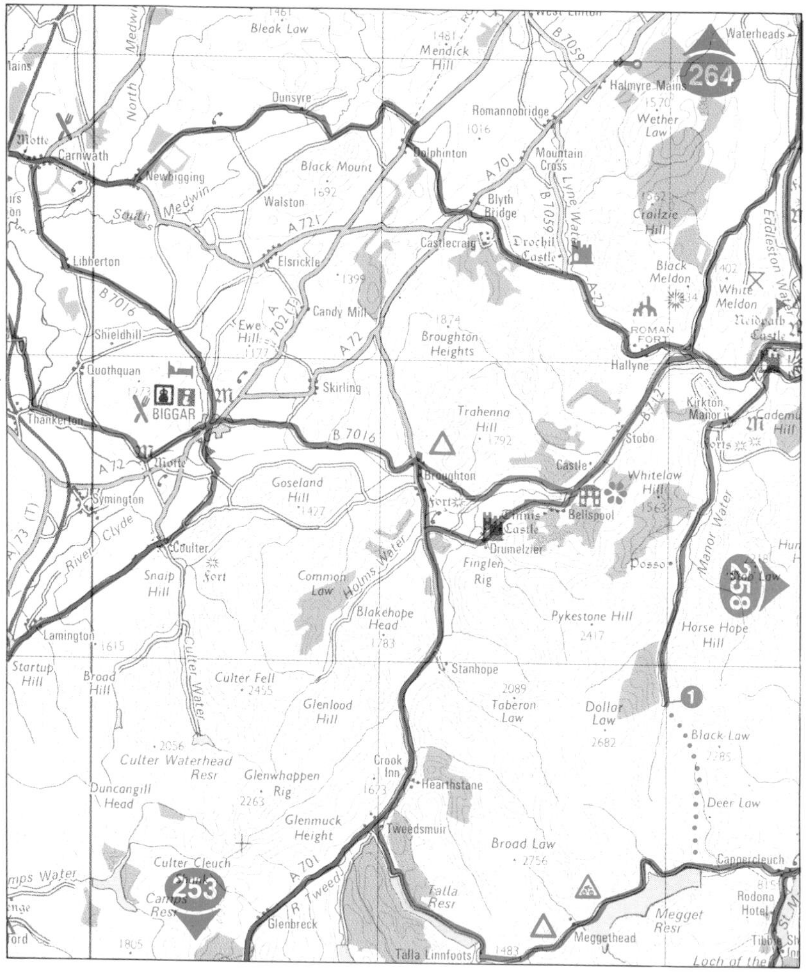

Tinto Hill has panoramic views in all directions: Ireland can be seen on a clear day; best approached from SW of Thankerton.

Tinnis Castle is a 16th-C ruin; **Drochil Castle** is a 16th-C fortressed manor house.

Neidpath Castle, begun in 13th C.

Biggar's museum recreates the atmosphere of a 19th-C village.

Many hill forts and settlements, for example on White Meldon and **Black Meldon**, and on Cademuir Hill; Milkieston Rings is a large Iron Age area just **E of A703** (name on page 258).

Remains of Roman Camp at Lyne (marked '**Roman Fort**').

Excellent views E and W from above S bank of the River Tweed (due S of **Neidpath Castle**).

Nearest is Edinburgh (see page 264).

B & B **Biggar**, 14 Cardon Drive.

Borders

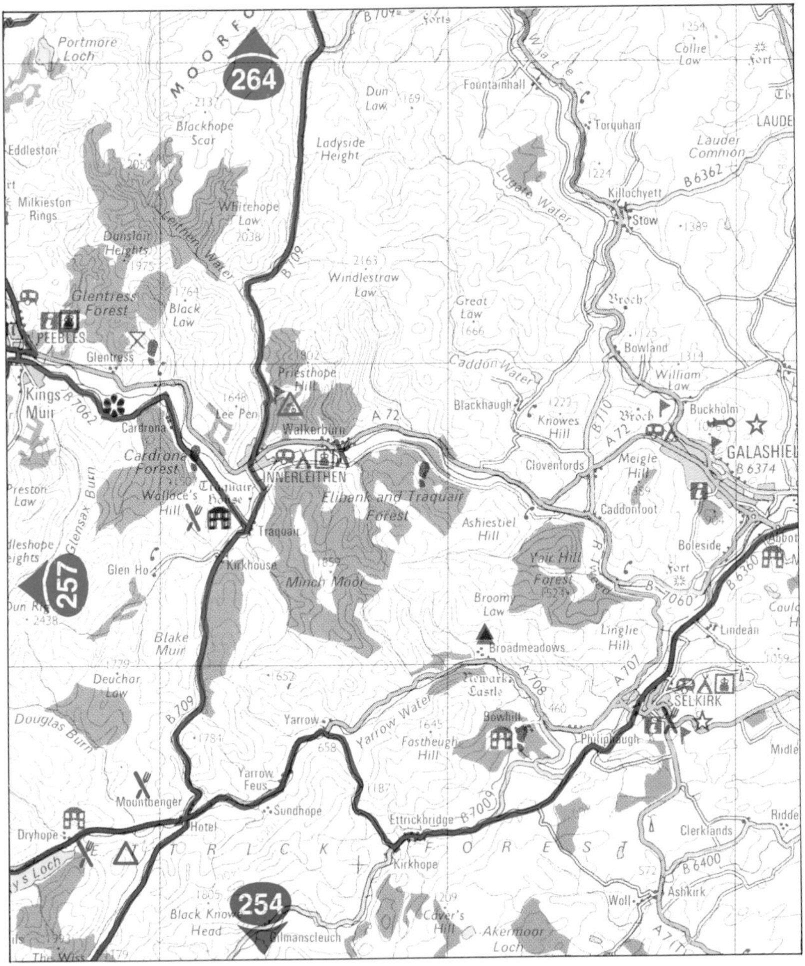

△ Some strenuous climbs, particularly at **Mountbenger**, where the road rises to 1,170 feet (357 m). B roads indicated are mostly peaceful and well-surfaced.

✗ Working brewhouse and cottage tea house at **Traquair House**; choices at **Innerleithen** and **Selkirk**; café on shore of **St Mary's Loch**; hotel meals, **Mountbenger**.

△ Wonderful downhill stretch on the **B709 into Innerleithen**.

Traquair House, dating from the 10th C, can claim to be the oldest inhabited house in Scotland.

☆ **Galashiels** The Tweed Mills were once part of the famous tweed industry hereabouts; relics of Sir Walter Scott in **Selkirk's** museum.

Galashiels Herbert Cycles, 5 Bridge Place.

▲ **Broadmeadows** Apply to The Warden, Yarrowford, Selkirk, TD7 5LZ.

Borders

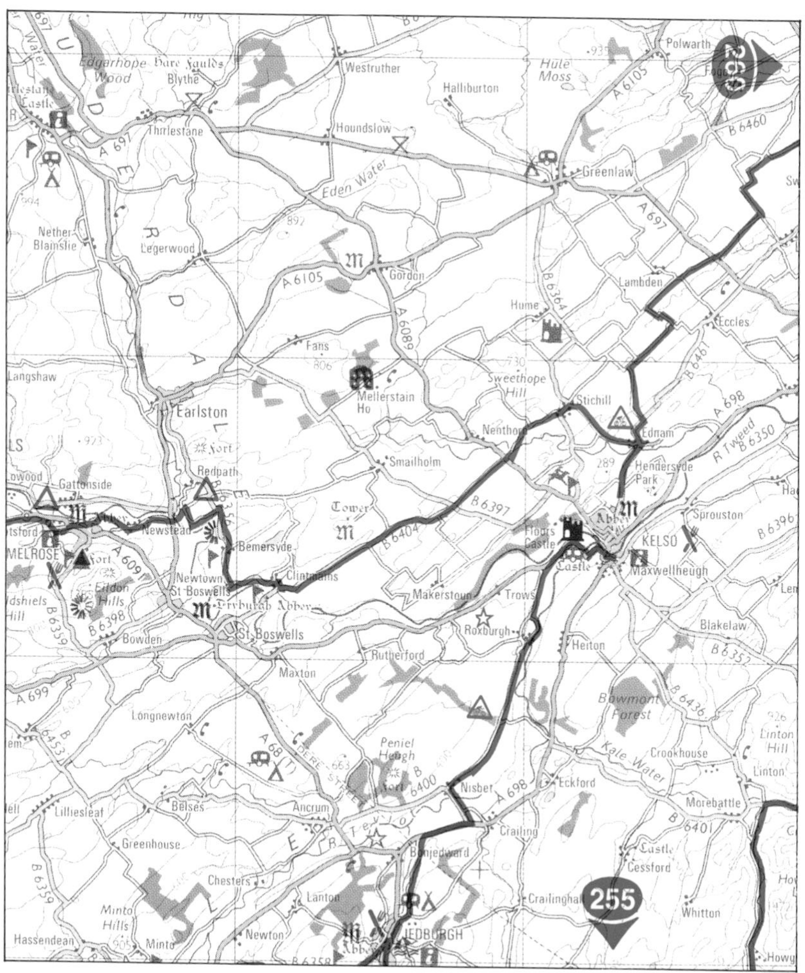

△ Climbs in the vicinity of **Melrose** and **Redpath**, otherwise gently undulating.

✗ Limited choices, **Melrose**, **Jedburgh**, **Kelso**.

From the **B6356** is Scott's View of the Tweed: the novelist's funeral cortège is said to have paused here. Fine views from the **Eildon Hills**.

Mellerstain, famous Adam mansion.

Swimming in the River Jed, **Jedburgh**.

Melrose Abbey, a Cistercian foundation, damaged by the English, interesting relics, inscriptions and museum in grounds; **Dryburgh Abbey** ruins; **Kelso Abbey**, now ruined; **Jedburgh Abbey**, mainly 12th–15th C.

Floors Castle, built by William Adam in 1721–25, with 19th-C additions.

☆ **Roxburgh**, once an important Scottish burgh, with a ruined castle.

▲ **Melrose** 089682 2521.

Borders/Northumberland

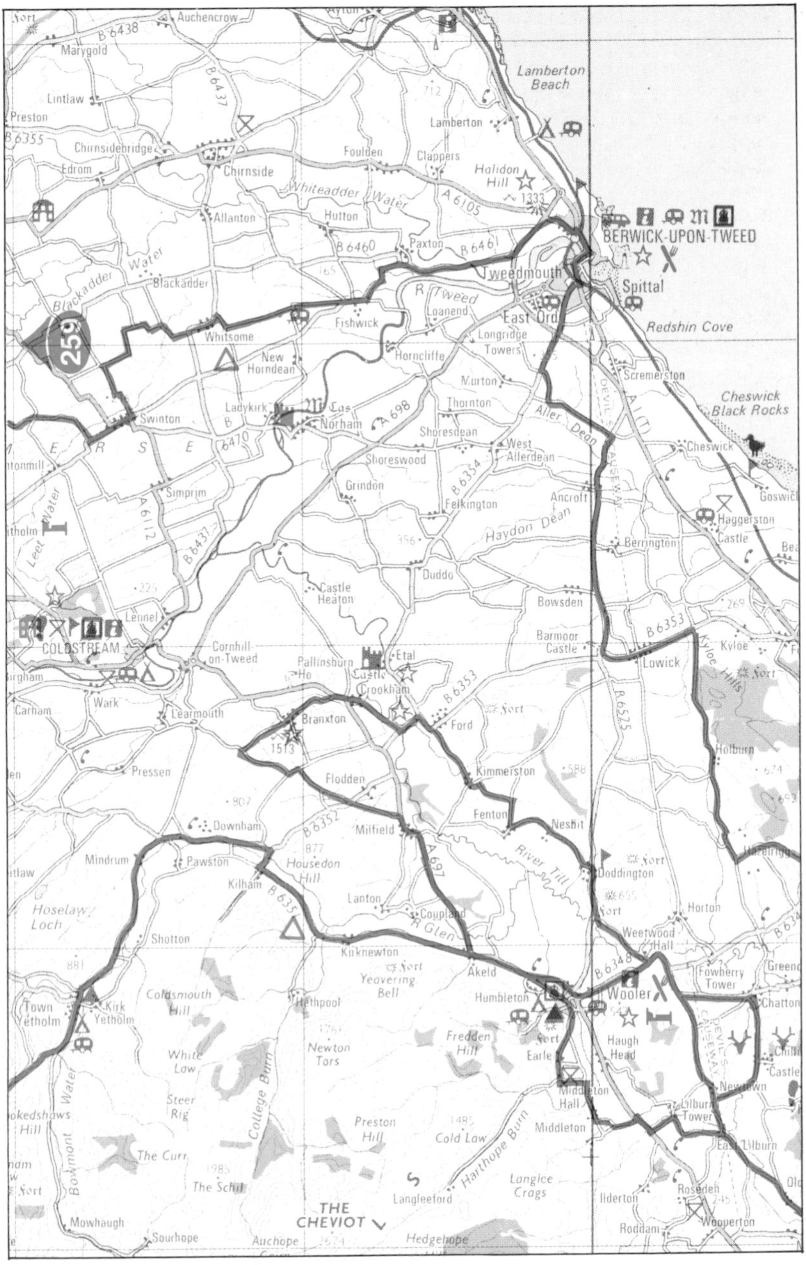

Auchencrow
B 6438
Marygold
Lintlaw
Preston
B 6355
Chirnsidebridge
Edrom
Chirnside
B 6437
Foulden
Clappers
Lamberton
Lamberton Beach
Halidon Hill
1333
Whiteadder Water
A 6105
Allanton
Hutton
B 6460
Paxton
B 6461
BERWICK-UPON-TWEED
Tweedmouth
Spittal
Blackadder Water
Blackadder
R Tweed
Loanend
East Ord
Redshin Cove
Whitsome
Fishwick
Longridge Towers
New Horndean
Horncliffe
Scremerston
Murton
Thornton
Ladykirk
Cas
Norham
A 698
Shoresdean
Cheswick Black Rocks
Swinton
B 6470
Aller Dean
West Allerdean
Cheswick
DEVIL'S CAUSEWAY
A 1(T)
M E R S E
Shoreswood
Grindon
B 6354
Simprim
Felkington
Ancroft
Goswick
A 6112
Leet Water
Haydon Dean
Haggerston Castle
B 6437
356
Berrington
Duddo
Castle Heaton
225
Lennel
Bowsden
269
COLDSTREAM
B 6353
Barmoor Castle
Kyloe
Cornhill-on-Tweed
Etal
Lowick
Kyloe Hills
Pallinsburn Ho
Castle
Crookham
B 6353
Fort
Carham
Wark
Learmouth
Ford
B 6525
Branxton
1513
Holburn
Pressen
Kimmerston
588
674
Flodden
807
Fenton
693
Downham
B 6352
Milfield
Nesbit
Mindrum
Pawston
877
Housedon Hill
A 697
River Till
Doddington
Fort
Kilham
B 6351
Lanton
655
Fort
Horton
Hoselaw Loch
Coupland
R Glen
Weetwood Hall
Shotton
Kirknewton
B 6348
881
Fort
Yeavering Bell
Akeld
Fowberry Tower
Town Yetholm
Kirk Yetholm
Colsmouth Hill
Hethpool
Humbleton
Wooler
Chatton
1767
Newton Tors
Fredden Hill
Fort
Earle
Haugh Head
DEVIL'S CAUSEWAY
White Law
College Burn
Middleton Hall
Newtown
Steer Rig
Lilburn Tower
Bowmont Water
Preston Hill
1485
Cold Law
Middleton
East Lilburn
The Curr
1985
The Schil
Harthope Burn
Langlee Crags
Ilderton
Roseden
245
Fort
Langleeford
THE CHEVIOT
Wooperton
Mowhaugh
Sourhope
Auchope
2674
Hedgehope
Roddam

Borders/Northumberland

Tough climbs through the **Cheviot Hills**, which are traversed by the B6351; network of peaceful but high-hedged lanes in **Ladykirk** vicinity.

Berwick-upon-Tweed, four hours from London by InterCity service: **Chathill** on Berwick–Newcastle line.

Berwick and **Coldstream**, choices; **Wooler**, limited choices, hotel meals; pub food, Collingwood Arms, **Coldstream**.

Glorious coastal road, **Bamburgh to Beadnell**.

Views to Holy Island and Lindisfarne Castle from coast in **Bamburgh** area.

The Grace Darling Museum, **Bamburgh**, run by the Royal National Lifeboat Institution, has maritime memorabilia, and tells the heroic story of a Farne Islands' lighthouse keeper's daughter. **Coldstream** Museum, local crafts, Coldstream Guards memorabilia; **Berwick**, museum of the King's Own Scottish Borderers.

Sea birds, **Cheswick** area.

Lennel, fine, mature parkland.

Chillingham Park, with its wild cattle.

The Hirsel, near **Coldstream**, residence of former prime minister Sir Alec Douglas Home (now Lord Home) and his forbears the Earls of Home: gardens only are open to the public.

Berwick, once much fought for by England and Scotland, offers a fine, peaceful 2 mile (3 km) walk around the town's walls from Meg Mount. The 18th-C town hall has a steeple. Three bridges span the Tweed at its estuary here, including one with 15 arches dating from 1620. The other two are the Royal Tweed Bridge (1928) and the Royal Border Railway Bridge (1847), the latter with an inscription celebrating this belated act of union between England and Scotland. **Halidon Hill** was the scene of a bloody battle when England re-took Berwick and **Flodden** saw James IV's disastrous defeat, and death, in 1513. General Monck raised the elite footguards regiment, the Coldstream Guards, at **Coldstream** in 1659.

Guest houses at **Wooler** and **Yetholm**.

Wooler 0668 81365.

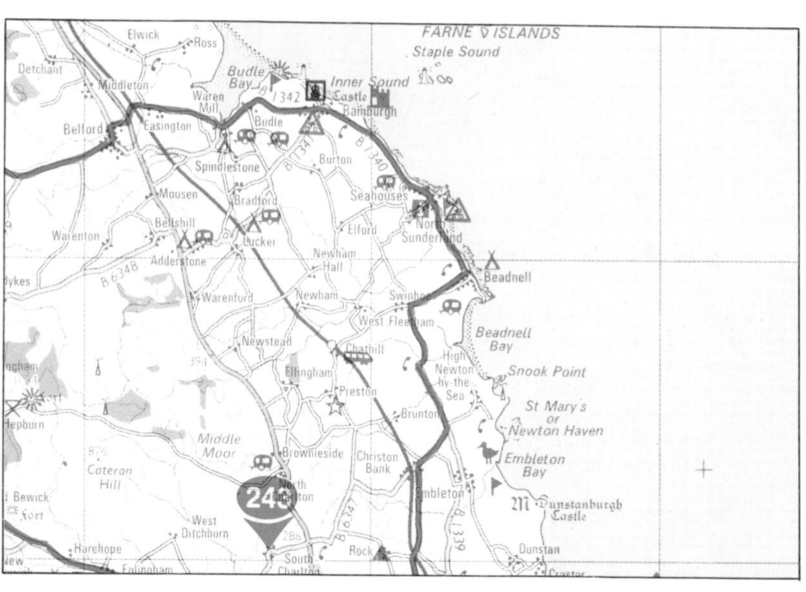

Strathclyde

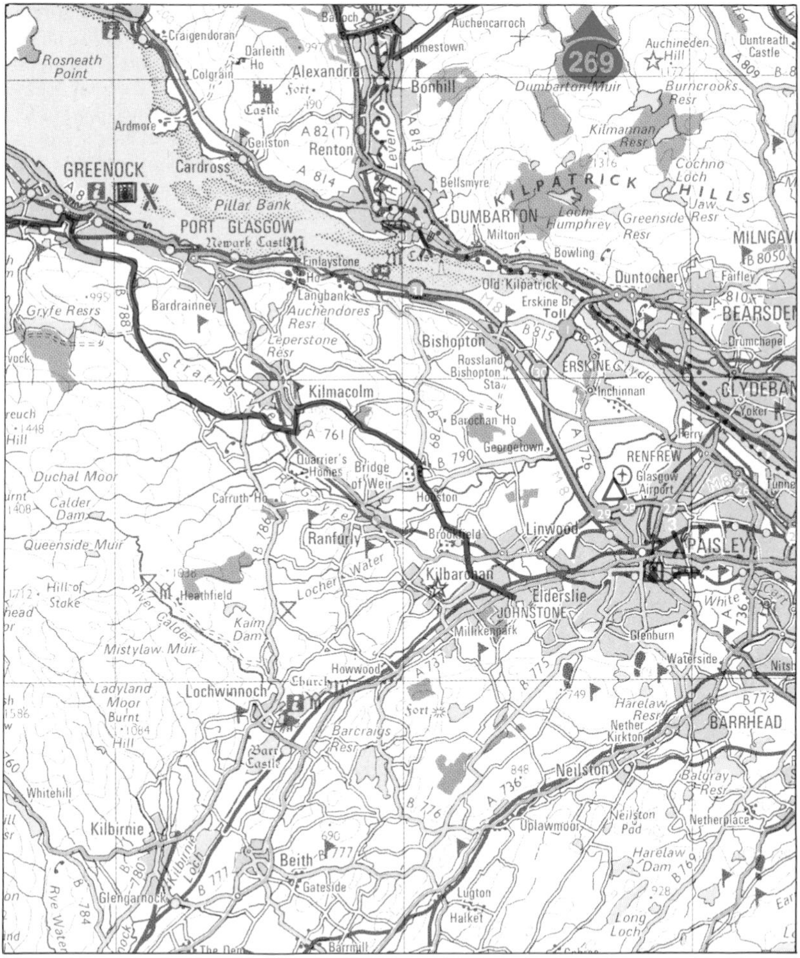

△ A-roads in the Greenock and Paisley areas are busy, particularly around **Glasgow Airport**.

Dumbarton on the branch line N from Glasgow; **Paisley St James** Station on the Glasgow–Largs branch line.

Choices, **Dumbarton**, **Greenock**, **Paisley**.

The McLean Museum, **Greenock**, has natural history, geology and shipping exhibits; priceless collection of Paisley shawls in **Paisley** Museum and Art Gallery (the town is one of the world's largest thread manufacturing centres).

☆ **Kilbarchan** is famed for tartan weaving. The home of a typical 18th-C handloom weaver is intriguingly re-created at The Weaver's Cottage.

† **Paisley** grew up around the Cluniac monastery founded here in 1163. The Abbey nave, dating from the 15th C, is still used as a parish church.

Strathclyde

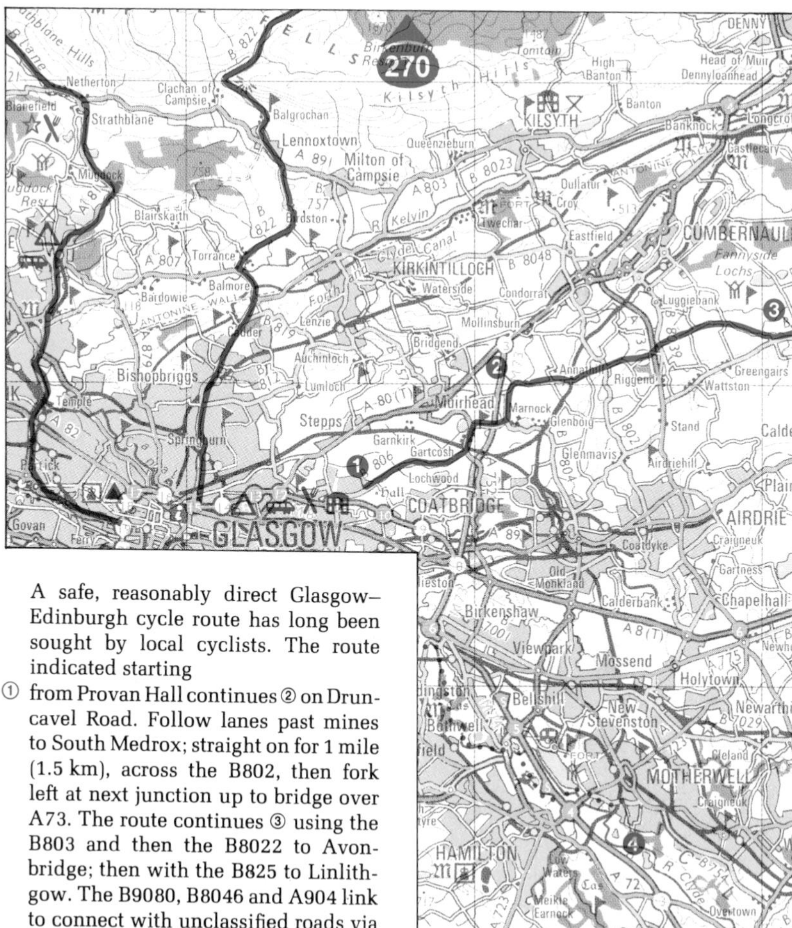

A safe, reasonably direct Glasgow–Edinburgh cycle route has long been sought by local cyclists. The route indicated starting

① from Provan Hall continues ② on Druncavel Road. Follow lanes past mines to South Medrox; straight on for 1 mile (1.5 km), across the B802, then fork left at next junction up to bridge over A73. The route continues ③ using the B803 and then the B8022 to Avonbridge; then with the B825 to Linlithgow. The B9080, B8046 and A904 link to connect with unclassified roads via Hopetoun and Society, then to Edinburgh as shown on page 264.

④ The River Clyde route, starting at Strathclyde Country Park, will eventually run as far as Balloch, N of Dumbarton on the A813; parts are already open, for example Glasgow Green to Carmyle.

△ East Kilbride (name not on map – it is **W of Motherwell**) has some useful cycle paths and subways. Avoid city traffic altogether by taking the train to **Milngavie**.

🚌 **Glasgow** is 5 hours from London.

✗ Choices in **Glasgow** and suburbs; café at **Blanefield**.

🏛 **Glasgow** 18th-C Pollock House contains the Burrell Collection; glimpse the bad old days at Tenement House, a restored 1890s tenement.

☆ Numerous antique shops at **Blanefield**; **Glasgow** has gardens, museums, a 12th-C cathedral and a 14th-C castle.

▲ **Glasgow** 041 332 2004.

Lothian

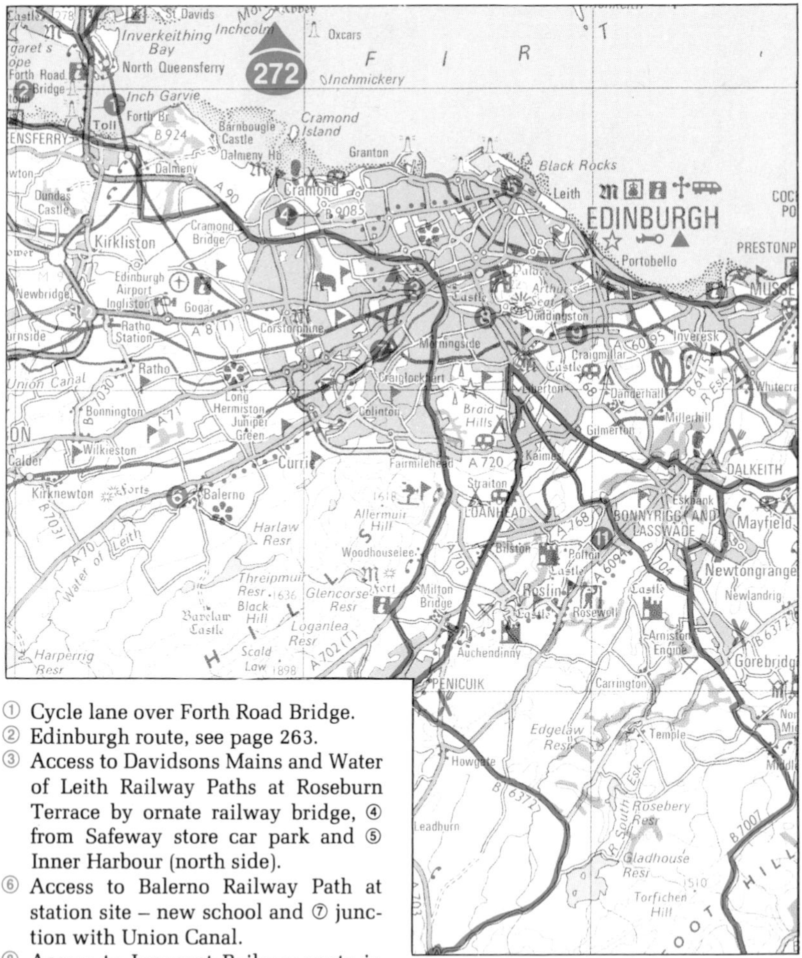

① Cycle lane over Forth Road Bridge.
② Edinburgh route, see page 263.
③ Access to Davidsons Mains and Water of Leith Railway Paths at Roseburn Terrace by ornate railway bridge, ④ from Safeway store car park and ⑤ Inner Harbour (north side).
⑥ Access to Balerno Railway Path at station site – new school and ⑦ junction with Union Canal.
⑧ Access to Innocent Railway route in Holyrood Park below Samson's Ribs and ⑨ Duddingston Road West.
⑩ Access to the Penicuik–Bonnington Railway Path at Penicuik Station site and ⑪ station site off B704.
△ Climbs in **Dalkeith** area.
🚌 **Edinburgh**, InterCity services from Waverley Station.
✗ Limited choice, **Penicuik**, **Dalkieth**, **Gorebridge**; choices, **Edinburgh**.
☆ **Edinburgh** museums, art galleries, churches.
♜ **Edinburgh** Castle, a fortress from earliest times – superb natural defensive position on the granite heights.
🏛 **Edinburgh** the Palace of Holyrood House, the Queen's official residence in Edinburgh.
🔧 **Edinburgh** Williamson, 26 Hamilton Place.
▲ **Edinburgh** Bruntisfield 031 447 2994; **Eglinton** 031 337 1120.

Lothian

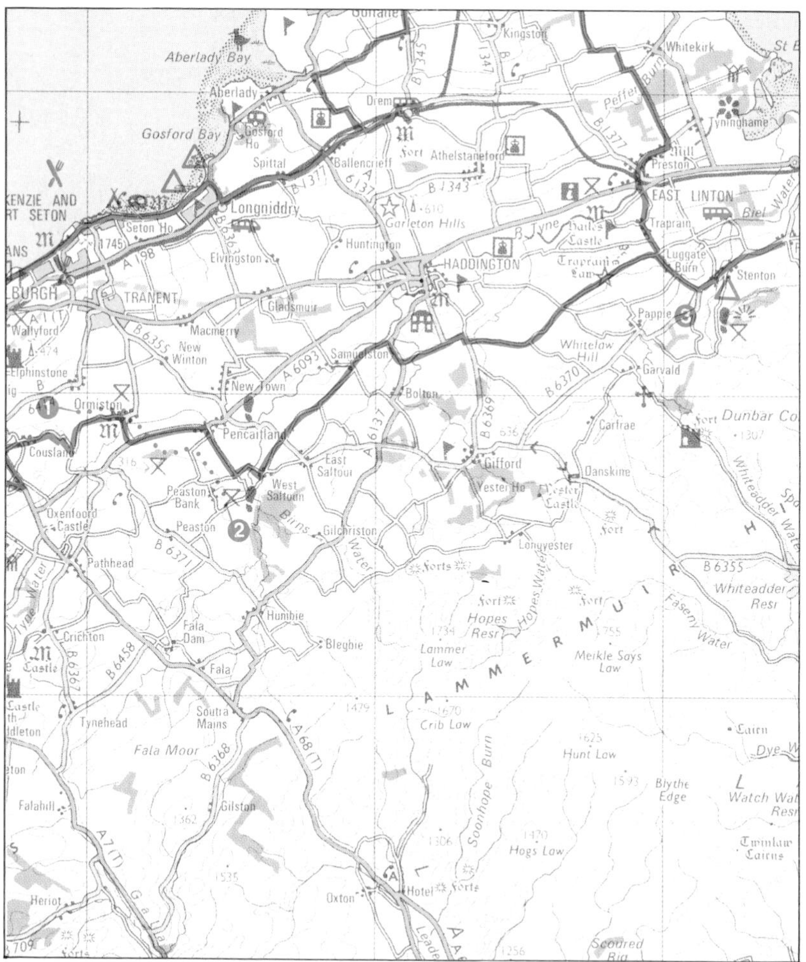

① and ② access as indicated to the Pencaitland Way, disused railway line route.

③ To continue to Dunbar, follow the B6370 to Pitcox – 2 miles (3 km) and fork right on to the unclassified road to Dunbar – about 4 miles (6.5 km). Don't go via Spott.

△ The coast road through **Port Seton** is busy at peak times – use inland alternative; steep climb into **Stenton**.

🚌 Dunbar (name off map), **Drem** and **Longniddry** are on the Newcastle upon Tyne–Edinburgh main line; **North Berwick** (name off map) is on a branch line from Drem.

✗ Choices, **Prestonpans** (name off map), **Port Seton** and **North Berwick**: well-placed inn at **Dirleton**, serves coffee.

☆ **Dirleton**, for many, Scotland's prettiest village. **North Berwick** became a seaside resort in the 19th C.

Strathclyde

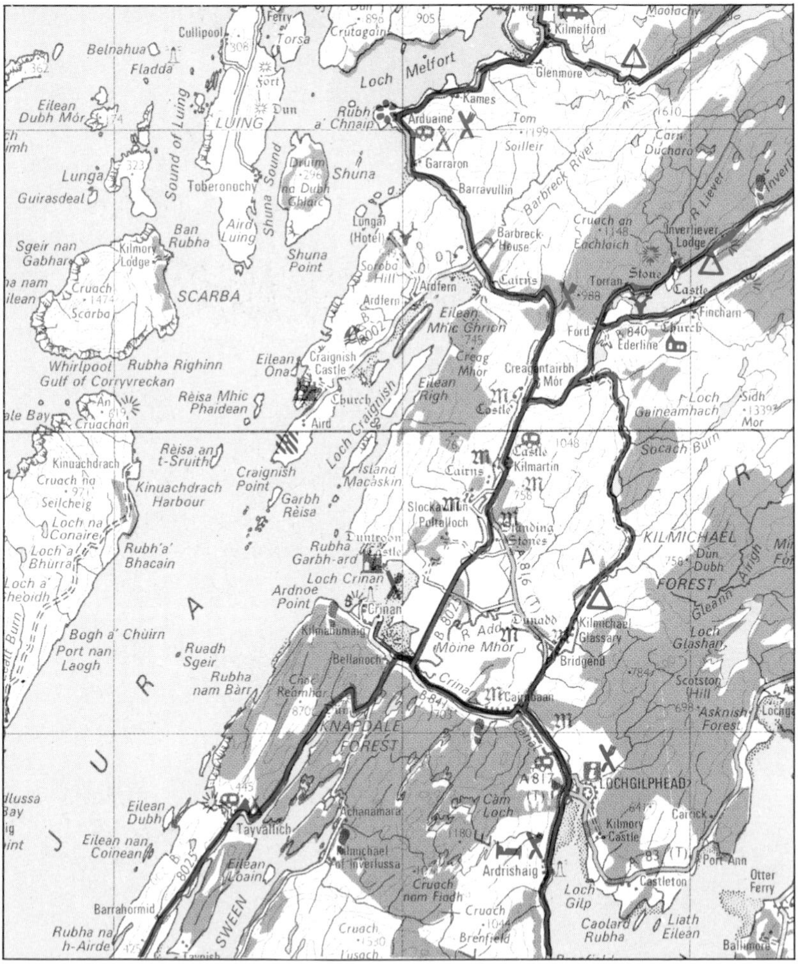

- △ The road from **Kilmelford to Moolachy** and Loch Avich is hilly, so is the road through **Inverliever Forest**. The track N from **Kilmichael Glassary** is surfaced, though narrow and gated.
- Nearest is Oban about 14 miles (22 km) N on the A816.
- **Lochgilphead**, **Ardrishaig**, limited choices; coffee shop at **Crinan**; fresh seafood at the Crinan Hotel, the Loch Melfort Hotel (**Arduaine**), and at hotels on Loch Awe; teas at **Ford.**
- Exceptionally rich collection of prehistoric monuments along the **A816 between Dunadd and Kilmartin**: standing stones at Dunadd, cup-and-ring marked rocks at Cairnbaan, chambered cairn and stone circle near Kilmartin.
- Sand and shingle beach at **Ardfern**, past Lunga Farm.
- Coastal gardens at **Arduaine**.

Strathclyde

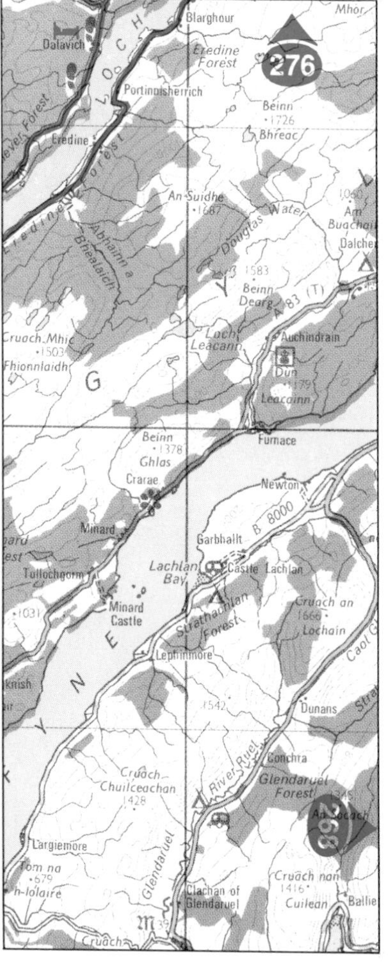

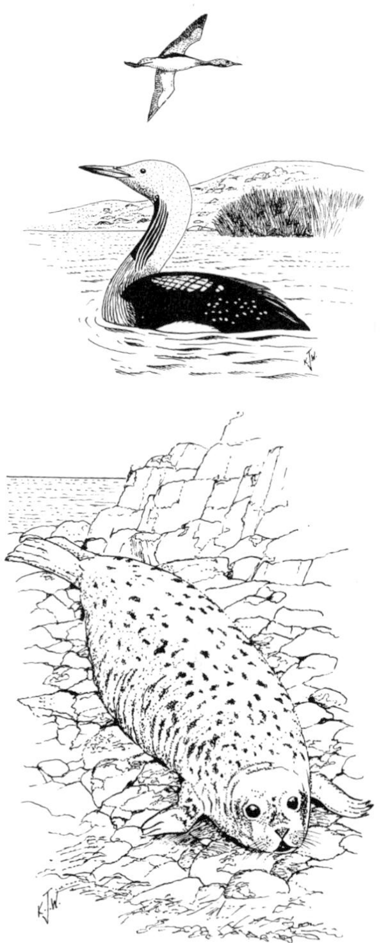

Two characteristic inhabitants of the west coast of Scotland – the grey seal and the great northern diver. The first, also known as the Atlantic seal, comes ashore only to breed and to bask. The second is a winter visitor to the north and west coasts.

- Black-throated divers and widgeons, lichens and rare plants, grey seals, otters and red deer are abundant, but typically at **Loch Awe**.
- Views up and down **Loch Awe** from roads on N and S shores.
- Standing stone off B845 **1 mile (1.5 km) after Ford**.
- B & B **Ardrishaig**, Canal House; **Dalavich**, forest village with timber holiday houses on stilts.

Strathclyde

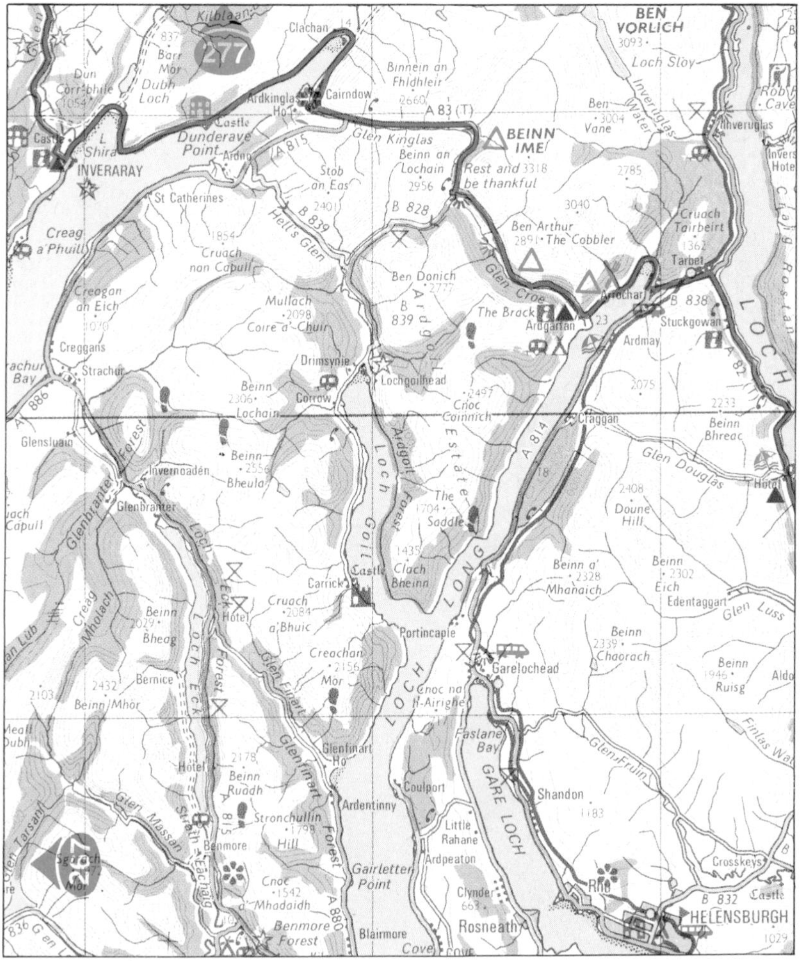

△ Long descent into **Arrochar**. Steep, winding climbs by **Ben Arthur** and **Beinn Ime**.

Helensburgh, **Garelochhead**, other stations on the line N from Glasgow.

Cafés, **Inveraray**; tea room, **Arrochar**; choices, **Helensburgh**.

Superb views in vicinity of **Ben Arthur**; **'Rest and be thankful'** is a famous viewpoint – stone seat inscribed with those words.

Swimming in **Loch Long** and **Loch Lomond**.

☆ **Inveraray**, beautiful small town, hereditary seat of Clan Campbell; **Arrochar**, centre for climbing.

Inveraray Castle rebuilt 1770, armoury, furnishings; **Dundarave** Castle is author Neil Munro's Doom Castle.

▲ **Inveraray** 0499 2454; **Ardgartan** Arrochar (03012) 362; **Inverbeg** Luss (043686) 635.

Central

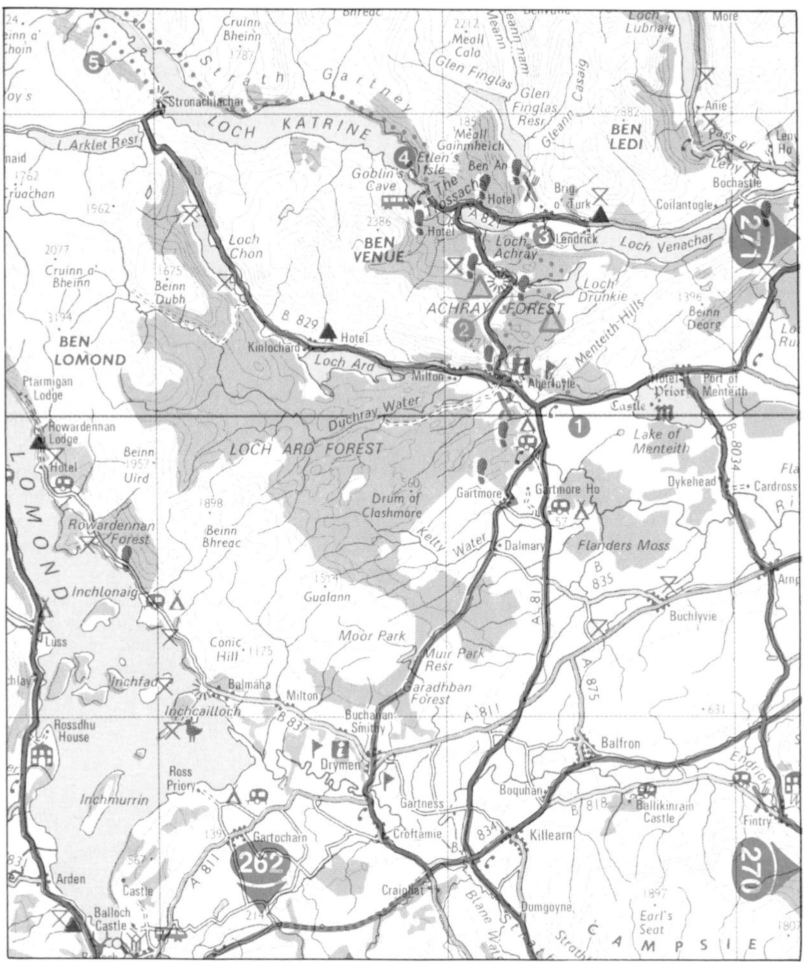

① Access to Achray Forest Cycle Trail at Forestry Commission car park entrance on A81 E of Aberfoyle, ② from A821 and ③ Achray Farm, near Brig o' Turk. Some restriction on direction of travel – see signs; trail open 10–6 Easter to end of September.

④ From Trossachs Pier continue ahead on N shore of Loch Katrine on Waterworks Drive, return ⑤ on S shore.

△ Climbs on **Achray Forest Trail**; climbing and traffic on **A821**. (Forest Trail recommended in season).

Balloch station, summer-only service to Glasgow; **Loch Katrine** ferry service from Trossachs Pier to Stronachlachar.

Pub meals, cafés, **Aberfoyle, The Trossachs**; coffee shop, **Flintry**.

▲ **Trossachs** 08776 227; **Loch Lomond** Arden (038985) 226; **Rowardennan** Balmaha (036087) 259; **Loch Ard** Kinlochard (08777) 256.

Central/Tayside

① From gate across unclassified road along Glen Artney take the path over the burn indicated as the footpath to Callander. Continue on this track, which is rough and hard going at times. At the ford ② it improves considerably until the first farm ③ is reached, from where the road is tarmac.

④ From Invergeldie continue to Loch Lednock Reservoir, which has flooded the line of the original track. Go round the head of the reservoir and in about ½ mile (0.8 km) head NW up the hill, over the pass and down Finglen to Ardeonaig.

△ Steep hill **NE from Bridge of Allan** on unclassified road; hard climb N through **Sma' Glen**; short but steep zig-zag at **NE end of Loch Tay**; **S shore of Loch Tay** is undulating.

Stirling and **Dunblane** on the Glasgow–Perth main line.

Choices **Callander**, **Stirling**, **Dunblane**, **Comrie**; **Carron Bridge** is a useful pub-stop before the remote road back to Stirling.

Going S down **Sma' Glen** is exciting; the **B827** is peaceful with an excellent surface; unclassified road **SE through Garrow** runs through a lovely, wild area almost unused by cars; memorable off-highway riding, **Glen Artney**.

Stirling Castle is outstanding of its kind, and gives real insights into the development of this historic city.

☆ **Callander** – none other than 'Tanochbrae' in the TV series *Dr Finlay's Casebook* – a busy holiday town in season. The Bracklinn Falls, on the Keltie 1½ miles (2.5 km) NE of the town, are popular with visitors. **Comrie** is a beautifully sited village, with Museum of Scottish Tartans.

Excellent wild campsite **SE of Garrow**.

▲ **Stirling** 0786 3442.

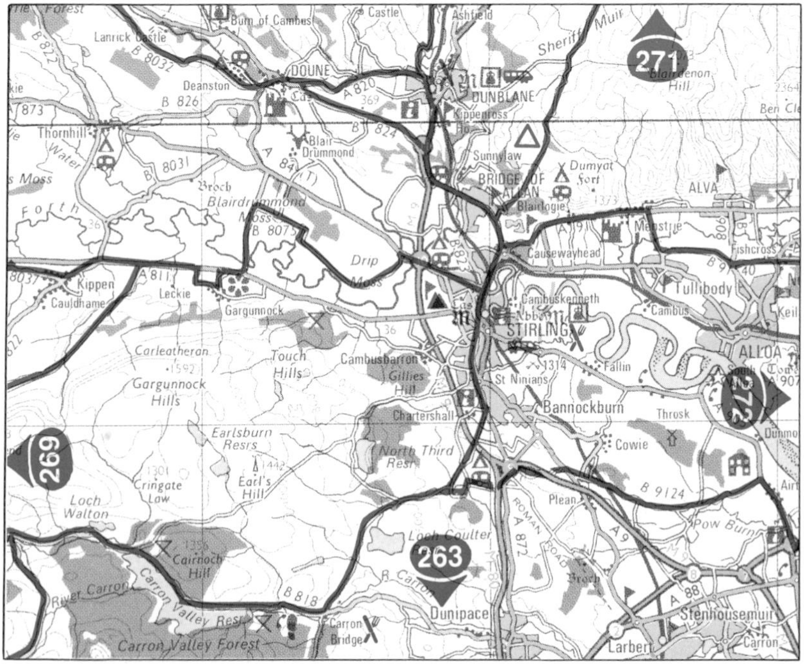

Central/Tayside

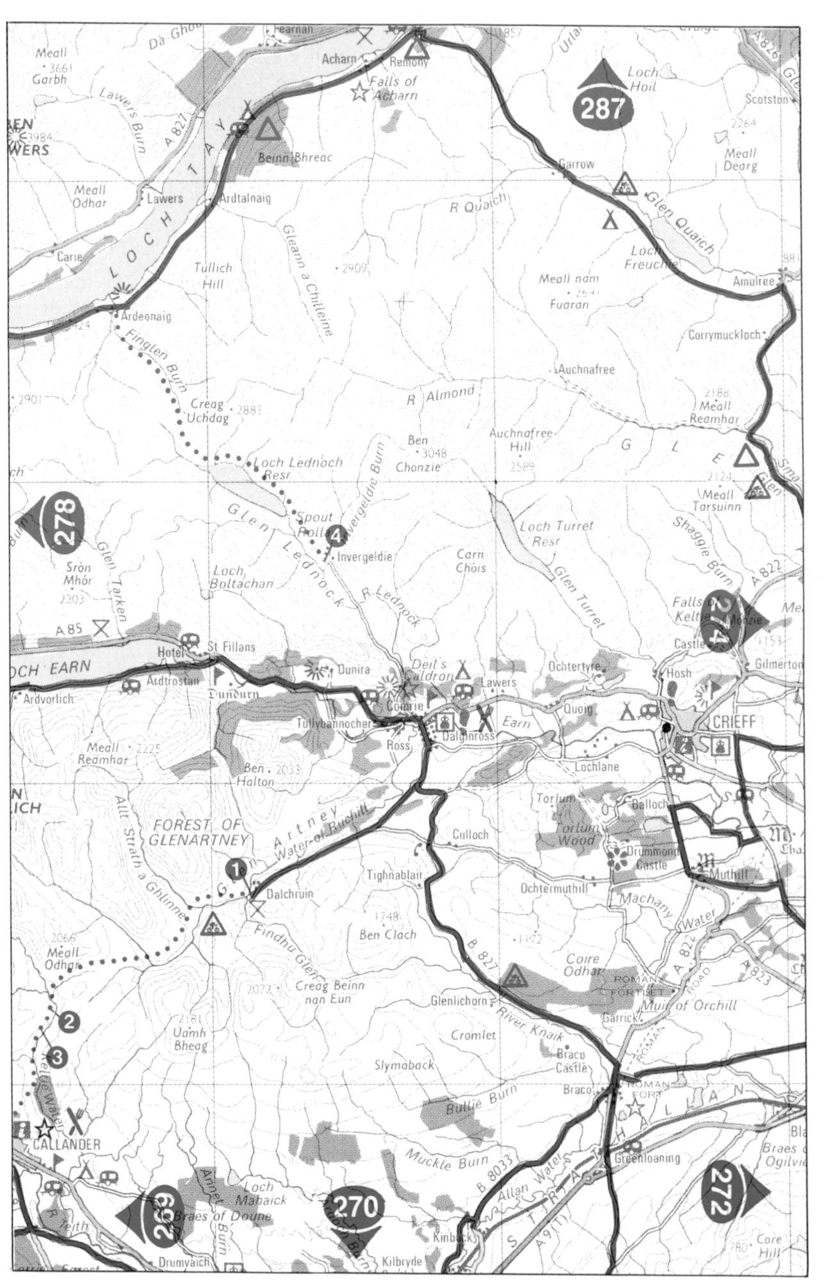

Central/Fife

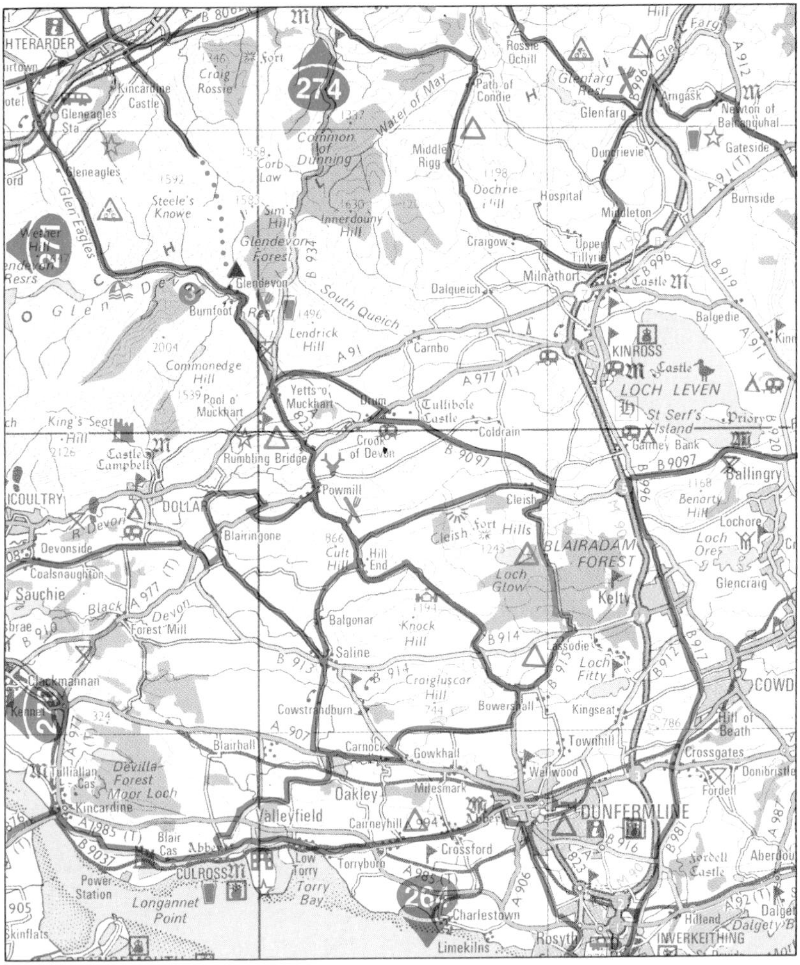

① and ② access as indicated to Glenrothes Railway Path.

③ Access to drover's road from youth hostel.

△ Severe ascents past Dunfermline up to **Lassodie**, in the vicinity of **Dollar**, **S from Path of Condie** and around **Glenfarg**; steep ascent/descent, **Cleish Hills** – ride with care; **Dunfermline to Culross** can be busy.

🚌 **Dunfermline**, half-hourly service to Edinburgh; **Inverkeithing**, **Burntisland** and other stations on the Edinburgh–Perth or Dundee lines; **Gleneagles Station** on the Stirling–Perth main line.

🍴 Salad bar at **Powmill**; cafés at **Falkland**, **Kirkcaldy**, **Glenrothes**; teas, **Glenfarg** Hotel; The Country Bite in the camp site, **Glen Devon**.

🍺 Good ale at the Tormakin, **Glendevon**; **Gateside**, comfortable pub; Bruce

Central/Fife/Tayside

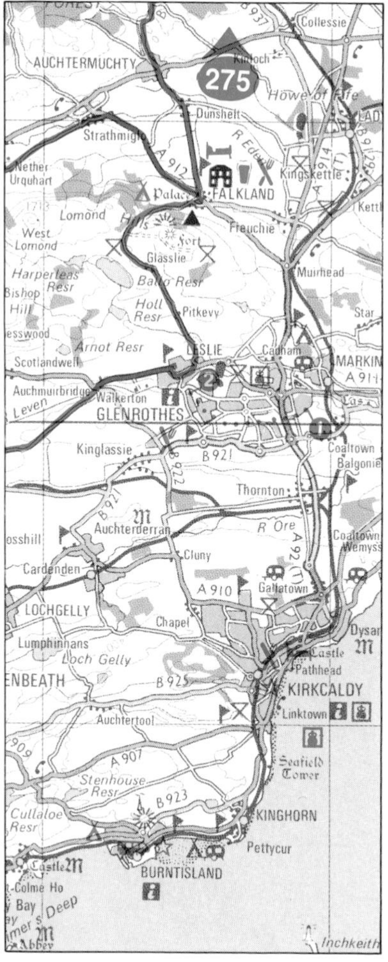

Arms, **Falkland**; Dundonald Arms, **Culross**.

Outside peak hours the road **from Gleneagles to Glendevon** is delightful; long downhill run from **Glen Devon to Yetts of Muckhart**; fine touring, **Ochil Hills**.

Views in Cleish Hills area.

Glendevon Bathing pool opposite camp site.

Picnic site on slopes of **Benarty Hill**.

Dunfermline is the birthplace of the famous philanthropist Andrew Carnegie. The weaver's cottage where he was born, and the Memorial Hall, have displays featuring his life and work. Pittencrieff house has costume collections and Dunfermline Museum has local and natural history exhibits. **Kirkcaldy** Museum and Art Gallery has archaeological and natural science collections; Industrial and Social History Museum, horse-drawn vehicles. **Culross**, Dunimarle Museum displays Napoleonic furniture, paintings, silver and other treasures.

Wild cattle in hollow of **Crook of Devon**.

☆ **Rumbling Bridge** spectacular sight of River Devon tumbling noisily through echoing bridge.

Kirkcaldy, with its linen industry, used to smell of rotting flax. The town was once the principal port of Fife and houses along Sailor's Walk have been well-restored by the National Trust for Scotland. **Culross** is a beautiful village with cobbled streets; the mill makes bobbins for the woollen industry. **Gleneagles**, perhaps Scotland's most famous hotel.

Mary, Queen of Scots was imprisoned on, and escaped from the smaller island marked on **Loch Leven** – boat trips there in summer. St Serf's Island, **Loch Leven**, harbours an ancient priory; the ruined 13th-C abbey at **Dunfermline** is Robert the Bruce's burial place.

Falkland Palace, an example of the French Renaissance style, was used by Mary Queen of Scots, boasts a real tennis court and once housed James IV's zoo. **Culross** Palace is 16th/17th C, with fine paintings and ceilings.

Castle Campbell, **Dollar**.

Hotels **Falkland, Kirkcaldy, Dunfermline**.

Camp sites, **Glen Devon, Burntisland**.

Falkland 03375 710; **Glen Devon** 025982 206.

Tayside

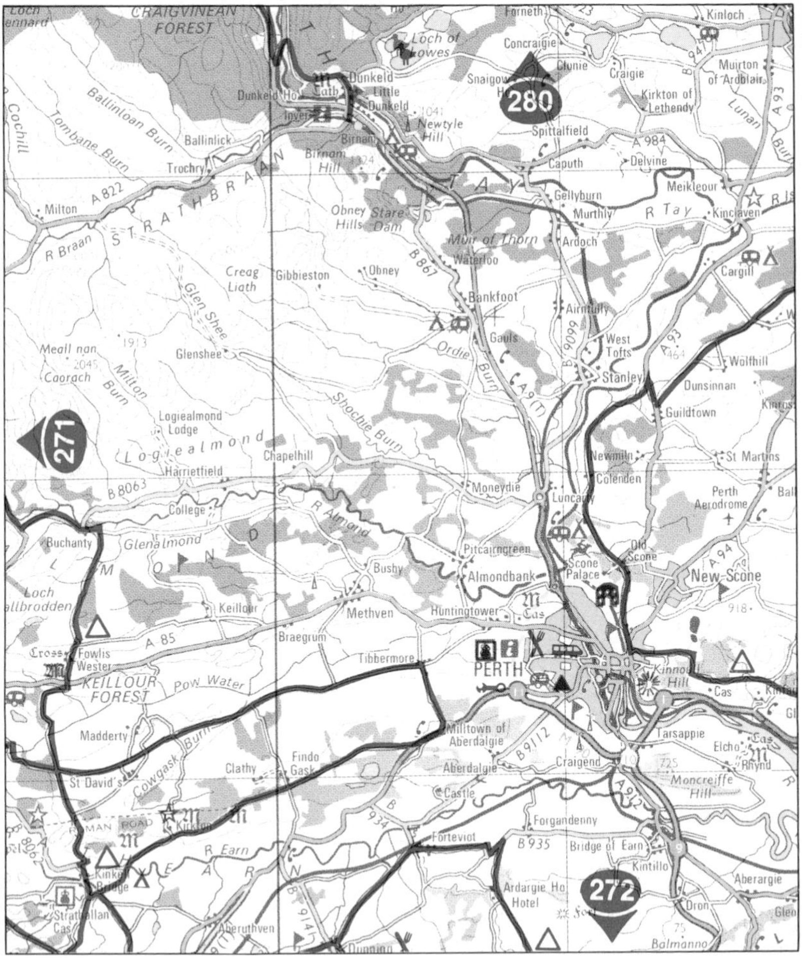

△ Hills **E of Kinnoull Hill**, with a steep climb at Kinfauns; steep climb N from **Fowlis Wester** and **S from Ardargie House Hotel**; gentle hills N and S of **Kinkell Bridge**.

🚌 Frequent services to **Perth** on InterCity routes from Stirling and Edinburgh.

✗ **Perth,** choices, and restaurant in Royal George Hotel; **Dunning**, choices.

☆ Sites of Roman signal stations in **Kirkton** area, and along Roman road.

🏛 **Scone Palace**, 19th-C with 16th-C gateway, home of Stone of Scone.

𝔐 The Cross at **Fowlis Wester** is 8th C and its 13th-C church has a Pictish stone.

☀ All-round views from **Kinnoull Hill**.

▣ **Perth**, with art gallery, near Perth Bridge.

🔧 **Perth**, Richards, 44 George Street.

⛺ Attractive site at **Kinkell Bridge**.

▲ **Perth** 0738 23658, view over town.

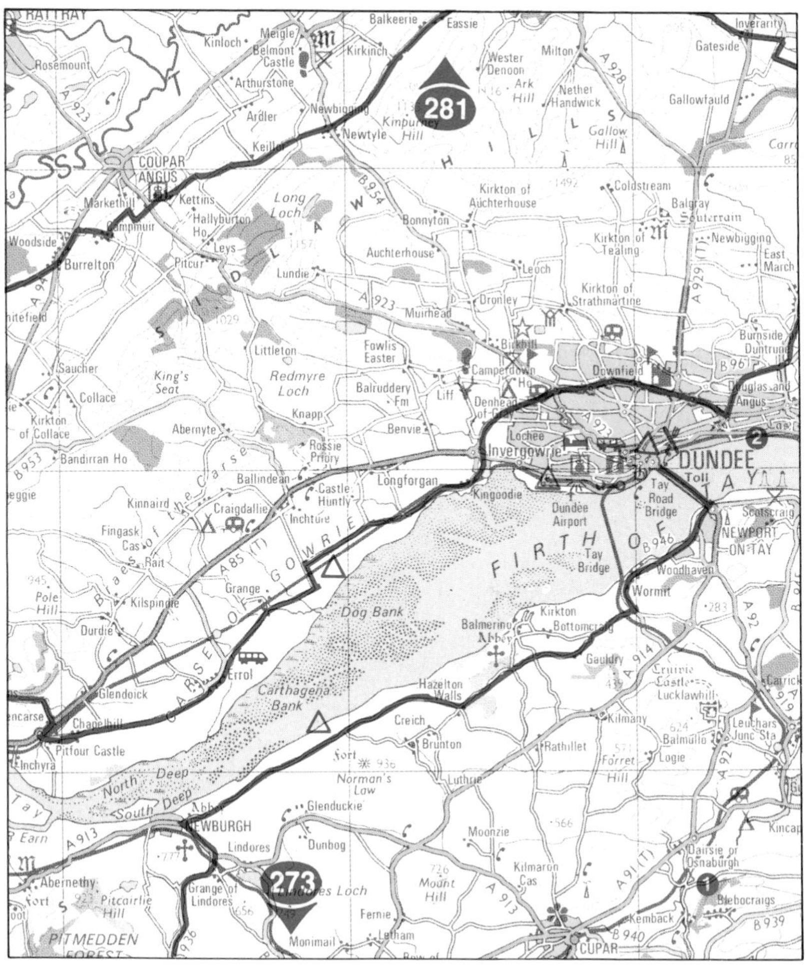

① St Andrews is about 5 miles (8 km) E on unclassified road through Strathkiness.

② Going E from Dundee, use the A930.

△ **Dundee**, set on the Law hill, has some sharp gradients; mostly easy riding along **Tay estuary**.

Dundee, 6 hours from London by InterCity service; **Errol** and **Invergowrie** on the Dundee to Perth line.

Choices, Dundee.

Dundee E is a lovely coastal ride.

Dundee William Wallace was a pupil at the grammar school and an inscription at the site of the former Dundee Castle notes that here he struck 'the first blow for Scottish independence'. He killed a man who had insulted him, was outlawed by the English, and consequently started his independence movement.

Dundee J. R. Nicholson, 2 Forfar Road.

Strathclyde

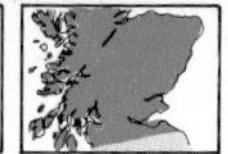

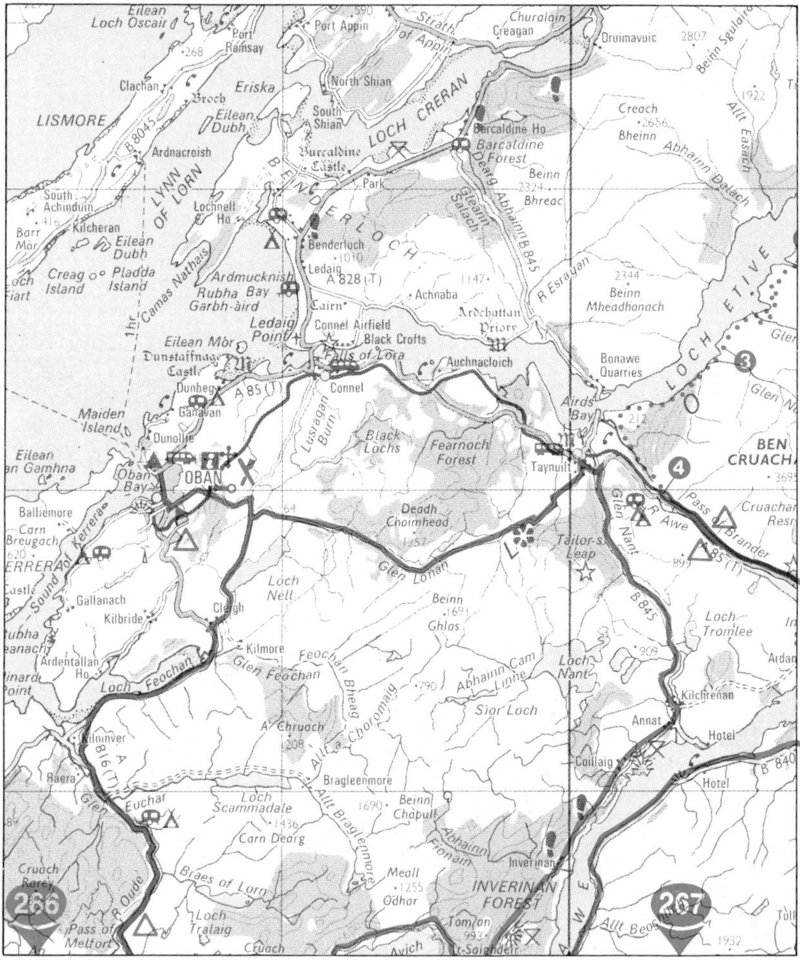

△ Hard climbs **E out of Oban, Pass of Melfort** and **Pass of Brander**. Traffic on **A85** in season – use alternatives.

Oban, Connel Ferry and **Taynuilt** on the Glasgow–Oban line. Oban is the starting point for most touring holidays in the West Highlands and islands. The choice of excursion and ferry services can be bewildering, and timetables and services change considerably. Some ferry services are delayed in summer, and there is considerable price variation between operators. If planning to visit the islands, investigate possibilities via tourist information.

Choices, **Oban**.

Memorable viewpoints on **Loch Awe**.

Bridge of Awe Well-placed camp site for the Glen Kinglass circuit, page 277.

Oban D. Graham, 9/15 Combie Street.

▲ **Oban** 0631 62025.

Strathclyde

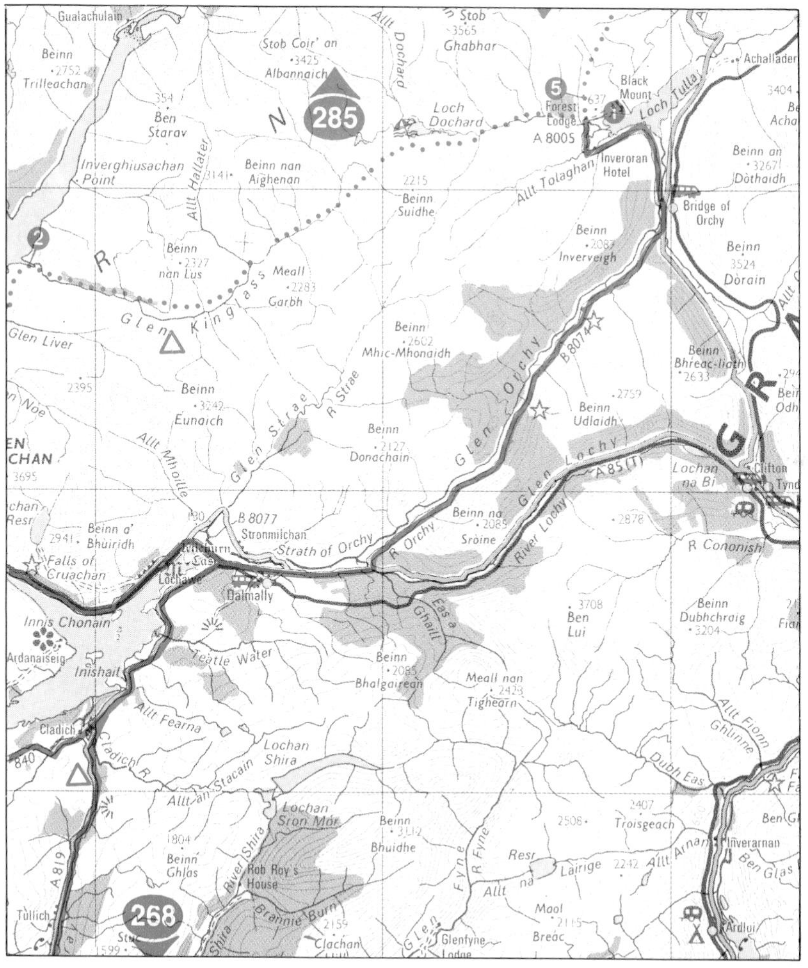

① At Forest Lodge cross the bridge and take the track along the right bank of the river down Glen Kinglass. The section mid-way along the glen is the most difficult; the track improves after Glen Kinglass Lodge. Reaching Loch Etive ② cross the bridge and head SW on rough track to ③ forestry road and ④ Bridge of Awe.

⑤ Access to the Old Glencoe Road from Forest Lodge is straight on through gate, up through woods on to moor. Track is part of West Highland Way.

△ Long climbs through **Glen Kinglass** and **S from Cladich**.

🚆 **Dalmally** and **Tyndrum Lower** on the Glasgow–Oban line; **Tyndrum Upper** and **Bridge of Orchy** on the Glasgow–Fort William–Mallaig line.

▲ One of the most magnificent cycle touring areas in Britain, with **Glen Kinglass** as classic rough-stuff.

Central/Tayside

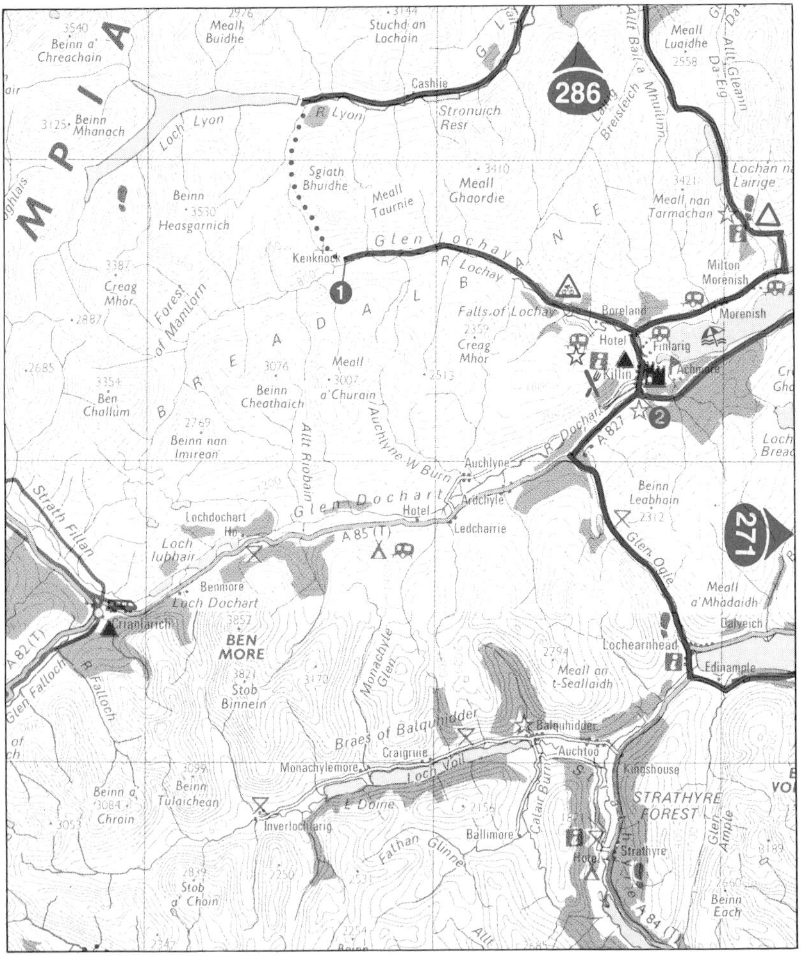

① Continue on extremely steep, rough track.

② Watch closely for the turning off the A827 S of Killin on to the unclassified road along the S shore of Loch Tay.

△ Very severe climbing on the unclassified road **N from the A827 near Milton Morenish**.

Crianlarich is the junction of the Glasgow–Oban and the Fort William/Mallaig–Glasgow lines.

Café and pub meals at **Killin**.

Glen Lochay is outstanding.

Swimming in **Loch Tay**.

☆ **Killin** The River Dochart makes a dramatic entry into Loch Tay here in a series of falls and rapids.

Finlarig Castle, **Killin**, where Black Duncan of the Cowl held sway; beheading pit close by.

▲ **Killin** 05672 546; **Crianlarich** 08383 260 – cycles for hire at hostel.

The River Dochart at Killin

Tayside

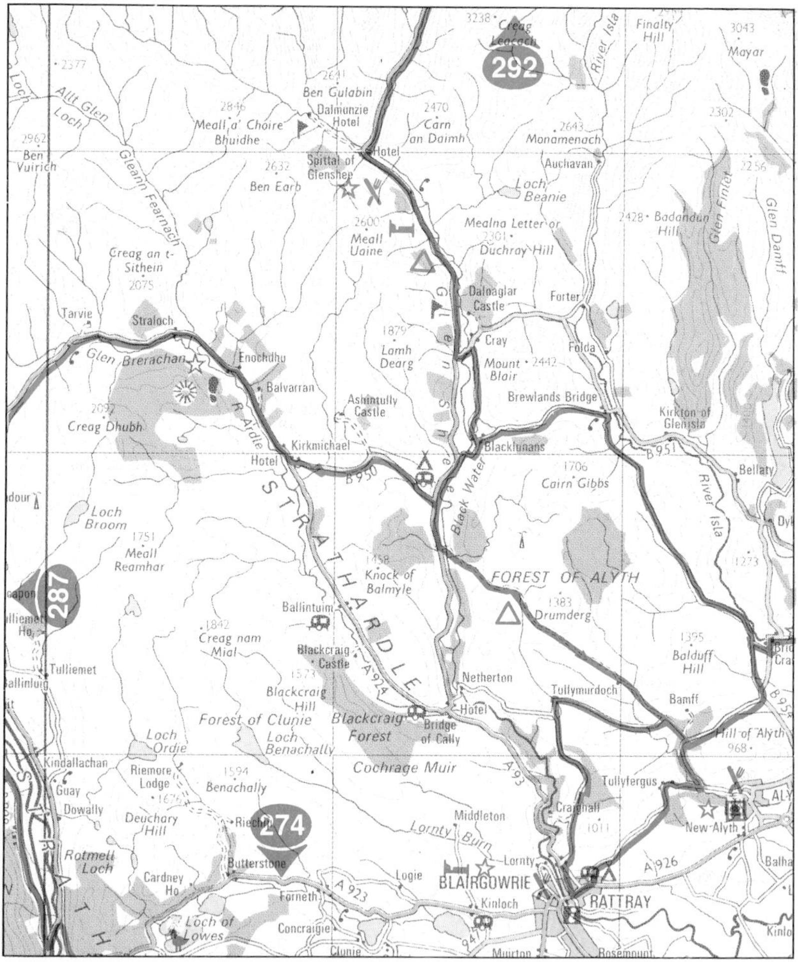

△ From Blairgowrie it is a long, often twisting climb up to and through Glen Shee. The present main road replaces an old highway, barely navigable now, but visible in places from the new road; mainly peaceful riding through farmland in **Alyth** area.

Snacks and meals in the hotel at **Spittal of Glenshee**; limited choices, **Alyth** and **Blairgowrie**.

Folk Museum, **Alyth**.

Loch of Lowes Public osprey hide in nature reserve.

☆ **Blairgowrie** has Roman and Pictish remains. **Alyth** is a pleasant sandstone town with a burn running through. **Spittal of Glenshee** is the hamlet, with a large hotel, where two streams join to form the Shee; in summer, a popular walking and pony trekking centre.

Some modestly priced hotels, **Blairgowrie** and along **Glen Shee**.

Tayside

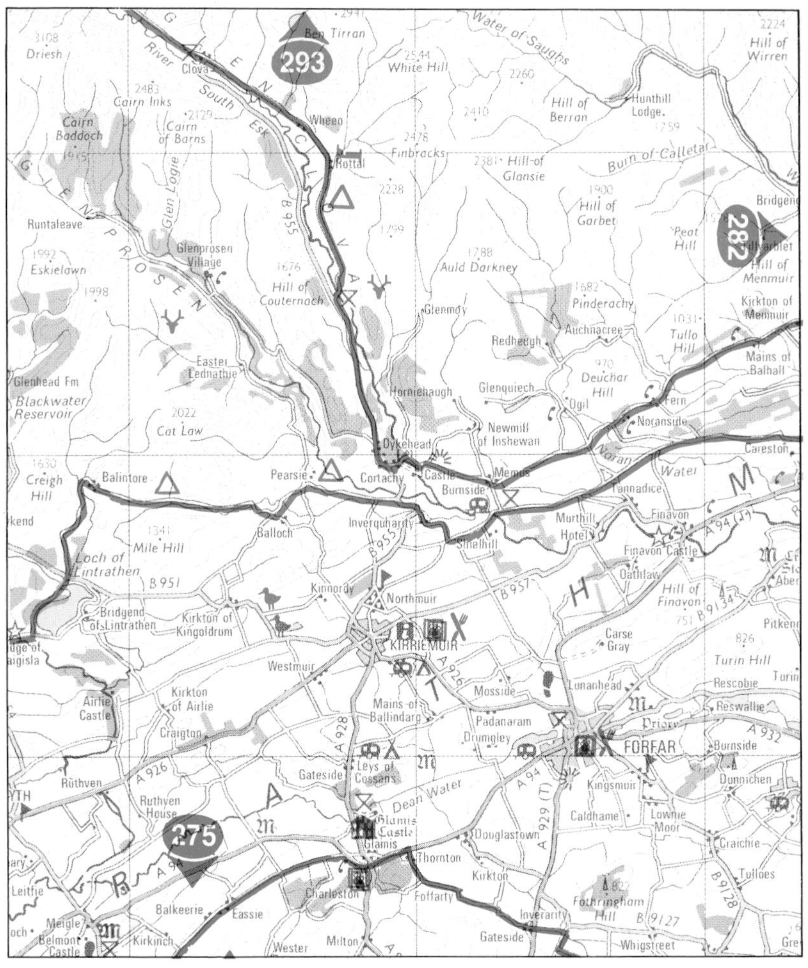

△ **N up Glen Clova** is a long, hard ride with many climbs, the road becoming rough and exposed in places; steep climbs to **Pearsie** and **Balintore**.

✗ Limited choices, **Kirriemuir**: snacks, teas and bar at the Royal Hotel, **Forfar**.

Fine views from **Cortachy Castle**.

Forfar Museum and Art Gallery with local history and flax industry exhibits; at **Glamis** Angus Folk Museum displays clothing, furnishings, domestic and farm implements in 19th-C cottages; Sir James Barrie, creator of Peter Pan, was born at 9 Brechin Road, **Kirriemuir**, now a museum of his life and work.

The Glens of **Clova** and **Prosen** were classic stalking and grouse country.

Glamis Castle, seat of the Earls of Strathmore, the family of Queen Elizabeth the Queen Mother.

Rottal Lodge, **Glen Clova**.

Tayside

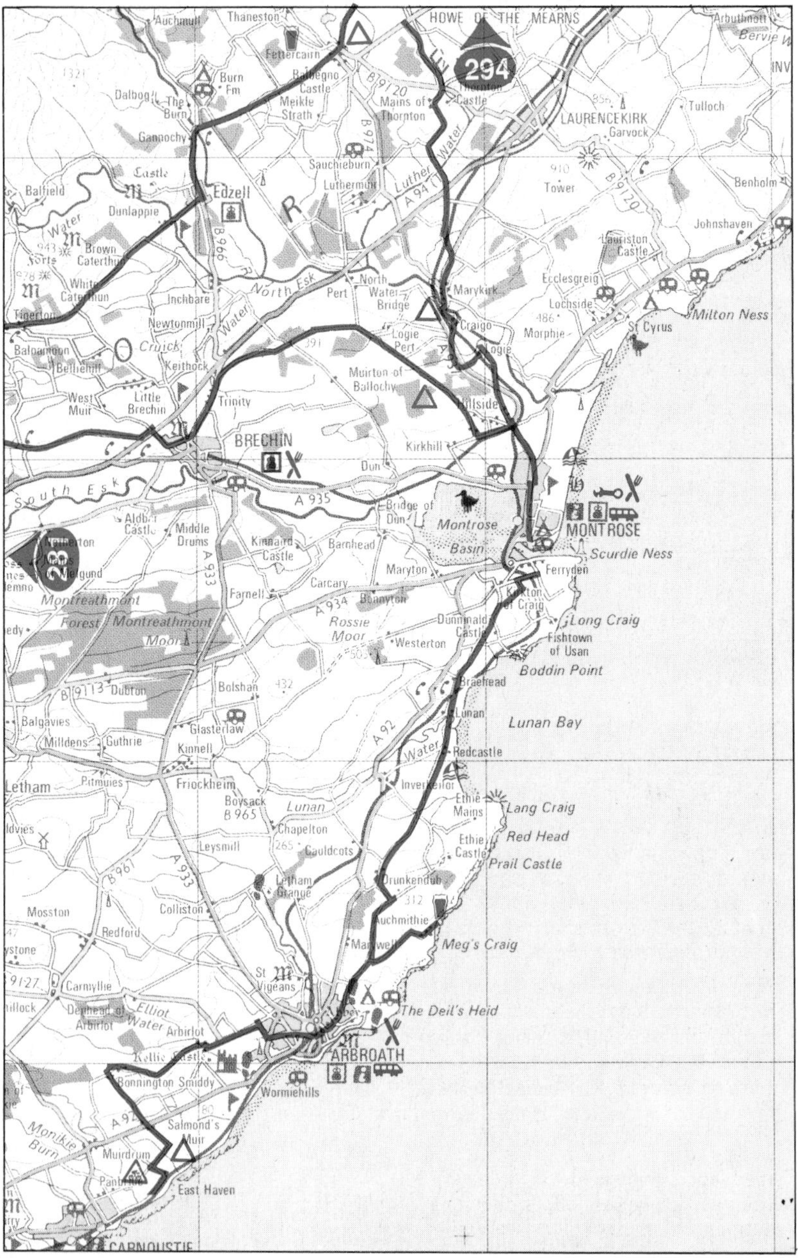

Auchmull
Thaneston
HOWE OF THE MEARNS
Arbuthnott
Bervie W
INV
Fettercairn
294
Burn Fm
Balbegno Castle
B 9120
Thornton Castle
Dalbog
The Burn
Meikle Strath
Mains of Thornton
856
Tulloch
LAURENCEKIRK
Garvock
Gannochy
B 974
Luther Water
Sauchieburn
910
Tower
B 9120
Castle
Luthermuir
A 94
Benholm
Balfield
Edzell
Dunlappie
Water
B 966
Johnshaven
943
Brown Caterthun
Lauriston Castle
978
White Caterthun
North Esk
North Water Bridge
Pert
Marykirk
Ecclesgreig
Inchbare
Lochside
Tigerton
Newtonmill
Craigo
486
Milton Ness
St Cyrus
Logie Pert
Logie
Morphie
391
Balnamoon
Cruick
Bellhiehill
Keithock
Muirton of Ballochy
West Muir
Little Brechin
Trinity
Hillside
BRECHIN
Kirkhill
Dun
South Esk
A 935
Bridge of Dun
Aldbar Castle
Middle Drums
Montrose Basin
MONTROSE
Kinnaird Castle
Barnhead
Scurdie Ness
A 933
Mains of Melgund
281
Maryton
Ferryden
Carcary
Farnell
Bonnyton
Kirkton of Craig
Montreathmont Forest
Montreathmont Moor
A 934
Rossie Moor
Dunninald Castle
Long Craig
Fishtown of Usan
Westerton
Boddin Point
432
B 9113
Dubton
Bolshan
Braehead
Balgavies
Glasterlaw
Lunan
Lunan Bay
Milldens
Guthrie
A 92
Kinnell
Water
Redcastle
Letham
Pitmuies
Friockheim
Inverkeilor
Boysack
B 965
Lunan
Ethie Mains
Lang Craig
Chapelton
Red Head
Leysmill
265
Cauldcots
Ethie Castle
Prail Castle
B 961
A 933
Letham Grange
Drunkendub
Mosston
Colliston
312
Auchmithie
Redford
Marywell
Meg's Craig
St Vigeans
Carmyllie
The Deil's Heid
Denhead of Arbirlot
Elliot Water
Arbirlot
ARBROATH
Kellie Castle
Bonnington Smiddy
Wormiehills
Monikie Burn
A 92
80
Salmond's Muir
Muirdrum
Panbride
East Haven
CARNOUSTIE

St Andrews

The A930 – **East Haven W to Dundee** – a relatively peaceful A road, most of the traffic taking the A92. The prevailing wind is from the SW, so riding the coastal route NE is usually satisfactory; climbs **N and NW from Montrose**; to avoid heavy climbing **N from Fettercairn**, take the B966 and A94 to Stonehaven, then the B979 to rejoin the route indicated on page 295. Avoid the A956.

Arbroath, **Montrose** and other stations on the east coast main line to Aberdeen.

Choices **Arbroath**, **Montrose** and **Brechin**.

There is a popular inn at **Auchmithie**, reached by a detour down the unclassified road indicated; the Ramsay Arms at **Fettercairn** offers generous portions with their bar lunches, and is a useful halt before the Cairn o' Mount climb (page 294).

This is thoroughly enjoyable **coastal riding**, with some fine views of St Andrews across the Firth of Tay.

Pleasant swimming on sandy beaches **N from Montrose** and at **Lunan Bay**.

Montrose Basin is a nature reserve.

Montrose has a long history, and several times saw interesting developments in Scottish history, such as the establishment of the first school in Scotland for teaching Greek in 1534. The Old Church and the Old Town Hall are graceful buildings and the museum offers some worthwhile insights to local history.

Montrose J. B. Keddie Cycles, 133 Murray Street.

Highland

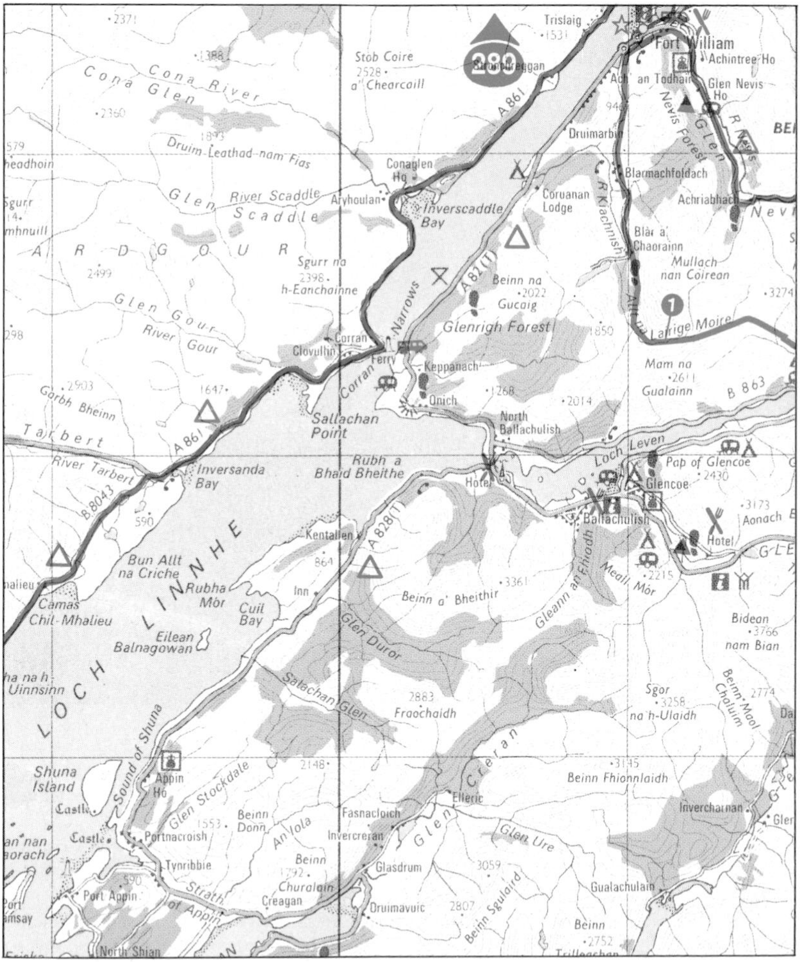

① Old military road, mainly following the route of pylons.

△ The **A82** and **A828 Fort William–Portnacroish** are busy during the holiday season, and the **A861** and **B8043** are preferable if the NW side of Loch Linhe can be planned into a tour.

Fort William on the Glasgow–Mallaig line; ferries **Fort William**–Camusnagaul (on the NW shore of Loch Linhe), Ballachulish–**Corran**.

Choices **Fort William**; limited choices **Ballachulish**; hotel food as marked.

Through Glen Nevis, round the foot of Ben Nevis.

☆ **Fort William** is a crowded tourist centre in summer; boat trips; the town is named after William III, during whose reign the earth fort was rebuilt in stone.

▲ **Glen Nevis** Fort William (0397) 2336; **Glencoe** Ballachulish (08552) 219.

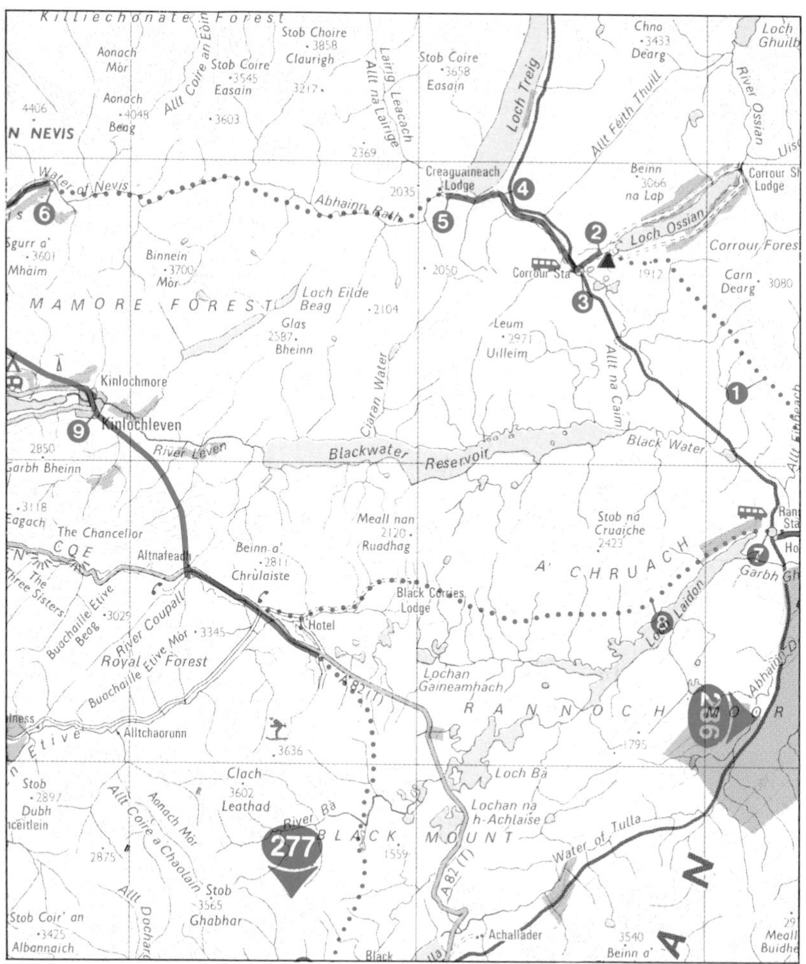

① The Road to the Isles: having crossed Allt Eigheach, soon leave river and follow NW along flank of Carn Dearg, past ruined Corrour Lodge to ② youth hostel. Rough road to Corrour Station, where ③ cross railway. Follow side of track and drop to Loch Treig ④. Round loch shore to Creaguaineach Lodge and ⑤ left down N bank of Abhainn Rath. Cross river at Luibeilt and follow left bank through pass to left of hill. N bank of Water of Nevis to ⑥.

⑦ Cross railway and follow N side of loch. In about a mile (1.5 km) bear right ⑧ to keep above loch as track swings due W.

⑨ Old Glencoe Road easily followed over Ba Bridge to A82.

Rannoch and **Corrour Stations** on the Glasgow–Fort William line.

▲ **Loch Ossian** bookings to SYHA, 7 Glebe Crescent, Stirling FK8 2JA.

Tayside

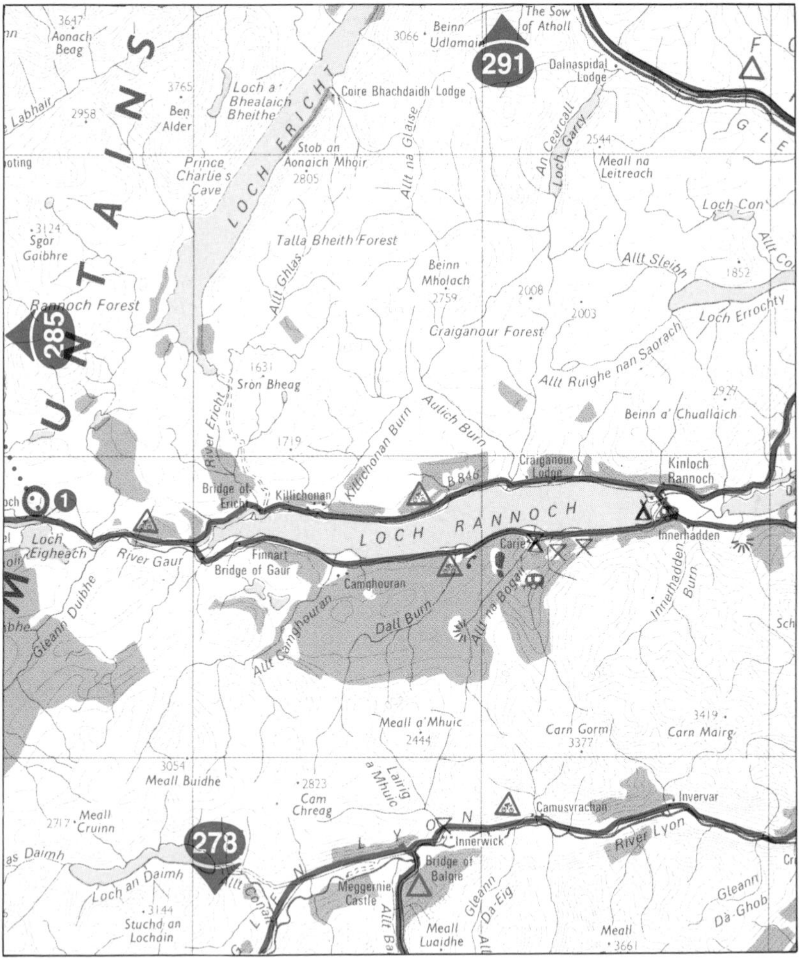

① Track leading off N from Loch Eigheach is the start of the Road to the Isles – see page 285. Go round hillside and continue to Allt Eigheach.

△ The dual carriageway section **through Glen Garry** is unfortunately unavoidable; Glen Garry is a 13-mile (20-km) climb to the watershed of Drumochter Pass; severe climb **S from Bridge of Balgie**.

▲ Through **Glen Lyon** and along **Loch Rannoch**: trees obscure the view along both shores of the loch at times – the N shore is perhaps the prettier ride. Beautiful, desolate ride from **W end of Loch Rannoch** along the lively River Gaur.

✻ The conspicuous conical peak seen to the S is **Schiehallion**, 3,554 feet (1,083 m).

⛺ Camping and picnicking, **S side of Loch Rannoch**.

Tayside

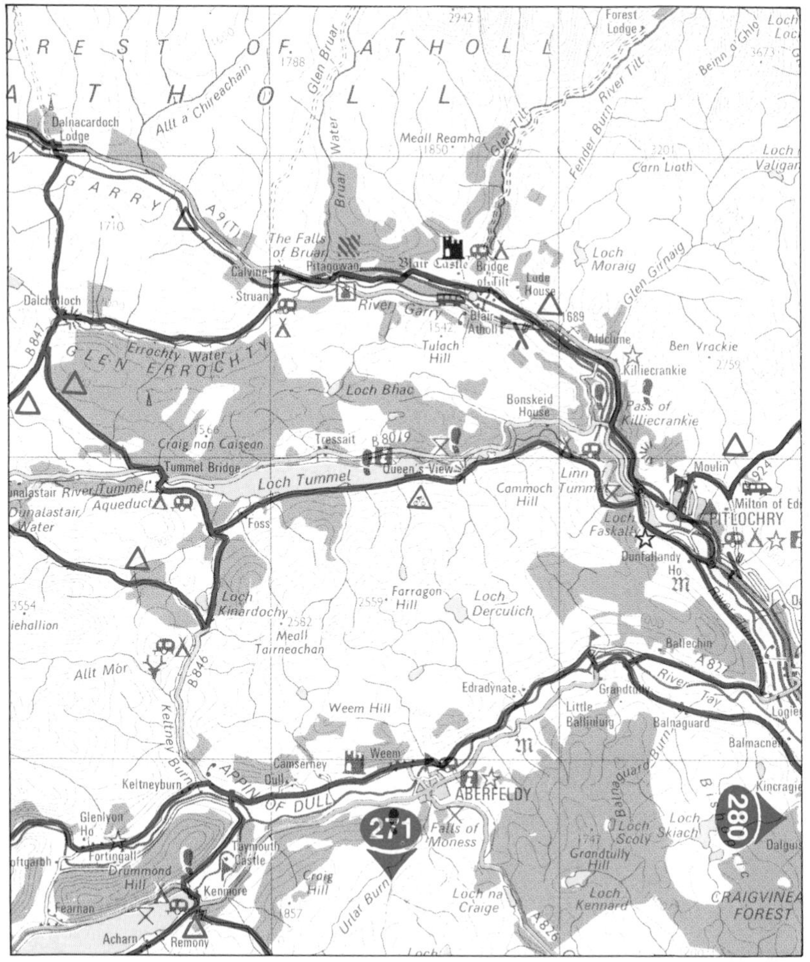

△ With the completion of the A9 improvement scheme at **Blair Atholl**, the old A9 is a relatively peaceful road. **Glen Garry** is a long climb – see page 286; severe climbs **NE from Pitlochry, between Tummel Bridge and Dalnacardoch Lodge, W from Loch Kinardochy** and **N on B847**.

🚃 **Pitlochry** and **Blair Atholl** on the Perth–Inverness main line.

✗ Choices **Pitlochry, Blair Atholl**.

⚠ Superb scenery throughout; **Queen's View** on the S shore of Loch Tummel is justly famous.

The Falls of Bruar Footpath leads N through woods, fine views of falls.

☆ On **Loch Faskally** near Pitlochry is a salmon pass with observation room.

Blair Atholl Castle, famous arms collection, paintings, Jacobite relics, china, natural history museum.

▲ **Pitlochry** 0796 2308.

Highland

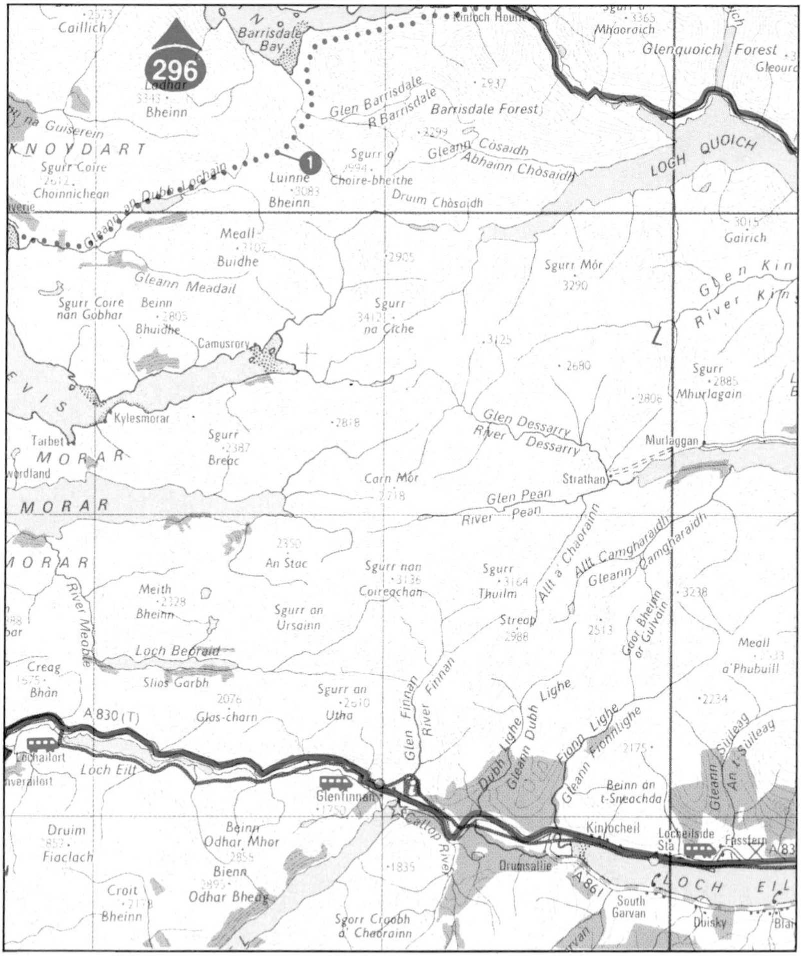

① Marked for reference only is the off-highway route known as the Rough Bounds of Knoydart, connecting the remote village of Inverie on the isolated peninsula N of Mallaig with the unclassified road that leads E to the A87 at Loch Garry. The remoteness of the Knoydart area, combined with unrideable condition of much of the route, plus the pass below Luinne Bheinn, can make the expedition

The familiar 'wild rhododendron', with its purple flowers, is common in this area.

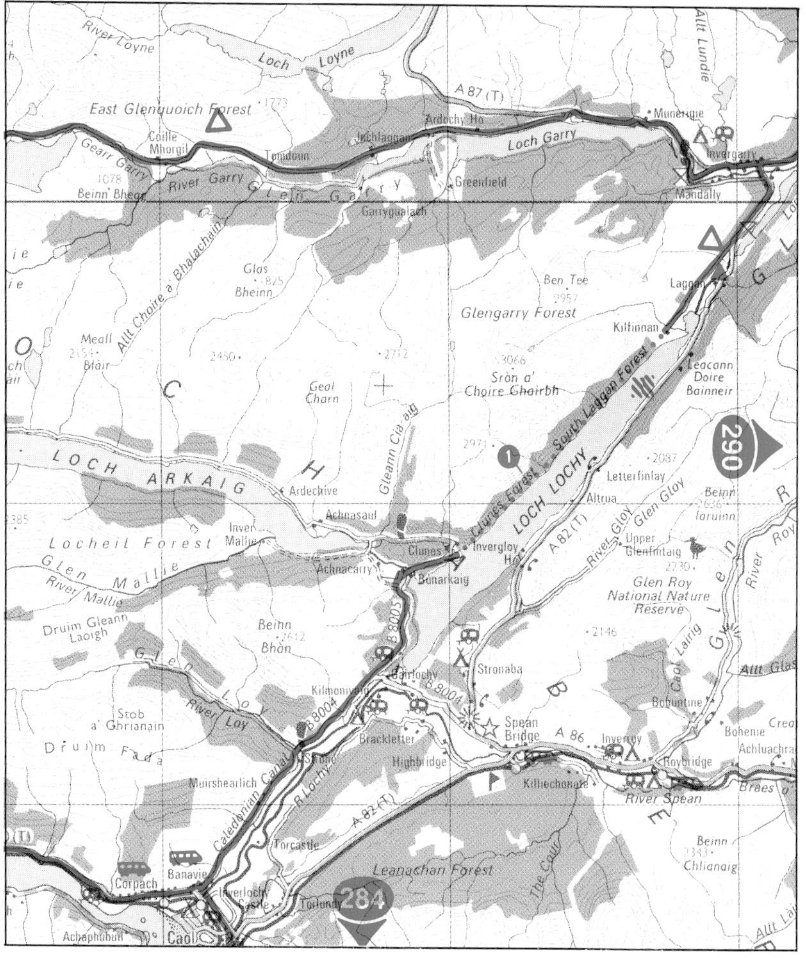

impractical for even the fittest and best-prepared. Do not consider undertaking this route unless truly experienced; large-scale maps and camping equipment essential; consult someone who has tackled the route before attempting it (the Rough Stuff Fellowship, address page 304, will assist).

🚌 **Lochailort**, **Glenfinnan** and **Locheilside** Station on the Fort William–Mallaig line.

① Loch-side track easily followed.

△ Climb **W along Glen Garry**; A82 carries heavy traffic in summer – linking stretch NE from **Laggan**.

🚌 **Roybridge**, **Spean Bridge**, **Banavie**, **Corpach** on Glasgow–Mallaig line.

Loch Lochy, Loch Ness and Loch Linhe, plus stretches of the Caledonian Canal (begun by Telford 1803) link the Atlantic and the North Sea.

▲ **Loch Lochy** Invergarry (08093) 239.

Highland

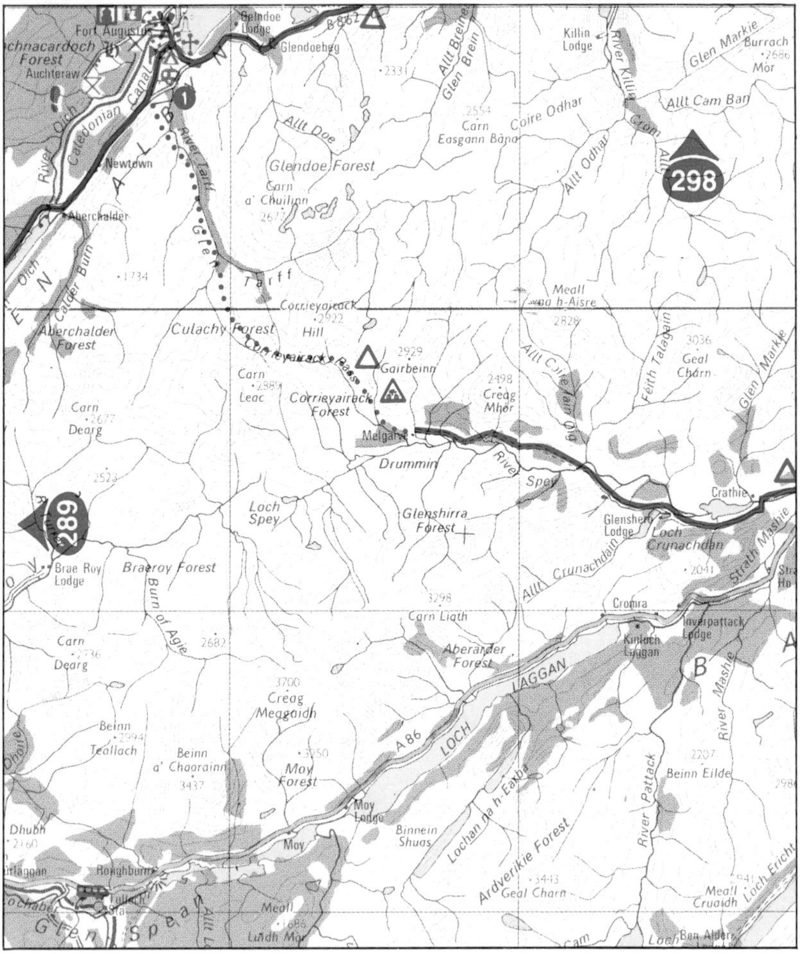

① Access to the Corrieyairack Pass at Loch Uanagan. Take track past Cullachy House, and up Glen Tarff to Lagan a' Bhainne Bridge. Through pass and down zig-zag to Melgarve, where surfaced road begins.

△ Severe climbs to summit of **Corrieyairack Pass** and **E from Crathie**.

Tulloch on the Glasgow–Fort William line.

Limited choice, **Fort Augustus**.

Although now spoilt by electricity pylons, the **Corrieyairack Pass** is still magnificent, with wide open views.

Fort Augustus The fort built here in the 18th C against Jacobite uprisings was named after Augustus, Duke of Cumberland.

Fort Augustus The Great Glen Exhibition gives insights into the past and present role of the huge natural fault which divides Scotland in two.

Highland

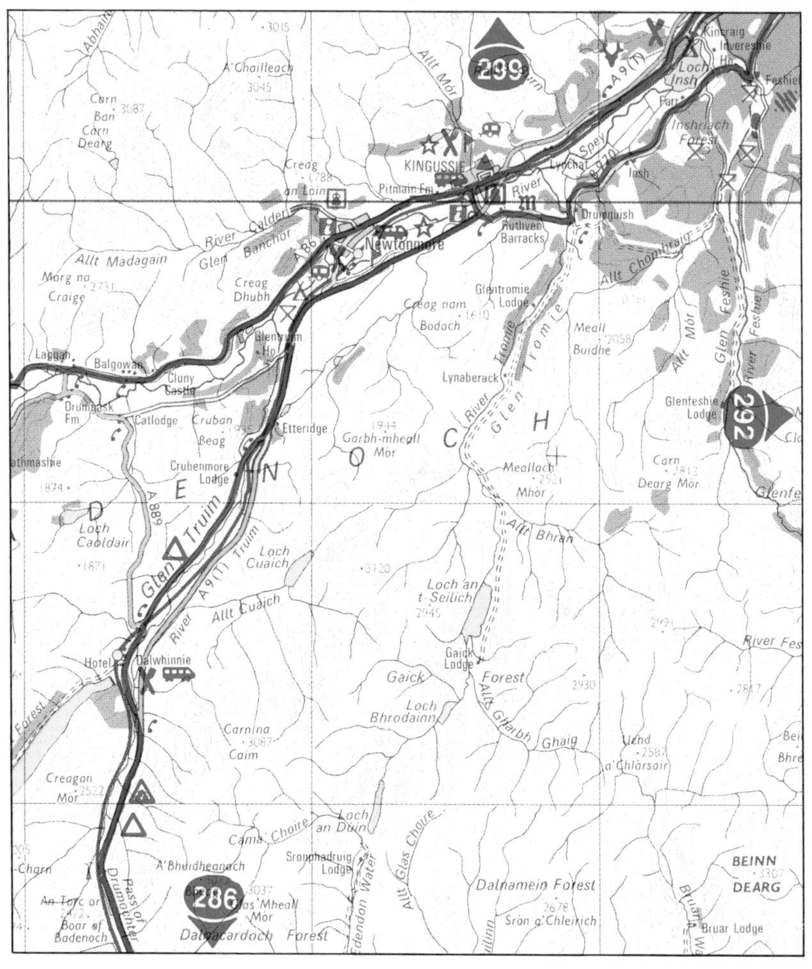

△ After the busy A9, quiet, well-surfaced roads **Dalwhinnie to Kingussie**; severe climb, **Drumochter Pass**.

Kingussie, **Newtonmore** and **Dalwhinnie** on the Perth–Inverness line.

Pubs and cafés at **Kingussie**; cafés, **Newtonmore**, **Dalwhinnie** and **Kincraig**.

The descent (going N) **from Drumochter Pass** is long and exhilarating.

Ruthven Barracks, outside **Kingussie**, where the clan chiefs gathered after Culloden.

Highland wildlife park, **Kincraig**.

☆ **Newtonmore**, once headquarters of Clan Macpherson; relics of their battles in clan museum. **Kingussie** attractive town, foot of Cairngorms.

Feshiebridge, glorious waterfalls.

Highland Museum, **Kingussie**.

Loch Insh, **Kincraig**, idyllic camp site.

▲ **Kingussie** 05402 506.

Highland/Tayside

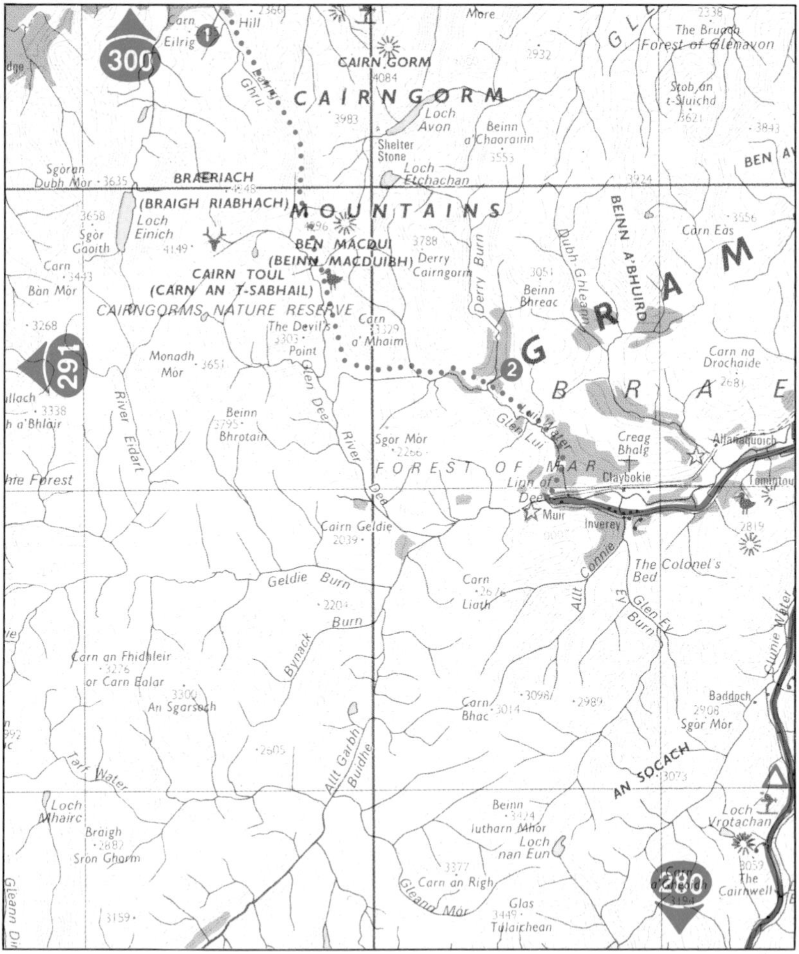

① The Lairig Ghru is signposted where it forks away from the Gleann Einich track, and is well indicated by cairns and signposts throughout. Proceed through the notorious boulder field, and up the pass, climbing to 2,771 feet (844 m). Continue past Pools of Dee and down through Glen Luibeg to ② Derry Lodge, from where there is a rough road to Linn of Dee. One of the most spectacular Scottish passes, a full day's journey in summer. Its popularity has increased considerably. The going is steep and rough and the scenery savagely impressive. The Corrour Bothy, on the southwards descent, may provide shelter.

△ Severest climbing to **Cairnwell Pass**, 2,199 feet (670 m), the highest main road pass in Britain.

✳ Chairlift to summit of **Cairnwell** for spectacular views.

Highland/Tayside/Grampian

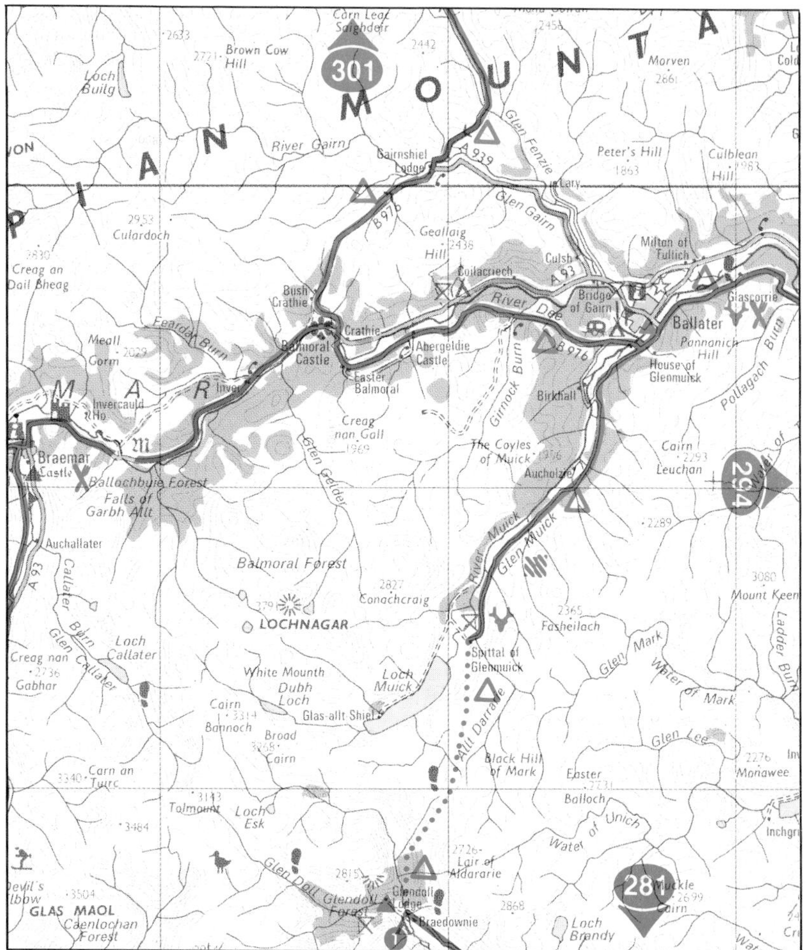

① The Capel Mounth: carry straight on from road end at Braedownie but do not cross bridge. Just over ½ mile (0.8 km) past bridge, ② take track right, winding steeply up hill. The track is well marked by cairns and leads over the pass, down past Loch Muick to the road at Spittal of Glenmuick.

△ Very severe climbs as marked on the **B976** and **A939**; going **S along Glen Muick** and mounting the pass **S of Spittal of Glenmuick**; **N from Glendoll Lodge** and going **into Ballater**.

Choices, **Ballater** and **Braemar**.

Glen Muick Impressive waterfall with salmon steps.

Spittal of Glenmuick Red deer often visible from the road; **Ballater** Monaltrie Wildlife Park.

▲ **Ballater** 0338 55227; **Glendoll Lodge** Clova (05755) 236, in unspoilt mountain area, many circular walks.

Grampian/Tayside

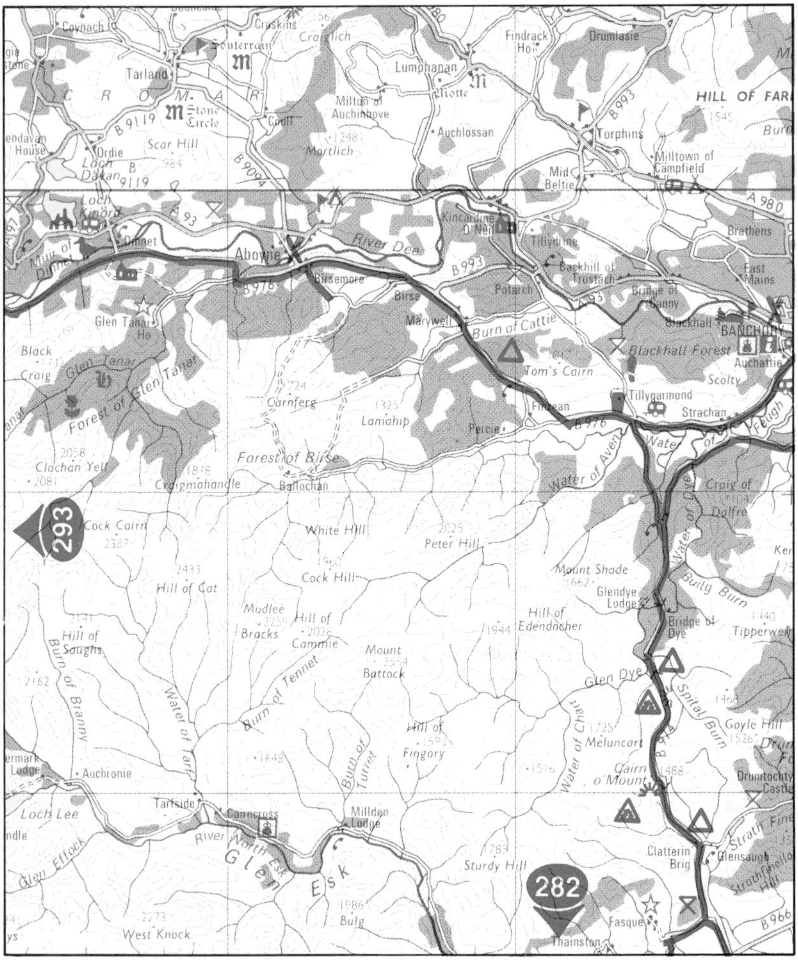

293

282

△ Steep climb **N to Cairn o' Mount**, with a steep descent and further severe climbs the other side; **B976** climbs N above **Drumhead to Marywell**.

Banchory, choices; **Aboyne**, limited choices.

Feughside Inn on the **B976**, refreshment after the Cairn o' Mount run.

Cairn o'Mount **N to Strachan** is a desolate, spectacular stretch.

Muir of Dinnet.

Forest of Glen Tanar, remnant of ancient Caledonian pine forest.

Crannog (ancient lake dwelling) and cross slab on **Loch Kinord** (above Muir of Dinnet).

From **Cairn o' Mount**.

Clatterin Brigg.

Detour to **Tarland** for ruined stone circle and souterrain (an earth-house).

B & B **Banchory**, 2 Alexandra Place, Watson Street.

Grampian

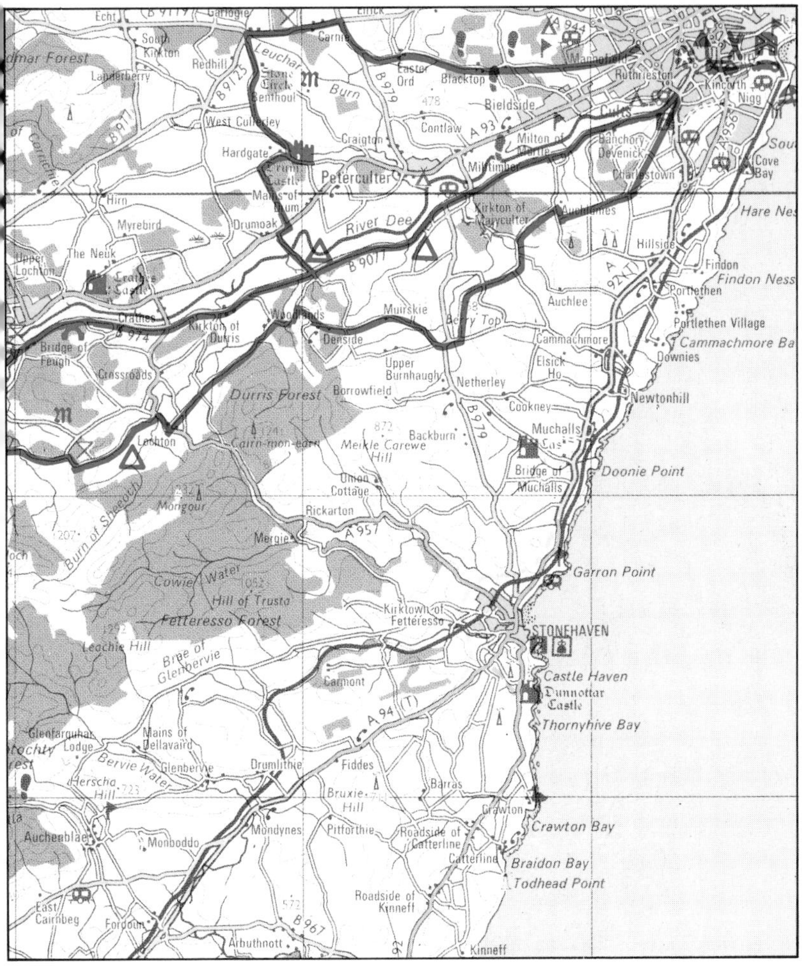

△ Gently rolling country **along River Dee**; hilly on minor road through **Lochton** and crossing the Dee.

Frequent service to **Aberdeen** on Intercity route from Dundee.

Aberdeen, choices, fish a speciality.

Twomiles (3 km) of sandy beaches at **Aberdeen**; approach via Beach Boulevard from Castle Hill.

Crathes Castle, rebuilt 16th-C tower-house with extensive gardens; **Drum Castle** with 13th-C tower and grounds.

Stone circles just **W of Lochton** (near The Nine Stanes) and at **Benthoul**.

Aberdeen the 16th-C turreted Provost Skene's House is now a museum; 16th-C King's College; 14th-C Cathedral of St Machar.

Bridge of Feugh above the rapids.

Aberdeen Anderson, 46–50 Rosemount Viaduct.

▲ **Aberdeen** 0224 646988.

Highland

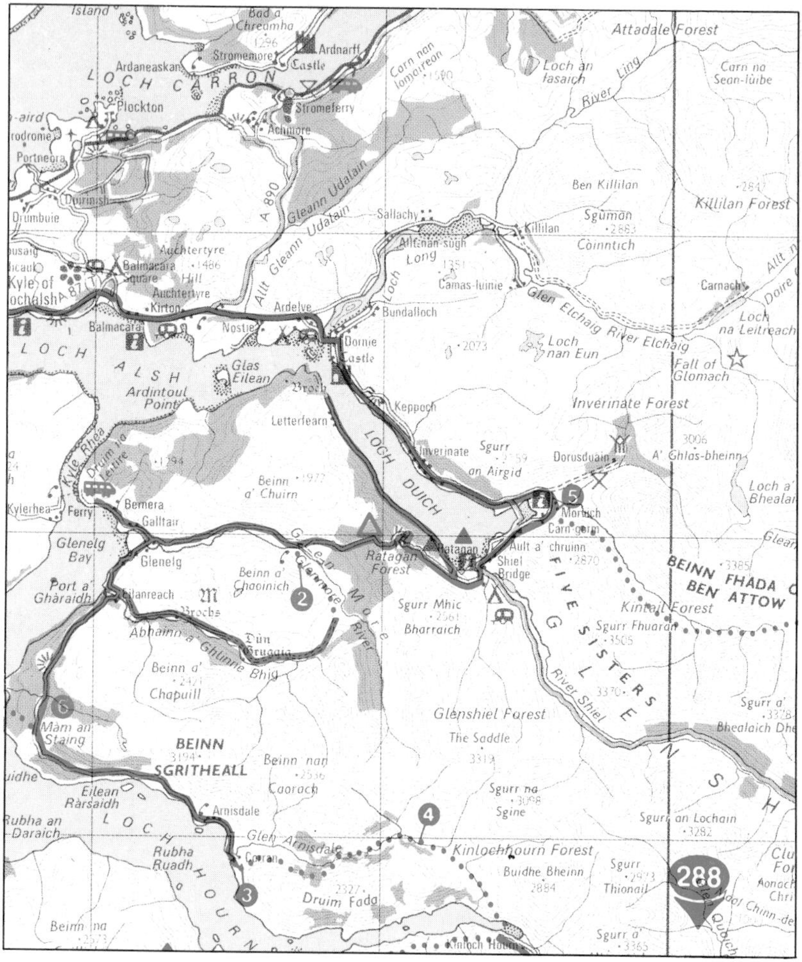

① From road end at Balvraid take rough track through pass, descending past Loch Iainmhic Aonghais and to left of Suardalan Bothy; boggy track round hillside and drop to Glenmore. Follow S bank of river and cross ② opposite telephone box to road.

③ From road end at Corran, take track across field from post office cottage, keeping to S bank of River Arnisdale. A rough, steep climb follows, then descend to waterfall. Go round left of lochs and along to river opposite ruined croft ④. Cross two streams and follow left bank up through pass; descend to Kinloch Hourn.

⑤ Access to Glen Affric route.

⑥ At Upper Sandaig cottages take track to Gavin Maxwell's cottage.

△ **Ratagan** Pass, strenuous either way.

Ferry to Skye, summer only.

▲ **Ratagan** Glenshiel (059981) 243.

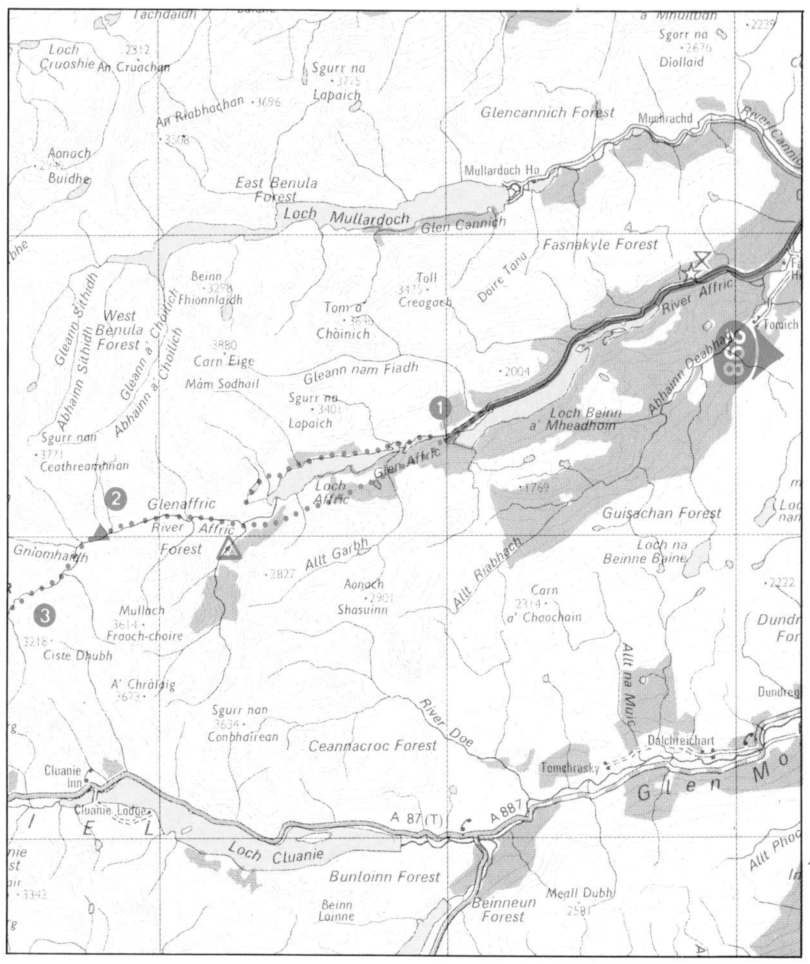

① From Affric Lodge (rough road here from Cannich) go past the car park and picnic area to the finger post indicating Kintail. Follow track along N side of Loch Affric (or forestry road along S side) and continue to the youth hostel at Alltbeithe ②. Keep SW up Fionngleann ③ past Camban Bothy. Climb the pass, and descend Gleann Lichd to Croe Bridge.

Glen Affric, one of the classic tracks. Despite hydro-electric developments between Cannich and Affric, this ride still offers the best of everything – if weather conditions are good.

▲ **Glen Affric** Allt Beathe, Glen Affric, Cannich Beauly, Inverness-shire 1V4 7ND. Extremely remote hostel, with no sleeping bags for hire; open May–Sept only, bookings at other times must go through Scottish YHA head office.

Highland

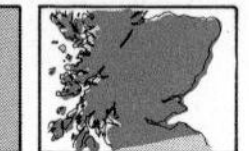

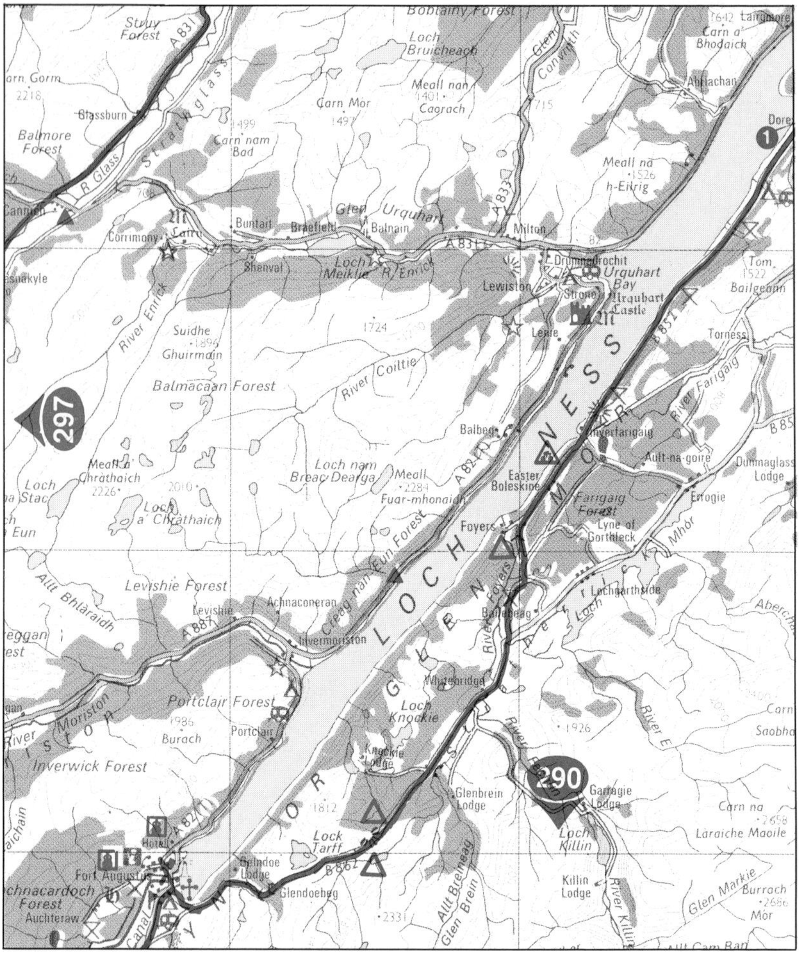

① Inverness 8 miles (13 km) NE on the B862.

△ **B862** is quiet, with a climb out of Fort Augustus, a steeper climb after Loch Tarff, and descent into Foyers.

✕ **Fort Augustus**, limited choices; Inchnacardoch Hotel, N of Fort Augustus.

⚠ Quiet scenic stretch along **SE shore of Loch Ness**, especially N of Foyers.

☀ Whitebridge Viewpoint **on the B862 E of Fort Augustus**.

▣ The Great Glen Exhibition at Fort Augustus (see also page 290) provides geographical and historical details of the area and the Loch Ness Monster.

☆ Detour to Stone Age **Corrimony Cairn**: chamber, passage, stone circle.

♜ **Urquhart Castle**, grandly sited ruin.

▲ **Loch Ness** Glenmoriston (0320) 51274; **Cannich**, Beauly, Inverness-shire IV4 7LT, May–Sept., otherwise head office.

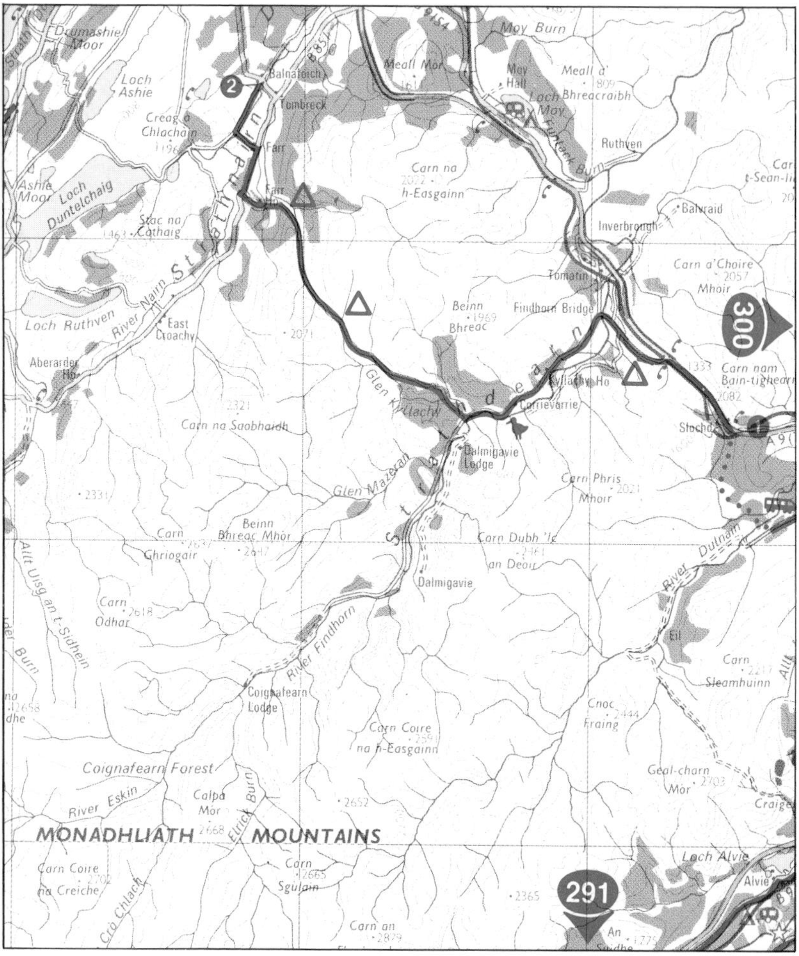

① Track connects with unclassified road leading to Carrbridge.

② Inverness 6 miles (10 km) N on the B861.

△ Severe climbs **NW from Glen Kyllachy**; **SE from Farr House**; **SE from Findhorn Bridge**.

Carrbridge is 4 miles (6 km) E.

On the **remote roads**, look for birdlife: capercaillie, crested tit, Scottish crossbill all breed in the area.

Scottish crossbill: crossed bill highly efficient for extracting pine cone seeds.

Highland/Grampian

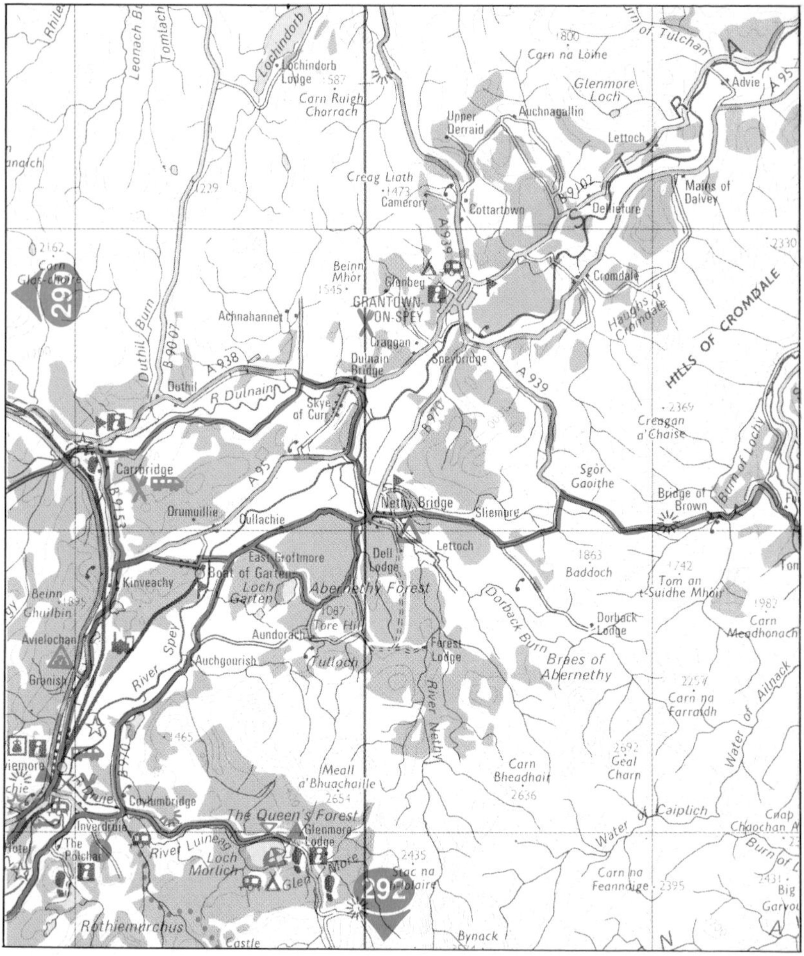

① The Lairig Ghru is signposted here.

△ Severe climbing **E from Nethy Bridge**.

Aviemore and **Carrbridge** on the Perth–Inverness main line.

Choices, Aviemore; cafés, **Grantown-on-Spey** and **Carrbridge**.

Aviemore to Carrbridge is a generally level valley-floor ride with splendid mountain views.

Swimming in **Loch Morlich** – sandy shore.

Spectacular views of the Cairngorm mountains in the **Inverdruie** area.

☆ **Aviemore** is the purpose-built centre for the Cairngorm ski area – wide range of tourist facilities all year.

Loch Morlich, lovely for picnics.

Aviemore Mountain Cycles, Mirtlefield, Grampian Road North.

▲ **Loch Morlich** Cairngorm (047986) 238; **Aviemore** 0479 810345 (cycles for hire).

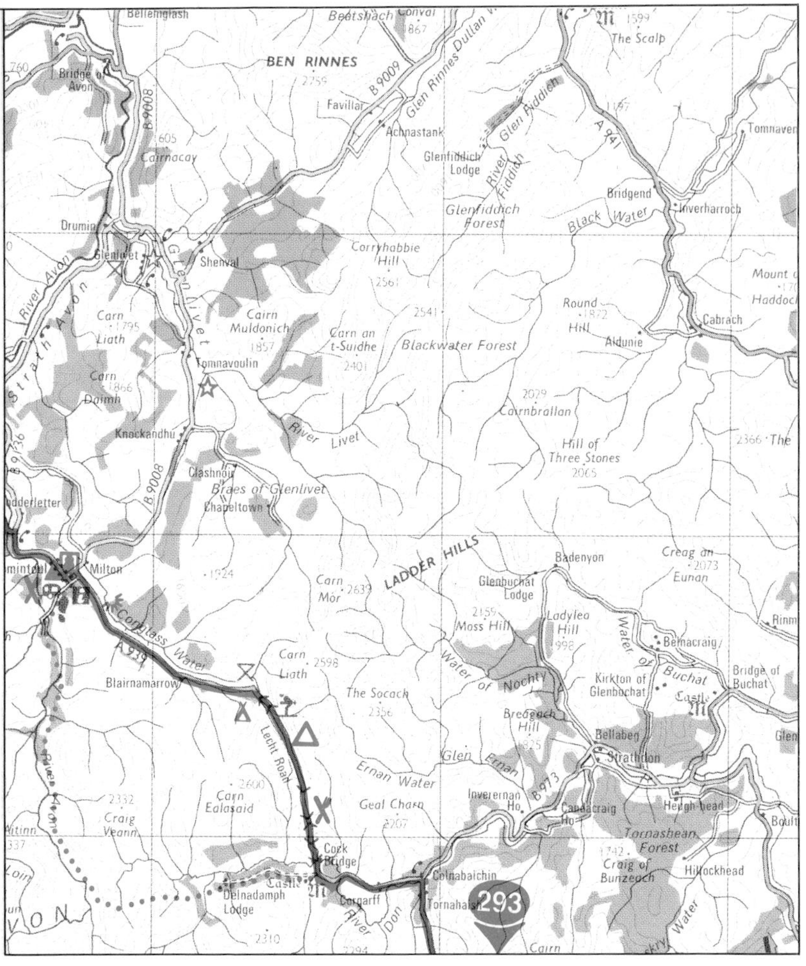

△ Several hills **SE from Tomintoul** are killers – between 1-in-8 and 1-in-5, and some several miles long. The wind can be a real problem, and the best direction of travel is anti-clockwise. The **Lecht Road**, one of the highest in Scotland, is especially exposed: from 1,344 feet (410 m) at Cock Bridge it rises steeply to 2,114 feet (644 m) at its highest point. From there, it is a long descent to Tomintoul.

A welcome café at the **Lecht** summit; limited choice, **Tomintoul**.

Tomintoul At the visitor centre, local wildlife, landscape, geology displays.

☆ **Tomnavoulin** Glenlivet whisky distillery, tours March–October.

Well of **Lecht** Stream and lovely pastoral setting for camp site.

▲ **Tomintoul**, Main Street, Tomintoul, Ballindalloch, Banffshire AB3 9HA, May-Sept, otherwise head office.

Highland

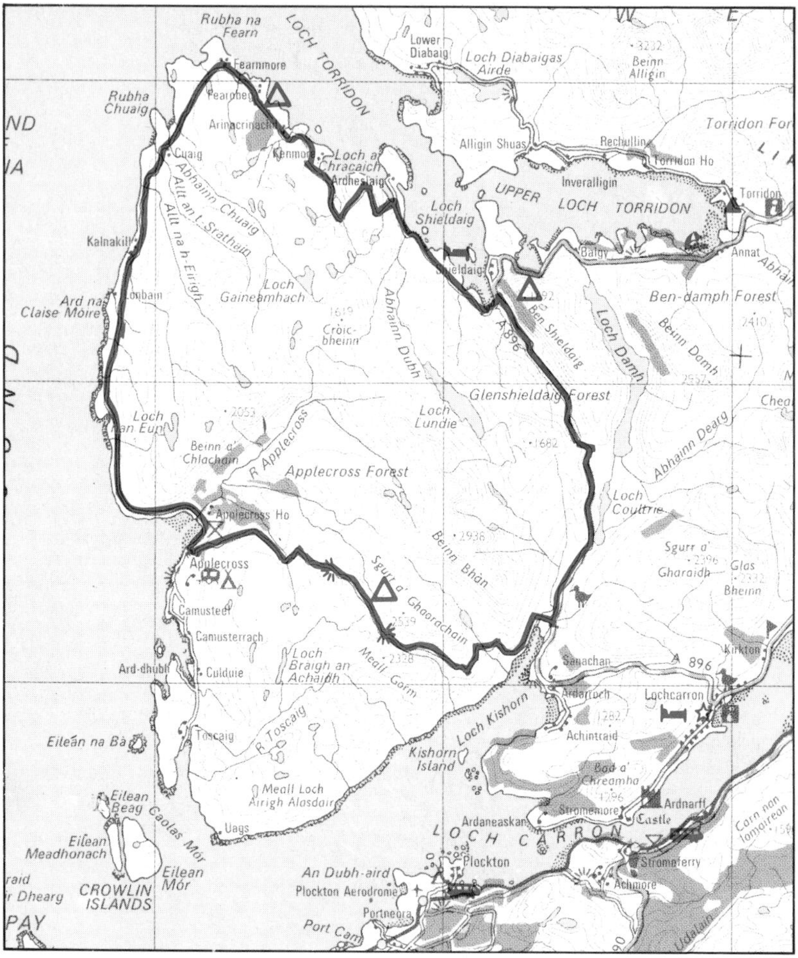

△ A very strenuous circuit overall: the **A896 SE from Shieldaig** is narrow, with a gradual climb, then a descent. From **junction N of Ardarroch** towards Applecross is a 4-mile (6-km) climb up to the Pass of Cattle with very steep gradients and several hairpin bends. Once past the summit, the lane descends quite gently. Almost continuous climbs and descents **between Fearnbeg and Shieldaig**. Do not attempt in bad weather.

Stromferry, **Plockton** and stations on the Inverness–Kyle of Lochalsh line.

Magnificent views on the descent from summit of **Pass of Cattle**, including mountains on Skye and seabirds.

Swimming in **Upper Loch Torridon**.

☆ **Lochcarron** Castle and crofts, latter with traditional tartan weaving.

B & B **Shieldaig** and **Lochcarron**.

▲ **Torridon** 044587 284.

Acknowledgements

Picture Credits
pages 2/3 Tim Hughes; 18 Tim Hughes; 31 Sarah King; 49 Aerofilms; 52 Tim Hughes; 82 Tim Hughes; 91 Aerofilms; 97 Aerofilms; 110 Tim Hughes; 115 Tim Hughes; 127 British Tourist Authority; 150 British Tourist Authority; 166 Tim Hughes; 194 Tim Hughes; 209 Tim Hughes; 217 David Hoffman; 219 Aerofilms; 221 British Tourist Authority; 225 Aerofilms; 231 Charlie Waite; 244 Tim Hughes; 279 British Tourist Authority; 283 Aerofilms.

Artwork Credits
page 14 James Robbins; 17 James Robbins; 33 Ken Wood; 63 Tony Graham; 69 Tony Graham; 77 Tony Graham; 89 Tony Graham; 92 Paul Saunders; 117 Ken Wood; 142 Tony Graham; 181 Ken Wood; 185 Ken Wood; 193 Paul Saunders; 207 Paul Saunders; 241 Ken Wood; 256 Paul Saunders; 267 Ken Wood; 288 Tony Graham; 299 Ken Wood. Artwork to maps by Nigel O'Gorman and Orrin Pollard.

Editorial and design
Editor Andrew Duncan; **assistant editor** Linda Hart; **contributing editors** Jayne Miller and John Nolan; **art editor** Mel Petersen; **designers** Arthur Brown and Brenda Breslan; special thanks to John Paddy Browne of Ordnance Survey's Cartographic Library.